COMPLETE GUIDE TO

PSYCHOTHERAPY DRUGS

AND

PSYCHOLOGICAL DISORDERS

By H. WINTER GRIFFITH, M.D.
Daniel Levinson, M.D.
Miriam L. Levinson, Pharm.D.

THE BODY PRESS/PERIGEE

The Body Press/Perigee Books
are published by
The Berkley Publishing Group
200 Madison Avenue
New York, NY 10016

ISBN: 0-399-52278-6
ISSN: 1090-4816

Printed in the United States of America

1 2 3 4 5 6 7 8 9 10

Contents

Why Use This Book?

INFORMATION FOR CHANGING TIMES

In years past, patients would come to their doctors for help with the attitude, "Do something to make me better." At that time, the doctors' attitude often was, "Do what I tell you, and things will get better—but don't ask too many questions. A little knowledge is a dangerous thing." Doctors had been trained to be authoritarian in their dealings with patients. However, these attitudes are self-defeating. Fortunately, they are changing, and enlightened professionals welcome this change as an important way to improve health care.

Many thoughtful and assertive patients wish to be more involved. They don't want to be passive and powerless in matters that affect their own bodies. They don't want instructions or advice that is incomplete or lacking in credibility. They seek—and sometimes demand—enough information so they can think for themselves and participate in making important medical decisions affecting them. This book is for those persons who want additional responsibility for their own mental health and that of their families.

BRIDGING THE INFORMATION GAP

The information in this book barely scratches the surface of all information in the scientific literature about psychological disorders and medications. It represents a small part of the knowledge doctors and other health care providers have acquired. In addition to a medical education, most doctors have extensive clinical experience—and ideally, a great deal of wisdom and compassion.

But somehow, and sometimes for justifiable reasons, a doctor's medical information does not get translated and transmitted in a usable form for the most important member of the health care team—the patient. Even when information is competently conveyed to the patient by a doctor, nurse or other health care professional, the patient and the family leave the doctor's office with no written material to reinforce and remind them of the information they have been given verbally. This book is intended to provide you with the missing material and to supplement information you have received from your doctor.

PROVIDING SIMPLE, CONCISE INFORMATION

Condensing the mass of psychological medical knowledge available into one volume has required much simplification. Major facts and concepts are included, but out of necessity, many details have been left out. The information provided is intended as a guide.

It is impossible to include all the factors and circumstances that affect each individual's psychological health. Thus, your doctor may take into account other factors not included here when making a precise diagnosis and recommending treatment for you.

HOW YOU WILL BENEFIT FROM THIS BOOK

Yet, armed with the introductory knowledge about psychological disorders and medications discussed in this book, you will be in a stronger position in the following ways:

- You can better understand each disorder and the medications used to treat it.
- You can more easily recognize circumstances when a doctor's help is necessary.
- You can learn useful facts about how to prevent potential problems.
- You can confirm the facts regarding the disorder, refresh your memory about what you have learned and help your family learn about and understand the disorder.
- You can review a list of ways you can help meet the treatment goals.
- You can discuss issues with the doctor if the treatment steps outlined in the book differ from what your doctor advises. Doctors do not always agree on the best course of treatment for a particular psychological illness.

What's in This Book

The book is divided into six sections (plus the index):

GENERAL INFORMATION

Included in this section is selected psychological information and other medical data that does not readily fit into the format that is used for the specific disorder charts and drug charts. This information is broader in its scope than that on the charts, but is important in understanding and learning about psychological problems. This section also includes a guide to the information blocks that appear on the disorder charts and the drug charts.

PSYCHOLOGICAL DISORDERS

Each psychological disorder is described on a separate one-page chart. The information blocks are the same for each disorder. These information blocks make it easy to quickly read the entire page or to find just the particular subject matter you want about the disorder, such as signs and symptoms. To help you understand what is included in the specific information blocks, read the Guide to the Disorder Charts, beginning on page 31.

PSYCHOTHERAPY DRUGS

Each drug is described on a two-page chart. The title of each chart is either the generic name of a drug or a drug class name. The information blocks are the same for each drug, which is helpful if you are looking for specific information about two or more drugs, such as side effects. You can quickly find that particular information and read only the facts you need. To help you understand what is included in the specific information blocks, read the Guide to the Drug Charts, beginning on page 38.

BRAND & GENERIC NAME DIRECTORY

On most of the drug charts, you will find a list of the pertinent brand and/or generic drug names as part of the information provided. However, on some of the drug charts, there are too many brand or generic names to be listed in the space allotted (e.g., Antidepressants, Tricyclic). On those particular charts, you will be referred to a page number in the Brand & Generic Name Directory for this information.

ADDITIONAL DRUG INTERACTIONS

On each drug chart is an information block that lists the possible interactions with other drugs. For some drugs, these possible interactions are numerous, and there is not sufficient space on the drug chart itself to include the complete list. In these instances, there will be a note indicating that the list is continued on a specific page in the Additional Drug Interactions section.

GLOSSARY

This section contains a wide range of medical words and terms and their definitions. Some of these words and terms are found in entries on the charts, and others are words and terms your doctor may use in discussing a psychological disorder or medications used to treat it.

About the Authors

H. Winter Griffith, M.D.

H. Winter Griffith, M.D., authored 25 medical books, including the *Complete Guide to Prescription & Nonprescription Drugs;* the *Complete Guide to Symptoms, Illness & Surgery; Complete Guide to Pediatric Symptoms, Illness & Medications;* and *Complete Guide to Sports Injuries,* each now published by The Body Press/Perigee Books. Others include *Instructions for Patients; Drug Information for Patients; Instructions for Dental Patients; Information and Instructions for Pediatric Patients; Vitamins, Minerals and Supplements;* and *Medical Tests—Doctor Ordered and Do-It-Yourself.* Dr. Griffith received his medical degree from Emory University in 1953. After 20 years in private practice, he established and was the first director of a basic medical science program at Florida State University. He then became an associate professor of family and community medicine at the University of Arizona College of Medicine. Until his death in 1993, Dr. Griffith lived in Tucson, Arizona.

Daniel Levinson, M.D.

Daniel Levinson, M.D., is board certified in family practice and is an associate professor of family and community medicine at the University of Arizona College of Medicine. Dr. Levinson recently completed a residency in psychiatry. He is a graduate of the University of Chicago (Pritzker) School of Medicine.

Miriam L. Levinson, Pharm.D.

Miriam L. Levinson, Pharm.D., is clinical specialist for drug information at Meriter Hospital in Madison, Wisconsin. She is a graduate of the University of Arizona College of Pharmacy.

About Psychological Disorders

Psychology involves the scientific study of the mental processes. It deals with the internal aspects of the mind (such as feelings, thoughts, memory and perception); the external aspects of the mind (such as speech and behavior); and the development of personality, intelligence and learning.

Psychological disorders encompass a variety of illnesses that are also described as mental health problems, emotional disturbances, behavioral problems and others. These terms are used interchangeably in this book. Psychological disorders include various degrees of impairment of behavior, thought, perception and emotion.

Everyone has to cope with an emotional or psychological problem at some time in life. Most of us experience depression over a loss, anxiety about starting a new job or grief following the death of a family member. Many of these problems are self-limited; there is usually a spontaneous recovery, or the problems respond to self-care.

How does good or normal mental health differ from mental illness? The "distress and disability definition" is one way to help diagnose a mental disorder. People are said said to have a mental disorder when (1) they feel distressed by their condition (2) the condition impairs their ability to pursue their life or (3) their behavior seriously interferes with the lives of others.

CAUSES OF PSYCHOLOGICAL DISORDERS

Psychological problems used to be thought of as caused by a weakness in character. But it has been discovered that the causes of mental health problems are complex. Evidence suggests that brain chemicals, genetic factors, environmental situations, medical history, mental history, medications, illnesses and other factors all play roles in causing these problems. In many cases, the exact cause of a particular disorder is unknown; there may be theories, but to date many of them are not proven or unproven.

Research continues into the causes, such as the role of genetics in mental disorders. Individuals with these disorders and their families seek information about the risk of their conditions to relatives and to unborn children.

Other research involves how the psychological factors are transformed into psychological changes. The mind-body connection is an important issue in medical studies. Psychological changes impact the body in different ways, such as the effect of stress on the body's immune system.

Research into the causes of these disorders can also lead to improvement in diagnosis and treatment, with new drugs developed and further advances made in therapeutic techniques.

SEVERE PSYCHOLOGICAL DISORDERS

A number of psychological disorders can be severe, persistent and disabling. People stricken with these disorders (e.g., schizophrenia) are impaired in their ability to function intellectually, emotionally and socially, and as a result, many of life's functions to grind to a halt. There is a profound impact on the patients, their families and often the community. These conditions can be fatal, as they lead to higher rates of suicide. Depressive conditions can be just as disabling as many chronic physical illnesses.

Severe mental illness is no respecter of persons; it affects people of all ages, races and walks of life (e.g., wealthy or poor, educated or high school dropouts). Although some of these people are residents of institutions, most live at home, but a number are considered homeless. In some cases, these disorders persist for a lifetime, continuously or intermittently; some individuals improve dramatically, while others continue to fail. There are multiple challenges in providing therapy and care for these individuals.

Considerable progress has been made in modes of treatment (medications, psychotherapy and others), but there is still a need for further improvement. In many communities, resources are limited, usually due to financial constraints; sometimes individuals who are mentally ill end up in the criminal justice system and are not referred to appropriate services for care; in addition, negative attitudes of the public and some medical professionals often present barriers to effective care.

DIAGNOSING PSYCHOLOGICAL DISORDERS

The stresses and strains attributed to routines of normal life do not require professional treatment. These episodes go away by themselves (like a common cold). Getting treatment for them is unnecessary and could cause more suffering than the original problem. However, when the problem is severe, incapacitating or of long duration, treatment is indicated. Often psychological problems fall somewhere between the normal stresses of life and the incapacitating ones. These are the ones that can be difficult to diagnose and for which it can be difficult to determine if treatment is warranted. Diagnosing psychological problems is difficult because the underlying problems are expressed in different ways by different individuals.

Some people cope with difficulties in life just fine and would not consider seeking treatment for an emotional problem. They use personal resources and "self-control" to manage such a situation. Other people worry constantly, and they may seek professional help for even minor unhappiness or what most would consider unimportant concerns. However, such people may experience substantial distress and disability, even when others consider their problems trivial. Neither the people who are coping nor those who are seeking help are wrong in handling the situation as they deem appropriate.

If you are experiencing symptoms but are undecided whether your symptoms are serious enough to seek professional help, you can discuss your problems with a family member or friend. Sometimes just talking about a problem or concern is sufficient to put your mind at ease. If the symptoms persist, seek professional help; don't ignore them. Many psychological disorders respond well to early treatment, so by seeking help you can avoid a major mental health problem.

Diagnosing a Psychological Disorder

Diagnosis of a psychological disorder is the first step on the road to recovery. The clinical interview starts the process. You will be asked about the symptoms you are having, about your past mental as well as physical and medical health, about your family and your upbringing, about your use of mind-altering substances and about your current lifestyle—work, marital status, friends, recreation and other aspects of your daily life. A physical examination and laboratory tests may be recommended. Sometimes specialized psychological testing will be needed to clarify the nature of your condition.

Many health care professionals use the definitions of mental health disorders found in the *Diagnostic and Statistical Manual of Mental Disorders*, 4th edition (DSM-IV), published by the American Psychiatry Association. This reference provides a set of standards to help doctors and other mental health care providers diagnose a specific psychological disorder based on criteria that have been carefully researched and tested. Each disorder is defined by describing the symptoms that are often present in persons with the disorder or the symptoms th⸱ ⸱ are not present, what behaviors are observable and the statements that are made in response to an interviewer's questions. The material in the book is based on current knowledge, and the definitions and criteria may change as more information about mental disorders is obtained. The DSM is periodically revised to reflect new knowledge.

The DSM-IV, of course, is not the final statement about diagnosis. Health care providers recognize that each patient is a unique individual and that they must use judgment, insight and empathy in making a diagnosis and recommending treatment. The DSM-IV describes fully developed conditions, while any one person is not likely to have all the manifestations. Also, existing conditions are frequently interpreted in a new light as a result of research.

MEDICAL PROBLEMS THAT MIMIC PSYCHOLOGICAL DISORDERS

There are some medical problems that can affect the central nervous system and cause symptoms that mimic those found in a psychological disorder. Your doctor will determine if your symptoms are being caused by a general medical disorder or some other problem and will treat it appropriately. Possibilities include:

Exposure to toxic substances—Such substances include lead, mercury, aluminum, manganese, arsenic and bromides. Ingestion of or environmental exposure to one of these may cause delirium, confusion, personality changes, hallucinations and behavioral changes.

Endocrine disorders—Problems involving the adrenal or thyroid glands or low blood sugar may cause a variety of mental status changes or changes in behavior.

Medications—Certain drugs (including nonprescription drugs) can affect mental functioning. Some drugs cause a toxic psychosis and others delirium or confusion. There are several drugs that have depression as a side effect.

Malignancies (cancer)—These diseases can sometimes cause mental status changes such as depression, anxiety attacks and dementia.

Others—There are other medical illnesses that can sometimes cause mental status changes. These include Wilson's disease, acute intermittent porphyria, Huntington's chorea, vitamin B-12 deficiency, pellagra, temporal lobe epilepsy, high or low calcium levels and low potassium or sodium levels.

Treatments for Psychological Disorders

Determining the appropriate treatment for a psychological disorder is dependent on many factors. You as the patient, your family and your doctor (or other health care provider) should work together as a team to find the best approach to relieve your symptoms. In some cases, people with a psychological disorder may not be aware the problem exists. They have lost touch with reality and often do not realize they are ill. Only to others (usually family members) are their symptoms noticeable. In these situations, the person with the disorder may not be able to cooperate at first with decisions about treatment.

An important decision about treatment is whether it will be inpatient (in a hospital or care facility) or outpatient treatment. For the majority of patients, there is no need for hospitalization. Indications for inpatient treatment include suicidal or homicidal behavior, inability to function (e.g., to feed or dress oneself), impulsive self-destructive behavior or inability to control emotional outbursts. Hospitalization also might be required for purposes of diagnostic evaluation (determining if the disabling symptoms are psychological or physiological).

Your doctor will explain the diagnosis, the treatment options that are right for you and the reasons for the choices. Treatments for psychological disorders include:

- No treatment or self-care.
- Medications only.
- Psychotherapy only.
- Medications and psychotherapy combined.
- Electroconvulsive therapy (combined with medications and/or psychotherapy).
- Rehabilitation or habilitation.
- Support groups, such as Alcoholics Anonymous (AA) or Al-Anon.

NO TREATMENT OR SELF-CARE

Many psychological problems are self-limiting and run their course without any treatment. Other psychological problems can be resolved fairly simply with self-care. Self-care includes a number of steps depending on the individual and the situation. Some approaches include changing a diet to exclude caffeine or to lose some extra weight, beginning an exercise program, talking to family or friends about the problem, keeping a diary or journal and writing down thoughts and feelings, trying to be optimistic (thinking positively and not negatively), finding things in life that are humorous, being more social, reaching out to help others and learning ways to manage the stresses encountered in personal relationships, work and other activities.

MEDICATIONS

Medications are used for treatment of many psychological disorders. Some medications relieve acute symptoms, while others relieve symptoms over a period of weeks to months. Medications can help prevent recurrences of the disorder, and in some cases will be needed for life.

PSYCHOTHERAPY

Psychotherapy is used to treat a variety of psychological disorders. It can be used alone or in conjunction with medications (combining treatment is helpful in many cases). In psychotherapy, you work with a qualified health care provider (therapist) who listens, talks and helps you solve your problems. Psychotherapy can be brief (just a few visits) or extend over a period of months or years. It can take the form of individual therapy (just you and the therapist), group therapy (with a therapist, you and other people with similar problems) or family or marriage therapy (with a therapist, you and family members or loved ones). There are a variety of approaches to psychotherapy, such as behavioral therapy, cognitive therapy or interpersonal therapy).

Most patients respond well to psychotherapy, but there are some who do not. Talk to your health care provider if you do not feel the treatment is effective. Another psychotherapy approach may be needed. Sometimes changing to a different therapist can be beneficial. You may find it easier to talk freely with one therapist than another.

ELECTROCONVULSIVE THERAPY (ECT)

ECT is used for patients with severe depression and other select disorders that have not responded to standard treatments. ECT uses an electric shock to induce a seizure that affects the central nervous system and helps bring relief of the symptoms. General anesthesia and special muscle-relaxing medicines are used to prevent physical harm and pain, and the effects are limited primarily to the brain. After the procedure, patients experience only mild discomfort as well as some short-term (1 to 2 weeks) memory impairment. When appropriately used, ECT has an 80 to 90% success rate. To prevent relapse, ECT "boosters" are sometimes recommended.

REHABILITATION OR HABILITATION

A severe mental illness is debilitating. Patients are often unable to perform the daily tasks necessary to function in life (cooking, cleaning, shopping, budgeting). They may not know how to be part of the community or how to develop friendships or find a job and perform it successfully. Rehabilitation services used in combination with clinical services (psychotherapy and medications) can help an individual reach the highest level of well-being possible. Rehabilitation services focus on the social skills, vocational status and independent living skills that an individual needs to function in his or her own environment. In general, these services help individuals with severe mental illness to obtain and hold a job, get along with other people and live as independently as possible. A variety of specialists may be involved, such as occupational therapists, speech therapists and vocational trainers.

Some people with severe mental illness never learned certain skills before the onset of their illness. They may have never been employed or never lived away from their parents. Services for these people are referred to as habilitation rather than rehabilitation.

SUPPORT GROUPS

There are various organizations and support groups that exist to help people with particular health problems, and many millions belong to these groups. Their goals are to provide support and encouragement, share information and let people know they are not alone in dealing with their particular problem. Some of the groups have a professional leader and formal structure, while others are more loosely structured. These self-help groups can provide participants with much-needed comfort, emotional support, information and understanding about their shared problem. They can help reduce a person's stress while increasing his or her self-confidence and self-esteem and providing a sense of belonging. For people with psychological problems, this type of group therapy can be very useful. Popular and well-known groups include Alcoholics Anonymous, Al-Anon, Narcotics Anonymous and Overeaters Anonymous. In larger communities, you can find a self-help group for almost any condition. Most are listed in the local telephone directory.

Professionals Who Treat Psychological Disorders

Many people with a psychological disorder can be treated by their regular health care provider. However, some people may need specialized treatment because the first treatment did not work, because they need a combination of treatments or because the condition is severe or it lasts a long time. Many times a second opinion or consultation is all that is needed. If a mental health professional provides treatment, it is usually on an outpatient basis (not in the hospital). If you think you need to see a mental health specialist, discuss it with your doctor. There is a wide range of professional (and lay) resources to choose from for mental health problems, and sometimes a team approach is needed.

GENERAL HEALTH CARE PROVIDERS

Physician—A medical doctor or doctor of osteopathy (M.D., D.O.) who has some training in treating mental or psychiatric disorders. A physician can review your medical history and medications for clues. He or she can refer you to other appropriate resources if necessary.

Physician assistant (P.A.)—An individual with medical training and some training in treating mental or psychiatric disorders.

Nurse practitioner—A registered nurse (R.N.) with additional training and some training in treating mental or psychiatric disorders.

MENTAL HEALTH SPECIALISTS

Psychiatrist—A physician (M.D., D.O.) who specializes in the diagnosis and treatment of mental or psychiatric disorders. As a physician, he or she can prescribe medications.

Psychologist—A person with a doctoral degree in psychology (Ph.D. or Psy.D.) and training in counseling, psychotherapy and psychological testing. A psychologist cannot prescribe medications.

Psychoanalyst—A person who may or may not be an M.D. who has had very specialized training in analysis at a psychoanalytic institute.

Social worker—A person with a degree in social work. A social worker with a master's degree (M.S.W.) often has specialized training in counseling.

Psychiatric nurse specialist—A registered nurse (R.N.), usually with a master's degree in psychiatric nursing, who specializes in treating mental or psychiatric disorders.

Counselor—A person with a degree in counseling, psychology or another related field who specializes in helping people with mental health problems.

OTHERS

Pastors—Clergy who may have formal training in counseling, though many do not. People often turn to their pastors for counseling and advice during periods of emotional distress.

Case managers—Individuals with diverse training and experience who provide advocacy and support to patients, usually outside of an office setting. They often link patients with needed services.

Pharmacists—People with degrees in pharmacy who dispense medications and who can provide counseling and answers to questions or concerns about them.

Therapists (occupational, physical, speech, sex or other)—People with a variety of educational backgrounds who provide special therapy depending on patients' needs.

When a Relative Has a Psychological Disorder

Once the diagnosis of a psychological disorder is made in a family member, the rest of the family goes through an emotional upheaval as well. Having a loved one with a psychological disorder can affect every aspect of family life. There may be changes in daily routines and social life, additional stresses on finances, restrictions on activities, worry about the future and a variety of other problems to be coped with.

Feelings of guilt and self-blame are common among family members of a person with a psychological disorder. They wonder if their behavior, feelings or actions caused this psychological problem. In addition, the person with the disorder often blames other family members for his or her behavior or actions. It is important for family members to recognize that they are not the cause of the problem. If these feelings of guilt or self-blame persist or seem overwhelming, counseling can help resolve them.

Education about the disorder is one key to helping everyone involved. Both the person with the disorder (if able to comprehend) and the family need to learn and understand what they can about the disorder itself. By learning about the disorder, family members can better communicate with the person, with each other and with the health care professionals who will be providing the treatment.

The age and family relationship of the person with the disorder make a difference. As patients, children, spouses or aging parents all differ in their needs and the levels of care required. Providing care can alter the relationship of a caregiver to the patient. What was once a loving relationship can be reduced to monitoring medications, providing for the patient's physical needs and keeping him or her safe from harm. It is important to try to maintain as many of the caring feelings as possible. This can be difficult, as frequently the patient is not aware of his or her behavior and how it may be hurtful to another person.

Family members providing home care (who are usually female) must look to their own needs as well as the patient's. It is common to feel alone, hopeless, fearful, angry, confused, stressed, resentful and overloaded. These feelings can sometimes lead to physical illness for a caregiver. Seek help from others before you reach "burn-out." Ask other family members for help and support, talk to the doctor or get counseling and join a support group for caregivers. Special daycare centers or programs for patients are available that will give a caregiver some needed time off (respite).

There are situations in which a person with a psychological disorder may be best cared for in an environment other than at home. This may be for the safety of the patient or may be best due to the severity of the symptoms or the effect of the home care on other family members. In some cases, the patient may do better outside the home. Making this decision with regard to a family member is one of the most difficult decisions the rest of the family will ever need to make, but it is sometimes the best solution. In reaching this decision, the family will have support and input from the health care professionals providing treatment.

While most therapists are happy to involve their family members, their first obligation is to the patient. In some cases, the patient may not wish to involve the family, and rules of confidentially give the patient the right to prohibit communication unless there is an emergency or the patient is not legally competent to make decisions.

Psychological Disorders in Children & Adolescents

Psychological disorders in children and adolescents vary—in the age at which they first appear, the types of symptoms and levels of impairment they produce and the long-term effects they have on the young person's development. These disorders are often the same as disorders found in adults, but some are specific to childhood or adolescence. There are emotional disturbances, such as depression and anxiety, behavioral problems characterized by disruptive and antisocial behavior and developmental impairments that limit a child's ability to think, learn, form social attachments or communicate effectively with others. Often parents think a child or adolescent will "outgrow" mental or behavior problems, but many of these problems, if untreated, carry on into adulthood.

The causes of psychological problems in children and adolescents involve both biological factors (genetic) and environmental factors (family and social environments). Factors that put children at risk of psychological disorders include:

- Genetic factors that can increase a young person's vulnerability to certain disorders.
- Biological factors, such as physical trauma or exposure to toxic chemicals or drugs.
- Poor prenatal care that leads to premature birth and low birth weight.
- Chronic physical illness, such as diabetes mellitus, asthma, epilepsy and AIDS.
- Cognitive impairments that result from mental illness and also from blindness or deafness.
- Persistent psychosocial situations (poverty, homelessness, inadequate schooling).
- Child abuse or neglect.
- Parental mental illness, which can sometimes cause family disruptions and inconsistent parenting (although many parents with a mental illness are fine parents).

RECOGNIZING AND TREATING PSYCHOLOGICAL DISORDERS

For parents, it is difficult to recognize whether their child has a psychological problem or is just going through an emotional, social, educational or behavioral development phase. There is great variability among children and adolescents in their pace of development. Also, young children are unable to explain or talk about their feelings or reasons for certain behaviors. Parents should not feel shy, guilty or hesitant about sharing their problems or concerns with a professional. Generally, parents should seek professional help or advice if:

- The parents' efforts to resolve a behavior problem don't appear to be working.
- The child's behavior is dysfunctional and persistent and is causing unhappiness.
- There are ongoing problems in school.
- There is a concern about substance abuse.
- An eating disorder is suspected.
- The child's behavior is very upsetting to the parents.

Generally, professionals evaluating a child's mental health look at the severity, duration and frequency of the problem; the age-appropriateness of the behavior; and the number of problems involved. The steps in diagnosing a psychological disorder in a child are similar to those for an adult (discussed earlier); the steps taken are age-appropriate.

Medical care professionals (usually professionals who are trained specifically to work with children, such as a pediatric psychiatrist) treat these disorders in children with psychotherapy (e.g., play therapy for young children) and medications or with combinations of the two. In many cases, the parents need special help and training in effective ways of handling their children with these disorders. Family therapy is usually recommended. In addition, support (self-help) groups are available in most communities for parents or other caregivers of children with psychological disorders.

DISORDERS THAT APPEAR IN THE DISORDER CHARTS

- Adjustment Disorder
- Anorexia Nervosa
- Anxiety
- Attention-Deficit Hyperactivity Disorder
- Bipolar Disorder (Manic-Depressive Disorder)
- Bulimia
- Dementia
- Depression
- Mental Retardation
- Obsessive-Compulsive Disorder
- Panic Disorder
- Phobias
- Post-Traumatic Stress Disorder
- Schizophrenic Disorders
- Sleep Disorders
- Somatoform Disorders
- Substance Abuse and Addiction

DISORDERS NOT INCLUDED IN THE DISORDER CHARTS

- **Autism**—A development disorder that appears in infancy or early childhood. It is characterized by self-absorption, inability to relate to others, avoidance of eye contact, playing alone, removal from reality and a wide range of other behaviors. However, many autistic people lead nearly normal lives, and some are uniquely gifted.
- **Conduct Disorder**—A personality disorder generally diagnosed in children. It is characterized by disruptive behaviors such as disobeying authority, stealing, lying and picking fights with other children.
- **Elective Mutism**—A rare disorder in children in which they withdraw by not speaking at all or speaking only to family members.
- **Gender Identity Disorder**—In children, a disorder characterized by a preference to be the opposite sex, which usually affects boys more than girls. Boys with the disorder are preoccupied with activities and clothing that are typically those of girls. In adolescents, this disorder is characterized by a person's persistent feelings of discomfort about his or her sexual identity.
- **Learning Disability (LD)**—An inability to read (dyslexia), write (dysgraphia) or do grade-appropriate mathematics (dyscalculia) in children of normal or above-average intelligence. Most experts feel that these disabilities stem from some form of minimal brain dysfunction.
- **Oppositional Defiant Disorder**—A childhood disorder characterized by a pattern of negative, hostile and defiant behavior. The child is usually argumentative, angry and resentful.
- **Overanxious Disorder**—A childhood anxiety disorder that varies among children in severity and is characterized by excessive worry about almost everything, extreme self-consciousness, inability to relax, a need for excessive reassurance and self-doubts.
- **Pica**—An eating disorder in which a child repeatedly eats nonnutritive substances (e.g., clay, paint. dirt).
- **Separation Anxiety**—A feeling of distress that occurs in a child when parted from his or her parents or home. It is part of a normal development phase for babies. Separation anxiety disorder is a condition in which the reaction to separation is greater than that expected or inappropriate for the child's level of development.
- **Other Disorders**—Manifested by problems in communication (stuttering), poor motor skills, eating disorders, tics, problems with elimination (bowel and urinary functions), behavior problems, etc.

Psychological Disorders in Older Persons

Most older citizens are mentally alert and are fully independent in their activities of daily living. However, as individuals age, they accumulate disabilities and diseases, and doctor visits increase. Functional impairments increase, creating a need for assistance with basic activities. There are many theories about the aging process, and medical studies are ongoing to help understand the age-related physiologic changes that occur. Today it is generally accepted by medical experts that the mind and mental functioning do not automatically deteriorate with aging. Though there are physical changes in the brain as people age that affect mental status, these changes do not mean that there is a general decline and that disorders like dementia are to be expected.

The psychological disorders in older adults are narrower in scope than those that are diagnosed in younger age groups. Psychological disorders such as phobias, obsessive-compulsive disorder, panic disorder and others are recognized at an earlier age and are diagnosed and treated long before a person reaches older age. The older population is more often affected with psychological disorders such as depression (with the added risk of suicide), dementia and anxiety. These are not caused by aging, but aspects of aging are risk factors for development of these disorders.

The elderly have the highest rate of suicide of any age group, and suicide is often preceded by depression. Grief, isolation, physical illness and other psychiatric disorders also put older adults at a higher risk of suicide.

COMMON PROBLEMS AFFECTING MENTAL STATUS IN LATER YEARS

Each developmental stage of life has its own types of stresses, and older age is no exception. Though many think this might be the best time in a person's life, aging has stresses and changes that can provoke a variety of emotional and psychological responses:

• **Physical Illness**—Cardiac disorders, lung disorders, arthritis, Parkinson's disease and stroke are among disorders often associated with aging. They can often produce psychological symptoms such as depression, sleep disturbances and confusion. Hospitalization can cause disorientation, delirium and confusion.

• **Medications**—Side effects and adverse reactions to medications are often more severe in older people. Also, because of the need to take several different medication, more drug interactions occur in older persons. Psychological reactions include confusion, forgetfulness, agitation, depression, anxiety, hallucinations or paranoia. Older persons are likely to take a number of medications whose effects on mental functioning are additive. Also, a person's ability to metabolize medications diminishes with age; a dose of medicine that is appropriate for a younger person may be excessive for an older person.

• **Sleep Problems**—People tend to sleep less as they get older, and the sleep is naturally lighter. Medications, caffeine use, alcohol consumption and physical ailments can contribute to sleep problems. Lack of sleep can affect daytime alertness and ability to function and can lead to confusion.

• **Hearing and Vision Problems**—Symptoms that seem to be associated with mental deterioration may be due to hearing or vision problems. Inappropriate answers to questions can be caused by a hearing loss, not dementia. Hearing loss is also associated with paranoia. Not being able to see clearly can result in confusion.

• **Alcoholism**—Older problem drinkers are either chronic, long-time abusers of alcohol or situational abusers, people who have turned to alcohol in response to the increased stresses associated with growing older. Alcohol can produce numerous mental and behavioral changes as well as a form of dementia.

• **Sexual Problems**—Many older people want and are able to lead a satisfactory sex life. Age may bring some changes, such as taking longer for a male to achieve an erection, and in women the decline in estrogen levels brings changes. For others, sexual dysfunction may be caused by illness, disability or medications. Concern with sexual function may lead to symptoms of depression or anxiety.

• **Grief and Bereavement**—As a person moves into the later years, losses are inevitable, including deaths of family members and friends, loss of one's job (retirement), often loss of income, loss of vitality, loss of some degree of health, changes in physical appearance (e.g., wrinkles and baldness) and sometimes a loss of one's familiar home environment. Some degree of grief and reactive depression is expected in response to these losses. Emotionally healthy older people work through such grief and return to their usual mood, outlook and activity levels. In some, however, the losses may lead to more severe depression that requires treatment.

• **Nutritional Deficiencies**—Older people may not eat properly for a variety of reasons: living alone and not cooking, no easy way to shop for groceries, lack of money, denture problems, etc. Continued nutritional deficiencies can lead to mental impairments.

• **Loneliness**—The elderly are more likely to be isolated from other people and social activities. For some, this isolation is acceptable as a trade-off for remaining independent. In others, being lonely and feeling separated and shut off leads to problems with depression, paranoia, neglect of self-care, alcohol abuse and possibly suicide.

• **Dependency**—Loss of independence is a major fear of older adults. A move to a grown child's home or to a care facility can be emotionally overwhelming. Reactions include depression, anxiety, anger and behavior changes such as withdrawal and infantilism (being childlike mentally and emotionally).

• **Abuse of the Elderly**—Physical neglect and physical injury of older adults occurs more frequently than reports indicate (perhaps as often as child abuse). The abuser is often a family member, and the older abused person is reluctant to tell anyone what is going on. The older person may become withdrawn, depressed or anxious. Also, older persons are often taken advantage of financially through theft, scams or inappropriate spending by guardians.

MEMORY & AGING

Memory is the component of mental functioning that most concerns older adults. They fear memory changes will contribute to a loss of independence and may be a sign of Alzheimer's disease. Studies have shown that memory functions may slow somewhat and that capabilities for learning and storing new information may be slightly affected, but memory for entrenched learning and personal information does not appear to be affected by aging. A person's later years can still be a period of learning and enjoying new accomplishments.

People who remain active intellectually and physically as they get older are the least likely to experience mental decline. There are many colleges and other organizations (e.g., elderhostel) that offer special courses to senior citizens; joining results in gratifying new experiences.

Older individuals and their families are often concerned that the least sign of mental changes could mean a diagnosis of dementia. Most often, there is no reason to be alarmed. "Benign forgetfulness" is a common trait of all ages. It is characterized by the inability to recall a name or some element of a prior experience when one thinks he or she should be able to do so. The person may recall many related features of the person or episode and know precisely what element or name is not being recalled. Usually the person will recall the name or element later, unexpectedly. A person with dementia will have no recall of the entire episode, as if it never happened, and can make only feeble, ineffective efforts to recall a name or episode.

DEMENTIA

Dementia is the loss of mental competence, a common and distressing disability of older persons. Dementia is not a feature of normal aging, but is a result of several disease processes. The most common form of dementia in older persons is Alzheimer's disease, which accounts for 50% of the cases. Other causes of dementia include vascular disease of the brain (blood clots, strokes or blood vessel narrowing), hereditary diseases (e.g., Huntington's chorea), infections and chronic alcoholism. Most causes of dementia are not reversible, although treatment may lessen their impact on the affected person.

Severe depression in older persons can mimic the manifestation of dementia (pseudodementia). With treatment of the depression, the symptoms usually disappear.

TREATMENT FOR OLDER ADULTS

Information about each psychological disorder is found on the charts in the Disorder Charts section. The basic information is the same for all age groups. It is important to recognize the signs and symptoms and seek medical help for any problem. Early diagnosis and treatment can head off complications and unnecessary mental suffering. Treatment is appropriate for persons of all ages. There is no age beyond which treatment is not appropriate. A person over age 90 can benefit from treatment of depression as much as someone younger.

There are medical professionals who have special training in dealing with the mental and emotional problems of older adults (geriatric medicine). They are concerned with mental health and adjustment problems associated with aging.

Steps in treating psychological disorders in older adults involve psychotherapy, medications or a combination of the two. Electroconvulsive therapy may be recommended for severe depression. Support groups are available in most communities for just about any disorder.

WHY SOME RESIST SEEKING HELP

There are many older people who suffer from emotional and psychological problems who do not seek help. Reasons include:

• Resistance to asking for help for a psychological problem (it's all right to ask for help for a physical ailment, but not for a psychological ailment).

• Reluctance to divulge personal feelings and family problems to someone.

• Lack of knowledge about what medical help is available for these problems.

• Feeling ashamed to admit that one has an emotional problem.

• Belief that one is too old for any treatment to be effective.

• Belief that one should be able to resolve the problem alone or that the problem will go away with time.

• Lack of money or a belief that money would be better spent on something or someone else.

Family members, friends or others who observe symptoms of a psychological disorder in an older person should encourage him or her to seek professional help. Treatment for such a problem can make huge differences in the life of an older person. The quality of life improves for the older person as well as the family.

What Are
Psychotherapy Drugs?

Psychotherapy drugs are medications prescribed for treating the symptoms of psychological disorders. Much of the time, these drugs do not bring about a cure, but will relieve the symptoms of the particular disorder being treated, just as the symptoms of illnesses such as arthritis, diabetes or a heart condition can be relieved by medications, but the medications will not cure the illnesses.

Each psychotherapy drug works a little differently, and some work only on specific psychological disorders and on specific symptoms. A diagnosis of the disorder by a health care professional is the first step in determining the best medication, its dosage, duration of use and maintenance therapy. In some cases, more than one medication may be prescribed depending on the symptoms and the disorder.

Psychotherapy drugs will not solve problems of living; they will not put money in the bank, make the kids behave, save a troubled marriage or miraculously bring you happiness. What these medications can do is relieve you of distress and stabilize your mental and emotional life so that you and your therapist can work more effectively on solving your problems.

In taking a medication, follow the instructions provided by the doctor or take as indicated on the label. Taking medications as directed will help relieve your symptoms. One of the reasons psychotherapy medications don't always work is that people do not take their medications regularly, and in some cases fail to take them at all. Reasons for noncompliance vary. There are side effects associated with most of the medications, and the cost may be high. Besides, people feel they should be able to recover "on their own" (they are "weak" if they can't), they have fears of becoming addicted to a medication and they may lack understanding that most of these medications will not work "right away." Talk to your doctor if you have any questions or concerns about staring a medication. If a medication does not provide the desired results, ask the doctor about an alternative. There is almost always another option.

Psychotherapy drugs are divided into different groups, usually named by the type of disorder being treated (e.g., antidepressants, which are used to treat depression). Within these groups, the drugs may be listed by class, such as benzodiazepines, or by generic name, such as clozapine. A medication can be listed in more than one group. For example, benzodiazepines are both antianxiety agents and sedative-hypnotic agents.

ANTIPSYCHOTICS
(ALSO CALLED NEUROLEPTICS)

Used primarily to treat symptoms of schizophrenic disorders or to treat psychosis associated with other psychiatric or physical diseases. Included in this drug group are chlorprothixene, clozapine, haloperidol, loxapine, molindone, risperidone, phenothiazines and thioxthixene. Patients who fail to respond to one type of antipsychotic may respond to another.

ANTIDEPRESSANTS

Used to treat the symptoms of various types of depression (such as bipolar disorder, dysthemic disorder and major depression). Included in this drug group are several drug classes and specific generic names: bupropion, carbamazepine, fluvoxamine, lithium, maprotiline, monoamine oxidase (MAO) inhibitors, nefazodone, serotonin reuptake inhibitors (paroxetine, fluoxetine and sertraline), trazodone, tricyclic antidepressants, valproic acid and venlafaxine. Patients may respond better to one of these medications than to another.

ANTIANXIETY AGENTS
(ALSO CALLED ANXIOLYTICS OR TRANQUILIZERS)

Used to treat anxiety and anxiety disorders. Included in this drug group are benzodiazepines, buspirone and meprobamate.

SEDATIVE-HYPNOTIC AGENTS

Used to treat sleep disorders such as insomnia. Included in this group are barbiturates, benzodiazepines, chloral hydrate, diphenhydramine, ethchlorvynol, hydroxyzine, triazolam and zolpidem.

CENTRAL NERVOUS SYSTEM STIMULANTS

Used to treat attention-deficit hyperactivity disorder, fatigue and other symptoms. Included in this group are amphetamines, caffeine, methylphenidate and pemoline.

MOOD STABILIZERS

Help smooth out extreme mood swings, particularly in bipolar (manic-depressive) disorder. These drugs include lithium, valproic acid and carbamazepine.

MISCELLANEOUS AGENTS

Used to treat various symptoms caused by psychological disorders, side effects from other medications and withdrawal symptoms. These include beta-adrenergic blocking agents, calcium channel blockers, disulfiram, naltrexone, tacrine, trimeprazine, and others that may be prescribed by your doctor.

General Information About Drugs

A drug cannot "cure." It aids the body's natural defenses to promote recovery. Likewise, a manufacturer or doctor cannot guarantee a drug will be useful for everyone. The complexity of the human body, individual responses in different people and in the same person under different circumstances, past and present health, age and gender influence how well a drug works.

All effective drugs produce desirable changes in the body, but a drug can also cause undesirable adverse reactions or side effects in some people. Despite uncertainties, the drug discoveries of recent years have given us tools to save lives and reduce discomfort. Before you decide whether to take a drug, you or your doctor must ask, "Will the benefits outweigh the risks?"

The purpose of this book is to give you enough information about the most widely used psychological drugs so you can make a wise decision. The information will alert you to potential or preventable problems. You can learn what to do if problems arise.

The information is derived from many authoritative sources and represents the consensus of many experts. Every effort has been made to ensure accuracy and completeness. Drug information changes with continuing observations by clinicians and users.

Information in this book applies to generic drugs in both the United States and Canada. Generic names do not vary in these countries, but brand names do.

BE SAFE! TELL YOUR DOCTOR

Some suggestions for wise drug use apply to all drugs. Always give your doctor or dentist complete information about the drugs you take, including your medical history, your medical plans and your progress while under medication.

MEDICAL HISTORY

Tell the important facts of your medical history including illness and previous experience with drugs. Include allergic or adverse reactions you have had to any medicine or other substance in the past. Describe the allergic symptoms you have, such as hay fever, asthma, eye watering and itching, throat irritation and reactions to food. People who have allergies to common substances are more likely to develop drug allergies.

List all drugs you take. Don't forget vitamin and mineral supplements; skin, rectal or vaginal medicines; eye drops and eardrops; antacids; antihistamines; cold and cough remedies; inhalants and nasal sprays; aspirin, aspirin combinations or other pain relievers; motion sickness remedies; weight-loss aids; salt and sugar substitutes; caffeine; oral contraceptives; sleeping pills or "tonics."

FUTURE MEDICAL PLANS

Discuss plans for elective surgery, pregnancy and breast-feeding. These conditions may require discontinuing or modifying the dosages of medicines you may be taking.

QUESTIONS

Don't hesitate to ask questions about a drug. Your doctor, nurse or pharmacist will be able to provide more information if they are familiar with you and your medical history.

YOUR ROLE

Learn the generic names and brand names of all your medicines. Write them down to help you remember. If a drug is a combination, learn the names of its generic ingredients.

TAKING A MEDICATION

Never take medicine in the dark! Recheck the label before each use. You could be taking the *wrong* drug! Tell your doctor about any unexpected new symptoms you have while taking medicine. You may need to change medicines or have a dose adjustment.

STORAGE

Keep all medicines out of children's reach. Store drugs in a cool, dry place, such as a kitchen cabinet or bedroom. Avoid medicine cabinets in bathrooms. They get too moist and warm at times. Keep medicine in its original container, tightly closed. Don't remove the label! If directions call for refrigeration, keep the medicine cool, but don't freeze it.

RESPONSE TO MEDICATIONS

Several weeks may pass after starting a medication before you notice improvement in your condition. Antidepressants, for example, often take 2 to 4 weeks before they take effect. Give your medications a chance to work before deciding they are not helping. However, if your condition is worsening rather than staying the same or gradually improving, call the doctor and discuss the situation.

ALCOHOL & MEDICATIONS

Alcohol and drugs of abuse defeat the purpose of many psychological medications. For example, alcohol causes depression; if you drink and are depressed, antidepressants will not relieve the depression. If you have a problem with drinking or drugs, discuss it with your doctor. There are many ways to help you conquer such a problem once you are willing to admit that you have a problem.

ALERTNESS

Many of the medicines used to treat psychological disorders may alter your alertness. If you drive, work around machinery, or must avoid sedation, discuss the problem with your doctor; usually there are ways (e.g., when you take the medicine) to manage the problem.

DISCARDING

Don't save leftover medicine to use later. Discard it before the expiration date shown on the container. Dispose safely to protect children and pets.

REFILLS

Refills must be ordered by your doctor or dentist, either in the first prescription or later. The pharmacy that originally filled the prescription can refill it without checking with your doctor or previous pharmacy (if your doctor has approved refills). If you go to a new pharmacy, you must have a new prescription, or the new pharmacist must call your doctor or original pharmacy to see if a refill is authorized.

If you need a refill, call your pharmacist and order your refill by prescription number and name.

Use one pharmacy for the whole family if you can. The pharmacist then has a record of all of your drugs and can communicate effectively with your doctor, you and your family. It is also valuable if you are taking several medications that interact with each other.

Most insurance plans limit a prescription to one month at a time. If you are to continue the medication beyond a month, *don't wait until you are completely out* of medication to call for a refill. The pharmacist may have to contact your doctor for refill approval, which may take several days, especially on weekends or during vacation times.

Compliance with Doctors' Recommendations

For medical purposes, *compliance* is defined as the extent to which a patient follows the instructions of a doctor and includes taking medications on schedule, keeping appointments and following directions for changes in life-style, such as changing one's diet or exercise.

Although the cost of obtaining medical advice and medication is one of the largest items in a family budget, many people defeat the health care process by departing from the doctor's recommendations. This failure to carry out the doctor's instructions is the single most common cause of treatment failure. Perhaps the instructions were not presented clearly, or you may not have understood them or realized their importance and benefits.

FACTORS THAT CAN CAUSE PROBLEMS WITH COMPLIANCE:

- Treatment recommendations that combine two or more actions (such as instructions to take medication, see a therapist and join a support group).
- Recommendations that require lifestyle changes (such as dieting).
- Recommendations that involve long-term regimens (such as taking a medication for life).
- Recommendations for very young patients or for the elderly (another person has to be responsible for following the instructions).

EXAMPLES OF NONCOMPLIANCE:

- Medications are forgotten or discontinued too soon. Forgetting to take a medication is the most common of all shortcomings, especially if a medication must be taken more than once a day. If you need to take a medication several times a day, set out a week's supply in an inexpensive pill box that you can carry with you.
- Side effects of medications are a common problem. Almost all medications have some unpleasant side effects. Often these disappear after a few days, but if they don't, let your doctor know right away. Side effects can often be controlled by changing to a similar medication or by adding medications that control the side effects.
- Not taking a drug because it is unpleasant (e.g., bad tasting). Ask your doctor about options.
- Cost is another reason why there are treatment failures; because of a tight budget, a person may take a medication less frequently than prescribed or just not purchase it. If you can't afford a medication, perhaps a less costly one can be prescribed or your doctor can find other ways to provide it.
- Laboratory tests, x-rays or other recommended medical studies are not obtained, perhaps due to concerns about costs or fear of the tests themselves.
- Recommendations about behavioral changes such as diet or exercise are ignored (old habits are difficult for anyone to change).
- Suggested immunizations are not obtained, sometimes due to fear of needles.
- Follow-up visits to the doctor are not made, or appointments are cancelled, perhaps due to problems finding transportation or long waiting times in the doctor's office.

COMMUNICATING WITH YOUR DOCTOR:

- If you don't understand something, *ask*.
- If there are reasons why you cannot follow a recommendation, *speak up*.
- If you have reservations or fears about treatment, *discuss them*.

Remember, it is your health and your money that are at issue. You and your doctor are—or should be—working together to make you well.

Checklist for Safer Use of All Medications

- Tell your doctor about *any* drug you take (even aspirin, allergy pills, cough and cold preparations, antacids, laxatives, vitamins, etc.) *before* you take *any* new drug.

- Learn all you can about drugs you may take *before* you take them. Information sources are your doctor, your nurse, your pharmacist, this book and other books in your public library.

- Don't take drugs prescribed for someone else—even if your symptoms are the same.

- Keep your prescription drugs to yourself. Your drugs may be harmful to someone else.

- Tell your doctor about any symptoms you believe are caused by a drug—prescription or nonprescription—that you take.

- Take only medicines that are *necessary*. Avoid taking nonprescription drugs while taking prescription drugs for a medical problem.

- Before your doctor prescribes for you, tell him about your previous experiences with any drug—beneficial results, side effects, adverse reactions or allergies.

- Take medicine in good light after you have identified it. If you wear glasses to read, put them on to check drug labels. It is easy to take the wrong drug at the wrong time, especially at night.

- Don't keep any drugs that change mood, alertness or judgment—such as sedatives, narcotics or tranquilizers—by your bedside. These cause many accidental deaths by overdose. You may unknowingly repeat a dose when you are half asleep or confused.

- Know the names of your medicines. These include the generic name, the brand name and the generic names of all ingredients in a drug mixture. Your doctor, nurse or pharmacist can give you this information.

- Study the labels on all nonprescription drugs. If the information is incomplete or if you have questions, ask the pharmacist for more details.

- If you must deviate from your prescribed dose schedule, tell your doctor.

- Shake liquid medicines before taking (if directed).

- Store all medicines away from moisture and heat. Bathroom medicine cabinets are sometimes unsuitable because of high humidity.

- If a drug needs refrigeration, don't freeze it.

- Obtain a standard measuring spoon from your pharmacy for liquid medicines. Kitchen teaspoons and tablespoons are not accurate enough.

- Follow diet instructions when you take medicines. Some work better on a full stomach, others on an empty stomach. Some drugs are more useful with special diets. For example, medicine for high blood pressure is more effective if accompanied by a sodium-restricted diet.

- Tell your doctor about allergies you have to any substance (e.g., food) or adverse reactions to medicines you've had in the past. A previous sensitivity to a drug may make it dangerous to prescribe again. People with other allergies, such as eczema, hay fever, asthma, bronchitis and food allergies, are more likely to be allergic to drugs.

- Finish all the prescribed medication. Don't save a few tablets "for next time."

- Prior to surgery, tell your doctor, anesthesiologist or dentist about any drug you have taken in the past few weeks. Advise them of any cortisone drugs you have taken within two years.

- If you become pregnant while taking any medicine, including birth control pills, tell your doctor immediately.

- Avoid *all* drugs while you are pregnant, if possible. If you must take drugs during pregnancy, record names, amounts, dates and reasons.

- If you see more than one doctor, tell each one about drugs others have prescribed.

- When you use nonprescription drugs, report it so the information is on your medical record.

- Store all drugs away from the reach of children.

- Note the expiration date on each drug label. Discard outdated ones safely. If no expiration date appears and it has been at least one year since taking the medication, it may be best to discard it.

- Pay attention to the information in the drug labels about safety while driving, piloting or working in dangerous places.

- Alcohol, cocaine, marijuana or other mood-altering drugs, as well as tobacco—mixed with some drugs—can cause a life-threatening interaction, prevent your medicine from being effective or delay your return to health. Common sense dictates that you avoid them during illness.

- Some medications are subject to theft. For example, a repair person in your home who is abusing drugs may ask to use your bathroom, and while there "check out" your medicine cabinet. Sedatives, stimulants and analgesics are especially likely to be stolen, but almost any medication is subject to theft.

- If possible, use the same pharmacy for all your medications. Every pharmacy keeps a "drug profile," and if it is complete, the pharmacist may stop medications that are likely to cause serious interactions. Also, having a record of all your medications in one place helps your doctor or an emergency room doctor get a complete picture in case of an emergency.

- If you have a complicated medical history or a condition that might render you unable to communicate (e.g.,diabetes or epilepsy), wear a Medic-Alert identification bracelet or neck tag. Call 800-344-3226 for information.

Therapies to Be Cautious About

There are a variety of products available (without the need of a prescription) that claim to have ingredients that will relieve the symptoms of many medical illnesses and promote health and well-being. These products are classified as dietary supplements (in accordance with the Health Education Act of 1994) and include plant extracts, enzymes, minerals and one hormone (melatonin). Some of these products are effective, others may be moderately effective and some are ineffective. The Food and Drug Administration (FDA) does not regulate these products as it does medications. The companies that make these supplements do not have to prove they are safe, and currently the supplements need not be manufactured according to any standards, such as actual amount of the active ingredients included. Standards will be established over the next few years. Medical claims are still permitted on the labels, although they cannot include claims to prevent or cure a disease. There are very few of these supplements that have undergone the medical studies and research that are necessary for regular prescription and nonprescription drugs. Information about their actions and effectiveness is lacking

As a consumer, don't be misled by advertising claims. If you are considering use of one of these products, seek out an independent information source, and buy only reputable brands that claim to be standardized. Follow the label instructions and heed any warnings; don't think that "more" is better (take only the recommended dosages). And monitor your reactions. If there is any problem, call your doctor.

Don't try to self-treat a serious illness (physical or psychological) or injury with these products. See your doctor or other health care provider.

If you are taking a prescription medication for a psychological disorder, do not use any of these products without your doctor's approval. There may be an interaction between the prescribed medication and a nonprescription product that could decrease the effectiveness of your psychotherapy drug or cause unwanted side effects. In addition, if you are being treated with psychotherapy, discuss the use of these products with your therapist before you take them. Some products may bring about changes in your mood or behavior that will make psychotherapy less effective or misdirected.

Following are brief summaries of a few of the well-known products that are promoted to improve symptoms that could pertain to emotional health or well-being.

CHROMIUM PICOLINATE

This is a patented form of chromium, a trace metal, that is promoted for weight loss. Chromium may play a role in how the body uses carbohydrates. Chromium deficiency in humans is rare. Much of the research supporting the claims that this substance promotes weight loss have come from the patent holder. Independent research does not show the same results.

COENZYME Q10

This supplement is marketed with claims that it can "strengthen the heart" and "inhibit the aging process." In the human body just about every cell produces this substance, which helps convert food into energy. Disagreement exists as to whether the product works when it is swallowed.

GINSENG

Ginseng has been around for many many years and is promoted as a supplement that will improve energy and endurance and relieve stress, high blood pressure, depression, edema, impaired memory, anemia, menopause symptoms and other problems. Supporting evidence for all these claims is scarce. There has been very little research on the effect of ginseng use in humans and whether it has any beneficial properties. The amount of ginseng in the products of different manufacturers varies. Some have 10 or 20 times as much as others.

LECITHIN

Manufacturers of lecithin, a supplement, claim it can help counteract ordinary memory lapses. To date, there have been no well-designed studies to support this. Lecithin, a fatty acid, is a food additive used in products such as ice cream, mayonnaise and margarine.

HERBAL TEAS

Many herb experts would say that, when consumed in reasonable amounts, major commercially packaged herbal teas are safe and that there are very few serious reactions to them. Complications come about when the teas are consumed in excess, are used for medicinal purposes or an uninformed consumer mistakenly uses unsafe herbs.

Most manufacturers of these products avoid therapeutic claims or, if they make them, skirt the issue with words such as "calming," "soothing" or "relaxing." The FDA is concerned about the safety of these products, as people have experienced serious illness and even death after consuming herbal teas.

Herbal remedies have been around for centuries, and about 25% of all prescription drugs sold in the United States are derived from plants. However, for many of the herbal remedies being sold today, there is still a lack of sufficient scientific evidence to prove their effectiveness. Much of the information about their healing qualities comes from historical data.

The herb industry is also concerned and will be conducting studies over the next few years to determine the safety and efficacy of these products.

MELATONIN

Melatonin is a hormone produced in the human body by the pineal gland and secreted at night. In most people, the melatonin levels are highest during the normal hours of sleep. The levels increase rapidly in the late evening, peaking after midnight and decreasing toward morning.

Melatonin, as a product, is marketed as a dietary supplement and is not reviewed by the FDA for effectiveness and safety. The melatonin products being sold are made from animal pineal glands or synthesized.

Some research studies have shown that taking melatonin before a flight and continuing for a few days after arrival at the destination have helped control jet lag symptoms of fatigue and sleep disturbances.

Other research studies have shown that taking melatonin about 2 hours before bedtime decreased the time needed to fall asleep and improved the quality of sleep (less wakefulness).

Other claims for melatonin—that it can slow aging, fight disease and enhance one's sex life—have been less studied and are more difficult to prove.

The correct dosage amounts are unknown, as are interactions with regular medications and the long-term effects of melatonin.

MISCELLANEOUS HERBS

Some products may have more beneficial effects than other supplements. These include chamomile for indigestion, ginger for nausea, ginko biloba for circulation (for the elderly, it may improve memory and concentration, reduce forgetfulness, etc.) and valerian for sleep problems. One should not rely on these products for regular medical treatment, and further research needs to be done about their actions and effects in humans.

Products that could do serious harm (as identified by the FDA) include chaparral, comfrey, ephedra, lobelia and yohimbe.

Information About Substances of Abuse

Each of the drug charts in this book contains a section listing the interactions of alcohol, marijuana and cocaine with the therapeutic drug in the bloodstream. These three drugs are singled out because of their widespread use and abuse. The information is factual, not judgmental.

The long-term effects of alcohol and tobacco abuse are numerous. They have been well publicized, and information is provided here as a reminder of the inherent dangers of these drugs.

Substances of potential abuse include those that are addictive and harmful. They usually produce a temporary, false sense of well-being. The long-term effects, however, are harmful and can be devastating to the body and psyche of the addict. See the information on the disorder chart for Substance Abuse & Addiction.

Refresh your memory frequently about the potential harm from prolonged use of any drugs or substances you take. Avoid unwise use of habit-forming drugs.

These are the most common substances of abuse:

TOBACCO (NICOTINE)

What it does: Tobacco smoke contains noxious and cancer-producing ingredients. They include nicotine, carbon monoxide, ammonia, and a variety of harmful tars. Carcinogens in smoke probably come from the tars. Most are present in chewing tobacco and snuff as well as smoke from cigarettes, cigars, and pipes. Tobacco smoke interferes with the immune mechanisms of the body.

Short-term effects of average amount: Relaxation of mood if you are a steady smoker. Constriction of blood vessels.

Short-term effects of large amount inhaled: Headache, appetite loss, nausea.

Long-term effects: Greatly enhanced chances of developing lung cancer. Impaired breathing and chronic lung disease (asthma, emphysema, bronchiectasis, lung abscess and others) much more likely. Heart and blood vessel disease more frequent and more severe when they happen. These include myocardial infarction (heart attack), coronary artery disease, heartbeat irregularities, generalized atherosclerosis (hardening of the arteries, making brain, heart, and kidney more vulnerable to disease), peripheral vascular disease such as intermittent claudication, Buerger's disease and others. Tobacco and nicotine lead to an increased incidence of abortion and significantly reduce the birth weight of children brought to term and delivered of women who smoke during pregnancy. Tobacco smoking not only causes higher frequency of lung cancer, but also increases the likelihood of developing cancer of the throat, larynx, mouth, esophagus, bladder, and pancreas. Carbon monoxide build-up in your blood can adversely affect the amount of oxygen delivered to the heart, brain and other vital organs.

ALCOHOL

What it does:

• Central Nervous System
Depresses, does *not* stimulate, the action of all parts of the central nervous system. It depresses normal mental activity and normal muscle function. Short-term effects of an average amount—relaxation, breakdown of inhibitions, euphoria, decreased alertness, insomnia. Short-term effects of large amounts—nausea, stupor, hangover, unconsciousness, even death. Alcoholism is associated with accidents of all types, marital and family problems, work impairment, legal problems and social problems. Continued abuse of alcohol may result in damage to peripheral nerves and cause various types of brain disorders, including loss of balance and dementia.

• Gastrointestinal System
Increases stomach acid, poisons liver function. Chronic alcoholism frequently leads to permanent damage to the liver and chronic pancreatitis.

• Heart and Blood Vessels
Decreased normal function, leading to heart diseases such as cardiomyopathy and disorders of the blood vessels and kidney, such as high blood pressure. Bleeding from the esophagus and stomach frequently accompany liver disease caused by chronic alcoholism.

• Unborn Fetus (teratogenicity)
Alcoholism in the mother carrying a fetus causes *fetal alcohol syndrome* (FAS), which includes the production of mental deficiency, facial abnormalities, slow growth and other major and minor malformations in the newborn.

Signs of Use:

Early signs: Prominent smell of alcohol on the breath, behavior changes (aggressiveness; passivity; lack of sexual inhibition (but does impair sexual function); poor judgment; outbursts of uncontrolled emotion, such as rage or tearfulness, blackouts.

Intoxication signs: Unsteady gait, slurred speech, poor performance of any brain or muscle function, stupor or coma in *severe* alcoholic intoxication with slow, noisy breathing, cold and clammy skin, heartbeat faster than usual.

Long-Term Effects:

In addition to all of the above effects, alcohol may cause the following:

Addiction: Compulsive use of alcohol. Persons addicted to alcohol have severe withdrawal symptoms when alcohol is unavailable. Even with successful treatment, addiction to alcohol (and other drugs that cause addiction) has a high tendency to relapse. Memories of euphoric feelings when intoxicated plus family, social, emotional, psychological and genetic factors probably are all important factors in producing the addiction.

Interference with expected or normal actions of many medications: Detailed on each drug chart in this book. Alcohol interacts with drugs such as sedatives, pain killers, narcotics, antihistamines, anticonvulsants, anticoagulants and others.

Liver disease: Usually cirrhosis; also, deleterious effects on the unborn child of an alcoholic mother.

Loss of sexual function: Impotence, erectile dysfunction, loss of libido.

Increased incidence of cancer: Mouth, pharynx, larynx, esophagus, liver and lung cancer.

Changes in blood: Makes clotting less efficient.

Heart disease: Decreased normal function leading to possible damage and disease.

Stomach and intestinal problems: Increased production of stomach acid.

MARIJUANA (CANNABIS, HASHISH)

What it does: Heightens perception, causes mood swings, relaxes mind and body.

Signs of use: Red eyes, lethargy, uncoordinated body movements.

Long-term effects or overdose: Decreased motivation. Possible brain, heart, lung and reproductive impairment. High doses may initiate symptoms of previously latent schizophrenia.

AMPHETAMINES

What they do: Speed up physical and mental processes to cause a false sense of energy and excitement. The moods are temporary and unreal.

Signs of use: Dilated pupils, insomnia, trembling.

Long-term effects or overdose: Violent behavior toward others, paranoia, inflammation of blood vessels, renal failure, possible death from overdose.

ANABOLIC STEROIDS

What they do: Enhance strength, increase muscle mass.

Signs of use: Significant mood swings, agressiveness.

Long-term effects or overdose: Possible heart problems, paranoid delusions and mania, liver and adrenal gland damage, infertility and impotence in men, male characteristics in females.

BARBITURATES

What they do: Produce drowsiness and lethargy.

Signs of use: Confused speech, lack of coordination and balance.

Long-term effects or overdose: Disrupt normal sleep pattern. Possible death from overdose, especially in combination with alcohol.

COCAINE

What it does: Stimulates the nervous system, heightens sensations and may produce hallucinations.

Signs of use: Trembling, intoxication, dilated pupils, constant sniffling.

Long-term effects or overdose: Ulceration of nasal passages where sniffed. Itching all over body, sometimes with open sores. Possible brain damage, pulmonary edema or hemorrhage, heart attack or heart rhythm disturbance. Paranoia, with attacks on others, or suicide are other consequences of using cocaine. Possible death from overdose.

OPIATES (CODEINE, HEROIN, METHADONE, MORPHINE, OPIUM)

What they do: Relieve pain, create temporary and false sense of well-being.

Signs of use: Constricted pupils, mood swings, slurred speech, sore eyes, lethargy, weight loss, sweating.

Long-term effects or overdose: Malnutrition, extreme susceptibility to infection, constipation, a need to increase drug amount to produce the same effects, delirium. Possible death from overdose.

PHENCYCLIDINE (PCP, ANGEL DUST)

What they do: Produce euphoria accompanied by a feeling of numbness.

Signs of use: Psychosis or violent behavior, dizziness, loss of motor skills, disorientation.

Long-term effects or overdose: Seizures, high or low blood pressure, rigid muscles. Possible death from overdose.

PSYCHEDELIC DRUGS (LSD, MESCALINE)

What they do: Produce hallucinations, either pleasant or frightening.

Signs of use: Dilated pupils, sweating, trembling, fever, chills.

Long-term effects or overdose: Lack of motivation, unpredictable behavior, narcissism, recurrent hallucinations without drug use ("flashbacks"). Possible death from overdose.

VOLATILE INHALANTS (GLUE, SOLVENTS, NITROUS OXIDE, OTHER VOLATILE COMPOUNDS)

What they do: Produce hallucinations, temporary false sense of well-being, possible unconsciousness.

Signs of use: Dilated pupils, flushed face, confusion, respiratory failure, coma.

Long-term effects or overdose: Permanent brain, liver and kidney damage. Possible death from overdose.

Mental Health Help from the Internet & World Wide Web

Mental health information is available on the Internet and the World Wide Web. This short introduction to an additional resource for information about mental health and psychological problems makes no attempt to cover all the aspects of how the Internet and the World Wide Web function or what is the best way to access them. That knowledge may be obtained by reading and researching computer literature or consulting with specially trained experts in the field.

Most people are probably aware of the Internet even if they are not users. It is becoming an important resource for gaining facts, obtaining additional information, sharing ideas and getting answers to questions about almost any subject.

On the Internet one can research a particular mental illness, the medications used in treatment, the different types of psychotherapy and other concerns a person might have concerning psychological disorders.

Resources on the Internet and the World Wide Web are growing and changing at a rapid rate. Some of these resources are sponsored by government, some by institutions such as universities, others by private organizations and still others by individuals. These resources can be helpful by providing information about issues of health and well-being. You can get online access to psychology and psychiatric journals, answers to questions, newsgroups, mental health forums and professional associations such as the American Psychological Association.

There are specific newsgroups and bulletin boards users can access to seek advice, support and help from other people with similar problems. There are forums for people with specific disorders, such as depression. This sort of interaction can be helpful to many who suffer from psychological disorders or for their family members who want to understand the disorders and be helpful and supportive.

In addition to providing information about psychological disorders, the Internet offers resources that provide consultation and therapy for some of these problems. Though this form of therapy can be helpful for some people, those seeking help need to recognize the limitations. Most of those offering help online list the cautions for potential users, such as the following:

• It is difficult for anyone to perform a thorough diagnosis without a complete family history and when the interview is short and not face-to-face. The person's facial expressions, manner of speaking, voice tones and body language all help a diagnostician reach a proper conclusion about what the problems really are.

• At this time, there are no standards about the extent and type of psychotherapy to be provided in these circumstances. Also, there may be no way for a person to know the qualifications of the person providing the therapy.

• People with serious psychological problems may decide that this therapy is sufficient and not look for other solutions that may be more helpful.

• There are usually costs involved for online therapy. Be sure you are aware of what these are before you begin.

• Though you don't need to identify yourself to receive therapy, confidentially could be a problem with the E-mail messages that are received, printed out and stored. Computer hackers can sometimes identify users who want to remain anonymous.

Resources for Additional Information

The following list provides names of national organizations and support groups that offer medical information by phone, mail or E-mail or on the World Wide Web. Some of the national organizations listed have local chapters. Check your telephone directory for telephone numbers and addresses for chapters in your area.

Aging

American Association of
  Retired Persons (AARP)
1909 K St., NW
Washington, DC 20049
202-872-4700

Elderhostel
80 Boylston St., Suite 400
Boston, MA 02116
617-426-8056
WWW page:
  http://www.elderhostel.org

National Institute on Aging
Information Office
Federal Building 6C12
Bethesda, MD 20892
310-496-1752

Alcoholism

Al-Anon Family Group Headquarters
1372 Broadway
New York, NY 10018-0862
212-302-7240

Alcoholics Anonymous
475 Riverside Dr.
New York, NY 10015
212-870-3400

Alcohol and Drug Helpline
800-821-4357

Alzheimer's Disease

Alzheimer's Association
919 N. Michigan Ave., Suite 1000
Chicago, IL 60611-1676
800-272-3900
800-572-6037 (in Illinois)

Alzheimer's Disease Education and
  Referral Center
800-438-4380

Anorexia Nervosa

Anorexia Nervosa and Related
  Eating Disorders
PO Box 5102
Eugene, OR 97405
503-344-1144

National Association of Anorexia and
  Associated Disorders
Box 271
Highland Park, IL 60035
847-831-3438

Anxiety

Anxiety Disorders Association of
  America
6000 Executive Blvd., Suite 513
Rockville, MD 20852
301-231-9350
Fax: 301-231-7392
E-mail: anxdis@aol.com

Attention-Deficit Hyperactivity Disorder

Attention Deficit Disorder Association
8091 S. Ireland Way
Aurora, CO 90016
800-487-2282

Children with Attention-Deficit Disorders

1859 N. Pine Island Rd., Suite 185
Plantation, FL 33322
305-587-3300

Bulimia Nervosa

See Anorexia Nervosa

Chronic Fatigue Syndrome

Chronic Fatigue Syndrome
PO Box 220398
Charlotte, NC 28222-0398
800-442-3437
Fax: 704-365-9755
WWW page:
http://www.ybi.com/cfids/tcaa.html

Depression

Depression Awareness, Recognition
    and Treatment Program
800-421-4211

National Depressive and Manic
    Depressive Association
Merchandise Mart, Box 3395
Chicago, IL 60654
800-82-NDMDA

National Foundation for
    Depressive Illness
245 7th Ave.
New York, NY 10001
800-248-4344

Drug Abuse

CSAT's National Drug Information
    Treatment and Referral Hotline
800-662-HELP
800-66-AYUDA (Spanish)

National Cocaine Hotline
800-262-2463

National Council on Alcoholism
    and Drug Dependency, Inc.
800-622-2255

Gambling, Pathological

See Impulse Control Disorders

Grief

Grief Recovery Hotline
800-445-4808

Impotence

Impotence Information Hotline
800-843-4315

Impulse Control Disorders

Gamblers Anonymous
PO Box 17173
Los Angeles, CA 90017
213-386-8789
Fax: 213-386-0300

Trichotillomania Learning Center
1215 Mission St., Suite 2
Santa Cruz, CA 95060
408-457-1004
Fax: 408-426-4383

Mental Health

National Mental Health Association
800-969-6642

National Institute of Mental Health
5600 Fishers Ln., Rm. 7C-02
Rockville, MD 20857
301-443-4513
WWW page:
    http://www.nimh.nih.gov

National Foundation for Mental Health
800-239-1263

National Clearinghouse on Family
    Support & Children's Mental Health
800-628-1696

Obsessive-Compulsive Disorder

Obsessive Compulsive Anonymous
PO Box 215
New Hyde Park, NY 11040
516-741-4901

Panic Disorder

Panic Disorder Information Line
800-64-PANIC

Phobias
Anxiety Disorders Association of
 America
6000 Executive Blvd., Suite 513
Rockville, MD 20852
301-231-9350

Schizophrenia
National Alliance for Research on
 Schizophrenia and Depression
60 Cutter Mill Rd., Suite 200
Great Neck, NY 11021
516-829-0091

Seasonal Affective Disorder
National Organization for Seasonal
 Affective Disorder
PO Box 40133
Washington, DC 20016

Sleep Disorders
American Sleep Disorders Association
1610 14th St., Suite 300
Rochester, MN 55901
507-287-6006

Stress Reduction
Association for Applied
 Psychophysiology & Biofeedback
10200 W. 44th Ave., Suite 304
Wheatridge, CO 80033
303-422-8436

Suicide, Information About
American Association of Suicidology
4201 Connecticut Ave., NW, Suite 310
Washington, DC 20008
202-237-2280

American Suicide Foundation
1045 Park Ave.
New York, NY 10028
800-273-4042

Therapy Information
American Academy of Child and
 Adolescent Psychiatry
3615 Wisconsin Ave., NW
Washington, DC 20016
202-966-7300

American Association of Geriatric
 Psychiatry
PO Box 376A
Greenbelt, MD 20768
310-220-0952

American Board of Hypnotherapy
1805 E. Garry Ave., # 100
Santa Ana, CA 92705
800-872-9996

American Psychiatry Association
1400 K St., NW
Washington, DC 20005
202-682-6000

American Psychological Association
750 First St., NW
Washington, DC 20002-4242
202-336-5500

Recovery, Inc.
116 South Michigan Ave.
Chicago, IL 60603
312-337-5661

Trichotillomania
See Impulse Control Disorders

Guide to Disorder Charts

The information about psychological disorders is organized in condensed, easy-to-read charts. Each disorder is described in a one-page format, as shown in the sample chart, *ANOREXIA NERVOSA*.

Major sections of the chart format are numbered and explained in the next few pages.

Most of the charts in this section refer to a psychological disorder. However, several of the charts refer to a emotional response, such as *GRIEF*, that is not considered a disorder. These charts are included because they can help you to recognize the expected symptoms, initiate self-care if needed and know when to seek professional help for symptoms that are getting worse or not not improving over a period of time.

1—CHART NAME

The charts are arranged alphabetically by the most-common name for each disorder or problem. Other names or terms for the disorder appear in parentheses following the main heading. For instance, dysthymia may also be referred to as low-grade depression. All names in this book, including alternate names, are cross-referenced in the index.

To find information about a specific psychological disorder, check the index.

2—GENERAL INFORMATION

This section includes seven topics: *Definition, Body Parts Involved, Sex or Age Most Affected, Signs and Symptoms, Causes, Risk Increases With,* and *How to Prevent.* Each is discussed separately.

3—DEFINITION

A short definition of the disorder is provided that is written in clear, easy-to-understand terms. Sometimes the definition must include information from other categories, such as causes, body parts involved and others. The definition may also include information of general interest, such as how common a disorder is or whether it is inherited.

4—BODY PARTS INVOLVED

For most psychological disorders, the central nervous system is the body part involved. The central nervous system (CNS) involves the brain and spinal cord. The CNS works in tandem with the peripheral nervous system (PNS), which consists of all the nerves that carry signals between the CNS and the rest of the body. The CNS consists of nerve cells or neurons and supporting tissue. The peripheral nervous system consists of nerve fibers extending from cells in the CNS.

ANOREXIA NERVOSA

 GENERAL INFORMATION

DEFINITION—A psychological eating disorder in which a person refuses to eat adequately—in spite of hunger—and loses enough weight to become emaciated. The illness usually begins with a normal weight-loss diet. The person eats very little and refuses to stop dieting after a reasonable weight loss. The person's body perception is distorted; the person continues to feel fat—even when emaciated.

BODY PARTS INVOLVED—All body cells.

SEX OR AGE MOST AFFECTED—Mostly female adolescents and young adults.

SIGNS & SYMPTOMS
- Weight loss of at least 15% of body weight without physical illness.
- High energy level despite body wasting.
- Intense fear of obesity.
- Depression.
- Appetite loss.
- Constipation.
- Cold intolerance.
- Refusal to maintain a minimum standard weight for age and height.
- Distorted body image. The person continues to feel fat—even when emaciated.
- Cessation of menstrual periods.

CAUSES—Unknown. Possible causes include family and internal conflicts (sexual conflicts); phobia about putting on weight; changes in fashion in U.S. (slimness is identified with beauty); a symptom of depression or personality disorder.

RISK INCREASES WITH
- Peer or social pressure to be thin.
- History of slight overweight.
- Perfectionistic, compulsive or overachieving personality.
- Psychological stress.
- Being an athlete, ballet dancer, cheerleader or model.

HOW TO PREVENT—Confront personal problems realistically. Try to correct or cope with problems with the help of counselors, therapists, family and friends. Develop a realistic attitude about weight.

 WHAT TO EXPECT

DIAGNOSTIC MEASURES
- Your own or others' observation of signs and symptoms.
- Medical history and physical exam by a doctor.
- Laboratory blood tests for anemia and electrolyte (e.g., sodium and potassium) imbalance.

APPROPRIATE HEALTH CARE
- Doctor's treatment.
- Psychotherapy or counseling for the patient and family.
- Treatment can usually be provided on an outpatient basis.
- Hospitalization during crises for intravenous or tube feeding.
- Psychiatric hospitalization for at least 2 to 3 weeks (sometimes).

PROBABLE OUTCOME—Treatable if the patient recognizes the emotional disturbance, wants help and cooperates with treatment. Without treatment, this disorder can cause permanent disability or even death. Persons with anorexia nervosa have a high rate of attempted suicide due to low self-esteem. Therapy may continue over several years. Relapses are common, especially when stressful situations occur.

POSSIBLE COMPLICATIONS
- Chronic anorexia nervosa caused by patient's resistance to treatment.
- Electrolyte disturbances or irregular heartbeat. These may be life-threatening.
- Osteoporosis.
- Suicide.

 HOW TO TREAT

GENERAL MEASURES
- The goal of treatment is for the patient to establish healthy eating patterns to regain normal weight. The patient can accomplish this with behavior modification training supervised by a qualified professional.
- For additional information, contact Anorexia Nervosa and Related Eating Disorders, PO Box 5102, Eugene, OR 97405; 503-344-1144.

MEDICATION—A variety of psychotherapy medications have some benefit, but there is no one medication that is consistently useful.

ACTIVITY—No restrictions, but avoid overexertion or compulsive exercise to lose weight.

DIET—A controlled refeeding program will be established. Vitamin and mineral supplements may be prescribed.

 CALL YOUR DOCTOR IF

- Life-threatening symptoms occur, including rapid, irregular heartbeat; chest pain; loss of consciousness. Call immediately. This is an emergency!
- You have symptoms of anorexia nervosa or observe them in a family member.
- Weight loss continues, despite treatment.

5—SEX OR AGE MOST AFFECTED

Some psychological disorders affect specific population groups only. Others affect all ages and both sexes indiscriminately. This section explains whether the disorder occurs more often in males or females or whether the incidence is about equal in both sexes. It also describes the age group usually affected. These are generalizations, and variations can occur with specific individuals.

Sometimes labels such as *adolescents* or *young adults* are used to describe age ranges. These labels are arbitrary terms used for people of specific ages, but they are commonly used in medical texts. Following are typical age classifications:

- Newborns (0 to 2 weeks)
- Infants (2 weeks to 1 year)
- Young children (1 to 5 years)
- Older children (5 to 12 years)
- Adolescents (12 to 20 years)
- Young adults (20 to 40 years)
- Middle-aged adults (40 to 60 years)
- Older adults (over 60 years)

6—SIGNS AND SYMPTOMS

Signs are observed. *Symptoms* are felt or experienced.

A sign may be observed by the person with the disorder or by someone else, or it may represent physical findings determined by laboratory tests, x-rays and other diagnostic measures. Symptoms are feelings only the person can describe.

Refer to the chart. The first item under this heading—weight loss of at least 15% of body weight without physical illness—is a sign. It can be observed by the person with anorexia and by others around him or her. The third item—intense fear of obesity—is a symptom that only the person can feel and describe. Other items—depression and appetite loss—are signs and symptoms. They can be observed by others, and they can be felt by the person.

Signs and symptoms are listed together in this book; no attempt is made to separate the two. On most charts, a wide range of possible signs and symptoms are listed. *It is unlikely that any patient will have all, or even most, of the possible signs and symptoms.* The presence or absence of signs and symptoms may vary according to:

- The age and sex of the person with the disorder.
- The extent of the disorder.
- The stage of the disorder.
- The person's medical and family history.
- The person's current state of health.

7—CAUSES

Many times the cause of a psychological disorder is unknown. For some disorders, the cause is a combination of factors, such as genetic and environmental factors. There are possible causes listed for some disorders. Ongoing medical research and studies are being conducted to find the causes of many of these psychological disorders. Until the causes are determined, no cures can be found.

8—RISK INCREASES WITH

Many disorders have known risk factors that can make them more likely to occur or increase their duration and intensity. Risk factors for psychological disorders will often differ from risk factors associated with physical disorders such as heart problems, in which smoking and obesity can play a role. Some risk factors for psychological disorders include:

- Age and personality type.
- Stress—either physical or emotional.
- Anxiety, depression and other mental or emotional problems.
- Fatigue or overwork.
- Presence of another psychological disorder.
- Childhood development factors.
- Recent or chronic illness.
- Recent surgery or injury.
- Genetic factors, such as family history or ethnic tendency toward a disorder.
- Use of drugs, such as alcohol, tobacco, caffeine, narcotics, psychedelics, hallucinogens, marijuana, sedatives, hypnotics or cocaine.
- Use of medications, whether prescription or nonprescription. Even necessary drugs cause adverse reactions and side effects that can complicate treatment and the outcomes of medical problems.
- Socioeconomic factors.

9—HOW TO PREVENT

Prevention can be of two types—prevention of the initial disorder or prevention of a relapse or recurrence after recovery.

Prevention of any medical problem is the *best treatment*. Researchers continue to discover ways to prevent, delay or diminish psychological disorders and other illnesses, disabilities and untimely deaths. These are included whenever available.

The causes and risk factors for a disorder often provide the best clues for prevention. Many psychological disorders, however, cannot be prevented at present.

10—WHAT TO EXPECT

This section includes four topics: *Diagnostic Measures, Appropriate Health Care, Possible Complications*, and *Probable Outcome*. Each is discussed separately below.

11—DIAGNOSTIC MEASURES

Your own observation of symptoms is usually the first—and often the most important—diagnostic measure. It is the first step toward medical treatment. For that reason, it is listed under this heading on most all disorder charts. In many people with psychological disorders, symptoms are first observed by other people.

A medical history and physical exam by a doctor are almost universal requirements before treatment for any disorder can begin. Even if a disorder is usually treated at home, a history and exam will be necessary if complications develop that require medical treatment.

There are hundreds of psychological tests (e.g., IQ tests, personality tests, cognitive functioning tests and others) and symptom rating scales that are used as aids for diagnosis. Since there are so many, specific tests are not discussed in this section.

Additional diagnostic measures may include laboratory studies and other medical tests. These are often done to rule out any organic reason for the symptoms. The most common include:

- Studies of bodily fluids, such as blood, serum, plasma or spinal fluid.
- Microscopic and chemical examination of excreted materials, such as urine or stools.
- CAT (computerized axial tomography) scans or x-rays of the affected body part.
- ECG (electrocardiogram), EEG (electroencephalogram) and EMG (electromyogram).

You may not undergo every diagnostic test listed on the chart; conversely, you may undergo tests not listed. Some tests are performed only if previous tests have not provided enough information. Others are performed only when complications develop. The medical diagnostic tests mentioned in this book are defined in the Glossary.

12—APPROPRIATE HEALTH CARE

Self-care is frequently listed as the first form of appropriate health care. It is an important part of care for almost all disorders. However, a psychological disorder should be diagnosed by a doctor before you attempt self-care.

Once your doctor makes a diagnosis and outlines a treatment program, self-care or home care is often important. The treatment measures outlined in this book are designed to guide you whether you are caring for yourself or taking care of someone else. Effective self-care includes maintaining a positive attitude about yourself and being determined to improve or heal.

A doctor's care is often necessary not only to diagnose and prescribe treatment for a psychological disorder, but to supervise self-care (or hospitalization, when necessary) and to provide additional treatment, such as psychotherapy. In addition, even minor psychological disorders sometimes develop complications and require a doctor's care.

Find a competent personal physician who communicates well with you and with whom you can establish a good rapport, mutual respect and trust. This is important for treatment of psychological disorders.

Psychotherapy, counseling or biofeedback training are usually recommended for psychological disorders. Counseling and therapy are also helpful in providing personal and family support, especially for disorders that represent major lifestyle adjustments.

13—PROBABLE OUTCOME

A very important concern with regard to any psychological disorder is represented by the patient's or family's question, "What is going to happen? How will this disorder affect our lives?" No one can completely predict the outcome of a disorder. The predictions in this section are guesses based on averages. Patients and doctors work toward optimal results, but medicine is an inexact science. Response to treatment depends on many variables, and there are many unanswered questions about health and disease.

Some disorders are considered incurable at present. The term *incurable* is a general one that includes everything from insignificant conditions that are mere annoyances to disorders that bring about complex life changes. Again, individual variations are common, but predictions are given in an attempt to answer patients' and families' most important questions. They will help you adopt optimistic but realistic expectations.

In almost all cases—no matter how serious the disorder—symptoms can be relieved or controlled to minimize dysfunction.

14—POSSIBLE COMPLICATIONS

Complications are additional medical, psychological or psychosocial problems triggered by or as a result of the original disorder. Complications sometimes occur despite accurate diagnosis and competent treatment. Some are preventable, and a few are inevitable, but most are rare if treatment is successful in relieving symptoms.

15—HOW TO TREAT

This section provides the information mentioned earlier that reminds you of instructions your doctor has given you. The information should not replace your doctor's instructions, because treatments vary a great deal between individuals. If the instructions don't seem to fit your problem, ask your doctor or nurse for instructions that apply uniquely to you.

The four major headings in this section include: *General Measures, Medication, Activity,* and *Diet.*

16—GENERAL MEASURES

The instructions under this heading can apply to home treatment or emphasize the importance of medical and psychotherapy treatment steps. They are not complete and may not apply to everybody, but they provide a good review of general measures that are helpful for most patients and their families.

17—MEDICATION

The information under this heading is about drugs your doctor may prescribe. In general, classes of drugs are mentioned rather than specific drug names. For example, antidepressant or antianxiety drugs are often listed as medications. In some instances, drugs are named by generic name (e.g., clozapine), with a brand name sometimes mentioned. For more information about each medication, see the drug chart for that generic name or class name.

18—ACTIVITY

Patients are often unsure whether activity will be restricted. For people with most psychological disorders, there are no restrictions. Exercise references are sometimes included, and when not specified otherwise, references to regular physical exercise mean *aerobic* exercise, such as walking.

19—DIET

Diet information is included for all the disorders. In the majority of cases, there is no special diet or diet restrictions. In other cases, there may be mention of a special diet or of beverages and foods that should be avoided. For specialized diets, consult your doctor or a dietitian.

20—CALL YOUR DOCTOR IF

For most psychological disorders, a phone call or visit to the doctor is recommended to establish a diagnosis for you or for a family member.

After diagnosis, when the course of a disorder differs from what is expected, your doctor will want to know. Many developing complications can be averted with prompt medical treatment. Specific symptoms may be listed that indicate complications.

Of course, if any other symptoms begin that you believe are related to your disorder or the drugs you take, call your doctor about them, too.

Remember, the information in this book is not for you to use to establish your own diagnosis and initiate treatment. Don't use it to replace diagnosis and treatment by a physician.

Guide to Drug Charts

The medication information in this book is organized in condensed, easy-to-read charts. Each medication is described in a two-page format, as shown in the sample chart below and opposite. The charts are arranged alphabetically by medication generic name, and in some instances, such as *ANTIDEPRESSANTS, TRICYCLIC,* by drug class name.

A generic name is the official chemical name for a drug. A brand name is a drug manufacturer's registered trademark for a generic drug. Brand names listed on the charts

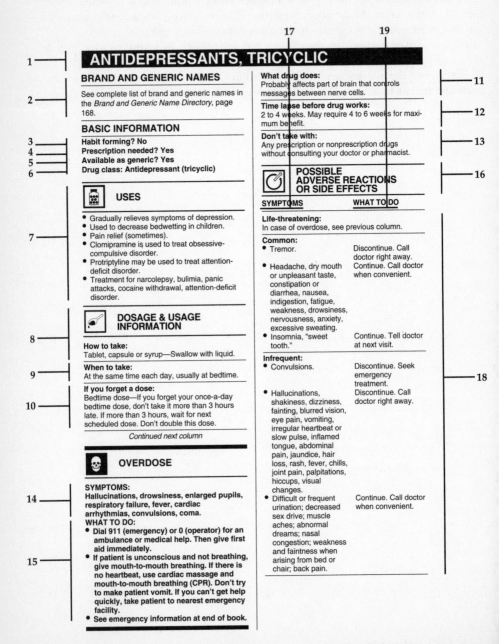

17   19

ANTIDEPRESSANTS, TRICYCLIC

1

BRAND AND GENERIC NAMES

2

See complete list of brand and generic names in the *Brand and Generic Name Directory,* page 168.

BASIC INFORMATION

3 Habit forming? No
4 Prescription needed? Yes
5 Available as generic? Yes
6 Drug class: Antidepressant (tricyclic)

USES

7
- Gradually relieves symptoms of depression.
- Used to decrease bedwetting in children.
- Pain relief (sometimes).
- Clomipramine is used to treat obsessive-compulsive disorder.
- Protriptyline may be used to treat attention-deficit disorder.
- Treatment for narcolepsy, bulimia, panic attacks, cocaine withdrawal, attention-deficit disorder.

DOSAGE & USAGE INFORMATION

8 **How to take:**
Tablet, capsule or syrup—Swallow with liquid.

9 **When to take:**
At the same time each day, usually at bedtime.

10 **If you forget a dose:**
Bedtime dose—If you forget your once-a-day bedtime dose, don't take it more than 3 hours late. If more than 3 hours, wait for next scheduled dose. Don't double this dose.

Continued next column

OVERDOSE

14 **SYMPTOMS:**
Hallucinations, drowsiness, enlarged pupils, respiratory failure, fever, cardiac arrhythmias, convulsions, coma.
WHAT TO DO:
- Dial 911 (emergency) or 0 (operator) for an ambulance or medical help. Then give first aid immediately.

15
- If patient is unconscious and not breathing, give mouth-to-mouth breathing. If there is no heartbeat, use cardiac massage and mouth-to-mouth breathing (CPR). Don't try to make patient vomit. If you can't get help quickly, take patient to nearest emergency facility.
- See emergency information at end of book.

What drug does:
Probably affects part of brain that controls messages between nerve cells. — 11

Time lapse before drug works:
2 to 4 weeks. May require 4 to 6 weeks for maximum benefit. — 12

Don't take with:
Any prescription or nonprescription drugs without consulting your doctor or pharmacist. — 13

POSSIBLE ADVERSE REACTIONS OR SIDE EFFECTS — 16

SYMPTOMS	WHAT TO DO
Life-threatening: In case of overdose, see previous column.	
Common:	
• Tremor.	Discontinue. Call doctor right away.
• Headache, dry mouth or unpleasant taste, constipation or diarrhea, nausea, indigestion, fatigue, weakness, drowsiness, nervousness, anxiety, excessive sweating.	Continue. Call doctor when convenient.
• Insomnia, "sweet tooth."	Continue. Tell doctor at next visit.
Infrequent:	
• Convulsions.	Discontinue. Seek emergency treatment.
• Hallucinations, shakiness, dizziness, fainting, blurred vision, eye pain, vomiting, irregular heartbeat or slow pulse, inflamed tongue, abdominal pain, jaundice, hair loss, rash, fever, chills, joint pain, palpitations, hiccups, visual changes.	Discontinue. Call doctor right away.
• Difficult or frequent urination; decreased sex drive; muscle aches; abnormal dreams; nasal congestion; weakness and faintness when arising from bed or chair; back pain.	Continue. Call doctor when convenient.

18

include those from the United States and Canada. A generic drug may have one or many brand names.

To find information about a generic drug, look it up in the alphabetical charts. To learn about a brand name, check the index first, where each brand name is followed by the name(s) of its generic ingredients and chart page numbers.

The chart design is the same for every drug. When you are familiar with the chart, you can quickly find information you want to know about a drug.

On the next few pages, each of the numbered chart sections below is explained. This information will guide you in reading and understanding the drug charts.

ANTIDEPRESSANTS, TRICYCLIC

18 — **Rare:**
Itchy skin; sore throat; involuntary movements of jaw, lips and tongue; nightmares; confusion; swollen breasts; swollen testicles.

Discontinue. Call doctor right away.

Driving, piloting or hazardous work:
Don't drive or pilot aircraft until you learn how medicine affects you. Don't work around dangerous machinery. Don't climb ladders or work in high places. Danger increases if you drink alcohol or take medicine affecting alertness and reflexes. — **29**

20 — 👉 **WARNINGS & PRECAUTIONS**

21 — **Don't take if:**
• You are allergic to any tricyclic antidepressant.
• You drink alcohol in excess.
• You have had a heart attack within 6 weeks.
• You have glaucoma.
• You have taken MAO inhibitors* within 2 weeks.
• Patient is younger than 12.

22 — **Before you start, tell your doctor:**
• If you will have surgery within 2 months, including dental surgery, requiring general or spinal anesthesia.
• If you have an enlarged prostate or glaucoma.
• If you have heart disease or high blood pressure.
• If you have stomach or intestinal problems.
• If you have an overactive thyroid.
• If you have asthma.
• If you have liver disease.

23 — **Over age 60:**
More likely to develop urination difficulty and serious side effects such as seizures, hallucinations, shaking, dizziness, fainting, headache, insomnia.

24 — **Pregnancy:**
Risk factors vary for drugs in this group. See category list on page 47 and consult doctor.

25 — **Breast-feeding:**
Drug may pass into milk. Avoid drug or discontinue nursing until you finish medicine. Consult doctor about maintaining milk supply.

26 — **Children & adolescents:**
Don't give to children younger than 12 except under medical supervision.

27 — **Prolonged use:**
Talk to your doctor about the need for follow-up medical examinations or laboratory studies to check complete blood cell count (white blood cell count, platelet count, red blood cell count, hemoglobin, hematocrit), blood pressure, eyes, teeth.

28 — **Skin, sunlight & heat:**
One or more drugs in this group may cause rash or intensify sunburn in areas exposed to sun or ultraviolet light (photosensitivity reaction). Avoid overexposure and use sunscreen. Notify doctor if reaction occurs.

Discontinuing:
• Don't discontinue without consulting doctor. Dose may require gradual reduction if you have taken drug for a long time. Doses of other drugs may also require adjustment.
• Withdrawal symptoms such as convulsions, muscle cramps, nightmares, insomnia, abdominal pain. Call your physician right away if any of these occur. — **30**

Others:
• May affect results in some medical tests.
• Advise any doctor or dentist whom you consult that you take this medicine. — **31**

⚕️ **POSSIBLE INTERACTION WITH OTHER DRUGS**

GENERIC NAME OR DRUG CLASS	COMBINED EFFECT
Anticoagulants*, oral	Possible increased anticoagulant effect.
Anticholinergics*	Increased anticholinergic effect.
Antihistamines*	Increased antihistamine effect.
Barbiturates*	Decreased antidepressant effect. Increased sedation.

— **32**

Continued on page 171

⚕️ **POSSIBLE INTERACTION WITH OTHER SUBSTANCES**

Alcohol: Beverages or medicines with alcohol.	Excessive intoxication. Avoid.
Beverages:	None expected.
Cocaine:	Increased risk of heartbeat irregularity.
Foods:	None expected.
Marijuana:	Excessive drowsiness. Avoid.
Tobacco:	Possible decreased tricyclic antidepressant effect.

— **33**

*See Glossary

1—GENERIC OR CLASS NAME

Each drug chart is titled by generic name, such as *CLOZAPINE*, or in some instances by the name of the drug class, such as *ANTIDEPRESSANTS, TRICYCLIC*.

Your drug container may show a generic name, a brand name or both. If you have only a brand name, use the index to find the drug's generic name(s) or drug class name and chart page numbers.

If your drug container shows no name, ask your doctor or pharmacist for the name, and record it on the container.

2—BRAND AND GENERIC NAMES

In the instances in which the drug chart is titled with a drug class name instead of a generic name, the generic and brand names all appear under the heading *BRAND AND GENERIC NAMES*. The brand names are in lower-case letters, and the generic names are in capital letters.

A brand name is usually shorter and easier to remember than the generic name.

The brand names listed for each generic drug in this book may not include all brands available in the United States and Canada. The most common ones are listed. New brands appear on the market, and brands are sometimes removed from the market. No list can reflect every change.

Inclusion of a brand name does not imply recommendation or endorsement. Exclusion does not imply that a missing brand name is less effective or less safe than the ones listed. Some generic drugs or drug class have too many brand names to list on one chart. A list of brand and generic names for those drugs is on the page indicated on the chart.

If you buy a nonprescription drug, look for generic names of the active ingredients on the container. Nonprescription drugs are described in this book under their generic components. They are also indexed by brand name.

Most drugs contain inert, or inactive, ingredients that are fillers, dyes or solvents for active ingredients. Manufacturers choose inert ingredients that preserve the drug without interfering with the action of the active ingredients.

Inert substances are listed on labels of nonprescription drugs. They do not appear on prescription drugs. Your pharmacist can tell you all active and inert ingredients in a prescription drug.

Occasionally, a tablet, capsule or liquid may contain small amounts of sodium, sugar or potassium. If you are on a diet that severely restricts any of these, ask your pharmacist or doctor to suggest another form.

BASIC INFORMATION

3—HABIT FORMING?

A drug habit can be physical or psychological. Either leads to drug dependence. Dependence occurs when there is a strong or compelling desire to continue taking the drug to experience its effects or to avoid the symptoms caused by its withdrawal.

4—PRESCRIPTION NEEDED?

"Yes" means a doctor must prescribe the drug, and that a pharmacist will dispense the drug to you. A prescription details information about how often the drug is to be taken, when it is to be taken, how much to take and other pertinent information. A drug may require a prescription for several reasons—it is dangerous, powerful or habit-forming or is for an illness or disorder that needs to be monitored by the doctor. The majority of the drugs included in this book require prescriptions. With many prescriptions, the pharmacist will also provide a drug information handout. Read it carefully, as well as the information in this book. If you still have questions, check with your doctor or pharmacist.

"No" means you can buy this drug without a doctor's prescription. A nonprescription (over-the-counter) drug has dosing and other instructions printed on the container label. Always read them carefully before you take the drug.

5—AVAILABLE AS GENERIC?

Some generic drugs have patent restrictions that protect the manufacturer or distributor of that drug. These drugs may be purchased only by brand name.

In recent years, drug manufacturers have marketed more drugs under generic names. Drugs purchased by generic name sometimes are less expensive than brand names.

Some states allow pharmacists to fill prescriptions by brand names or generic names. This allows patients to buy the least expensive form of a drug.

A doctor may specify a brand name because he or she trusts a known source more than an unknown manufacturer of generic drugs. You and your doctor should decide together whether you should buy a medicine by generic or brand name.

Generic drugs manufactured in other countries are not subject to regulation by the U.S. Food and Drug Administration. All drugs manufactured in the United States are subject to regulation.

6—DRUG CLASS

Drugs that possess similar chemical structures and similar therapeutic effects are grouped into classes. Most drugs within a class produce similar benefits, side effects, adverse reactions and interactions with other drugs and substances. For example, all the generic drugs in the drug class antidepressants, tricyclic, will have similar effects on the body.

Some information on the charts applies to all drugs in a class. For example, a reference may be made to sedative-hypnotic agents. The index lists the class—sedative-hypnotic agents—and lists drugs in that class.

The names for classes of drugs are not standardized, so classes listed in other references may vary from the classes in this book.

7—USES

This section lists the disease or disorder for which a drug is prescribed.

Most uses listed are approved by the U.S. Food and Drug Administration. Some uses are listed if experiments and clinical trials indicate effectiveness and safety. Still, other uses are included that may not be officially sanctioned, but for which doctors commonly prescribe the drug.

The use for which your doctor prescribes the drug may not appear. You and your doctor should discuss the reason for any prescription medicine you take. You alone will probably decide whether to take a nonprescription drug. This section may help you make a wise decision.

DOSAGE & USAGE INFORMATION

8—HOW TO TAKE

Drugs are available in tablets, capsules, liquids, suppositories, injections, transdermal patches (see Glossary), aerosol inhalants and topical forms such as drops, sprays, creams, ointments and lotions. This section gives general instructions for taking each form.

This information supplements drug label information. If your doctor's instructions differ from the suggestions, follow your *doctor's* instructions.

Instructions are left out for how *much* to take. Dose amounts can't be generalized. Dosages of prescription drugs must be individualized for you by your doctor. Nonprescription drugs have instructions on the labels regarding how much to take.

9—WHEN TO TAKE

Dose schedules vary for medicines and for patients.

Drugs prescribed on a schedule should usually be taken at approximately the same times each day. Some *must* be taken at regular intervals to maintain a steady level of the drug in the body. If the schedule interferes with your sleep, consult with your doctor.

Instructions to take on an empty stomach mean the drug is absorbed best in your body this way. Many drugs must be taken with liquid or food because they irritate the stomach.

Instructions for other dose schedules are usually on the label. Variations in standard dose schedules may apply because some medicines interact with others if you take them at the same time.

10—IF YOU FORGET A DOSE

Suggestions in this section vary from drug to drug. Most tell you when to resume taking the medicine if you forget a scheduled dose.

Establish habits so you won't forget doses. Forgotten doses decrease a drug's therapeutic effect.

11—WHAT DRUG DOES

This is a simple description of the drug's action in the body. The wording is generalized and may not be a complete explanation of the complex chemical process that takes place.

12—TIME LAPSE BEFORE DRUG WORKS

The times given are approximations. Times vary a great deal from person to person, and from time to time in the same person. The figures give you some idea of when to expect improvement or side effects.

13—DON'T TAKE WITH

Some drugs create problems when taken in combination with other substances. Most problems are detailed in the Interaction column of each chart. This section may mention substances that don't appear in the Interaction column, and it also reminds you to always check with your doctor or pharmacist before starting any new drug if you are already taking one. On some charts, an interaction is singled out if the combination is particularly harmful.

OVERDOSE

14—SYMPTOMS

The symptoms listed are most likely to develop with accidental or purposeful overdose. Overdosage may not cause all symptoms listed. Sometimes symptoms are identical to ones listed as side effects. The difference is intensity and severity. You will have to judge. Consult a doctor or poison control center if you have any doubt.

15—WHAT TO DO

If you suspect an overdose, whether symptoms are apparent or not, follow instructions in this section. Expanded instructions for emergency treatment for overdose are on the inside back cover.

16—POSSIBLE ADVERSE REACTIONS OR SIDE EFFECTS

Adverse reactions or side effects are symptoms that may occur when you take a drug. They are effects on the body other than the desired therapeutic effect.

The term *side effects* implies expected and usually unavoidable effects of a drug. Side effects have nothing to do with the drug's intended use. For example, many drugs used for psychological disorders cause a dry mouth. The dry mouth is a side effect that is usually harmless and does not affect the drug's therapeutic potential. Many side effects disappear in a short time without treatment, or there are ways to cope with the problem (e.g., sucking sugarless hard candy or chewing sugarless gum for a dry mouth).

The term *adverse reaction* is more significant. A number of drugs can cause a serious adverse allergic reaction in some people (including hives, rash and severe itch).

Some adverse reactions can be prevented, which is one reason this information is included in the book. Most adverse reactions are minor and last only a short time. With many drugs, adverse reactions that might occur will frequently diminish in intensity as time passes.

The majority of drugs, used properly for valid reasons, offer benefits that outweigh potential hazards.

17—SYMPTOMS

Symptoms of commonly known side effects and adverse reactions are listed. Other drug responses may be listed under *Prolonged use, Skin, sunlight & heat* or *Others*. You may experience a symptom that is not listed. It may be a side effect or adverse reaction to the drug, or it may be another symptom of the disorder. If you are unsure, call your doctor.

18—FREQUENCY

This is an estimation of how often symptoms occur in persons who take the drug. The four most common categories of frequency can be found under the *SYMPTOMS* heading and are as follows. **Life-threatening** means seek emergency treatment immediately. **Common** means these symptoms are expected and sometimes inevitable. **Infrequent** means the symptoms occur less often. **Rare** means symptoms seldom occur.

19—WHAT TO DO

Follow the instructions provided opposite the symptoms that apply to you. If you are unsure, concerned or confused, *always* call your doctor or check with your pharmacist.

20—WARNINGS & PRECAUTIONS

Read these entries to determine special information that applies to you.

21—DON'T TAKE IF

This section lists circumstances when drug use is not safe. On some drug labels and in formal medical literature, these circumstances are called *contraindications*.

22—BEFORE YOU START, TELL YOUR DOCTOR

This section lists conditions, especially disease conditions, under which a drug should be used only with caution and supervision.

23—OVER AGE 60

As a person ages, physical changes occur that require special considerations. Liver and kidney functions decrease, metabolism slows and the prostate gland enlarges in men.

Most drugs are metabolized or excreted at a rate dependent on kidney and liver functions. Small doses or longer intervals between doses may be necessary to prevent unhealthy concentration of a drug. Toxic effects and adverse reactions occur more frequently and cause more serious problems in older people.

24—PREGNANCY

The best rule to follow during pregnancy is to avoid all drugs, including tobacco and alcohol. Any medicine—prescription or nonprescription—requires medical advice and supervision.

This section will alert you if there is evidence that a drug harms the unborn child. Lack of evidence does not guarantee a drug's safety.

The definitions of the pregnancy risk categories of drugs used by the Food and Drug Administration (FDA) are listed on page 47.

25—BREAST-FEEDING

Many drugs filter into a mother's milk. Some drugs have dangerous or unwanted effects on the nursing infant. This section suggests ways to minimize harm to the child.

26—CHILDREN & ADOLESCENTS

Many drugs carry special warnings and precautions for children and adolescents because of their size and immaturity. In medical terminology, children are those from ages 1 to 12 years and adolescents are ages 12 to 20 years.

27—PROLONGED USE

With the exception of immediate allergic reactions, most drugs produce no ill effects during short periods of treatment. However, relatively safe drugs taken for long periods may produce unwanted effects. These are listed. Drugs should be taken in the smallest effective dose and for the shortest time possible. Nevertheless, some diseases and conditions require an indefinite period of treatment. Listed also are follow-up medical examinations and laboratory tests recommended when a drug is taken for long periods. Your doctor may want to change drugs occasionally or alter your treatment regimen to minimize problems.

The words "functional dependence" sometimes appear in this section. This does not mean physical or *psychological addiction*. Sometimes a body function ceases to work naturally because it has been replaced or interfered with by the drug. The body then becomes dependent on the drug to continue the function. If the medicine is discontinued, withdrawal symptoms are likely.

28—SKIN, SUNLIGHT & HEAT

Many drugs cause *photosensitivity*, which means increased skin sensitivity to ultraviolet rays from sunlight or artificial rays from a sunlamp, resulting in rashes or other skin disorders. This section will alert you to this potential problem. In hot weather dehydration is possible and can create serious risks if fluid intake is not adequate and some medications affect the body's ability to maintain normal body temperature.

29—DRIVING, PILOTING OR HAZARDOUS WORK

Any drug that alters moods or that decreases alertness, muscular coordination or reflexes may make these activities particularly hazardous. The effects may not appear in all people, or they may disappear after a short exposure to the drug. If this section contains a warning, use caution until you determine how a new drug affects you.

30—DISCONTINUING

Some patients stop taking a drug when symptoms begin to go away, although complete recovery may require longer treatment. Many conditions are never cured and require lifelong treatment to maintain optimal health. Bipolar (manic-depressive) disorder and many psychoses are examples of conditions that will almost certainly recur if medications are stopped without your doctor's approval. These are similar to illnesses such as diabetes mellitus, arthritis and thyroid disorders, for which treatment is usually life-long.

Other patients continue taking a drug when it is no longer needed. This section gives warnings about prematurely discontinuing. Some drugs cause symptoms days or weeks after they have been discontinued.

31—OTHERS

Warnings and precautions appear here if they don't fit into the other categories. This section includes special instructions and reminders; warnings to persons with chronic illness and other information.

32—POSSIBLE INTERACTION WITH OTHER DRUGS

Drugs interact in your body with other drugs, whether prescription or nonprescription. Interactions affect absorption, elimination or distribution of either drug. The chart lists interactions by generic drug name, drug class or drug-induced effect. An asterisk (*) beside a drug class name in this column reminds you to "See Glossary" in the back of the book, where additional information is provided such as generic names of drugs in a drug class or whether there is a chart in this book for that particular drug class.

If a drug class appears, the drug may interact with several or all generic drugs in that class. Drugs in each class that are included in the book are listed in the index. Frequently drugs that are not included on the individual charts in this book appear in the Interaction column.

Drug interactions are sometimes beneficial. You may not be able to determine from the chart which interactions are good and which are bad. Don't guess. Consult your doctor if you take drugs that interact. Some combinations are fatal.

Some drugs have too many interactions to list on one chart. The additional interactions appear on the continuation page indicated at the bottom of the list.

Testing has not been done on all possible drug combinations. It is *important* to let your doctor or pharmacist know about any drugs you take, *both prescription and nonprescription.*

33—POSSIBLE INTERACTION WITH OTHER SUBSTANCES

The substances listed here are repeated on every drug chart. All people eat food and drink beverages. Many adults consume alcohol. People use cocaine and smoke tobacco or marijuana. This section shows possible interactions between these substances and each drug.

Pregnancy Risk Category Information

The pregnancy risk category assigned to a medication identifies the potential risk for that particular drug to cause birth defects or death to an unborn child (fetus). These categories are assigned by applying the definitions of the Food and Drug Administration (FDA) to the available clinical information about the drug. Most drugs are tested only on animals and not on humans for safety during pregnancy, because such testing would subject unborn children to unnecessary risks.

It is best to avoid all drugs during pregnancy, but this rating system can help you and your doctor to assess the risk-to-benefit ratio should drug treatment become necessary. You and your doctor should discuss these benefits and risks carefully before any drug treatment is initiated. You should not take any medications (including nonprescription drugs such as laxatives or cold remedies) without your doctor's approval.

Definitions of the drug categories, labeled A, B, C, D, and X, are listed below:

- A: Adequate studies in pregnant women have failed to show a risk to the fetus in the first trimester of pregnancy, and there is no evidence of risk in later trimesters.

- B: Animal studies have not shown an adverse effect on the fetus, but there are no adequate studies in pregnant women; or animal studies have shown an adverse effect on the fetus, but adequate studies in pregnant women have not shown a risk to the fetus.

- C: Animal studies have shown an adverse effect on the fetus, but there are no adequate studies in humans; or there are no studies in animals or women. The drug may be used by pregnant women only if its benefits outweigh its potential risks.

- D: There is evidence of risk to the human fetus, but the potential benefits of use by pregnant women may be acceptable despite the potential risks (e.g., a woman might take such a drug in a life-threatening situation or for a serious disease for which safer drugs cannot be used or are ineffective).

- X: Studies in animals and humans show fetal abnormalities, or reports of adverse reactions indicate evidence of fetal risk. The risks involved clearly outweigh potential benefits, and the drug is contraindicated for pregnant women.

Psychological
Disorders

ADJUSTMENT DISORDERS

 GENERAL INFORMATION

DEFINITION—Excessive emotional or behavioral symptoms in response to a stressful situation in one's life. The individual is unable to adjust as expected to changes in life, which in turn causes impaired functioning in daily life.

BODY PARTS INVOLVED—Nervous system.

SEX OR AGE MOST AFFECTED—Both sexes, women more than men; adolescents and adults.

SIGNS & SYMPTOMS
- There must be an identifiable stressor. It may seem minor, or even positive, such as a job promotion, or negative, as with a small financial loss.
- The symptoms or behavior changes occur within 3 months of onset of the stressor and last no more than 6 months after the end of the stressor.
- Other psychological disorders are not present (e.g., major depression, anxiety disorder, personality disorder, etc.).
- Symptoms vary from person to person (often more severe in adolescents and the elderly), and include sleeping problems, restlessness, irritability, loss of concentration, fatigue, increased startle reaction, tension, depression, anxiety, withdrawal and inhibition. There can be feelings of fear, rage, guilt and shame, and denial of the stressful event (acting as if it never occurred).

CAUSES—A disruption in the normal process of adapting to a stressful event.

RISK INCREASES WITH
- The degree of undesirable change a stressor causes.
- Whether the stressor was sudden or expected.
- The unique importance of the stressor in the individual's life.
- Lack of support systems (e.g., family, friends; religious, cultural and social ties).
- The degree of vulnerability of the individual to stressful life experiences.

HOW TO PREVENT—No specific preventive measures known.

 WHAT TO EXPECT

DIAGNOSTIC MEASURES
- Observation of symptoms by you or others.
- Medical history, behavior history, physical exam and psychological evaluation by a doctor.

APPROPRIATE HEALTH CARE
- Self-care.
- Professional treatment.

PROBABLE OUTCOME—Usually resolved by adapting to the changed situation or the stressor ends. Treatment can help in cases where self-care does not alleviate the symptoms. These disorders are common and usually temporary.

POSSIBLE COMPLICATIONS
- Difficulty maintaining relationships or jobs.
- Lingering problems in adolescents.
- Self-treatment using alcohol or drugs to overcome undesired symptoms and feelings.
- Chronic anxiety and depression.

 HOW TO TREAT

GENERAL MEASURES
- Self-care, psychotherapy and in some cases medications, depending on severity of disorder and impact on life-style.
- For family/friends—Helping the person adapt to and cope with the event, and helping foster a change to prevent a recurrence.
- For yourself—Learning to cope with stress, keeping a journal about your stressors and feelings, talking to a friend, joining a support group, and taking good care of your physical health (diet, exercise, sleep).
- Psychotherapy—Several therapy methods are effective and often needed for a brief period. Family therapy (including marital counseling) may be recommended for some.

MEDICATION—Since adjustment disorders are usually of short duration, medications are normally not necessary. A medication may be prescribed short term for insomnia or for other specific symptoms, depending on their severity.

ACTIVITY—No restrictions. A routine physical exercise program is recommended. Physical exertion helps reduce anxiety and stress.

DIET—Eat a nutritionally balanced diet to maintain optimum health.

 CALL YOUR DOCTOR IF

- You or a family member has symptoms of an adjustment disorder.
- Symptoms continue or worsen after treatment is started.
- New, unexplained symptoms develop. Drugs used in treatment may produce side effects.

ALCOHOLISM

GENERAL INFORMATION

DEFINITION—A psychological and physiological dependence on alcohol resulting in chronic disease and disruption of interpersonal, family and work relationships.

BODY PARTS INVOLVED—Brain; nervous system; liver; heart.

SEX OR AGE MOST AFFECTED—Both sexes, but occurs 4 times more often in men than in women. Alcoholism in children is increasing.

SIGNS & SYMPTOMS
Early stages:
- Low tolerance for anxiety.
- Need for alcohol at the beginning of the day, or at times of stress.
- Insomnia; nightmares.
- Habitual Monday-morning hangovers, and frequent absences from work.
- Preoccupation with obtaining alcohol and hiding drinking from family and friends.
- Guilt or irritability when others suggest drinking is excessive.
Late stages:
- Frequent blackouts; memory loss.
- Delirium tremens (tremors, hallucinations, confusion, sweating, rapid heartbeat). These occur with alcohol withdrawal.
- Liver disease (yellow skin or eyes).
- Neurological impairment (numbness and tingling in hands and feet, declining sexual interest and potency, confusion, coma).
- Congestive heart failure (see Glossary).

CAUSES—Not fully understood, but include:
- Personality factors, especially dependency, anger, mania, depression or introversion.
- Family influences, especially alcoholic or divorced parents.
- Hereditary factors.
- Social and cultural pressure to drink.
- Body chemistry disturbances (perhaps).

RISK INCREASES WITH
- Cultural factors. Some ethnic groups have high alcoholism rates—for either social or biological reasons.
- Use of recreational drugs.
- Crisis situations, including unemployment, frequent moves or loss of friends or family.
- Environmental factors such as ready availability, affordability and social acceptance of alcohol in the culture group, work group or social group.
- Too much free unconstructed time, as with retirement.

HOW TO PREVENT
- Use alcohol in moderation—if at all—to provide a healthy role model. Set limits, drink slowly, dilute drinks and don't drink alone.
- Help a spouse, friend or co-worker to admit when an alcohol problem exists, and seek help.

WHAT TO EXPECT

DIAGNOSTIC MEASURES
- Medical history and physical examination.
- EEG (see Glossary) and laboratory studies of blood and liver function.

APPROPRIATE HEALTH CARE
- Self-care. The first and most difficult step of treatment is admitting the problem exists.
- Psychotherapy, behavioral therapy and medications are often combined in treatment.
- May require detoxification (see Glossary).
- Join Alcoholics Anonymous or other groups.

PROBABLE OUTCOME—With abstinence (absence of alcohol), sobriety is a way of life. The lifestyle change is difficult, and relapses occur. If determined, you can give up alcohol.

POSSIBLE COMPLICATIONS
- Chronic and progressive liver disease, gastric erosion, heart or stomach inflammation.
- Neuritis, tremors, seizures, memory loss and brain impairment; falls at home.
- Effects of "hangover" (headache, nausea, vomiting, thirst, overall drugged feeling).
- Impotence and other sexual problems.
- Mental and physical damage to the fetus if a woman drinks during pregnancy (fetal alcohol syndrome).
- Loss of job, friends and breaking up of family.
- Traffic accidents due to driving while impaired.
- Premature death.

HOW TO TREAT

GENERAL MEASURES
- Treatment involves short-term care that stops the drinking and long-term help to change the problems that caused the alcoholism.
- Join a local Alcoholics Anonymous or other support group, and attend regularly.
- Reassess your lifestyle to identify and alter factors that encourage drinking.

MEDICATION—Your doctor may prescribe disulfiram (Antabuse), which causes unpleasant physical symptoms when alcohol is consumed, or naltrexone, which lessens the pleasure of alcohol. Drugs used for withdrawal symptoms include benzodiazepines, tranquilizers, antipsychotics and anticonvulsants (if seizures occur).

ACTIVITY—Don't drink and drive.

DIET—Eat a normal, well-balanced diet. Vitamin supplements may be recommended.

☎ CALL YOUR DOCTOR IF

You or a family member has symptoms of alcoholism.

ALZHEIMER'S DISEASE

GENERAL INFORMATION

DEFINITION—A brain disorder characterized by gradual mental deterioration. A rapidly progressive form begins in adults around ages 36 to 45. A more gradual form, with slow development of symptoms, begins around ages 65 to 70.

BODY PARTS INVOLVED—Brain; nervous system; liver; heart.

SEX OR AGE MOST AFFECTED—Both sexes, beginning in the 40s and 50s.

SIGNS & SYMPTOMS
Early stages:
- Forgetfulness of recent events.
- Increasing difficulty performing intellectual tasks, such as usual work, balancing a checkbook or maintaining a household.
- Personality changes, including poor impulse control and poor judgment.

Later stages:
- Difficulty doing simple tasks, such as choosing clothing, solving problems.
- Failure to recognize familiar persons.
- Disinterest in personal hygiene or appearance.
- Difficulty feeding self.
- Belligerence and denial that anything is wrong.
- Loss of usual sexual inhibitions.
- Wandering away.
- Anxiety and insomnia.

Advanced stages:
- Complete loss of memory, speech and muscle function (including bladder and bowel control), necessitating total care and supervision.
- Extreme belligerence and hostility.

CAUSES—Irreversible damage to or loss of brain cells for unknown reasons.

RISK INCREASES WITH
- Family history of Alzheimer's disease.
- Aging.

HOW TO PREVENT—No specific preventive measures.

WHAT TO EXPECT

DIAGNOSTIC MEASURES
- Your own or others' observation of symptoms.
- Medical history and physical exam by a doctor.
- X-rays of the brain, including CAT scan (see Glossary) to rule out other conditions.

APPROPRIATE HEALTH CARE
- Doctor's treatment.
- Psychotherapy or counseling for family members.
- Care by a health facility, such as a nursing home, when home care becomes impossible.

PROBABLE OUTCOME—This condition is currently incurable, and treatment is directed to relieving the symptoms. Research into causes and treatment continues, so there is hope for eventual treatment and a cure.

POSSIBLE COMPLICATIONS
- Decreased resistance to infections, especially pneumonia and meningitis.
- Seizures and coma (rare).

HOW TO TREAT

GENERAL MEASURES
- If a family member has this disease, don't take his or her hostile personally.
- If you care for a family member with the disease, try to obtain help so you can get away often. Don't feel guilty about needing a respite—even if the patient resents it.
- Join or start a support group for families of Alzheimer's victims. Contact the Alzheimer's Association for information at 800-272-3900.
- Caregivers can help reduce some of the patient's behaviors by:
  Repetition: Patients with memory problems may benefit from from frequent, simple reminders.
  Reassurance: A brief, firm chat may help a patient with anxiety, verbal outbursts or agitation.
  Redirection: Distract a patient who is frustrated or agitated. A short walk can be helpful.

MEDICATION—Many medications are being studied. Some are useful to control symptoms such as agitation. The prescription drug tacrine (Cognex) may help some patients.

ACTIVITY—As much as possible. As the condition progresses, all activity will eventually require supervision.

DIET—Regular diet. Feeding assistance will eventually be necessary.

CALL YOUR DOCTOR IF

- You or a family member has symptoms of Alzheimer's disease.
- Signs of infection occur, such as fever, chills, muscle aches or headache.
- You care for someone with Alzheimer's disease, and you fear you are about to lose emotional control.

ANOREXIA NERVOSA

GENERAL INFORMATION

DEFINITION—A psychological eating disorder in which a person refuses to eat adequately—in spite of hunger—and loses enough weight to become emaciated. The illness usually begins with a normal weight-loss diet. The person eats very little and refuses to stop dieting after a reasonable weight loss. The person's body perception is distorted; the person continues to feel fat—even when emaciated.

BODY PARTS INVOLVED—All body cells.

SEX OR AGE MOST AFFECTED—Mostly female adolescents and young adults.

SIGNS & SYMPTOMS
- Weight loss of at least 15% of body weight without physical illness.
- High energy level despite body wasting.
- Intense fear of obesity.
- Depression.
- Appetite loss.
- Constipation.
- Cold intolerance.
- Refusal to maintain a minimum standard weight for age and height.
- Distorted body image. The person continues to feel fat—even when emaciated.
- Cessation of menstrual periods.

CAUSES—Unknown. Possible causes include family and internal conflicts (sexual conflicts); phobia about putting on weight; changes in fashion in U.S. (slimness is identified with beauty); a symptom of depression or personality disorder.

RISK INCREASES WITH
- Peer or social pressure to be thin.
- History of slight overweight.
- Perfectionistic, compulsive or overachieving personality.
- Psychological stress.
- Being an athlete, ballet dancer, cheerleader or model.

HOW TO PREVENT—Confront personal problems realistically. Try to correct or cope with problems with the help of counselors, therapists, family and friends. Develop a realistic attitude about weight.

WHAT TO EXPECT

DIAGNOSTIC MEASURES
- Your own or others' observation of signs and symptoms.
- Medical history and physical exam by a doctor.
- Laboratory blood tests for anemia and electrolyte (e.g., sodium and potassium) imbalance.

APPROPRIATE HEALTH CARE
- Doctor's treatment.
- Psychotherapy or counseling for the patient and family.
- Treatment can usually be provided on an outpatient basis.
- Hospitalization during crises for intravenous or tube feeding.
- Psychiatric hospitalization for at least 2 to 3 weeks (sometimes).

PROBABLE OUTCOME—Treatable if the patient recognizes the emotional disturbance, wants help and cooperates with treatment. Without treatment, this disorder can cause permanent disability or even death. Persons with anorexia nervosa have a high rate of attempted suicide due to low self-esteem. Therapy may continue over several years. Relapses are common, especially when stressful situations occur.

POSSIBLE COMPLICATIONS
- Chronic anorexia nervosa caused by patient's resistance to treatment.
- Electrolyte disturbances or irregular heartbeat. These may be life-threatening.
- Osteoporosis.
- Suicide.

HOW TO TREAT

GENERAL MEASURES
- The goal of treatment is for the patient to establish healthy eating patterns to regain normal weight. The patient can accomplish this with behavior modification training supervised by a qualified professional.
- For additional information, contact Anorexia Nervosa and Related Eating Disorders, PO Box 5102, Eugene, OR 97405; 503-344-1144.

MEDICATION—A variety of psychotherapy medications have some benefit, but there is no one medication that is consistently useful.

ACTIVITY—No restrictions, but avoid overexertion or compulsive exercise to lose weight.

DIET—A controlled refeeding program will be established. Vitamin and mineral supplements may be prescribed.

CALL YOUR DOCTOR IF

- Life-threatening symptoms occur, including rapid, irregular heartbeat; chest pain; loss of consciousness. Call immediately. This is an emergency!
- You have symptoms of anorexia nervosa or observe them in a family member.
- Weight loss continues, despite treatment.

ANXIETY

GENERAL INFORMATION

DEFINITION—A vague, uncomfortable feeling of fear, dread or danger from an unknown source. For some it may be a one-time episode; other persons become constantly anxious about everything. A certain amount of anxiety is normal and helps improve performance and allows people to avoid dangerous situations.

Several types of anxiety are recognized, including acute situational anxiety (which is usually short-term), generalized anxiety disorder, and adjustment disorder with anxious mood. (See also separate charts on Adjustment Disorders, Panic Disorder, Post-Traumatic Stress Disorder, Phobias, Obsessive-Compulsive Disorder and Stress). Generalized anxiety is defined as unrealistic or excessive anxiety for 6 months or longer. Anxiety is the most common mental health problem in U.S.

BODY PARTS INVOLVED—Central nervous system; endocrine system.

SEX OR AGE MOST AFFECTED—Females more than males, mainly adults ages 20-45.

SIGNS & SYMPTOMS
● Feeling that something undesirable or harmful is about to happen (edginess and apprehension).
● Dry mouth; swallowing difficulty; hoarseness.
● Rapid breathing and heartbeat, palpitations.
● Twitching or trembling.
● Muscle tension; headaches; backache.
● Sweating.
● Difficulty concentrating.
● Dizziness or faintness.
● Nausea; diarrhea; weight loss.
● Sleeplessness.
● Irritability.
● Fatigue.
● Nightmares.
● Memory problems.
● Sexual impotence.

CAUSES—Activation of the body's defense mechanisms for fight or flight. Excess adrenaline is discharged from the adrenal glands, and adrenaline breakdown products (catecholamines) eventually affect various parts of the body. Attempts to avoid the anxiety leads to more anxiety.

RISK INCREASES WITH
● Stress from any source (such as social or financial problems).
● Family history of anxiety.
● Fatigue or overwork.
● Recurrence of situations that have previously been stressful or harmful.
● Medical illness.
● Unrealistic perfectionism.
● Withdrawal from drugs or alcohol.

HOW TO PREVENT
● Practice relaxation techniques or meditation.
● Consider lifestyle changes to reduce stress.

WHAT TO EXPECT

DIAGNOSTIC MEASURES
● Your own observation of symptoms.
● Medical history and physical exam by a doctor.
● Laboratory studies to rule out medical conditions that produce anxiety, such as hyperthyroidism, anemia, hypoglycemia and diabetes.

APPROPRIATE HEALTH CARE
● Self-care.
● Doctor's treatment.
● Psychotherapy or counseling.

PROBABLE OUTCOME—Generalized anxiety can be controlled with treatment. Overcoming anxiety often results in a richer, more satisfying life.

POSSIBLE COMPLICATIONS
● Impaired social and occupational functioning.
● A sudden increase in anxiety may lead to panic and violent escape behavior.
● Dependence on drugs.
● Heart arrhythmias.

HOW TO TREAT

GENERAL MEASURES
● Obtain therapy to understand the specific but unconscious threat or source of stress.
● Learn techniques, including biofeedback and relaxation therapy, to reduce muscle tension.
● Follow a regular energetic fitness routine using aerobic exercise if possible.
● For additional information, contact Anxiety Disorders Association of America, 6000 Executive Blvd., Suite 513, Rockville, MD 20852; 301-231-9350.

MEDICATION—Your doctor may prescribe:
● Antianxiety drugs on a short-term basis.
● Antidepressants for panic disorders.

ACTIVITY—Stay active. Physical exertion helps reduce anxiety.

DIET—No special diet. Avoid caffeine and other stimulants, as well as alcohol.

CALL YOUR DOCTOR IF

● You have symptoms of anxiety and self-treatment has failed.
● You have a sudden feeling of panic.
● New, unexplained symptoms develop. Drugs used in treatment may produce side effects.

ATTENTION-DEFICIT HYPERACTIVITY DISORDER (ADHD)

GENERAL INFORMATION

DEFINITION—A pattern of behavior in children characterized by short attention spans and impulsivity, with or without hyperactivity. It is implicated in learning disorders and estimated to affect 5-10% of school-aged children.

SEX OR AGE MOST AFFECTED—Boys are affected 10 times more often than girls. The symptoms can appear at ages 4-7 and peak at 8-10; may continue into adulthood.

SIGNS & SYMPTOMS
- Squirms in seat; fidgets with hands or feet.
- Unable to stay seated when required to do so.
- Easily distracted.
- Blurts out answers before a question is finished.
- Difficulty waiting turn in games and lines.
- Difficulty following instructions.
- Unable to sustain attention in work or play activities.
- Shifts from one uncompleted project to another.
- Difficulty playing quietly.
- Talks excessively.
- Interrupts or intrudes on others.
- Doesn't appear to listen.
- Loses items necessary for tasks.
- Often engages in dangerous activities without considering consequences.

CAUSES—Unknown. Many theories proposed, but none proven or disproven. It is thought to be of biologic origin.

RISK INCREASES WITH—Family history of the disorder.

HOW TO PREVENT—No preventive measures known.

WHAT TO EXPECT

DIAGNOSTIC MEASURES
- Care must be taken in diagnosis, and no specific test is available. Many of the behavioral problems are common to all children. Usually 8 out of the 14 signs and symptoms above should be present for diagnosis. Formal educational and psychological assessment is necessary.
- A social history, medical history and school reports are necessary to aid in diagnosis.

APPROPRIATE HEALTH CARE
- Doctor's treatment and counseling for parents and child.
- Behavior and cognitive therapies (see Glossary for both). These therapies involve the child with self-monitoring, role playing and self-recording. They focus on strategies that alter the undesired behavior. A combination of these techniques and psychostimulant medications seem to have the greatest affect on controlling the symptoms.

PROBABLE OUTCOME—In some cases, the behavior disappears completely at puberty. In others, hyperactivity diminishes with age. However, a number of these children grow into troubled teenagers and adults.

POSSIBLE COMPLICATIONS
- Child may not grow out of difficulties. Later problems may occur, such as academic failure, antisocial behavior and sometimes criminal behavior.
- Problems may carry on to adulthood, with a high incidence of personality disorders.

HOW TO TREAT

GENERAL MEASURES
- Help your child at home by providing a structured environment, well-defined behavior limits and consistent use of parenting techniques. Get professional assistance if help is needed.
- Stay in close contact with the child's teacher. Arrange for extra lessons or tutoring if the child needs help with school subjects.
- For additional information, contact Attention Deficit Disorder Association, 8091 S. Ireland Way, Aurora, CO 90016; 800-487-2282.

MEDICATION—Your doctor may prescribe stimulant drugs, such as methylphenidate (Ritalin), which appear to have a calming affect on children with the disorder. These drugs have unpleasant side effects, such as sleep disturbances, depression, headache, stomach ache, loss of appetite and stunted growth.

ACTIVITY—Structure your child's activity to the extent possible.

DIET—Diets that remove all food additives, special elimination diets or megavitamin therapy have been suggested. Most medical research indicates these diets benefit very few children. Many parents, however, report dramatic changes in behavior after this treatment. This change may result from the extra attention the child receives with preparation of special meals. Discuss any special diets with the doctor.

CALL YOUR DOCTOR IF

- You believe your child has symptoms of attention deficit hyperactivity disorder.
- Symptoms don't improve, or worsen after treatment is begun.
- New, unexplained symptoms develop. Drugs used in treatment may produce side effects.

BIPOLAR DISORDER
(Manic-Depressive Disorder)

 GENERAL INFORMATION

DEFINITION—A disorder that is characterized by extreme mood swings, and the relationship between the moods and what is actually happening in the person's life is not direct. Periods of unexplainable elation and overactivity (mania) alternate on an irregular, but cyclical, basis with deep depression. Periods of normal behavior (that can last for a short time or for years) occur in between the mania and the depression.

BODY PARTS INVOLVED—Nervous system.

SEX OR AGE MOST AFFECTED—Both sexes. The peak age is 20 to 25; onset after 60 is rare.

SIGNS & SYMPTOMS
Mania:
• Accelerated energy levels; euphoric mood.
• Getting up earlier and earlier in the morning (some may not sleep at all for 3-4 days).
• Easily distracted and restless (which can cause work output to fall). Enthusiastically start (but rarely finish) new projects.
• May go on spending sprees.
• May become sexually promiscuous.
• Often irritable and has attacks of rage.
• Speech becomes rapid, wild and illogical.
• May have a very high opinion of one's abilities and exaggerated thinking (grandiosity).
• May forget to eat; may lose weight and become exhausted.
• May develop delusions of grandeur or intense anger at one's inability to carry out wild schemes.
Depression:
• Becomes increasingly withdrawn; has disturbed sleep; late rising becomes a habit.
• May stay in one's room (afraid to face the world); lacks self-esteem.
• Self-neglect.
• Decreased sex drive.
• Slowing of speech and movement.
• Imagined problems multiply.
• Excessive worrying about imagined illnesses. See chart on Depression for other symptoms.

CAUSES—Exact cause is unknown. Biologic, psychological and hereditary factors may play a part. Extreme stress or a death may trigger a sudden episode of mania or depression.

RISK INCREASES WITH—Family history of bipolar disorder.

HOW TO PREVENT—No known measures.

 WHAT TO EXPECT

DIAGNOSTIC MEASURES—Medical history and physical exam by a doctor (sometimes a psychiatrist). Psychological testing.

APPROPRIATE HEALTH CARE
• Psychotherapy or counseling along with drug treatment achieves the best results.
• Hospitalization or inpatient care at a treatment center may be required for severe symptoms.
• Electroconvulsive therapy (ECT) (see Glossary) may be used for patients who fail to respond to medication.

PROBABLE OUTCOME—May be restored to nearly normal health with long-term therapy that reduces the frequency and severity of episodes. Many famous executives, scientists and government leaders have this disorder.

POSSIBLE COMPLICATIONS
• Relapse (especially if medication is stopped).
• Job loss; marital problems.
• Failure to improve.
• Suicide.

 HOW TO TREAT

GENERAL MEASURES
• Comply with the medication regimen provided by your doctor. Schedule regular office visits to monitor the effectiveness of the treatment and to watch for side effects.
• Do not discontinue medication when you feel better. This may cause a relapse that may not respond well to medication.
• Counseling can provide the methods needed to help you cope with the disorder. Family members should learn to recognize signs of an impending episode and how to help the person.
• Seek support groups. Contact social agencies for help. Call the local suicide-prevention hot line if you feel suicidal.
• For additional information, contact National Depressive and Manic Depressive Association, Merchandise Mart, Box 3395, Chicago, IL 60654; 800-82-NDMDA.

MEDICATION—Your doctor may prescribe lithium, valproic acid or carbamazepine (Tegretol). Antipsychotic medications may be necessary for more severe symptoms.

ACTIVITY—No restrictions. Maintain daily activities—even if you don't feel like it.

DIET—Eat a normal, well-balanced diet—even if you have no appetite. Vitamin and mineral supplements may be necessary. Your doctor may advise you to avoid caffeine, as it is a stimulant.

 CALL YOUR DOCTOR IF

• You or a family member has symptoms of depression or mania.
• You feel suicidal or hopeless.

BULIMIA NERVOSA

GENERAL INFORMATION

DEFINITION—A psychological eating disorder characterized by abnormal perception of body image, constant craving for food and binge eating, followed by self-induced vomiting or laxative use.

BODY PARTS INVOLVED—Brain and central nervous system; kidneys; liver; endocrine system; gastrointestinal tract.

SEX OR AGE MOST AFFECTED—Usually female adolescents or young adults.

SIGNS & SYMPTOMS—Recurrent episodes of binge eating (rapid consumption of a large amount of food in a short time, usually less than 2 hours), plus at least 3 of the following:
* Preference for high-calorie convenience foods during a binge.
* Secretive eating during a binge. Patients are aware that the eating pattern is abnormal, and they fear being unable to stop eating.
* Termination of an eating binge with purging measures, such as laxative use or self-induced vomiting.
* Depression and guilt following an eating binge.
* Repeated attempts to lose weight with severely restrictive diets, self-induced vomiting and use of laxatives or diuretics.
* Frequent weight fluctuations of more than 10 pounds from alternately fasting and gorging.
* No underlying physical disorder.

CAUSES—Unknown. Thought to be largely emotional.

RISK INCREASES WITH
* Strict, compulsive, perfectionistic family environment.
* Anorexia nervosa.
* Depression.
* Stress, including lifestyle changes, such as moving or starting a new school or job.
* Personality disorders.
* Neurotic preoccupation with being physically attractive.
* Being a ballet dancer, model, cheerleader or athlete (especially a gymnast).

HOW TO PREVENT
* Encourage rational attitude about weight.
* Enhance self-esteem.
* Avoid overly high self-expectations.
* Avoid stress.

WHAT TO EXPECT

DIAGNOSTIC MEASURES
* Your own or others' observation of symptoms. Many patients are secretive, and parents/spouses may be unaware of this condition.
* Medical history and physical exam by a doctor.
* Laboratory blood studies, including measurement of electrolyte (e.g., sodium and potassium) levels.

APPROPRIATE HEALTH CARE
* Doctor's treatment.
* Psychotherapy or counseling that may include hypnosis or biofeedback training.
* Treatment in an eating disorder facility (sometimes).
* Hospitalization (in severe cases).

PROBABLE OUTCOME—Outcome is variable; patients can learn to control the bulimia with counseling, psychotherapy, biofeedback training and individual or group psychotherapy.

POSSIBLE COMPLICATIONS
* Fluid and electrolyte imbalance from vomiting; dental disease from vomiting gastric acid; stomach rupture (rare); malnutrition.
* Without treatment, complications can be fatal.
* Relapse.

HOW TO TREAT

GENERAL MEASURES
* The goal of treatment is for the patient to establish healthy eating patterns to regain normal weight. The patient can accomplish this with behavior modification training supervised by a qualified professional.
* Those who stay in therapy have the best chance to improve.
* See Resources for Additional Information.

MEDICATION—Medication is usually not necessary for this disorder. However, antidepressants are sometimes helpful.

ACTIVITY—No restrictions. Don't overexercise to lose weight.

DIET
* If hospitalization is necessary—Intravenous fluids may be prescribed. During recovery, vitamin and mineral supplements will be necessary until signs of deficiency disappear and normal eating patterns are established.
* For outpatient therapy—Supervision and regulation of eating habits; a food diary may be maintained; feared foods will be reintroduced.

CALL YOUR DOCTOR IF

* You have symptoms of bulimia or you suspect your child or spouse has bulimia.
* The following occur during treatment:
  Rapid, irregular heartbeat or chest pain.
  Loss of consciousness.
  Cessation of menstrual periods.
  Repeated vomiting or diarrhea.
  Continued weight loss, despite treatment.

CHRONIC FATIGUE SYNDROME

GENERAL INFORMATION

DEFINITION—A disorder characterized primarily by profound fatigue. There is usually an abrupt onset of symptoms that come and go for at least six months. It is unknown whether chronic fatigue syndrome represents one or many disorders. It is difficult to diagnose, because there is no specific laboratory test or defined set of signs and symptoms. Currently, the major criteria used to define cases are: (1) persistent of recurring fatigue that does not resolve with bed rest and is severe enough to reduce average daily activity by at least 50% for at least 6 months, and (2) satisfactory exclusion of other chronic clinical conditions, including preexisting psychiatric disease. Other signs and symptoms aid in the diagnosis.

BODY PARTS INVOLVED—Endocrine system; muscles; gastrointestinal system; central nervous system.

SEX OR AGE MOST AFFECTED—Primarily young adults between 20 and 40. Women outnumber men about 2 to 1.

SIGNS & SYMPTOMS
- Fatigue.
- Low-grade fever.
- Pharyngitis.
- Painful lymph glands.
- Sore throat.
- Generalized muscle weakness.
- Muscle aches.
- Headaches.
- Sleep disturbances (hypersomnia or insomnia).
- Joint pain.
- Neuropsychological complaints (photophobia, forgetfulness, irritability, confusion, difficulty concentrating, depression, vision changes).

CAUSES—Unknown. Immunological abnormalities may be involved. Many theories center on an infectious agent, especially Epstein-Barr (EB) virus, but proof is lacking.

RISK INCREASES WITH—Unknown.

HOW TO PREVENT—Unknown.

WHAT TO EXPECT

DIAGNOSTIC MEASURES
- No specific medical test is available. The 2 major criteria mentioned under Definition plus about 8 of the other signs and symptoms are necessary to establish the diagnosis.
- Medical history and social history plus physical exam by a doctor.
- Laboratory blood and urine studies as necessary to rule out other disorders.

APPROPRIATE HEALTH CARE
- Self-care after diagnosis.
- Doctor's treatment.
- Psychotherapy may be helpful for some patients.

PROBABLE OUTCOME—Generally very slow improvement over months or years.

POSSIBLE COMPLICATIONS—None specific to the disorder. Symptoms are usually most severe during the first 6 months.

HOW TO TREAT

GENERAL MEASURES
- Basic management involves four areas:
  1. Validation of the diagnosis and your education about the disorder.
  2. General treatment measures.
  3. Treatment of specific symptoms.
  4. Experimental therapy.
- Try to remain optimistic.
- Keep involved in life; don't isolate yourself.
- Sometimes a change of scenery can help. Take a vacation if possible.
- Be patient with family and friends and their understanding and acceptance of your disorder.
- Join a local or national support group.
- For additional information, contact Chronic Fatigue Syndrome, PO Box 220398, Charlotte, NC 28222-0398; 800-442-3437.

MEDICATION
- Medications must be individually tailored, but may include pain medicine, local injections, antidepressants or others.
- Other experimental medication therapies are being studied.

ACTIVITY
- Rest if you feel tired.
- Exercise is important. Begin a gradual program that may be just 3-5 minutes a day to start with. Increase the activity by about 20% about every 2-3 weeks. Setbacks will occur, so don't be discouraged.

DIET—Try to maintain good nutrition, even if appetite is decreased. Eat a low-fat, high-fiber diet. Take vitamin supplements.

CALL YOUR DOCTOR IF

- You or a family member has signs and symptoms of chronic fatigue syndrome.
- Symptoms worsen after treatment is started.
- New or unexplained symptoms develop. Drugs used in treatment may cause side effects.

CHRONIC PAIN DISORDER
(Somatoform Pain Disorder)

 GENERAL INFORMATION

DEFINITION—Perceived pain that continues longer than 6 months without an accompanying injury or illness. There may be a medical problem, but it does not fully explain the pain. Patients have often tried numerous medications and a variety of doctors in seeking a solution. Standard pain treatments bring only minimal relief.

BODY PARTS INVOLVED—Nervous system; muscles; joints; gastrointestinal tract. Almost any body part may be involved.

SEX OR AGE MOST AFFECTED—Both sexes, but more common in women. May begin at any age, but most often occurs during adolescence and young adulthood.

SIGNS & SYMPTOMS
• Pain that is described as stinging, burning, aching. The pain may come and go and may vary in intensity, duration, location and radiating pattern (moving from one body part to another).
• The pain may begin suddenly and increase in severity over days to weeks.
• Anxiety and depression.

CAUSES—The exact cause is unknown. It appears to be of psychological origin and may result from translation of emotions into physical pain rather than expressing them in other ways.

RISK INCREASES WITH—A family history of illnesses and painful injuries.

HOW TO PREVENT—No specific preventive measures known.

 WHAT TO EXPECT

DIAGNOSTIC MEASURES
• Your own observation of symptoms.
• Medical history, behavior history, physical exam and psychological evaluation by a doctor.

APPROPRIATE HEALTH CARE
• Doctor's treatment.
• May be referred to a special pain treatment center for help.
• Treatment is usually provided on an outpatient basis. Hospitalization or inpatient care may be recommended in rare cases.

PROBABLE OUTCOME—Treatment can be effective for some patients and bring about a gradual change; for others, the prognosis is guarded and the chronic pain may continue.

POSSIBLE COMPLICATIONS
• Difficulty maintaining personal relationships and jobs.
• Addiction to narcotic pain medications.
• Chronic anxiety and depression.
• Noncompliance with treatment.

 HOW TO TREAT

GENERAL MEASURES
• Treatment requires a trusting relationship between the doctor and patient. It is important that you as the patient be a partner in the effort to relieve the chronic pain.
• Treatment is focused on achieving pain relief, improving any depressive symptoms, increasing normal functioning and reducing pain-related behavior.
• Steps in treatment may include counseling, biofeedback, hypnosis and prescription of medications in some cases. Group therapy can be helpful.
• The family or other significant persons in the patient's life should also be involved in the therapy in order to understand the problem and what they can do to help the patient.

MEDICATION—Standard pain medications or sedatives do not cure chronic pain disorder. Your doctor may prescribe a tricyclic antidepressant. These drugs appear to help with pain relief and relieving the symptoms of depression.

ACTIVITY—Normally no restrictions unless directed by your doctor.

DIET—Eat a nutritionally balanced diet to maintain optimum health.

 CALL YOUR DOCTOR IF

• You or a family member has symptoms of chronic pain disorder.
• Symptoms continue or worsen after treatment is started.
• New, unexplained symptoms develop. Drugs used in treatment may produce side effects.

DELUSIONAL DISORDERS

GENERAL INFORMATION

DEFINITION—Disorders characterized by consistent delusions, while other mental functioning is apparently unaffected. A delusion is a persistent belief held by an individual despite ample evidence proving it is false. (A belief that is shared by a group or a culture is not considered delusional.)

BODY PARTS INVOLVED—Nervous system.

SEX OR AGE MOST AFFECTED—Females slightly more frequently than males; usually affects ages 35-55.

SIGNS & SYMPTOMS
Delusional disorders (previously called paranoia) are classified by the type of delusion that is most prominent in the individual:
- Erotomanic—A belief that a particular person (often someone rich and famous such as a movie star or politician) is deeply in love with one. This delusion can lead to "stalking."
- Grandiose—A belief that one is very special or has very important talents or abilities.
- Jealous—A mistaken belief that one's spouse or lover is unfaithful despite no reasonable cause.
- Persecutory—A belief that one is a victim of an organized plot, others are out to "get" one or one is being spied on or cheated.
- Somatic—A belief that one has some dread disease, is dying or has some physical defect. Often the person feels that he or she has a foul-smelling body odor or is infested with insects or parasites.
- Mixed—More than one type of delusion is present without one type predominating.

CAUSES—The causes are unknown. Several theories have been suggested, but unproven.

RISK INCREASES WITH
- Lower socioeconomic status.
- Recent immigration to this country.
- Old age, with impaired hearing or other physical disabilities that limit social contacts.

HOW TO PREVENT—No specific prevention measures known.

WHAT TO EXPECT

DIAGNOSTIC MEASURES
- Your own or others' observation of symptoms.
- Physical exam and mental tests by a doctor (diagnosis is difficult, as patients don't feel they have any problem. Outside of delusions, they may behave and function in a normal manner).

APPROPRIATE HEALTH CARE
- Doctor's treatment.
- Medication and psychotherapy.

PROBABLE OUTCOME
- Treatment may be effective for some who can build a trusting relationship with their therapists. People with delusional disorders feel that accepting medications is an admission that their beliefs are false. Also, side effects of medications can frighten them into discontinuing the treatment.
- Some people are forced into treatment by legal action. Such people may not improve.
- Others may not accept treatment, but continue to function fairly normally in day-to-day life. The delusions remain chronic; they can wax or wane over time.

POSSIBLE COMPLICATIONS
- Delusions can dominate a person's life and lead to loss of job or family and to marital conflicts and difficulties with friends and colleagues.
- Sexual problems and depression.
- Legal problems if delusions lead to behaviors such as stalking or violence to others.
- Financial problems (all one's money may be spent in support of the delusion).
- Suicide (often to escape "persecuters").

HOW TO TREAT

GENERAL MEASURES
- Medication is usually the treatment of choice.
- Psychotherapy may be helpful for some individuals who are willing to cooperate.
- Counseling is recommended for family members to help them understand and cope. This may be particularly true with the spouses of persons with jealous delusional disorder.
- Family and friends should not try to argue or talk the individual out of the beliefs with logical reasoning. It will do no good. They can explain to the delusional person that they do not believe or accept the delusion, but that this does not imply disrespect.

MEDICATION
- Antipsychotic medication is usually prescribed; it can relieve some of the delusional symptoms.
- Depression can be treated with antidepressants and antianxiety medications.

ACTIVITY—Full activity.

DIET—No special diet.

CALL YOUR DOCTOR IF

- You or a family member has symptoms of delusional disorder.
- During treatment, delusional symptoms worsen or do not improve.
- New, unexplained symptoms develop. Drugs used in treatment may produce side effects.

DEMENTIA (Senility)

GENERAL INFORMATION

DEFINITION—Mental impairment caused by a variety of diseases that produce brain deterioration and loss of normal psychological functions.

BODY PARTS INVOLVED—Brain.

SEX OR AGE MOST AFFECTED—Older adults.

SIGNS & SYMPTOMS
- Forgetfulness, especially of recent events.
- Unpredictable, sometimes violent, behavior.
- Confusion.
- Loss of interest in normal activities.
- Disorientation, especially at night.
- Poor personal hygiene and appearance.
- Depression; sleep disturbances.
- Poor judgment.
- Incontinence (late stage).

CAUSES—Degeneration and loss of the gray matter from the brain. The causes include:
- Alzheimer's disease (its underlying cause is not known). See separate chart on Alzheimer's.
- Inadequate blood supply to the brain due to blood clots, hypertension or atherosclerosis.
- Severe head injury or repeated head injury (e.g., from boxing).
- Brain tumor.
- AIDS.
- Parkinson's disease, Huntington's chorea and some hereditary disorders.
- Secondary dementias caused by hypothyroidism, syphilis, normal-pressure hydrocephalus, vitamin B deficiency and some medications. These may be reversible with treatment of the primary disorder.

RISK INCREASES WITH
- High blood pressure or atherosclerotic disease.
- Age over 60.

HOW TO PREVENT
- Seek early medical treatment for underlying causes.
- Protect yourself from head injury. Wear seat belts in vehicles. Wear protective head gear for riding bicycles and motorcycles and participating in contact sports.
- To prevent atherosclerosis, don't smoke; also, eat a diet low in fat, exercise regularly and reduce stress whenever possible. Ask your doctor about other preventive steps to take.

WHAT TO EXPECT

DIAGNOSTIC MEASURES
- Observation of symptoms by others.
- Medical history and physical exam by a doctor.
- Laboratory blood studies, EEG (see Glossary); x-rays of the head (to rule out potentially reversible causes).

APPROPRIATE HEALTH CARE
- Doctor's treatment.
- Home care if symptoms are mild to moderate.
- Nursing home care, if the disorder is too advanced for home care.
- Psychotherapy or counseling for family members.
- Occupational therapy.

PROBABLE OUTCOME—Primary dementia is currently considered incurable and progressive. Medicine may help a few to keep the condition from worsening, but cannot restore lost brain function.

POSSIBLE COMPLICATIONS—Infections, constipation, falls and injuries and poor nutrition. These occur because the ill person cannot care for himself or herself.

HOW TO TREAT

GENERAL MEASURES—Family members can help:
- Notice early behavior changes, and seek prompt medical care.
- Provide simple reminders, such as a clock, daily calendar or name tag. Help the person with personal hygiene.
- Minimize changes in the person's daily routine and environment.
- Encourage social activities and contacts. Consider adult day care.
- Treat the person with respect and kindness.
- Provide a protected, nonjudgmental environment when the patient cannot provide self-care. When home care is no longer possible, find a good extended care facility.
- Visit the patient often—even if he or she doesn't seem to recognize you.
- See Resources for Additional Information.

MEDICATION—Your doctor may prescribe medication appropriate to treat the underlying condition or drugs to treat the behavioral symptoms if other treatment has failed.

ACTIVITY—Encourage as much activity as possible. Accident-proof the home. Take precautions against the patient's wandering.

DIET—Provide a well-balanced diet.

CALL YOUR DOCTOR IF

You observe symptoms of dementia in a family member.

DEPRESSION

 GENERAL INFORMATION

DEFINITION—A continuing feeling of sadness, despondency or hopelessness most days and most of every day for at least 2 weeks with accompanying symptoms. Major depression occurs in about 1 in 10 Americans.

BODY PARTS INVOLVED—Nervous system.

SEX OR AGE MOST AFFECTED—Both sexes, but more commonly in women; all ages.

SIGNS & SYMPTOMS
- Loss of interest; boredom; inability to enjoy.
- Hopelessness; listlessness and fatigue.
- Insomnia; excessive or disturbed sleeping.
- Social isolation; feeling of not being useful or needed.
- Appetite loss or overeating; constipation.
- Loss of sex drive.
- Difficulty making decisions; difficulty concentrating; unexplained crying bouts.
- Intense guilt over minor or imaginary events.
- Irritability; restlessness; thoughts of suicide.
- Various pains, such as headache or chest pain, without evidence of disease.

CAUSES
- Depressive illness has no single obvious cause. Biological factors (physical illness, hormonal disorders, some drugs) play a part.
- Social and psychological factors play a part.
- Inherited disorders may contribute (bipolar disorder or manic-depressive disorder runs in families).
- May relate to the number of disturbing events in a person's life all at one time.

RISK INCREASES WITH
- Unexpressed anger or other emotion.
- Compulsive, rigid, perfectionist or highly dependent personality.
- Family history of depression, alcoholism.
- Failure in occupation, marriage or other relationships; death or loss of a loved one.
- Loss of something important (job, home, etc).
- Job change or move to a new area.
- Surgery, such as mastectomy for cancer.
- Major illness or disability.
- Passing from one life stage to another, such as menopause or retirement.
- Use of some drugs, such as reserpine, beta-adrenergic blockers or benzodiazepines.
- Withdrawal from stimulant drugs, such as cocaine, amphetamines or caffeine.
- Some diseases, such as diabetes mellitus, cancer of the pancreas and hormonal disorders.

HOW TO PREVENT
- Anticipate and prepare for major life changes.
- Avoid risk factors when feasible.

 WHAT TO EXPECT

DIAGNOSTIC MEASURES
Evaluation by a health care professional (sometimes a psychiatrist). Psychological testing.

APPROPRIATE HEALTH CARE
- Self-care for mild depression.
- Psychotherapy or counseling along with medication appears to obtain the best results for moderate to severe depression.
- Hospitalization for severe depression.
- Electroconvulsive therapy (see Glossary) if other measures fail.

PROBABLE OUTCOME—Spontaneous recovery often, but professional help shortens the duration and helps you learn to cope in the future. Recurrence is common. Recovery rate is high, despite one's pessimism when depressed.

POSSIBLE COMPLICATIONS
- Suicide. Warning signs include withdrawal from family and friends, neglect of personal appearance, mention of wanting "to end it all" or being "a burden," evidence of a suicide plan (e.g., buying a gun or making a will), sudden cheerfulness.
- Failure to improve.

 HOW TO TREAT

GENERAL MEASURES
- If symptoms are mild to moderate, try self-care ideas: Talk to friends and family; exercise regularly; eat a balanced, low-fat diet; avoid alcohol; maintain normal routines (if overscheduling is a problem, though, try to slow down); see fun movies; try relaxation techniques; take a vacation if possible; write down your feelings in a journal or diary; try to work out interpersonal problems (it's best, however, to avoid making major decisions at this time); stay as active as possible. Seek support group help.
- Delegate responsibilities until improved.
- Call suicide-prevention hotline if you feel suicidal.
- See Resources for Additional Information.

MEDICATION—Your doctor may prescribe:
- Antidepressant drugs to accompany therapy.
- Lithium or other mood stabilizers for alternating mania and depression.

ACTIVITY—No restrictions. Maintain daily activities—even if you don't feel up to them.

DIET—Eat a normal, well-balanced diet—even if you have no appetite.

 CALL YOUR DOCTOR IF

- You have symptoms of depression.
- You feel suicidal or hopeless.

DISSOCIATIVE DISORDERS

GENERAL INFORMATION

DEFINITION—A group of psychological illnesses that involve a sudden change in a person's state of consciousness, identity, behavior, thoughts, feelings and perception of external reality that cause that particular mental function to be separated or cut off from the mind as a whole.

BODY PARTS INVOLVED—Nervous system.

SEX OR AGE MOST AFFECTED—Females more than males; young to middle-aged adults.

SIGNS & SYMPTOMS
- Amnesia—Inability to recall important personal information.
- Fugue—Episode of altered consciousness that causes a person to act or wander away from home or work and not remember it afterward.
- Identity disorder (previously called multiple personality disorder)—Presence of 2 or more distinct personalities, each one unique and unchanging, each of which dominates at different times.
- Depersonalization disorder—A state of feeling unreal; feeling as if you are an outside observer of your mental processes and body.
- Somnambulism—Walking while sleeping.

CAUSES
- Physical, emotional, verbal or sexual abuse in childhood.
- Sudden and severe trauma; unexpected exposure to someone's being killed or severely injured (as in a car accident).
- Overuse of dissociation (daydreaming or not concentrating) when coping with life's problems.

RISK INCREASES WITH—See Causes.

HOW TO PREVENT
- Child abuse prevention through parent education and reporting of suspected cases to proper agencies.
- Crisis intervention and emotional support for persons involved in trauma and natural or human-caused disasters.

WHAT TO EXPECT

DIAGNOSTIC MEASURES
- Observation of symptoms by you or others.
- Medical history and physical exam.
- Laboratory blood tests to rule out any problems with drugs, alcohol or chemical substances.
- Imaging studies such as CT scan or MRI (see Glossary for both) to check for any physical problems.
- EEG (see Glossary) to study the activity of the brain.
- Psychological testing to help diagnose the disorder and to rule out other mental problems.

APPROPRIATE HEALTH CARE
- Psychotherapy or counseling for the patient and family.
- Treatment can usually be provided on an outpatient basis.
- Steps in treatment may involve hypnosis, behavior modification and drug therapy.
- Hospitalization may be necessary during a crisis or a severe episode.

PROBABLE OUTCOME
- Effective treatment can produce full or partial recovery for many patients.
- Some patients may have a spontaneous improvement or recovery.
- Without treatment, patients with identity disorder go through life with many emotional and mood problems, but can appear to be functioning in a healthy manner.

POSSIBLE COMPLICATIONS
- Self-inflicted injuries.
- Suicide attempts.
- Substance abuse or chemical dependency.
- The disorder may become a chronic condition.

HOW TO TREAT

GENERAL MEASURES
- Treatment goals include learning to adapt to and cope with the functions of daily living, control the symptoms of the disorder and prevent a worsening of the problem or a relapse.
- Learn all you can about the disorder, and study the experience of others who have recovered.
- Support groups or group therapy are helpful.
- Seek instruction in self-hypnosis and relaxation techniques.
- Keep a personal diary, and write in it daily. Review it with the doctor during office visits.

MEDICATION—No medication will cure a dissociative disorder, but different drugs may be prescribed that help with specific symptoms:
- Antidepressants for depression.
- Benzodiazepines for anxiety and insomnia.
- Propranolol for flashbacks or other symptoms.
- Antipsychotic drugs for severe symptoms.
- Other drugs if an additional medical problem is diagnosed.

ACTIVITY—No restrictions. Activities should be based on your physical condition.

DIET—No special diet.

CALL YOUR DOCTOR IF

- You or a family member has symptoms of a dissociative disorder.
- Symptoms continue or worsen after treatment is started.
- New, unexplained symptoms develop. Drugs used in treatment may produce side effects.

DYSTHYMIA (Low-Grade Depression)

GENERAL INFORMATION

DEFINITION—A chronic depressive mood with symptoms that are milder, but longer lasting, than those of a major depressive episode. The onset of dysthymia is often unnoticed, and many people are not aware of the change in their lives. Symptoms may begin in childhood or in adolescence and continue over years or decades.

BODY PARTS INVOLVED—Nervous system.

SEX OR AGE MOST AFFECTED—Both sexes; late teens, youth to middle age.

SIGNS & SYMPTOMS—Dysthymia may be diagnosed if several of the following signs and symptoms have been present for most of the day, for most days, for two years or more (one year for children or teens), with no more than two months symptom free:
- Poor appetite or eating too much.
- Sleep problems (too much or too little sleep).
- Lack of energy; feeling tired all the time.
- Preoccupation with failure, inadequacy, and negative thoughts (hopelessness).
- Feelings of self-pity; pessimistic attitude.
- Lack of productivity at home and work.
- Trouble with concentration and making decisions.
- Lack of interest or enjoyment in pleasurable activities or social activities.
- Irritability.
- Crying for no reason.
- Overcritical or complaining.
- Skeptical.

CAUSES—Probably due to a combination of genetic factors, development factors and psychosocial factors (job loss, divorce).

RISK INCREASES WITH
- Family history of depressive illnesses.
- Alcohol dependency or abuse may be a contributor to the depression, or depression may give people a reason to start drinking.

HOW TO PREVENT
No specific preventive measures. Anticipate and prepare for major life changes where possible.

WHAT TO EXPECT

DIAGNOSTIC MEASURES
- Your own observation of symptoms.
- Medical history and physical exam by a doctor.

APPROPRIATE HEALTH CARE
- Doctor's treatment.
- Psychotherapy or counseling (may be combined with antidepressant medications). Several techniques are effective in treating dysthymia, such as cognitive or behavior therapy (focuses on changing negative thought patterns into positive ones), interpersonal therapy (focuses on building better relationships) and cultural analysis (deals with the role of society in contributing to low self-esteem and powerless feelings).
- Vocational counseling for some patients to be sure their work suits their temperament.

PROBABLE OUTCOME—The majority of people are helped with treatment. It may take several months before symptoms show improvement. Sometimes it's not until one has been treated and is feeling better that one realizes how depressed he or she has been.

POSSIBLE COMPLICATIONS
- Chronic recurrence; major depression.
- Alcohol abuse or dependency.

HOW TO TREAT

GENERAL MEASURES
- Join a support group. They help many people with sharing problems and fostering friendships.
- Avoid alcohol. If you need help stopping, ask your doctor, or contact an Alcoholics Anonymous group in your community.
- Reduce emotional stress in your life. Learn techniques to cope with stress.
- Additional information is available from the National Institute of Mental Health (NIMH), 9000 Rockville Pike, Bethesda, MD 20892, 800-232-3472.

MEDICATION—Your doctor may prescribe antidepressants. The medication may be needed for several months or several years. If one medication doesn't work, it is possible that another will.

ACTIVITY—No restrictions. A routine physical exercise program is recommended.

DIET—Eat a nutritionally balanced diet to help maintain optimum health.

CALL YOUR DOCTOR IF

- You or a family member has symptoms of dysthymia.
- Symptoms worsen or don't improve despite treatment.
- You have thoughts of death or suicide.

GRIEF (Bereavement)

GENERAL INFORMATION

DEFINITION—The emotional reaction following the death of a loved person, a divorce, loss of a body part or function, loss of self-esteem (such as losing a job) or other significant loss. Grief is a normal, appropriate reaction to loss. Grieving people gradually adjust to their loss and begin to make positive plans for the future. There are no guidelines for the normal duration of grieving. Occasionally grief is so intense or prolonged that professional help is needed.

BODY PARTS INVOLVED—Nervous system.

SEX OR AGE MOST AFFECTED—Both sexes, all ages.

SIGNS & SYMPTOMS
Recognized expressions of grief:
• Feelings of sadness, numbness, pain, anger, despair, guilt (these feelings can come and go for months, and may be overwhelming at times).
• Sudden crying spells.
• Hallucinations (such as a sense of having seen or heard the dead person).
• Anxiety and depression.
• Unwillingness to accept the loss; for example, maintaining the dead person's room or clothing as if he or she is expected to return.
• Insomnia.
• Nervousness or hyperactivity.
• Gastrointestinal problems.
• Tiredness, agitation, tearfulness.
• Increased intake of alcohol, tranquilizers and other drugs is common (but may cause problems).

CAUSES—Grief follows a loss.

RISK INCREASES WITH—An existing emotional problem, such as depression; social isolation; strong feelings of guilt or anger due to one's relationship with the dead person.

HOW TO PREVENT—Grieving should not be prevented or denied. It is a normal and expected response to a loss, and should be encouraged by open expression of feeling and social recognition of the loss.

WHAT TO EXPECT

DIAGNOSTIC MEASURES—In cases of prolonged grief or reactions, a physical examination and medical history will rule out medical illness.

APPROPRIATE HEALTH CARE
• Self-care.
• Doctor's treatment or other professional help, if needed.

PROBABLE OUTCOME—With time, the grief lessens and adjustment begins. The feelings of grief may return unpredictably, and will probably recur occasionally for years.

POSSIBLE COMPLICATIONS
• Difficulty maintaining relationships and jobs.
• Excess use of alcohol or tranquilizer drugs.
• Chronic anxiety and depression.
• Grieving expressions that may need medical help:
    Severe depression or panic attacks.
    Excessive feelings of guilt, bitterness, or remorse.
    Prolonged grief (usually more than 2 years). A person may build a life around the grief and never accept the loss.
    Talk about or threats of suicide.

HOW TO TREAT

GENERAL MEASURES
• Hold a memorial service or funeral for the loved one.
• Express your feelings following the loss. Don't keep them "bottled up" inside. Look to family and friends for help and support.
• Join a grief support group. They are available in most communities. Many people find comfort in sharing their feelings with others who have had similar experiences.
• Don't expect your feelings of grief to follow any pattern or a particular timetable.
• Slowly begin to rebuild your life; meet new people, and interest yourself in new activities.
• Avoid the overuse of alcohol or medications to suppress the emotions you are feeling.
• Seek professional counseling or psychotherapy help if you or your family thinks it is needed. Therapy can help bring about a healthy resolution of grief.

MEDICATION—Your doctor may prescribe medications, such as sedatives or antidepressants, for a short time; in most cases, drugs are not needed.

ACTIVITY—Normally no restrictions unless directed by your doctor.

DIET—Eat a nutritionally balanced diet to maintain optimum health.

CALL YOUR DOCTOR IF

• You or a family member has symptoms of prolonged or intense grief.
• You want information about grief support groups.

HYPOCHONDRIASIS

GENERAL INFORMATION

DEFINITION—A disorder characterized by person's conviction that he or she has a serious or fatal disease, despite evidence to the contrary from thorough medical examinations and tests. The person becomes quite informed and knowledgeable about illnesses, diagnoses and treatment, usually as a result of multiple medical evaluations and numerous contacts with health care professionals.

BODY PARTS INVOLVED—Brain.

SEX OR AGE MOST AFFECTED—Both sexes, all ages.

SIGNS & SYMPTOMS—Anxiety and persistent reports of symptoms involving any body part. Preoccupation with the possibility of heart disease or cancer is common. Symptoms may change, but the person's belief that a serious condition exists does not. Frequently reported symptoms include insomnia, sexual dysfunction and gastrointestinal discomfort, such as bloating, belching and cramps. Symptom complaints may shift and change and be very specific, general or vague.

CAUSES—Possibly a complication of other psychological disorders, but the cause is uncertain. Hypochondriasis is more common in people who had a true organic illness in childhood or were closely involved with a sick relative.

RISK INCREASES WITH—Unknown.

HOW TO PREVENT—No specific measures known. In childhood, don't reward illness by giving a child special privileges and undue attention for being sick. Provide adequate love and support during healthy periods.

WHAT TO EXPECT

DIAGNOSTIC MEASURES
• Medical history and physical exam by a doctor.
• Medical testing as needed to rule out an organic disease.
• Psychological evaluation.

APPROPRIATE HEALTH CARE
• Doctor's treatment.
• Psychotherapy or counseling with the patient and the family. It is very difficult for a person with hypochondriasis to accept the conclusion that a preceived health problem is not a serious organic illness.
• Regular follow-up visits with the doctor can help the patient deal with the symptoms.

PROBABLE OUTCOME—Generally resistant to treatment. Most patients maintain a lifelong belief that they have a serious disease, and they change doctors frequently.

POSSIBLE COMPLICATIONS
• Wasting money on unnecessary—and sometimes dangerous—medical care.
• Insisting on unnecessary surgical procedures or medications.

HOW TO TREAT

GENERAL MEASURES
• For family members—Persons with hypochondriasis are often difficult to live with because of their constant worry and demands for attention. Realize that the person really suffers, and try to be supportive. Reward positive behavior that is not related to physical complaints. Don't encourage the "sick role."
• For patients—Try to focus on other aspects or problems of life rather than on these symptoms. Make an effort to avoid going to different doctors continuously and having repeat medical tests.

MEDICATION—Medication usually is not necessary for this disorder. Your doctor may prescribe mild tranquilizers for a short time.

ACTIVITY—No restrictions.

DIET—No special diet. Avoid alcohol.

CALL YOUR DOCTOR IF

• You or a family member has symptoms of hypochondriasis and wants professional help to overcome the problem.
• New, unexplained symptoms develop. Tranquilizers used in treatment may produce side effects or dependence.

IMPULSE CONTROL DISORDERS

GENERAL INFORMATION

DEFINITION—A group of disorders characterized by a person's inability to resist an impulse or temptation to do something that ultimately proves harmful to the person or to others.

BODY PARTS INVOLVED—Nervous system.

SEX OR AGE MOST AFFECTED—Both sexes, more frequently males; different age groups.

SIGNS & SYMPTOMS
- Pathological (compulsive) gambling—Inability to stop gambling. The time and money spent on gambling progressively increases. Sufferers feel a "high" from the gambling experience.
- Kleptomania—Repeated failure to resist the impulse to steal objects that are not wanted or needed, with little thought given to the consequences.
- Trichotillomania—Compulsive plucking or tugging at the hair and pulling it out. Usually results in small bald patches on the scalp. An individual may pull out all the hair on the head and the rest of the body.
- Pyromania—A persistent impulse to set fires. One obtains a relief of tension (or pleasure) from setting fire to something and watching it burn.
- Explosive disorder—Uncontrolled violent behavior that is completely out of proportion to any known cause. Can lead to personal assault, (serious injury or murder) and property damage.

CAUSES
- The exact causes of these disorders are unknown. Theories involve genetics; childhood developmental problems; behavioral, sociological and biological factors.
- These disorders serve as a way to relieve painful thoughts or feelings by people who are unable to acknowledge or express normal emotions. They take action instead.

RISK INCREASES WITH
- Family history of similar problems.
- Presence or history of other mental disorder.

HOW TO PREVENT—No known preventive measures.

WHAT TO EXPECT

DIAGNOSTIC MEASURES
- The observation of symptoms by you or others.
- Medical history, behavior history, physical exam and psychological evaluation by a doctor.

APPROPRIATE HEALTH CARE
- Long-term psychotherapy for the patient, often involving the family.
- Treatment is usually provided on an outpatient basis. Hospitalization or inpatient care may be recommended in some cases.

PROBABLE OUTCOME—Therapy can be effective for some patients and bring about a gradual change in behavior; for others, the prognosis is guarded; for some, the outcome is poor.

POSSIBLE COMPLICATIONS
- Difficulty maintaining personal relationships and jobs.
- Anxiety and depression.
- Noncompliance with treatment.
- Pathological gambling can cause financial disaster for the patient and family.
- Some of these disorders can lead to property destruction, injury to self and others, arrest and imprisonment.

HOW TO TREAT

GENERAL MEASURES
- Treatment requires a trusting relationship between the therapist and patient. This can be difficult, as motivation for treatment often comes from someone other than the person involved (such as a family member, an employer or the criminal justice system).
- Psychological treatment steps may include family and group therapy, group living situations and self-help groups. Behavior-changing techniques involve the learning of social skills, reinforcement of appropriate behavior, setting limits on inappropriate behavior, learning to express feelings, self-analysis of behavior and accountably for actions.
- Pathological gamblers should contact Gamblers Anonymous for support and help.
- Trichotillomania patients can obtain additional information from Trichotillomania Learning Center,1215 Mission St., Suite 2, Santa Cruz, CA 95060; 408-457-1004.

MEDICATION—No medication will cure or treat an impulse control disorder. Drugs may be prescribed for treatment of additional illnesses:
- Antidepressants for depression or anxiety.
- Clomipramine (Anafranil) or fluoxetine (Prozac) for compulsive disorders.
- Antipsychotic drugs for psychoses.
- Mood stabilizers for explosive disorders.

ACTIVITY—No restrictions.

DIET—No special diet.

CALL YOUR DOCTOR IF

- You or a family member has symptoms of an impulse control disorder.
- The problem behavior continues or worsens after treatment is started.

MENTAL RETARDATION

 GENERAL INFORMATION

DEFINITION—A below-average intellectual functioning (an IQ of less than 70) as assessed by a standard IQ test. An IQ of 80-130 is considered normal; 100 is average. The impaired intellectual function results in an inability to cope with the normal responsibilities of life. Retardation is classified as mild (IQ 50-70), moderate (IQ 35-49), severe (20-34) or profound (IQ less than 20). Mild retardation is the most common form (over 80% of cases).

BODY PARTS INVOLVED—Nervous system.

SEX OR AGE MOST AFFECTED—Males more often than females; usually diagnosed at birth or during the early school years.

SIGNS & SYMPTOMS
- Many mildly retarded children are not identified until they enter school. Mental tasks such as math are done more slowly, reading ability is impaired and emotions may be more childlike. May have hyperactivity and/or repetitive involuntary movements.
- May have development delays including speech and language problems, delayed motor skills, sensory defects (slow in responding to people, sounds, toys, etc.), neurological impairments.
- May have seizures, fecal and urinary incontinence, problems with hearing.
- Profoundly and severely retarded children are often diagnosed at birth.

CAUSES
- Genetic—Inborn errors of metabolism or chromosome disorders. Down syndrome is the most frequent genetic disorder causing mental retardation.
- Intrauterine—Congenital infections, placental-fetal malfunction, complications of pregnancy (infections, preeclampsia, eclampsia, maternal alcohol or drug abuse or malnutrition).
- Perinatal (just before or at birth)—Prematurity, postmaturity, birth injury, metabolic disorders.
- Postnatal (after birth)—Endocrine or metabolic disorders, infection, trauma, toxic and other causes of brain damage, abuse.

RISK INCREASES WITH
- Poor prenatal care.
- Family history of mental retardation.
- Lower socioeconomic status.

HOW TO PREVENT
- In some cases, a cause is not determined, and there are no known preventive measures.
- Genetic counseling and prenatal genetic diagnosis will help in some cases.
- Proper prenatal care helps, as does avoidance of alcohol or drugs of abuse by pregnant women.
- New treatments and technology are undergoing study that may further reduce the incidence of mental retardation.

 WHAT TO EXPECT

DIAGNOSTIC MEASURES
- Your own observation of signs in a child.
- Physical exam and mental tests by a doctor.

APPROPRIATE HEALTH CARE
- Special training as appropriate for level of retardation.
- Doctor's treatment for associated medical, emotional or behavior problems.
- Counseling for family.
- Care facility or group home for some.

PROBABLE OUTCOME
- Mildly retarded people can learn to lead independent, productive lives.
- Moderately retarded people are trainable, but often require protective care (e.g., group home).
- More severely and profoundly retarded people usually require continuous care.

POSSIBLE COMPLICATIONS
- Emotional and behavior problems in the child.
- Coping stresses placed on the family.
- Sexual or other exploitation of the person.

 HOW TO TREAT

GENERAL MEASURES
- Most families raise these children at home.
- Special training, education, and behavior modification will enhance the child's skills. The retardation cannot be reversed, but much can be done to maximize the child's potential.
- Family support is vital; therapy is helpful to learn to accept and cope with the demands and time-consuming task of caring for the child.
- Support groups for families are important. Join one in your community.
- Additional information is available from the Association for Retarded Citizens, 500 E. Border St., Suite 300, Arlington, TX 76010; phone 817-261-6003.

MEDICATION—Your doctor may prescribe medications for associated medical problems such as anticonvulsants for seizures. In general, care for retarded people is educational, not medical.

ACTIVITY—As fully active as child's physical condition permits.

DIET—No special diet.

 CALL YOUR DOCTOR IF

- You are concerned with your child's development.
- Following diagnosis of mental retardation, any new or unusual signs or symptoms occur in the child or you feel unable to cope.

OBSESSIVE-COMPULSIVE DISORDER (OCD)

GENERAL INFORMATION

DEFINITION—A disorder characterized by recurrent, intrusive thoughts (obsessions) and repetitive, ritualistic behaviors (compulsions). The disorder usually begins in adolescence and waxes and wanes throughout life, never going completely away and sometimes becoming more severe. New cases after age 50 are rare.

BODY PARTS INVOLVED—Nervous system.

SEX OR AGE MOST AFFECTED—Both sexes; adolescents and young adults; rarely starts after age 50.

SIGNS & SYMPTOMS
- Obsessions and/or compulsions consume many hours a day and cause significant distress or impairment. The obsessions (thoughts) are recurrent, and attempts to ignore or resist them are unsuccessful.
- Obsessions include thoughts of violence; fear of harming a family member or a friend or of self-injury such as jumping off a bridge (these are never acted out, however); fears of infection (from germs, dirt, etc.); doubts (Is the front door shut, locked? Is the iron on?); excessive orderliness or symmetry; constant brooding (over a word, phrase or unanswerable question such as the meaning of life).
- Compulsions (actions) are repetitive, purposeful behaviors in response to the thoughts (obsessions) in an attempt to neutralize them.
- Compulsions include checking in response to doubt (locks, doors, windows); excessive handwashing; counting over and over to a certain number; hoarding; repeating, such as dressing rituals.

CAUSES
- Exact cause of the disorder unknown. It may be connected to an imbalance in a brain chemical called serotonin. Serotonin is involved in sending impulses from one nerve cell to the next and in regulating repetitive behavior.
- Certain forms of brain damage (e.g., encephalitis) can result in obsessions.

RISK INCREASES WITH
- Phobias; panic attacks; major depression.
- Schizophrenia; organic brain syndrome.
- Family history of the disorder.

HOW TO PREVENT—No specific prevention methods known.

WHAT TO EXPECT

DIAGNOSTIC MEASURES
- Medical history and exam by a doctor.
- There are no medical tests to diagnose the disorder. Often the patient's description of the behavior offers the best clues to diagnosis.

APPROPRIATE HEALTH CARE
- Treatment is aimed at reducing anxiety, resolving inner conflicts, relieving depression, learning ways of dealing with stress, building self-esteem and understanding the behavior.
- Behavioral therapy (usually a process known as "exposure and response prevention") is used in treatment and is usually combined with medications to achieve satisfactory results.
- Group therapy (sometimes).
- Family therapy is important to help educate relatives.

PROBABLE OUTCOME—Effective and specific therapy is now available, and though it may not lead to a total cure, it can reduce disabling symptoms considerably.

POSSIBLE COMPLICATIONS
- Incapacity to develop and maintain normal work and personal relationships.
- Depression; psychosis.
- Anxiety and paniclike episodes.
- Housebound lifestyle; indecisiveness.

HOW TO TREAT

GENERAL MEASURES
- This is a complex disorder that requires professional help.
- Joining a support group is helpful for some.
- See Resources for Additional Information.

MEDICATION
- Antidepressants, such as clomipramine (Anafranil), fluoxetine (Prozac), paroxetine (Paxil) or fluvoxamine (Luvox) may be prescribed. Complete benefits may not be seen for 10-12 weeks. About 10% of patients are unable to tolerate the side effects of the medications, but an adverse response to one does not mean there will be problems with others.
- Antianxiety or tranquilizer drugs may be prescribed.

ACTIVITY—No restrictions.

DIET—With use of some medications, a diet free of tyramine (see Glossary) may be necessary to prevent precipitation of hypertensive crisis. The doctor will advise you if this is necessary.

CALL YOUR DOCTOR IF

- You or a family member has symptoms of obsessive-compulsive disorder.
- Symptoms continue or worsen after an adequate treatment time has elapsed.
- New, unexplained symptoms appear. Drugs used in treatment may produce side effects.

PANIC DISORDER

GENERAL INFORMATION

DEFINITION—A severe, spontaneous form of anxiety that is recurrent and unpredictable. Most attacks last 2-10 minutes, but some may extend over an hour or two. This type of anxiety occurs with attacklike symptoms (often during sleep), while chronic anxiety (generalized anxiety) is a persistent state of anxiety.

BODY PARTS INVOLVED—Central nervous system; heart; lungs; skin; hands; feet.

SEX OR AGE MOST AFFECTED—Twice as many females as males; young adults, ages 25-44.

SIGNS & SYMPTOMS
Physical symptoms:
• Palpitations, rapid heartbeat; chest pains.
• Shortness of breath; choking feeling; hyperventilation; weakness or faintness; fainting (occasionally); sweating and trembling.
• Numbness and tingling around the mouth, hands and feet.
• Muscle spasm or contractions in the hands and feet.
• Feeling of "butterflies" in the stomach.
Emotional symptoms:
• Intense fear of losing one's mind (fear of going crazy); fear of dying; sense of terror, doom or dread.
• Feelings of unreality, loss of contact with people and objects.

CAUSES
• The brain's "alarm system" appears to be influenced by a complex interaction of biologic factors, genetics, illnesses, drugs and one's own personal history of traumatic events.
• A variety of disorders can simulate panic attacks (heart rhythm problems, angina, respiratory illness, asthma, obstructive pulmonary disease, endocrine disorders, seizure disorders, stimulating drugs and withdrawal from certain drugs).

RISK INCREASES WITH
• Stress; feelings of guilt; fatigue or overwork; illness; alcohol or drug abuse.
• History of other psychiatric problems; family history of panic disorder.

HOW TO PREVENT—There are no specific measures to prevent a first panic attack; therapy helps prevent additional episodes.

WHAT TO EXPECT

DIAGNOSTIC MEASURES
• Medical history and exam by a doctor.
• Laboratory tests as needed to rule out other disorders.

APPROPRIATE HEALTH CARE
• Self-care.
• Doctor's treatment if the cause is organic or symptoms are prolonged.
• Psychotherapy (cognitive or behavioral therapy) or counseling and/or medications.

PROBABLE OUTCOME—For many, this disorder may run a limited course, with a few attacks and long periods of remission. For others, treatment with psychotherapy and/or medication is effective.

POSSIBLE COMPLICATIONS
• Chronic anxiety or depression.
• Phobias, including agoraphobia, a fear of being alone or being in public places.
• Drug dependency.

HOW TO TREAT

GENERAL MEASURES
• Talk to a friend or family member about your feelings. This sometimes defuses your anxiety.
• Keep a journal or diary about your anxious thoughts or emotions. Consider the causes and possible solutions.
• Join a self-help group. Call your local mental health society for referrals.
• Learn relaxation techniques. For some people, meditation is effective.
• Reduce stress in your life where possible.
• For hyperventilation symptoms, cover the mouth and nose with a small paper bag and breathe into it for a few minutes.

MEDICATION—Your doctor may prescribe an antidepressant, benzodiazepine or beta-blocking agent. The medicine may be slowly reduced or discontinued after 6 months to a year to determine if the panic attacks will return. If not, the medicine can be discontinued.

ACTIVITY
• Get physical exercise regularly.
• Get adequate rest at night.

DIET—Consider giving up caffeine (coffee, tea, soft drinks). You may experience withdrawal symptoms of headache or tiredness, but they will stop in a few days.

CALL YOUR DOCTOR IF

• You or a family member has symptoms of panic disorder that don't diminish with self-treatment.
• Treatment program fails after 8 weeks.
• New, unexplained symptoms develop.

PARAPHILIAS (Sexual Deviations)

GENERAL INFORMATION

DEFINITION—A group of disorders in which unusual or bizarre objects or acts are required for sexual enjoyment. These disorders are sorted into three types: (1) a preference for nonhuman objects for sexual arousal, (2) repetitive sexual activity with human beings involving real or simulated suffering and humiliation, and (3) repetitive sexual activity with nonconsenting partners. For diagnosis, the behaviors must have been present for more than 6 months and must cause significant distress and impairment.

BODY PARTS INVOLVED—Central nervous system.

SEX OR AGE MOST AFFECTED—Both sexes, but mostly males; usually begins in adolescence.

SIGNS & SYMPTOMS
- Fetishism—A person is sexually aroused by nonliving objects (common objects are female underwear, boots and shoes).
- Transvestism—Sexual excitement is achieved by cross-dressing (male dressing as a female).
- Sadism and masochism—One intentionally inflicts pain on another person or asks for the infliction of pain or humiliation in order to be sexually aroused.
- Exhibitionism—A male exposes his genitals in a public place. Always performed for an unknown woman, where sexual intercourse is impossible; seems designed to surprise and shock the woman.
- Frotteurism—Involves illicit sexual touching or rubbing (rubbing the penis against a woman's clothing).
- Voyeurism—Sexual excitement is achieved by watching people undress or participate in sexual behavior.
- Pedophilia—A person fondles a child sexually or attempts intercourse with a child.

CAUSES—Unknown. Theories involve the psychosexual development or behavioral development of the individual.

RISK INCREASES WITH—Unknown.

HOW TO PREVENT—No preventive measures known.

WHAT TO EXPECT

DIAGNOSTIC MEASURES
- Observation of symptoms by yourself or by other people.
- Medical history, behavior history, physical exam and psychological evaluation by a doctor.

APPROPRIATE HEALTH CARE
- Long-term psychotherapy for the patient, often involving the family.
- Treatment is usually provided on an outpatient basis. Hospitalization or inpatient care may be recommended in rare cases.

PROBABLE OUTCOME—Therapy can be effective for some patients and bring about a gradual change in behavior; for others, prognosis is guarded; for some, the outcome is poor.

POSSIBLE COMPLICATIONS
- Difficulty maintaining personal relationships and jobs.
- Drug abuse.
- Anxiety and depression.
- Noncompliance with treatment

HOW TO TREAT

GENERAL MEASURES
- Treatment requires a trusting relationship between the therapist and patient. This can be difficult, as motivation for treatment often comes from someone other than the person involved.
- Psychological treatment steps may include family and group therapy, self-help groups. Behavior-changing techniques involve the learning of social skills, reinforcement of appropriate behavior, setting limits on inappropriate behavior, learning to express feelings, self-analysis of behavior and accepting accountably for actions.

MEDICATION—No medication will cure or treat a sexual disorder. Drugs that reduce testosterone may be prescribed to decrease the intensity of the sexual urges and help with self-control.

ACTIVITY—Normally no restrictions unless directed by your doctor.

DIET—Eat a nutritionally balanced diet to maintain optimum health.

CALL YOUR DOCTOR IF

- You or a family member has symptoms of a sexual disorder.
- Behaviors continue or worsen after treatment is started.

PERSONALITY DISORDERS

 GENERAL INFORMATION

DEFINITION—A group of conditions that are not illnesses, but ways of behaving. They are classified according to the predominant symptoms (see Signs & Symptoms). Characteristics include relatively fixed, inflexible and maladaptive patterns of behavior that cause trouble with relationships, work and the law. Individuals with these conditions feel their behavior patterns are "normal" and "right."

BODY PARTS INVOLVED—Nervous system.

SEX OR AGE MOST AFFECTED—Both sexes; personality disorders usually appear in adolescence or early adulthood.

SIGNS & SYMPTOMS
- Paranoid—Shows unwarranted suspiciousness and distrust of others; is defensive, oversensitive.
- Schizoid and schizotypal—Cold emotionally; has difficulty forming relationships; is withdrawn, shy, superstitious, socially isolated.
- Compulsive—Perfectionist, rigid in habits, indecisive; needs control.
- Histrionic—Dependent, immature, excitable, vain; constantly craves stimulation and attention; communicates by appearances or behavior.
- Narcissistic—Has an exaggerated sense of one's own importance; is preoccupied with power; lacks interest in others; demands attention; feels entitled to special consideration.
- Avoidant—Fears and overreacts to rejection; has low self-esteem; is socially withdrawn, dependent.
- Dependent—Passive, overaccepting, unable to make decisions; lacks confidence.
- Passive-aggressive—Stubborn, sulking; fears authority; procrastinates; is chronically late, argumentative, helpless, clinging.
- Antisocial—Selfish, callous, promiscuous, impulsive, reckless, unable to learn from experience; fails at school and work.
- Borderline—Impulsive; has unstable and intense interpersonal relationships; displays inappropriate anger, fear and guilt; lacks self-control; has identity problems; may self-mutilate (cut or burn oneself to relieve tension); is suicidal (sometimes).

CAUSES—Unknown. Theories include biological, social development and psychological factors.

RISK INCREASES WITH
- History of abuse as a child.
- Family history of mood disorders.

HOW TO PREVENT—Healthy parenting.

 WHAT TO EXPECT

DIAGNOSTIC MEASURES
- Observation of symptoms by other people.
- Medical history, behavior history, physical exam and psychological evaluation by a doctor.

APPROPRIATE HEALTH CARE
- Long-term psychotherapy for the patient, often involving the family.
- Treatment is usually provided on an outpatient basis. Hospitalization or inpatient care may be recommended in rare cases.

PROBABLE OUTCOME—Therapy can be effective for some patients and bring about a gradual change in personality and behavior; for others, prognosis is guarded; for some, the outcome is poor.

POSSIBLE COMPLICATIONS
- Difficulty maintaining personal relationships and jobs; anxiety and depression.
- Drug abuse.
- Noncompliance with treatment.
- Suicide.

 HOW TO TREAT

GENERAL MEASURES
- Treatment requires a trusting relationship between the therapist and patient. This can be difficult, as motivation for treatment often comes from someone other than the person with the disorder.
- Psychological treatment may include family and group therapy, group living situations and self-help groups. Behavior-changing techniques involve the learning of social skills, reinforcement of appropriate behavior, setting limits on inappropriate behavior, learning to express feelings, self-analysis of behavior and accepting accountably for actions.

MEDICATION—No medication will cure or treat a personality disorder. Drugs may be prescribed for treatment of additional illnesses:
- Antidepressants for depression; anxiety medications.
- Antipsychotic drugs for psychoses.

ACTIVITY—No restrictions.

DIET—No special diet.

 CALL YOUR DOCTOR IF

- You or a family member has symptoms of a personality disorder.
- Symptoms continue or worsen after treatment is started.
- New, unexplained symptoms develop. Drugs used in treatment may produce side effects.

PHOBIAS

GENERAL INFORMATION

DEFINITION—A type of anxiety involving persistent, irrational or an exaggerated fear of a particular object, situation, activity, setting or even a bodily function (none of which is basically dangerous or an appropriate source of anxiety). Most people with phobias recognize that the fear is inappropriate to the situation. Phobias are classified as:
• Social (fear of embarrassment in social situations, such as public speaking or using a public bathroom).
• Agoraphobia (fear of being alone or fear of public places).
• Simple (fear of a particular type of stimulus, such as animals, insects, heights, flying, closed places, etc.).

BODY PARTS INVOLVED—Nervous system.

SEX OR AGE MOST AFFECTED—Females more than males; usually late adolescence or young adulthood.

SIGNS & SYMPTOMS—The following anxiety symptoms occur when exposed to, or thinking of, the phobic stimulus:
• Palpitations.
• Sweating.
• Tremors.
• Flushing.
• Nausea.
• Negative thoughts and scary images.

CAUSES—Exact cause is unknown. Possibly a learned response (conditioning), such as being raised by someone with a similar fear or having an early frightening experience that has become associated with the object or situation. Other theories focus on the phobia as having a symbolic meaning.

RISK INCREASES WITH
• Family history of anxiety.
• Separation anxiety in childhood.
• Presence of another psychiatric disorder.
• Perfectionistic personality.

HOW TO PREVENT—No specific preventive measure to prevent the phobia. Techniques are available to prevent or control the reaction.

WHAT TO EXPECT

DIAGNOSTIC MEASURES
• Your own observation of symptoms.
• Medical and social history and physical exam by a doctor (sometimes).

APPROPRIATE HEALTH CARE
• Self-care.
• Psychotherapy or counseling for severe phobias and for phobias that are lifestyle restricting. Several different types of therapy are used, such as desensitization or flooding (see Glossary for both).
• Clinics to deal with fear of flying are available in many communities.

PROBABLE OUTCOME
• Simple phobias—Some spontaneously stop as a person ages; others don't cause any impairment if the object can be avoided (such as snakes); some diminish as people go through their fearful situations (such as flying); and others can be cured with treatment.
• Social phobias—May be resolved with treatment; medication is often helpful.
• Agoraphobia—Person becomes more and more homebound without treatment; often associated with panic disorder.

POSSIBLE COMPLICATIONS
• Lifestyle constrictions brought on by avoidance of the phobic stimulus. Agoraphobia in particular restricts an individual's activities and is severely disabling.
• Dependence on drugs or alcohol to overcome anxiety.

HOW TO TREAT

GENERAL MEASURES
• If you feel your fear taking hold:
  Shift your thoughts from negative ("The dog will bite") to something realistic and positive ("The dog is on a leash").
  Do something manageable—count backward from 1000, read a book, talk aloud, take deep measured breaths.
  Shift your thoughts to pleasant ones.
  Practice relaxation techniques.
• Join a support group if available.
• For additional information, contact Anxiety Disorders Association of America, 6000 Executive Blvd., Suite 513, Rockville, MD 20852; 301-231-9350.

MEDICATION—Medications are sometimes helpful for treatment of phobias.

ACTIVITY—No restrictions.

DIET—No special diet. Avoid caffeine.

CALL YOUR DOCTOR IF

• You or a family member has symptoms of a phobia that are not helped with self-care.
• Symptoms of the phobia return after treatment.

POSTPARTUM DEPRESSION
(Postnatal Depression)

GENERAL INFORMATION

DEFINITION—Emotional changes following the birth of a baby. Such changes affect almost half of all new mothers. "Baby blues" are most common 3 to 10 days following delivery (but can occur any time in the first year) and usually last anywhere from 48 hours to 2 weeks. In some women, the depression is more pronounced, and rarely there is extreme depression.

BODY PARTS INVOLVED—Brain.

SEX OR AGE MOST AFFECTED—Females.

SIGNS & SYMPTOMS
The symptoms vary in intensity, but can include:
* Feelings of sadness, hopelessness or gloom.
* Appetite and weight loss (or a weight gain).
* Sleep disturbances or frightening dreams.
* Loss of energy; fatigue; irritability; anxiety.
* Slow speech and thought.
* Frequent headaches and other physical discomforts.
* Confusion about one's ability to improve life.
* Fears about own health and infant's health.

CAUSES
* It is common for mothers to experience some degree of mild depression during the first weeks after birth. Pregnancy and birth involve sudden hormonal changes that affect emotions.
* Additionally, the 24-hour responsibility for a newborn infant represents a major psychological and lifestyle adjustment for most mothers, even if it is not the first child.
* These physical and emotional stresses are usually accompanied by inadequate rest until the baby's routine stabilizes, so fatigue and depression are not unusual.

RISK INCREASES WITH
* Stress and lack of sleep; poor nutrition.
* Postpartum blues following a previous pregnancy.
* Lack of support from one's partner, family or friends.
* Preexisting psychological disorder.

HOW TO PREVENT
Cannot be prevented, but can be minimized with rest, an adequate diet and a strong emotional support system.

WHAT TO EXPECT

DIAGNOSTIC MEASURES
* Your own observation of symptoms.
* Medical exam by a doctor (sometimes).

APPROPRIATE HEALTH CARE
* Self-care for mild symptoms.
* Severe postpartum depression requires professional help (psychotherapy and/or drugs).

PROBABLE OUTCOME—This depression is usually very short-lived. With time and support from family, mild symptoms disappear quickly. More severe symptoms can be treated with medications and/or psychotherapy.

POSSIBLE COMPLICATIONS
* Lack of bonding between mother and infant, which is harmful to both.
* More severe depression; the mother may not be able to care for herself or the baby.
* Serious depression that may be accompanied by aggressive feelings toward the baby, a loss of pride in one's appearance and home, loss of appetite or overeating, withdrawal, suicide.

HOW TO TREAT

GENERAL MEASURES
* Don't feel guilty if you have mixed feelings about motherhood. Adjustment and bonding take time.
* Schedule frequent outings, such as walks and short visits with friends or family. These help prevent feelings of isolation.
* Put your baby in a separate room to sleep. You will sleep more restfully.
* Ask for daytime help from family or friends who will shop for you or babysit while you rest.
* If you feel depressed, share your feelings with your partner or a friend who is a good listener. Talking with other mothers can help you keep problems in perspective.

MEDICATION
* Any medication use must be carefully considered if you are breast-feeding.
* A short-term mild sedative may be prescribed.
* Antidepressant drugs may be recommended for more severe symptoms. These are effective when used for 3 to 4 weeks.

ACTIVITY
* Resume your normal activities as soon as possible. Avoid getting too fatigued.
* Exercise regularly (as your recovery from childbirth permits).

DIET—Eat a normal, well-balanced diet. Avoid alcohol and caffeinated beverages.

CALL YOUR DOCTOR IF

* Postpartum depression does not improve after 2 weeks, the symptom level increases or additional life changes occur, such as divorce, a career change or a move.
* You have suicidal urges or aggressive feelings toward the baby. Seek help promptly.

POST-TRAUMATIC STRESS DISORDER (PTSD)

GENERAL INFORMATION

DEFINITION—A type of anxiety seen in people who have experienced an event that would be extremely distressing to most human beings. Such events (natural disasters, murder, rape, war, imprisonment, torture, accidents) produce psychological stress in anyone. Some people do not recover normally. PTSD is characterized by a persistent reexperiencing of the trauma and associated symptoms. The symptoms may begin right after the event or may develop several months later.

BODY PARTS INVOLVED—Central nervous system.

SEX OR AGE MOST AFFECTED—Both sexes; all ages (children often are affected).

SIGNS & SYMPTOMS
- Recurrent, intrusive and distressing recollections of the event.
- Recurrent dreams relating to the event.
- A sense of reliving the event (flashbacks).
- Chronic anxiety.
- Insomnia.
- Difficulty concentrating.
- Memory impairment.
- A sense of personal isolation.
- Diminished interest in activities.
- Phobic reactions to situations or avoidance of activities that recall memories of the event.
- Emotional effects (irritability, restlessness, tremulousness, explosive outbursts of behavior, a deadening of feelings, painful guilt feelings).

CAUSES—Exposure to an overwhelming event. A variety of factors seem to combine to produce PTSD:
- The event's suddenness and unexpectedness.
- The bloodiness and brutalality of the event.
- More prolonged and chronic stress during the event.
- Psychological and constitutional strengths and weaknesses of the victim.
- Bodily injury (especially head injury).
- Type and availability of social support.

RISK INCREASES WITH—A history of childhood neglect or a dysfunctional family, alcoholic parents or childhood abuse, low educational achievement.

HOW TO PREVENT—Crisis intervention immediately after a traumatic event may prevent the development of PTSD.

WHAT TO EXPECT

DIAGNOSTIC MEASURES
- Your own or others' observation of symptoms.
- Medical history and physical exam by a doctor.
- Laboratory and medical tests as needed to rule out any brain disorder.
- Psychiatric exam and psychological testing.

APPROPRIATE HEALTH CARE
- Psychotherapy and counseling. Several different methods of therapy are available, including behavior therapy, desensitization (see Glossary for both), hypnosis and others. Individual or group therapy as needed.
- Psychiatric hospitalization if patient is suicidal or is severely dysfunctional in activities of daily living.

PROBABLE OUTCOME—For some patients, the symptoms disappear spontaneously after 6 months; some patients can be helped with treatment; in others, the disorder may run a chronic course for months or years.

POSSIBLE COMPLICATIONS
- Chronic PTSD, which can lead to loss of job, marital conflicts and disability.
- Injury to oneself during a reenactment of the trauma.
- Drug or alcohol dependency.
- Suicide.

HOW TO TREAT

GENERAL MEASURES
- Make a commitment to yourself to work on the problem.
- Learn relaxation techniques. They are particularly helpful, especially in helping with sleep problems.
- Support groups are highly effective and available through Veterans Affairs centers and community crisis centers.

MEDICATION—Your doctor may prescribe antianxiety or antidepressant drugs for short periods of time. No specific drug is available to treat PTSD.

ACTIVITY—No restrictions. A routine physical exercise program is helpful in relieving some stress.

DIET—No special diet.

CALL YOUR DOCTOR IF

- You or a family member has symptoms of post-traumatic stress disorder.
- Symptoms don't improve or worsen after treatment begins.
- New, unexplained symptoms develop. Drugs used in treatment may produce side effects.

SCHIZOPHRENIC DISORDERS

GENERAL INFORMATION

DEFINITION—A group of emotional disorders including catatonic, paranoid, disorganized, undifferentiated and residual schizophrenia. *Schizo* means split, and *phrenia* refers to the mind. Schizophrenia is often referred to as split personality disorder, because the person's thoughts and feelings do not relate to each other in a logical fashion. The person can't tell fact from fantasy, and therefore behaves irrationally.

BODY PARTS INVOLVED—Nervous system.

SEX OR AGE MOST AFFECTED—Affects both sexes equally; onset is usually between ages 15 and 25.

SIGNS & SYMPTOMS
The following symptoms may take months or years to become apparent.
- Becoming more withdrawn and introverted.
- Losing motivation.
- Severe limitations of emotions, or inappropriate expression of emotions.
- Delusions (fixed false, unreal beliefs).
- Hallucinations (a sensory experience that originates in the mind, e.g., hearing voices or seeing things that are not present).
- Disordered thinking that is shown in disorganized or disjointed speech.
- A belief that other people hear and "steal" one's thoughts or that one is being controlled by others.
- Paranoid schizophrenia—Predominantly suspicious and paranoid behavior.

CAUSES—Exact cause is unknown. Inheritance appears to play a role, and environmental factors may be involved.

RISK INCREASES WITH—Family history of schizophrenia.

HOW TO PREVENT—No specific preventive measures known.

WHAT TO EXPECT

DIAGNOSTIC MEASURES
- Observation of symptoms by others.
- Medical history, behavior history, physical exam and psychological evaluation by a doctor.
- There is no specific test to diagnose schizophrenia. To confirm the diagnosis, the symptoms must have occurred for at least 6 months at some time in the person's life. Some medical tests are conducted to rule out other possible illnesses.

APPROPRIATE HEALTH CARE—Treatment is usually provided on an outpatient basis. Hospitalization or inpatient care is necessary in some cases.

PROBABLE OUTCOME—Treatment is effective for most patients and enables them to return to varying degrees of independence. About 30% return to normal lives and occupations. Sometimes the condition completely disappears.

POSSIBLE COMPLICATIONS
- Life-long disability.
- Self-inflicted injuries; suicide.
- Hostile behavior toward others.
- Relapse, neglect, vagrancy or imprisonment.

HOW TO TREAT

GENERAL MEASURES
- The goal of therapy is to help the person get back in touch with reality. Treatment begins with medications to reduce the symptoms.
- Once the symptoms are controlled, treatment continues with psychotherapy and rehabilitation, which will help the person regain normal skills and behavior patterns.
- The family or other significant persons in the patient's life should also be involved in the therapy in order to understand the problem and what they can do to help the patient. Schizophrenia patients are sometimes difficult to live with.

MEDICATION
- Antipsychotic medications are usually prescribed. Some are taken orally, while others may be injected. If side effects are too severe with one drug or the symptoms are not controlled, a different drug is prescribed. Dosages are reduced as symptoms disappear. For most patients, the medication may need to be taken for life.
- Sedating drugs such as benzodiazepines may be necessary at the beginning of treatment.

ACTIVITY—Normally no restrictions unless directed by your doctor.

DIET—Eat a nutritionally balanced diet to maintain optimum health.

CALL YOUR DOCTOR IF

- A family member has symptoms of schizophrenia.
- Symptoms continue or worsen after treatment is started.
- New, unexplained symptoms develop. Drugs used in treatment may produce side effects.

SEASONAL AFFECTIVE DISORDER (SAD)

 GENERAL INFORMATION

DEFINITION—A seasonal disruption of mood that occurs during the winter months and ceases with the advent of spring. Symptoms usually begin in September, when the days begin to shorten, and last through the winter into March, when the days begin to lengthen. Light plays a big part in the origin of the disorder and in its treatment. In rarer instances, the seasonal disorder symptoms occur in the summer months and may be caused by an intolerance to heat.

BODY PARTS INVOLVED—Nervous system.

SEX OR AGE MOST AFFECTED—More common in women; affects adults and children.

SIGNS & SYMPTOMS
Experienced at the start of winter:
● Depression, tiredness, sluggishness.
● Increased appetite (especially for carbohydrates); weight gain.
● Irritability; needing more sleep; feeling less cheerful; socializing less.
● Difficulty coping with life as a result of these changes.

CAUSES—The pineal gland (one of the body's "clocks") in the brain releases a hormone, melatonin, which can adversely affect our moods. Very little melatonin is secreted in light (daytime), and its peak production is usually at night, between 2 and 3 a.m. Winter months (with their longer nights) cause extra production of melatonin, so the level in the body is increased. The average nighttime illumination in homes or offices is not adequate to counteract this affect.

RISK INCREASES WITH
● Geographical location (people in northern or cloudy latitudes are more susceptible).
● Other depressive illness.

HOW TO PREVENT—No measures known.

 WHAT TO EXPECT

DIAGNOSTIC MEASURES
● Medical history and physical exam by a doctor.
● Diagnosing SAD can be difficult. The same symptoms can arise from other types of depression. Laboratory blood studies may be done to rule out other medical disorders. Diagnosis usually requires a three-year mood disturbance pattern, with the onset occurring in the autumn and a remission in the spring.

APPROPRIATE HEALTH CARE
● Self-care and/or doctor's treatment.
● Therapies continue to evolve for treatment of

people with moderate to severe symptoms, but they usually involve extending the day artificially with light therapy (phototherapy). The duration and intensity of the light therapy may vary between individuals and need to be worked out with you and your medical team. Even though light sources are commercially available, it is recommended that they not be used without medical advice. Examples include:
　Exposure to specialized light sources.
　Installing a computerized system of lighting in a patient's bedroom that creates an artificial dawn. The light goes from very dim to bright, like a sunrise.
　Wearing a visor cap with small battery-powered lights that provide illumination that falls directly on the eyes.
● For some patients the light therapy doesn't work, and other forms of treatment such as drugs or psychotherapy may be necessary.

PROBABLE OUTCOME—With correct diagnosis and treatment, symptoms can be minimized.

POSSIBLE COMPLICATIONS—Continuation of the symptoms and lifestyle disruptions.

 HOW TO TREAT

GENERAL MEASURES
● Mild symptoms may be resolved with simple measures: Keep drapes and blinds open in your house; sit near windows and gaze outside frequently; turn on bright lights on cloudy days; keep a diary or journal of your mood changes so that any changes or patterns can be evaluated; don't isolate yourself (visit friends, see shows, etc.).
● For more information, contact the National Organization for Seasonal Affective Disorder, PO Box 40133, Washington, DC 20016. See Resources for Additional Information.

MEDICATION—Antidepressants may be prescribed for patients who do not respond to other forms of therapy.

ACTIVITY
● Stay as active as your energy permits. Physical activity is usually always therapeutic.
● Get outside as much as possible, especially in the early morning light.
● Try to take a vacation in the winter months instead of the summer.

DIET—Eat a normal, well-balanced diet to maintain optimum health.

 CALL YOUR DOCTOR IF

You or a family member has symptoms of seasonal affective disorder.

SEXUAL DYSFUNCTION, FEMALE

GENERAL INFORMATION

DEFINITION—Female sexual dysfunction involving an inability to experience sexual pleasure (arousal dysfunction) or an inability to achieve orgasm (orgasmic dysfunction).

BODY PARTS INVOLVED—Brain and central nervous system; autonomic nervous system.

SEX OR AGE MOST AFFECTED—Sexually active females.

SIGNS & SYMPTOMS
- Lack of sexual desire; inability to enjoy sex.
- Lack of vaginal lubrication.
- Failure to achieve orgasm, even when sexually aroused.

CAUSES
- Inadequate or ineffective foreplay.
- Psychological problems, including depression, poor self-esteem, sexual abuse or incest, feelings of shame or guilt about sex, fear of pregnancy, stress and fatigue.
- Two-career marriage (work, children and household tasks leave little energy for sex).
- Acute illness or chronic illness.
- Inexperience or inadequate information about sexuality on the part of either partner.
- Repressed anger toward the sexual partner resulting from feelings of being used as a sexual object, physical or emotional abuse, jealousy or fears of disloyalty or lack of true intimacy.
- Sexual abuse as a child or adult.
- Abuse of drugs, including alcohol.
- Gynecologic factors (infection or disorder).
- Aging (sexual desire may decline).
- Having children (hormonal changes in pregnancy cause many women to lose interest in sex).
- Surgery on the reproductive organs.

RISK INCREASES WITH
- Use of some medications, such as MAO inhibitors, antidepressants, beta-adrenergic blockers, narcotics, barbiturates and, for some women, use of birth control pills.
- Discrepancies between partners in expectations and attitudes toward sex.
- Proximity of other people (children, mother-in-law) in the home.

HOW TO PREVENT
- Talk with your partner about your needs.
- Seek counseling to resolve feelings.

WHAT TO EXPECT

DIAGNOSTIC MEASURES
- Your own observation of symptoms.
- Medical history and physical exam by a doctor.
- Tests may include laboratory blood tests and other studies to rule out physical causes.

- If no physical problems are found, a detailed sexual history is the most important tool for determining an appropriate treatment program.

APPROPRIATE HEALTH CARE
Possible treatment methods:
- For childhood sexual abuse problems—Psychotherapy or counseling.
- For arousal dysfunction—Relaxation techniques, sensate focus exercises, counseling (usually with a sex therapist).
- For orgasmic problems—Self-stimulation (masturbation), new behavior patterns, sexual homework with partner (with guidance by a sex therapist).
- For medication-caused problems—Changing dosage, discontinuing, trying a new medication.
- Other problems—Family therapy, sensate conditioning, referral to sex therapist.

PROBABLE OUTCOME—Best predictors of positive outcome are the desire to change and an overall healthy relationship. Arousal dysfunction is more difficult to treat, and outcomes may vary.

POSSIBLE COMPLICATIONS
- Permanent inability to enjoy sex.
- Damage to interpersonal relationships.

HOW TO TREAT

GENERAL MEASURES
Self-help suggestions for you and your partner:
- Admit the problem, and try to establish open communication with your partner. Pretending that you are aroused or have orgasms leaves the problem unsolved.
- Reduce stress in your life where possible.
- Find ways to spend time together as a couple that is nonsexual; go on regular dates. Spend time just touching or cuddling that doesn't necessarily lead to sex.
- Age does not stop sexual enjoyment. You are never too old for sexual desire and activities.

MEDICATION—Medication is not necessary unless the sexual problem is due to some underlying medical condition. There is no known aphrodisiac that is effective and safe.

ACTIVITY—No restrictions. Exercise regularly to reduce stress, and improve your self-image. A healthy body and mind promote enjoyable sex.

DIET—Eat a well-balanced diet. Vitamin and mineral supplements may be helpful. Weight-loss program may be recommended if either partner is overweight. Avoid alcohol.

CALL YOUR DOCTOR IF

You have sexual problems and want help in resolving them.

SEXUAL DYSFUNCTION, MALE EJACULATORY DISORDERS

GENERAL INFORMATION

DEFINITION—Male orgasm and ejaculation following brief sexual stimulation and prior to satisfactory arousal and orgasm in the sexual partner. This is a common disorder affecting all age groups and usually caused by psychological problems.

BODY PARTS INVOLVED—Central nervous system; reproductive system.

SEX OR AGE MOST AFFECTED—Males; adolescents and adults.

SIGNS & SYMPTOMS
• Repeated episodes of premature ejaculation.
• Feelings of self-doubt, inadequacy and guilt.

CAUSES
• Poor relationship or communication with the sexual partner.
• Fear of impregnating the partner.
• Fear of contracting a sexually transmitted disease.
• Anxiety about sexual performance.
• Cultural or religious conflicts.
• Belief that sex is sinful or dirty.
• Rarely may be due to underlying neurological disorder (e.g., prostatitis).

RISK INCREASES WITH—See Causes.

HOW TO PREVENT—See suggestions under General Measures.

WHAT TO EXPECT

DIAGNOSTIC MEASURES
• Your own observation of signs.
• Medical history and physical exam by a doctor.
• Any laboratory test results are usually normal, since most males with this problem are healthy individuals.

APPROPRIATE HEALTH CARE
• Self-care after diagnosis.
• Doctor's treatment if self-help measures fail.
• Counseling from a qualified sex therapist if other methods are not successful.

PROBABLE OUTCOME—Usually curable in most males within 6 months after recognition and treatment.

POSSIBLE COMPLICATIONS
• Low self-esteem.
• Damage to marital or interpersonal relationships.

HOW TO TREAT

GENERAL MEASURES
The following methods are recommended by sex researchers and therapists Masters and Johnson. These measures usually lead to ejaculatory control for 5 to 10 minutes or longer:
• Sensate-focus exercises, in which each partner caresses the other's body without intercourse to learn relaxed, pleasurable aspects of touching.
• Mutual physical examination of each other's bodies to acquaint both partners thoroughly with anatomy. This helps reduce shameful feelings about sex.
• Stop-and-start technique in which the man is stimulated through controlled intercourse or masturbation until he feels an impending ejaculation. Stimulation is stopped, then resumed in 20 to 30 seconds.
• Squeeze technique in which the woman squeezes her partner's penis with her thumb and forefinger when he feels an impending ejaculation. When ejaculatory feelings pass, intercourse is resumed. This is repeated as often as necessary until the man can control ejaculation to the satisfaction of both partners.

MEDICATION—Medicine usually is not necessary for this disorder.

ACTIVITY—No restrictions.

DIET—Eat a normal, well-balanced diet. Vitamin supplements may be recommended.

CALL YOUR DOCTOR IF

You or a family member has had repeated episodes of premature ejaculation and wants professional guidance to solve the problem.

SEXUAL DYSFUNCTION, MALE IMPOTENCE

GENERAL INFORMATION

DEFINITION—A consistent inability to achieve or maintain an erection of the penis, which is necessary to have sexual intercourse. (The occasional periods of impotence that occur in just about all adult males are not considered dysfunctional.) Impotence is not inevitable with aging. The capacity for erection is retained, though a man may need more stimulation to achieve erection or more time between erections, and sometimes erections may be less firm or full.

BODY PARTS INVOLVED—Male reproductive system; nervous system; vascular system.

SEX OR AGE MOST AFFECTED—Male adolescents and adults, but most commonly men over 45.

SIGNS & SYMPTOMS
- Inability to achieve an erection.
- Inability to maintain an erection for the normal duration of intercourse (erection may be too weak, too brief or too painful).

CAUSES—
Physical causes include:
- Diabetes mellitus.
- Atherosclerosis (hardening of the arteries).
- Medications (antihypertensives, antipsychotics, antihistamines, anti-ulcer drugs, sedatives).
- Disorders of the central nervous system, such as spinal cord injury, multiple sclerosis, stroke or syphilis.
- Endocrine disorders that involve the pituitary, thyroid, adrenal or sexual glands.
- Alcoholism; drug or substance abuse.
- Decreased circulation to the penis from any cause or genital illness.
- Hormone imbalance (rare).
- Surgery (prostate, back or genital surgery).
Psychological causes include:
- Guilt feelings.
- A poor relationship with the sexual partner.
- Psychological disorders, including depression, anxiety, stress and psychosis.
- Lack of sexual information or understanding of the emotional aspects of sexuality and information about female anatomy.
Situational or environmental causes include:
- Presence of other people in the home.
- Rushed or routine lovemaking.
- Smoking.

RISK INCREASES WITH
- Problems listed under Causes.
- Recent illness that has lowered strength.
- Recent major surgery, especially cardiovascular or prostate surgery.

HOW TO PREVENT
- Maintain good communication with partner.
- Don't drink more than 1 or 2 alcoholic drinks—if any—a day. Don't abuse drugs.
- If you have diabetes, adhere to treatment.
- Maintain overall good health.
- If a new medication is prescribed, ask doctor or pharmacist if it can cause erection problems.

WHAT TO EXPECT

DIAGNOSTIC MEASURES
- Your own observation of symptoms.
- Medical history and physical exam by a doctor. Medical tests as needed for diagnosis of any underlying disorder. Tests at a special diagnostic center to measure erections.

APPROPRIATE HEALTH CARE
- Self-care after diagnosis.
- Doctor's treatment.
- Psychotherapy or counseling (alone or with your partner) from a qualified sex therapist.
- If medication is the cause, a change in medication or dosage amounts may help.
- Self-administered penile injection therapy or other drugs may be prescribed.
- Use of vacuum erectile device may be recommended for some patients.
- Surgery to implant an inflatable or noninflatable penile prosthesis (sometimes).

PROBABLE OUTCOME—Spontaneous recovery or recovery after brief counseling in many cases with psychological origins. For other cases with physical origins, treatment and improvement in the underlying disorder may improve sexual performance.

POSSIBLE COMPLICATIONS
- Depression and loss of self-esteem.
- Marital problems or breakdown of close personal relationships.

HOW TO TREAT

GENERAL MEASURES
- Don't be hesitant about discussing the problem, exploring your needs and asking for help. Your partner's understanding is critical to solving the problem.
- For more information, call Impotence Information Center, 800-843-4315 or 800-543-9632.

MEDICATION—Your doctor may prescribe oral medications or ones to be injected into the penis (they help some males to achieve an erection).

ACTIVITY—No restrictions.

DIET—Eat a normal, well-balanced diet. Vitamin supplements may be recommended.

CALL YOUR DOCTOR IF

You or a family member has symptoms of impotence, especially if you take medications or have disorders listed under Causes.

SLEEP DISORDERS

GENERAL INFORMATION

DEFINITION—Difficulty falling asleep or remaining asleep, intermittent wakefulness, early-morning awakening or a combination of these. Insomnia affects all age groups, but is more common in the elderly. Insomnia may be transient due to a life crisis or lifestyle change or chronic due to medical or psychological problems or drug intake.

BODY PARTS INVOLVED—Nervous system.

SEX OR AGE MOST AFFECTED—Both sexes, all ages

SIGNS & SYMPTOMS
- Restlessness when trying to fall asleep.
- Brief sleep followed by wakefulness.
- Normal sleep until very early in the morning (3 a.m. or 4 a.m.), then wakefulness (often with frightening thoughts).
- Periods of sleeplessness alternating with periods of excessive sleep or sleepiness at inconvenient times.

CAUSES
- Depression. This is usually characterized by early-morning wakefulness.
- Overactivity of the thyroid gland.
- Anxiety caused by stress.
- Sexual problems, such as impotence or lack of a sex partner.
- Noisy environment (including a snoring partner).
- Allergies and early-morning wheezing.
- Heart or lung conditions that cause shortness of breath when lying down.
- Painful disorders, such as fibromyositis (muscle inflammation) or arthritis.
- Urinary or gastrointestinal problems that require urination or bowel movements during the night.
- Consumption of stimulants, such as coffee, tea or cola drinks, during the evening.
- Watching stimulating TV shows before going to bed.
- Use of some medications, including dextroamphetamines, cortisone drugs or decongestants.
- Erratic work hours.
- New environment or location.
- Jet lag after travel.
- Lack of physical exercise.
- Alcoholism.
- Drug abuse, including overuse of sleep-inducing drugs.
- Withdrawal from addictive substances.

RISK INCREASES WITH—Stress, obesity, smoking.

HOW TO PREVENT—Establish a lifestyle that fosters healthy sleep patterns. Avoid causes of sleep disorder.

WHAT TO EXPECT

DIAGNOSTIC MEASURES
- Your own observation of symptoms.
- Medical history and physical exam by a doctor.
- Laboratory thyroid studies, EEG (see Glossary).
- Tests in a sleep-study laboratory (sometimes).

APPROPRIATE HEALTH CARE
- Self-care after diagnosis.
- Doctor's treatment; if the cause is psychological, psychotherapy or counseling.

PROBABLE OUTCOME—Most persons can establish good sleep patterns if the underlying cause of insomnia is treated or eliminated.

POSSIBLE COMPLICATIONS
- Temporary insomnia may become chronic.
- Increased daytime sleepiness can affect all aspects of your life.

HOW TO TREAT

GENERAL MEASURES
- Seek ways to minimize stress. Learn and practice relaxation techniques.
- Treat any underlying drug use or medical cause.
- Don't use stimulants for several hours before bedtime.
- Relax in a warm bath before bedtime.
- Don't turn your bedroom into an office or a den. Create a comfortable sleep setting.
- Turn off your mind. Focus on peaceful and relaxing thoughts. Play soft music or relaxation tapes. Set a rigid sleep schedule.
- Use mechanical aids such as ear plugs, eye shades or an electric blanket.

MEDICATION
- Long-term use of sleep inducers may be counterproductive or addictive. Your doctor may prescribe sleep-inducing drugs for a short time if temporary insomnia is interfering with your daily activities; you have a medical disorder that regularly disturbs sleep; you need to establish regular sleep patterns.
- Melatonin, a nonprescription product, may help some people with insomnia. Ask your doctor.

ACTIVITY—Exercise regularly to create healthy fatigue, but not within 2 hours of going to bed.

DIET—Don't eat within 3 hours of bedtime if indigestion is a problem. A glass of warm milk before bedtime may help. Avoid caffeine.

CALL YOUR DOCTOR IF

You or a family member has symptoms of a sleep disorder.

SOMATOFORM DISORDERS

GENERAL INFORMATION

DEFINITION—A group of disorders in which there are physical symptoms for which no medical cause can be found. Included in this group are somatization disorder, conversion disorder and body dysmorphic disorder. Hypochondriasis and chronic pain disorder (somatoform pain disorder) are also classified as somatoform disorders, but are covered in separate charts.

BODY PARTS INVOLVED—Nervous system.

SEX OR AGE MOST AFFECTED—Both sexes, females more often then males; usually ages 20-30.

SIGNS & SYMPTOMS
• Somatization disorder—Multiple physical symptoms that recur over a period of several years with no medical basis. The patient has usually consulted numerous doctors for treatment and medications. The symptoms often involve neurological problems (double vision), gynecological problems (painful menstruation) or gastrointestinal problems (abdominal pain).
• Conversion disorder—Loss or change of a physical function (paralysis of an arm, blindness, seizures). The symptom is not intentionally produced or faked.
• Body dysmorphic disorder—Preoccupation with an imagined defect in a normal-appearing person. The defect may be very minor, but the concern is greatly exaggerated. The focus is often on skin wrinkles and blemishes, facial hair, or shape of the nose, mouth, jaw or breasts.
• See also chart on Chronic Pain Disorder.

CAUSES—The specific causes of the disorders are unknown, but they are presumed to be psychological in origin.

RISK INCREASES WITH
• Family history of similar disorders.
• History of other psychiatric illness.
• History of child abuse and/or sexual abuse.
• Underlying emotional problems that are not confronted.
• Family or personal history of alcoholism.
• Psychological stress.
• Psychosocial problems (e.g., conversion disorder may symbolize a patient's desire to do something and the defense against that wish).

HOW TO PREVENT—No measures known.

WHAT TO EXPECT

DIAGNOSTIC MEASURES
• Your own or others' observation of symptoms.
• Medical history, behavior history, physical exam and psychological evaluation by a doctor.

APPROPRIATE HEALTH CARE
• Doctor's treatment.
• Treatment is usually provided on an outpatient basis. Hospitalization or inpatient care may be recommended in rare cases.

PROBABLE OUTCOME—Treatment can be effective for some patients and bring about a gradual change; for others, the prognosis is poor and the disorder may continue. For some, symptoms may resolve spontaneously.

POSSIBLE COMPLICATIONS
• Difficulty maintaining personal relationships and jobs.
• The somatoform disorder becomes a way of life, with the patient going from one doctor to another.
• Chronic anxiety and depression.
• Undertaking needless surgery.
• Noncompliance with treatment.

HOW TO TREAT

GENERAL MEASURES
• Treatment requires a trusting relationship between the doctor and patient. It is important that you as the patient be a partner in the effort to relieve the symptoms.
• Treatment is focused on achieving symptom relief, improving any depressive symptoms, increasing normal functioning and reducing symptom-related behavior. A patient needs to recognize that the symptoms will neither seriously worsen nor lead to death.
• Steps in treatment will include counseling. Group therapy may be helpful.
• The family or other significant persons in the patient's life should also be involved in the therapy in order to understand the problem and what they can do to help the patient.

MEDICATION—Medications will be prescribed as necessary for any associated medical or psychiatric problem. There are no specific medications to treat somatoform disorders.

ACTIVITY—Normally no restrictions unless recommended by your doctor.

DIET—Eat a nutritionally balanced diet to maintain optimum health.

CALL YOUR DOCTOR IF

• You or a family member has symptoms of a somatoform disorder.
• Symptoms continue or worsen after treatment is started.

STRESS

GENERAL INFORMATION

DEFINITION—The physical, mental and emotional reactions experienced as the result of changes and demands in one's life. The changes can be both large and small. Everyone responds to life's changes differently. Positive stress can be a motivator, while negative stress can set in when these changes and demands overwhelm the person.

BODY PARTS INVOLVED—All parts of the body.

SEX OR AGE MOST AFFECTED—Both sexes, adolescents and adults.

SIGNS & SYMPTOMS
- Physical—Muscle tension, headache, chest pain, upset stomach, diarrhea or constipation, racing heartbeat, cold clammy hands, fatigue, profuse sweating, rashes, rapid breathing, shaking, tics, jumpiness, poor or excessive appetite, weakness, tiredness, dizziness.
- Emotional—Anger, low self-esteem, depression, apathy, irritability, fear and phobic responses, difficulty concentrating, guilt, worry, agitation, anxiety, panic.
- Behavioral—Alcohol or drug abuse, increase in smoking, sleep disorders, overeating, memory loss, confusion.

CAUSES—When faced with a stressful situation, the body responds by increasing the production of certain hormones, causing changes in the heart rate, blood pressure, metabolism and physical activity.

RISK INCREASES WITH
Changes in lifestyle and disruptions in one's normal routine can bring about stress.
Some of the common causes of stress are:
- Recent death of a loved one (spouse, child, friend).
- Loss of anything valuable to you.
- Injuries or severe illnesses.
- Getting fired or changing jobs.
- Recent move to a new city or state.
- Sexual difficulties between you and your partner.
- Business or financial reverses or taking on a large debt, such as to purchase a new home.
- Regular conflict between you and a family member, close friend or business associate.
- Constant fatigue brought about by inadequate rest, sleep or recreation.

HOW TO PREVENT
- To help prevent negative stress, try to take charge of those aspects of your life that you can manage.
- Since stress cannot always be prevented, learn techniques to cope to protect your mental and physical health. Educate yourself about stress by reading articles and books.

WHAT TO EXPECT

DIAGNOSTIC MEASURES
- Your own observation of symptoms.
- Medical history and physical exam by a doctor, if necessary.

APPROPRIATE HEALTH CARE
- Self-care.
- Doctor's treatment (occasionally).
- Psychotherapy or counseling if needed.

PROBABLE OUTCOME—Usually resolved with self-treatment or professional therapy.

POSSIBLE COMPLICATIONS—Chronic stress can play a role in many health problems, including accidents, arthritis, asthma, cancer, colds, colitis, diabetes, endocrine disorders, fatigue, headaches, backaches, digestive problems, skin disorders, heart disease, high blood pressure, insomnia, muscle aches, sexual dysfunction, ulcers.

HOW TO TREAT

GENERAL MEASURES
Here are some tips to help reduce stress:
- Learn a meditation technique, and practice it regularly, daily if possible. There are many methods available.
- Take a short time away from any stressful situation you encounter during a day.
- Learn and practice a muscle-tensing and muscle-relaxing technique.
- Avoid taking your problems home or to bed with you. At the end of the day, spend a few minutes reviewing your entire day's experiences, event by event, as if you're replaying a tape. Release all negative emotions you have harbored (anger, feelings of insecurity or anxiety). Relish all good energy or emotion (loving thoughts, praise, good feelings about your work or yourself). Reach decisions about unfinished events, and release mental or muscular tension. Now you're ready for a relaxing and emotionally healing sleep.
- Join a support group in your community.

MEDICATION—Your doctor may prescribe tranquilizers or antidepressants for a short time.

ACTIVITY—Adopt an exercise program. People in good physical condition are less likely to suffer the negative effects of stress.

DIET—Eat a normal, well-balanced diet. Vitamin supplements may be recommended.

CALL YOUR DOCTOR IF

You or a family member has stress problems.

SUBSTANCE ABUSE & ADDICTION

GENERAL INFORMATION

DEFINITION—Preoccupation with mood-altering substances (drugs, alcohol, food) in which there is a loss of self-control and a compulsion to continue despite adverse personal and social consequences.

BODY PARTS INVOLVED—Central nervous system; liver; kidneys; blood.

SEX OR AGE MOST AFFECTED—Both sexes, all ages except early childhood.

SIGNS & SYMPTOMS—Depends on the substance of abuse. Most produce:
- A temporary pleasant mood.
- Relief from anxiety.
- False feelings of self-confidence.
- Increased sensitivity to sights and sounds (including hallucinations).
- Altered activity levels—either stupor and sleeplike states or frenzies.
- Unpleasant or painful symptoms when the abused substance is withdrawn.

CAUSES—Substances of abuse may produce addiction or dependence. The most common substances of abuse include:
- Nicotine.
- Alcohol.
- Marijuana.
- Amphetamines; barbiturates.
- Cocaine.
- Opiates, including codeine, heroin, methadone, morphine and opium.
- Psychedelic or hallucinogenic drugs, including PCP ("angel dust"), mescaline and LSD.
- Volatile substances, such as glue, solvents and paints that are inhaled.

RISK INCREASES WITH
- Illness that requires prescription pain relievers or tranquilizers.
- Family history of drug abuse.
- Genetic factors. Some persons may be more susceptible to addiction.
- Excess alcohol consumption.
- Fatigue or overwork.
- Poverty.
- Psychological problems, including depression, dependency or poor self-esteem.

HOW TO PREVENT
- Don't socialize with persons who use and abuse drugs.
- Seek counseling for mental health problems, such as depression or chronic anxiety, before they lead to drug problems.
- Develop wholesome interests and leisure activities.
- After surgery, illness or injury, stop prescription pain relievers or tranquilizers as soon as possible. Don't use more than you need.

WHAT TO EXPECT

DIAGNOSTIC MEASURES
- Observation of symptoms by you and others.
- Medical history and physical exam by a doctor; laboratory blood tests.

APPROPRIATE HEALTH CARE
- Doctor's treatment.
- Psychotherapy or counseling.
- Hospitalization for drug withdrawal symptoms.

PROBABLE OUTCOME—Curable with strong motivation, good medical care and support from family and friends.

POSSIBLE COMPLICATIONS
- Sexually transmitted diseases in addicts who share needles or practice careless sexual behavior while under the influence of drugs.
- Severe infections, such as endocarditis, hepatitis or blood poisoning, from intravenous injections with nonsterile needles.
- Malnutrition.
- Accidental injury to oneself or others while in a drug-induced state.
- Loss of job or family.
- Irreversible damage to body organs.
- Death caused by overdose.

HOW TO TREAT

GENERAL MEASURES
- Admit you have a problem.
- Seek professional help.
- Be open and honest with your family and good friends, and ask their help. Avoid friends who tempt you to resume your habit.
- Join self-help groups such as Narcotics Anonymous.
- See Resources for Additional Information.

MEDICATION—Your doctor may prescribe:
- Disulfiram (Antabuse) for alcoholism. This drug produces severe illness when alcohol is consumed.
- Naltrexone, which blocks the effect of opiates.
- Methadone for narcotic abuse. This drug is a less potent narcotic that is used to decrease the severity of physical withdrawal symptoms or allows a return to a normal life.

ACTIVITY—No restrictions. Exercise regularly.

DIET—Eat a normal, well-balanced diet that is high in protein. Vitamin supplements may be necessary if you suffer from malnutrition.

CALL YOUR DOCTOR IF

You abuse or are addicted to drugs and want help or new, unexplained symptoms develop. Drugs in treatment may produce side effects.

SUICIDE

GENERAL INFORMATION

DEFINITION
• Completed suicide—Death by one's own hand.
• Attempted suicide—Potentially fatal actions that do not result in death and nonfatal, attention-gaining attempts (e.g., superficial cuts on wrists). Attempted suicide is ten times more frequent than completed suicide.

BODY PARTS INVOLVED—Nervous system.

SEX OR AGE MOST AFFECTED—Males complete more suicides; females make more suicide attempts. Suicide rate is highest in those over 65 and in those ages15 to 24 years.

SIGNS & SYMPTOMS
• Hopelessness about the future.
• Suicidal thoughts with organized plan and intent—Suicide note, giving away personal possessions, quitting a job, making a will.
• Major depression—Change in sleep pattern, loss of interest, loss of energy, loss of concentration, loss of appetite, diminished psychomotor activity, guilt, suicidal thoughts.
• Psychosis—Hearing voices telling one to harm oneself (command hallucinations).

CAUSES
• Combination of psychiatric illness and social circumstances. Many suicidal people have active psychiatric illness.
• Major depression and bipolar disorder.
• Alcoholism and drug abuse disorders.
• Schizophrenia and other psychotic disorders.

RISK INCREASES WITH
Psychiatric risk factors:
• Mood disorders (major depression, bipolar depression), alcoholism, drug abuse, psychotic disorders, personality disorders.
• Family history of suicide.
• History of previous suicide attempt.
• Medical diagnosis of terminal illness (cancer, AIDS), chronic intractable pain, chronic and disabling illness (e.g., renal dialysis).
• Hopelessness about future.
Psychosocial/demographic risk factors:
• Sex—Males three times females.
• Age—Adolescent and geriatric populations (males peaking at 75 years, females peaking at 55 years).
• Race—Native American, Caucasian.
• Marital status—in order of risk: single, divorced, widowed, married.
Psychological risk factors:
• History of recent loss (loved one, job, etc.).
• Loss of social supports.
• Important dates (holidays, birthdays, anniversaries, etc.).

HOW TO PREVENT
• For yourself—Recognize your symptoms of depression; talk to someone about your feelings; get professional help; avoid alcohol or drugs; call suicide hotline number.
• For family/friends—Listen to and talk with the suicidal person about the problem; help person get professional help; do not leave person alone; remove guns and drugs from house; call suicide hotline number. In adolescents, watch for behavior changes (social, school, family).

WHAT TO EXPECT

DIAGNOSTIC MEASURES—All who make suicide threats, gestures or attempts should have physical and psychological examinations.

APPROPRIATE HEALTH CARE
• Hospitalization if severely depressed, intoxicated, psychotic or have made serious suicide attempt.
• Outpatient treatment if no evidence of severe depression, psychosis or intoxication and person has strong family support.
• A suicidal person may require a legal guardian until improved.

PROBABLE OUTCOME—The keys to a favorable course and prognosis are early recognition of risk factors; early diagnosis and treatment of a psychiatric disorder; follow-up.

POSSIBLE COMPLICATIONS
• There can be a brief period of increased suicide risk as depression resolves and patient's energy and initiative return.
• 15% of suicidal, depressed patients will ultimately complete suicide.

HOW TO TREAT

GENERAL MEASURES
• Treatment for underlying psychiatric and medical illness and any drug or substance abuse problem.
• Possibly electroconvulsive therapy (see Glossary) for severely depressed, acutely suicidal patients.

MEDICATION—Antidepressants, antipsychotics or antianxiety medications will be prescribed as needed.

ACTIVITY—As directed by your doctor.

DIET—As directed by your doctor.

CALL YOUR DOCTOR IF

You have serious thoughts of suicide or a family member is threatening suicide. Talk to someone immediately. Call a suicide hotline in your area. This is an emergency!

Psychotherapy Drugs

AMPHETAMINES

BRAND AND GENERIC NAMES

See complete list of brand and generic names in the *Brand and Generic Name Directory*, page 168.

BASIC INFORMATION

Habit forming? Yes
Prescription needed? Yes
Available as generic? Yes
Drug class: Central nervous system stimulant

USES

- Prevents narcolepsy (attacks of uncontrollable sleepiness).
- Controls hyperactivity in children under special circumstances.

DOSAGE & USAGE INFORMATION

How to take:
- Tablet—Swallow with liquid.
- Extended-release capsules and tablets—Swallow each dose whole with liquid; do not crush.

When to take:
- At the same times each day.
- Short-acting form—Don't take later than 6 hours before bedtime.
- Long-acting form—Take on awakening.

If you forget a dose:
- Short-acting form—Take up to 2 hours late. If more than 2 hours, wait for next dose (don't double this dose).
- Long-acting form—Take as soon as you remember. Wait 20 hours for next dose.

What drug does:
- Hyperactivity—Decreases motor restlessness and increases ability to pay attention.
- Narcolepsy—Increases motor activity and mental alertness; diminishes drowsiness.

Continued next column

OVERDOSE

SYMPTOMS:
Rapid heartbeat, hyperactivity, high fever, hallucinations, suicidal or homicidal feelings, convulsions, coma.
WHAT TO DO:
- Dial 911 (emergency) or 0 (operator) for an ambulance or medical help. Then give first aid immediately.
- See emergency information at end of book.

Time lapse before drug works:
15 to 30 minutes (short-acting).

Don't take with:
Any other medicine without consulting your doctor or pharmacist.

POSSIBLE ADVERSE REACTIONS OR SIDE EFFECTS

SYMPTOMS	WHAT TO DO
Life-threatening:	
In case of overdose, see previous column.	
Common:	
• Irritability, nervousness, insomnia, euphoria. signs of addiction*.	Continue. Call doctor when convenient.
• Dry mouth.	Continue. Tell doctor at next visit.
• Fast, pounding heartbeat.	Discontinue. Call doctor right away.
Infrequent:	
• Dizziness, reduced alertness, blurred vision, unusual sweating.	Discontinue. Call doctor right away.
• Headache, diarrhea or constipation, appetite loss, stomach pain, nausea, vomiting, weight loss, diminished sex drive, impotence.	Continue. Call doctor when convenient.
Rare:	
• Rash; hives; chest pain or irregular heartbeat; uncontrollable movements of head, neck, arms, legs.	Discontinue. Call doctor right away.
• Mood changes, swollen breasts.	Continue. Call doctor when convenient.

WARNINGS & PRECAUTIONS

Don't take if:
- You are allergic to any amphetamine.
- You will have surgery within 2 months, including dental surgery, requiring general or spinal anesthesia.

Before you start, tell your doctor:
- If you plan to become pregnant within medication period.
- If you have glaucoma.
- If you have diabetes.
- If you have a history of substance abuse.
- If you have heart or blood vessel disease or high blood pressure.
- If you have overactive thyroid, anxiety or tension.
- If you have a severe mental illness (especially children).

Over age 60:
Adverse reactions and side effects may be more frequent and severe than in younger persons.

Pregnancy:
Decide with your doctor if drug benefits justify risk to unborn child. Consult doctor. Risk category C (see page 47).

Breast-feeding:
Drug passes into milk.

Children & adolescents:
Not recommended for children under 12.

Prolonged use:
- Habit forming.
- Talk to your doctor about the need for follow-up medical examinations or laboratory studies to check blood pressure, growth charts in children, reassessment of need for continued treatment.

Skin, sunlight & heat:
No problems expected.

Driving, piloting or hazardous work:
Don't drive or pilot aircraft until you learn how medicine affects you. Don't work around dangerous machinery. Don't climb ladders or work in high places. Danger increases if you drink alcohol or take medicine affecting alertness and reflexes.

Discontinuing:
May be unnecessary to finish medicine, but don't suddenly stop. Follow doctor's instructions.

Others:
- This is a dangerous drug and must be closely supervised. Don't use for appetite control or depression. Potential for damage and abuse.
- During withdrawal phase, may cause prolonged sleep of several days.
- Don't use for fatigue or to replace rest.

 POSSIBLE INTERACTION WITH OTHER DRUGS

GENERIC NAME OR DRUG CLASS	COMBINED EFFECT
Antidepressants, tricyclic*	Decreased amphetamine effect.
Antihypertensives*	Decreased antihypertensive effect.
Beta-adrenergic blocking agents*	High blood pressure, slow heartbeat.
Carbonic anhydrase inhibitors*	Increased amphetamine effect.
Central nervous system (CNS) stimulants*, other	Excessive CNS stimulation.
Doxazosin	Decreased doxazosin effect.
Furazolidine	Sudden and severe high blood pressure.
Haloperidol	Decreased amphetamine effect.
Monoamine oxidase (MAO) inhibitors*	May severely increase blood pressure.
Phenothiazines*	Decreased amphetamine effect.
Prazosin	Decreased prazosin effect.
Sodium bicarbonate	Increased amphetamine effect.
Sympathomimetics*	Seizures.
Thyroid hormones*	Heartbeat irregularities.

 POSSIBLE INTERACTION WITH OTHER SUBSTANCES

INTERACTS WITH	COMBINED EFFECT
Alcohol:	Decreased amphetamine effect. Avoid.
Beverages: Caffeine drinks.	Overstimulation. Avoid.
Cocaine:	Dangerous stimulation of nervous system. Avoid.
Foods:	None expected.
Marijuana:	Frequent use— Severely impaired mental function.
Tobacco:	None expected.

*See Glossary

BRAND AND GENERIC NAMES

See complete list of brand and generic names in the *Brand and Generic Name Directory*, page 168.

BASIC INFORMATION

Habit forming? No
Prescription needed? Yes
Available as generic? Yes
Drug class: Antidepressant (tricyclic)

USES

- Gradually relieves symptoms of depression.
- Used to decrease bedwetting in children.
- Pain relief (sometimes).
- Clomipramine is used to treat obsessive-compulsive disorder.
- Protriptyline may be used to treat attention-deficit disorder.
- Treatment for narcolepsy, bulimia, panic attacks, cocaine withdrawal, attention-deficit disorder.

DOSAGE & USAGE INFORMATION

How to take:
Tablet, capsule or syrup—Swallow with liquid.

When to take:
At the same time each day, usually at bedtime.

If you forget a dose:
Bedtime dose—If you forget your once-a-day bedtime dose, don't take it more than 3 hours late. If more than 3 hours, wait for next scheduled dose. Don't double this dose.

Continued next column

OVERDOSE

SYMPTOMS:
Hallucinations, drowsiness, enlarged pupils, respiratory failure, fever, cardiac arrhythmias, convulsions, coma.
WHAT TO DO:
- **Dial 911 (emergency) or 0 (operator) for an ambulance or medical help. Then give first aid immediately.**
- **If patient is unconscious and not breathing, give mouth-to-mouth breathing. If there is no heartbeat, use cardiac massage and mouth-to-mouth breathing (CPR). Don't try to make patient vomit. If you can't get help quickly, take patient to nearest emergency facility.**
- **See emergency information at end of book.**

What drug does:
Probably affects part of brain that controls messages between nerve cells.

Time lapse before drug works:
2 to 4 weeks. May require 4 to 6 weeks for maximum benefit.

Don't take with:
Any prescription or nonprescription drugs without consulting your doctor or pharmacist.

POSSIBLE ADVERSE REACTIONS OR SIDE EFFECTS

SYMPTOMS	WHAT TO DO
Life-threatening: In case of overdose, see previous column.	
Common:	
• Tremor.	Discontinue. Call doctor right away.
• Headache, dry mouth or unpleasant taste, constipation or diarrhea, nausea, indigestion, fatigue, weakness, drowsiness, nervousness, anxiety, excessive sweating.	Continue. Call doctor when convenient.
• Insomnia, "sweet tooth."	Continue. Tell doctor at next visit.
Infrequent:	
• Convulsions.	Discontinue. Seek emergency treatment.
• Hallucinations, shakiness, dizziness, fainting, blurred vision, eye pain, vomiting, irregular heartbeat or slow pulse, inflamed tongue, abdominal pain, jaundice, hair loss, rash, fever, chills, joint pain, palpitations, hiccups, visual changes.	Discontinue. Call doctor right away.
• Difficult or frequent urination; decreased sex drive; muscle aches; abnormal dreams; nasal congestion; weakness and faintness when arising from bed or chair; back pain.	Continue. Call doctor when convenient.

Rare:

Itchy skin; sore throat; involuntary movements of jaw, lips and tongue; nightmares; confusion; swollen breasts; swollen testicles.	Discontinue. Call doctor right away.

WARNINGS & PRECAUTIONS

Don't take if:
- You are allergic to any tricyclic antidepressant.
- You drink alcohol in excess.
- You have had a heart attack within 6 weeks.
- You have glaucoma.
- You have taken MAO inhibitors* within 2 weeks.
- Patient is younger than 12.

Before you start, tell your doctor:
- If you will have surgery within 2 months, including dental surgery, requiring general or spinal anesthesia.
- If you have an enlarged prostate or glaucoma.
- If you have heart disease or high blood pressure.
- If you have stomach or intestinal problems.
- If you have an overactive thyroid.
- If you have asthma.
- If you have liver disease.

Over age 60:
More likely to develop urination difficulty and serious side effects such as seizures, hallucinations, shaking, dizziness, fainting, headache, insomnia.

Pregnancy:
Risk factors vary for drugs in this group. See category list on page 47 and consult doctor.

Breast-feeding:
Drug may pass into milk. Avoid drug or discontinue nursing until you finish medicine. Consult doctor about maintaining milk supply.

Children & adolescents:
Don't give to children younger than 12 except under medical supervision.

Prolonged use:
Talk to your doctor about the need for follow-up medical examinations or laboratory studies to check complete blood counts (white blood cell count, platelet count, red blood cell count, hemoglobin, hematocrit), blood pressure, eyes, teeth.

Skin, sunlight & heat:
One or more drugs in this group may cause rash or intensify sunburn in areas exposed to sun or ultraviolet light (photosensitivity reaction). Avoid overexposure and use sunscreen. Notify doctor if reaction occurs.

Driving, piloting or hazardous work:
Don't drive or pilot aircraft until you learn how medicine affects you. Don't work around dangerous machinery. Don't climb ladders or work in high places. Danger increases if you drink alcohol or take medicine affecting alertness and reflexes.

Discontinuing:
- Don't discontinue without consulting doctor. Dose may require gradual reduction if you have taken drug for a long time. Doses of other drugs may also require adjustment.
- Withdrawal symptoms such as convulsions, muscle cramps, nightmares, insomnia, abdominal pain. Call your physician right away if any of these occur.

Others:
- May affect results in some medical tests.
- Advise any doctor or dentist whom you consult that you take this medicine.

POSSIBLE INTERACTION WITH OTHER DRUGS

GENERIC NAME OR DRUG CLASS	COMBINED EFFECT
Anticoagulants*, oral	Possible increased anticoagulant effect.
Anticholinergics*	Increased anticholinergic effect.
Antihistamines*	Increased antihistamine effect.
Barbiturates*	Decreased antidepressant effect. Increased sedation.

Continued on page 171

POSSIBLE INTERACTION WITH OTHER SUBSTANCES

Alcohol: Beverages or medicines with alcohol.	Excessive intoxication. Avoid.
Beverages:	None expected.
Cocaine:	Increased risk of heartbeat irregularity.
Foods:	None expected.
Marijuana:	Excessive drowsiness. Avoid.
Tobacco:	Possible decreased tricyclic antidepressant effect.

---

*See Glossary

BARBITURATES

BRAND AND GENERIC NAMES

See complete list of brand and generic names in the *Brand and Generic Name Directory*, page 168.

BASIC INFORMATION

Habit forming? Yes
Prescription needed? Yes
Available as generic? Yes, for some
Drug class: Sedative-hypnotic agent, anitconvulsant

USES

- Reduces likelihood of seizures (tonic-clonic seizure pattern and simple partial) in epilepsy.
- Preventive treatment for febrile seizures.
- Reduces anxiety or nervous tension.
- As an ingredient in combination drugs to treat gastrointestinal disorders, headaches and asthma.
- Aids sleep at night (on a short-term basis).

DOSAGE & USAGE INFORMATION

How to take:
- Capsule—Swallow with liquid. If you can't swallow whole, open capsule and take with liquid or food. Instructions to take on empty stomach mean 1 hour before or 2 hours after eating.
- Elixir—Swallow with liquid.
- Rectal suppositories—Remove wrapper and moisten suppository with water. Gently insert into rectum, pointed end first. If suppository is too soft, chill in refrigerator or cool water before removing wrapper.
- Tablet—Swallow with liquid or food to lessen stomach irritation. If you can't swallow whole, crumble tablet and take with liquid or food.

Continued next column

OVERDOSE

SYMPTOMS:
Deep sleep, trouble breathing, weak pulse, coma.
WHAT TO DO:
- Dial 911 (emergency) or 0 (operator) for an ambulance or medical help. Then give first aid immediately.
- If patient is unconscious and not breathing, give mouth-to-mouth breathing. If there is no heartbeat use cardiac massage and mouth-to-mouth breathing (CPR). Don't try to make patient vomit. If you can't get help quickly, take patient to emergency facility. See emergency facts at end of book.

When to take:
At the same times each day.

If you forget a dose:
Take as soon as you remember up to 2 hours late. If more than 2 hours, wait for next scheduled dose (don't double this dose).

What drug does:
May partially block nerve impulses at nerve-cell connections.

Time lapse before drug works:
60 minutes; will take several weeks for maximum antiepilepsy effect.

Don't take with:
- Nonprescription drugs without consulting doctor or pharmacist.
- See Interaction column and consult doctor.

POSSIBLE ADVERSE REACTIONS OR SIDE EFFECTS

SYMPTOMS	WHAT TO DO
Life-threatening: In case of overdose, see previous column.	
Common: Dizziness, drowsiness, clumsiness, unsteadiness. signs of addiction*.	Continue. Call doctor when convenient.
Infrequent: Confusion, headache, irritability, feeling faint, nausea, vomiting, depression, nightmares, trouble sleeping.	Continue, but call doctor right away.
Rare: Agitation, slow heartbeat, difficult breathing, bleeding sores on lips, fever, chest pain, unexplained bleeding or bruising, muscle or joint pain, skin rash or hives, thickened or scaly skin, white spots in mouth, tightness in chest, face swelling, sore throat, yellow eyes or skin, hallucinations, unusual tiredness or weakness.	Continue, but call doctor right away.

WARNINGS & PRECAUTIONS

Don't take if:
- You are allergic to any barbiturate.
- You have porphyria.

Before you start, tell your doctor:
- If you have epilepsy.
- If you have kidney or liver damage.
- If you have asthma.
- If you have anemia.
- If you have chronic pain.
- If you will have surgery within 2 months, including dental surgery, requiring general or spinal anesthesia.

Over age 60:
Adverse reactions and side effects may be more frequent and severe than in younger persons. Use small doses.

Pregnancy:
Risk to unborn child outweighs drug benefits. Don't use. Risk category D (see page 47).

Breast-feeding:
Drug passes into milk. Avoid drug or discontinue nursing until you finish medicine. Consult doctor for advice on maintaining milk supply.

Children & adolescents:
Use only under doctor's supervision.

Prolonged use:
- May cause addiction, anemia, chronic intoxication. Unlikely to occur with the usual anticonvulsant or sedative dosage levels.
- May lower body temperature, making exposure to cold temperatures hazardous.
- Talk to your doctor about the need for follow-up medical examinations or laboratory studies to check blood sugar, kidney function.

Skin, sunlight & heat:
No problems expected.

Driving, piloting or hazardous work:
Don't drive or pilot aircraft until you learn how medicine affects you. Don't work around dangerous machinery. Don't climb ladders or work in high places. Danger increases if you drink alcohol or take medicine affecting alertness and reflexes.

Discontinuing:
If you become addicted, don't stop taking barbiturates suddenly. Seek medical help for safe withdrawal.

Others:
- May affect results in some medical tests.
- Barbiturate addiction is common. Withdrawal effects may be fatal.
- Advise any doctor or dentist whom you consult that you take this medicine.

POSSIBLE INTERACTION WITH OTHER DRUGS

GENERIC NAME OR DRUG CLASS	COMBINED EFFECT
Anticoagulants, oral*	Decreased effect of anticoagulant.
Anticonvulsants*	Changed seizure patterns.
Antidepressants, tricyclic*	Decreased antidepressant effect. Possible dangerous oversedation.
Antidiabetic, agents, oral*	Increased effect of barbiturate.
Antihistamines*	Dangerous sedation. Avoid.
Aspirin	Decreased aspirin effect.
Beta-adrenergic blocking agents*	Decreased effect of beta-adrenergic blocker.
Carbamazepine	Decreased carbamazepine effect.
Carteolol	Increased barbiturate effect. Dangerous sedation.
Clozapine	Toxic effect on the central nervous system.
Contraceptives, oral*	Decreased contraceptive effect.
Cortisone drugs*	Decreased cortisone effect.

Continued on page 172

POSSIBLE INTERACTION WITH OTHER SUBSTANCES

INTERACTS WITH	COMBINED EFFECT
Alcohol:	Possible fatal oversedation. Avoid.
Beverages:	None expected.
Cocaine:	Decreased barbiturate effect.
Foods:	None expected.
Marijuana:	Excessive sedation. Avoid.
Tobacco:	None expected.

*See Glossary

BENZODIAZEPINES

BRAND AND GENERIC NAMES

See complete list of brand and generic names in the *Brand and Generic Name Directory*, page 169.

BASIC INFORMATION

Habit forming? Yes
Prescription needed? Yes
Available as generic? Yes, for most
Drug class: Tranquilizer (benzodiazepine), anticonvulsant

 USE

- Treatment for anxiety disorders.
- Treatment for muscle spasm.
- Treatment for seizure disorders.
- Treatment for alcohol withdrawal.
- Treatment for insomnia (short-term).

 DOSAGE & USAGE INFORMATION

How to take:
- Tablet or capsule—Swallow with liquid. If you can't swallow whole, crumble tablet or open capsule and take with liquid or small amount of food.
- Extended-release capsule—Swallow capsule whole. Do not open or chew.
- Oral suspension—Dilute dose in water, soda or sodalike beverage or small amount of food such as applesauce or pudding.
- Sublingual tablet—Do not chew or swallow. Place under tongue until dissolved.

When to take:
At the same time each day, according to instructions on prescription label.

Continued next column

 OVERDOSE

SYMPTOMS:
Drowsiness, weakness, tremor, stupor, coma.
WHAT TO DO:
- **Dial 911 (emergency) or 0 (operator) for an ambulance or medical help. Then give first aid immediately.**
- **If patient is unconscious and not breathing, give mouth-to-mouth breathing. If there is no heartbeat, use cardiac massage and mouth-to-mouth breathing (CPR). Don't try to make patient vomit. If you can't get help quickly, take patient to nearest emergency facility.**
- **See emergency information at end of book.**

If you forget a dose:
Take as soon as you remember up to 2 hours late. If more than 2 hours, wait for next scheduled dose (don't double this dose).

What drug does:
Affects limbic system of brain, the part that controls emotions.

Time lapse before drug works:
May take 6 weeks for full benefit; depends on drug when treating anxiety.

Don't take with:
Any other medicine without consulting your doctor or pharmacist.

 POSSIBLE ADVERSE REACTIONS OR SIDE EFFECTS

SYMPTOMS	WHAT TO DO
Life-threatening:	
In case of overdose, see previous column.	
Common:	
Clumsiness, drowsiness, dizziness. signs of addiction*.	Continue. Call doctor when convenient.
Infrequent:	
• Hallucinations, confusion, depression, irritability, rash, itch, vision changes, sore throat, fever, chills.	Discontinue. Call doctor right away.
• Constipation or diarrhea, nausea, vomiting, difficult urination, vivid dreams, behavior changes, abdominal pain, headache, dry mouth.	Continue. Call doctor when convenient.
Rare:	
• Slow heartbeat, breathing difficulty.	Discontinue. Seek emergency treatment.
• Mouth, throat ulcers; jaundice.	Discontinue. Call doctor right away.
• Decreased sex drive.	Continue. Call doctor when convenient.

 WARNINGS & PRECAUTIONS

Don't take if:
- You are allergic to any benzodiazepine.
- You have myasthenia gravis.
- You are an active or recovering alcoholic.
- Patient is younger than 6 months.

Before you start, tell your doctor:
- If you have liver, kidney or lung disease.
- If you have diabetes, epilepsy or porphyria.
- If you have glaucoma.

Over age 60:
Adverse reactions and side effects may be more frequent and severe than in younger persons. You may need smaller doses for shorter periods of time. You may develop increased sedation or agitation or difficulty walking.

Pregnancy:
Risk factors vary for drugs in this group. See category list on page 47 and consult doctor.

Breast-feeding:
Drug passes into milk. Avoid drug or discontinue nursing until you finish medicine. Consult doctor for advice on maintaining milk supply.

Children & adolescents:
Use only under medical supervision.

Prolonged use:
May impair liver function.

Skin, sunlight & heat:
- One or more drugs in this group may cause rash or intensify sunburn in areas exposed to sun or ultraviolet light (photosensitivity reaction). Avoid overexposure and use sunscreen. Notify doctor if reaction occurs.
- Hot weather, heavy exercise and sweating may reduce excretion and cause overdose in some people with one or more of these drugs.

Driving, piloting or hazardous work:
Don't drive or pilot aircraft until you learn how medicine affects you. Don't work around dangerous machinery. Don't climb ladders or work in high places. Danger increases if you drink alcohol or take medicine affecting alertness and reflexes.

Discontinuing:
Don't discontinue without consulting doctor. Dose may require gradual reduction if you have taken drug for a long time. Doses of other drugs may also require adjustment.

Others:
- Blood sugar may rise in diabetics, requiring insulin adjustment.
- Don't use for insomnia more than 4-7 days.
- Caution—Keep in safe secure place to avoid theft.
- Advise any doctor or dentist whom you consult that you take this medicine.

 POSSIBLE INTERACTION WITH OTHER DRUGS

GENERIC NAME OR DRUG CLASS	COMBINED EFFECT
Anticonvulsants*	Change in seizure pattern.
Antidepressants, tricyclic*	Increased sedative effect of both drugs.
Antihistamines*	Increased sedative effect of both drugs.
Central nervous system (CNS) depressants*	Increased sedative effect.
Cimetidine	Increased benzodiazepine effect.
Clozapine	Toxic effect on the central nervous system.
Contraceptives, oral*	Increased benzodiazepine effect.
Disulfiram	Increased benzodiazepine effect.
Erythromycins*	Increased benzodiazepine effect.
Fluoxetine	Increased sedative effect.
Fluvoxamine	Increased sedative effect.
Ketoconazole	Increased benzodiazepine effect.
Levodopa	Possible decreased levodopa effect.
Molindone	Increased tranquilizer effect.
Monoamine oxidase (MAO) inhibitors*	Convulsions, deep sedation, rage.
Narcotics*	Increased sedative effect of both drugs.
Nefazodone	Increased effect of nefazodone and alprazolam.

Continued on page 172

 POSSIBLE INTERACTION WITH OTHER SUBSTANCES

INTERACTS WITH	COMBINED EFFECT
Alcohol:	Heavy sedation. Avoid.
Beverages:	None expected.
Cocaine:	Decreased benzodiazepine effect.
Foods:	None expected.
Marijuana:	Heavy sedation. Avoid.
Tobacco:	Decreased benzodiazepine effect.

*See Glossary

BETA-ADRENERGIC BLOCKING AGENTS

BRAND AND GENERIC NAMES

See complete list of brand and generic names in the *Brand and Generic Name Directory*, page 169.

BASIC INFORMATION

Habit forming? No
Prescription needed? Yes
Available as generic? Yes, for some.
Drug class: Beta-adrenergic blocker

 USES

- Treats anxiety disorders.
- Treats social phobia.
- Treats akathisia* associated with antipsychotic medications.
- Treats tremors (some types).
- Treats violent behavior in demented person.
- Reduces frequency of vascular headaches (does not relieve headache pain).
- Nonpsychiatry uses—Treats heart problems.

 DOSAGE & USAGE INFORMATION

How to take:
Tablet, liquid or extended-release capsule—Swallow with liquid. If you can't swallow whole, crumble tablet or open capsule and take with liquid or food. Don't crush capsule or extended-release tablet.

When to take:
With meals or immediately after.

If you forget a dose:
Take as soon as you remember. Return to regular schedule, but allow 3 hours between doses.

Continued next column

 OVERDOSE

SYMPTOMS:
Weakness, slow or weak pulse, blood pressure drop, fainting, difficulty breathing, convulsions, cold and sweaty skin.
WHAT TO DO:
- **Dial 911 (emergency) or 0 (operator) for an ambulance or medical help. Then give first aid immediately.**
- **See emergency information at end of book.**

What drug does:
- Blocks certain actions of sympathetic nervous system.
- Lowers heart's oxygen requirements.
- Slows nerve impulses through heart.
- Reduces blood vessel contraction in heart, scalp and other body parts.

Time lapse before drug works:
1 to 4 hours.

Don't take with:
Nonprescription drugs or drugs in Interaction column without consulting doctor or pharmacist.

 POSSIBLE ADVERSE REACTIONS OR SIDE EFFECTS

SYMPTOMS	WHAT TO DO
Life-threatening:	
Congestive heart failure (severe shortness of breath, rapid heartbeat); severe asthma.	Discontinue. Seek emergency treatment.
Common:	
• Pulse slower than 50 beats per minute.	Discontinue. Call doctor right away.
• Drowsiness, fatigue, numbness or tingling of fingers or toes, dizziness, diarrhea, nausea, weakness.	Continue. Call doctor when convenient.
• Cold hands or feet; dry mouth, eyes and skin.	Continue. Tell doctor at next visit.
Infrequent:	
• Hallucinations, nightmares, insomnia, headache, difficult breathing, joint pain, anxiety, chest pain.	Discontinue. Call doctor right away.
• Confusion, reduced alertness, depression, impotence, abdominal pain.	Continue. Call doctor when convenient.
• Constipation.	Continue. Tell doctor at next visit.
Rare:	
• Rash, sore throat, fever.	Discontinue. Call doctor right away.
• Unusual bleeding and bruising; dry, burning eyes.	Continue. Call doctor when convenient.

BETA-ADRENERGIC BLOCKING AGENTS

 WARNINGS & PRECAUTIONS

Don't take if:
- You are allergic to any beta-adrenergic blocker.
- You have asthma.
- You have hay fever symptoms.
- You have taken a monoamine oxidase (MAO) inhibitor* in the past 2 weeks.

Before you start, tell your doctor:
- If you have heart disease or poor circulation to the extremities.
- If you have hay fever, asthma, chronic bronchitis, emphysema.
- If you have overactive thyroid function.
- If you have impaired liver or kidney function.
- If you will have surgery within 2 months, including dental surgery, requiring general or spinal anesthesia.
- If you have diabetes or hypoglycemia.

Over age 60:
Adverse reactions and side effects may be more frequent and severe than in younger persons.

Pregnancy:
Risk factors vary for drugs in this group. See category list on page 47 and consult doctor.

Breast-feeding:
Drug passes into milk. Avoid drug or discontinue nursing until you finish medicine. Consult doctor for advice on maintaining milk supply.

Children & adolescents:
Not recommended.

Prolonged use:
Talk to your doctor about the need for follow-up medical examinations or laboratory studies to check blood pressure, ECG*, kidney function, blood sugar.

Skin, sunlight & heat:
No problems expected.

Driving, piloting or hazardous work:
Don't drive or pilot aircraft until you learn how medicine affects you. Don't work around dangerous machinery. Don't climb ladders or work in high places. Danger increases if you drink alcohol or take medicine affecting alertness and reflexes.

Discontinuing
Don't discontinue without consulting doctor. Dose may require gradual reduction if you have taken drug for a long time. Doses of other drugs may also require adjustment. Angina may result from abrupt discontinuing.

Others:
- May mask diabetic hypoglycemia symptoms.
- May affect results in some medical tests.
- Advise any doctor or dentist whom you consult that you take this medicine.

 POSSIBLE INTERACTION WITH OTHER DRUGS

GENERIC NAME OR DRUG CLASS	COMBINED EFFECT
Angiotensin-converting (ACE) inhibitors*	Increased anti-hypertensive effects of both drugs. Dosages may require adjustment.
Antidiabetics*	Increased anti-diabetic effect.
Antihistamines*	Decreased antihistamine effect.
Antihypertensives*	Increased anti-hypertensive effect.
Anti-inflammatory drugs, nonsteroidal (NSAIDs)*	Decreased anti-hypertensive effect of beta blocker.
Betaxolol eyedrops	Possible increased beta blocker effect.
Calcium channel blockers*	Additional blood pressure drop.
Clonidine	Additional blood pressure drop. High blood pressure if clonidine stopped abruptly.
Dextrothyroxine	Possible decreased beta blocker effect.

Continued on page 172

POSSIBLE INTERACTION WITH OTHER SUBSTANCES

INTERACTS WITH	COMBINED EFFECT
Alcohol:	Excessive blood pressure drop. Avoid.
Beverages:	None expected.
Cocaine:	Irregular heartbeat; decreased beta-adrenergic effect. Avoid.
Foods:	None expected.
Marijuana:	Daily use—Impaired circulation to hands and feet.
Tobacco:	Possible irregular heartbeat.

*See Glossary

BUPROPION

BRAND NAMES

Wellbutrin

BASIC INFORMATION

Habit forming? No
Prescription needed? Yes
Available as generic? No
Drug class: Antidepressant

 ## USES

Relieves severe depression. (Has less effect on sexual functioning than some other antidepressants and may be more acceptable to some patients.)

 ## DOSAGE & USAGE INFORMATION

How to take:
Tablets—Swallow with liquid. If you can't swallow whole, crumble tablet and take with liquid or food. May take with food to lessen stomach irritation.

When to take:
At the same times each day, according to instructions on prescription label.

If you forget a dose:
Take as soon as you remember up to 2 hours late. If more than 2 hours, wait for next scheduled dose (don't double this dose). Do not take more often than every 6 hours.

What drug does:
Blocks certain chemicals that are necessary for nerve transmission in the brain.

Time lapse before drug works:
3 to 4 weeks.

Don't take with:
Any other medicine without consulting your doctor or pharmacist.

 ## OVERDOSE

SYMPTOMS:
Confusion, agitation, seizures, coma.
WHAT TO DO:
• Dial 911 (emergency) or 0 (operator) for an ambulance or medical help. Then give first aid immediately. Do not induce vomiting.
• See emergency information at end of book.

 ## POSSIBLE ADVERSE REACTIONS OR SIDE EFFECTS

SYMPTOMS	WHAT TO DO
Life-threatening:	
In case of overdose, see previous column.	
Common:	
• Excitement, anxiety, insomnia, restlessness. constipation, loss of appetite, dry mouth, dizziness, nausea or vomiting.	Continue. Call doctor when convenient.
• Confusion, heart-beat irregularity, severe headache.	Discontinue. Call doctor right away.
Infrequent:	
Rash, blurred vision, drowsiness, chills, fever, hallucinations, fatigue, nightmares.	Discontinue. Call doctor right away
Rare:	
Fainting, seizures.	Discontinue. Call doctor right away.

WARNINGS & PRECAUTIONS

Don't take if:
- You have anorexia nervosa or bulimia.
- You have had recent head injury.
- You have a brain or spinal cord tumor.

Before you start, tell your doctor:
- If you have manic phases to your illness.
- If you abuse drugs.
- If you have seizures.
- If you have liver, kidney or heart disease.

Over age 60:
See Interaction column and consult doctor.

Pregnancy:
No proven harm to unborn child, but avoid if possible. Risk category B (see page 47).

Breast-feeding:
Drug passes into milk. May cause adverse reactions. Avoid drug or discontinue breast-feeding. Consult doctor about maintaining milk supply.

Children & adolescents:
Effect not documented. Consult your doctor.

Prolonged use:
Talk to your doctor about the need for follow-up medical examinations or laboratory studies to check kidney function, liver function and serum bupropion levels in blood.

Skin, sunlight & heat:
No problems expected.

Driving, piloting or hazardous work:
Don't drive or pilot aircraft until you learn how medicine affects you. Don't work around dangerous machinery. Don't climb ladders or work in high places. Danger increases if you drink alcohol or take medicine affecting alertness and reflexes.

Discontinuing:
Don't discontinue without doctor's approval. Dose may require gradual reduction to avoid adverse effects.

Others:
- May affect results in some medical tests.
- Advise any doctor or dentist whom you consult that you take this medicine.

POSSIBLE INTERACTION WITH OTHER DRUGS

GENERIC NAME OR DRUG CLASS	COMBINED EFFECT
Antidepressants, tricyclic*	Increased risk of major seizures.
Carbamazepine	Increased carbamazepine effect and risk of seizures.
Cimetidine	Increased bupropion effect.
Clozapine	Increased risk of major seizures.
Fluoxetine	Increased risk of major seizures.
Haloperidol	Increased risk of major seizures.
Levodopa	Increased levodopa effect and risk of seizures.
Lithium	Increased risk of major seizures.
Loxapine	Increased risk of major seizures.
Molindone	Increased risk of major seizures.
Monoamine oxidase (MAO) inhibitors*	Increased risk of bupropion toxicity.
Phenothiazines*	Increased risk of major seizures.
Phenytoin	Increased phenytoin effect and risk of seizures.
Thioxanthenes*	Increased risk of major seizures.
Trazodone	Increased risk of major seizures.

POSSIBLE INTERACTION WITH OTHER SUBSTANCES

INTERACTS WITH	COMBINED EFFECT
Alcohol:	Increased risk of seizures. Avoid.
Beverages: Coffee, tea, cocoa.	Increased side effects such as restlessness, insomnia.
Cocaine:	Increased risk of seizures. Avoid.
Foods:	No special problems expected.
Marijuana:	Increased risk of seizures. Avoid.
Tobacco:	No special problems expected.

*See Glossary

BUSPIRONE

BRAND NAMES

BuSpar

BASIC INFORMATION

Habit forming? Probably not
Prescription needed? Yes
Available as generic? No
Drug class: Antianxiety agent

 USES

- Treats chronic anxiety disorders with nervousness or tension. Not intended for treatment of ordinary stress of daily living. Causes less sedation than some anti-anxiety drugs. Not useful for acute anxiety.
- Useful in agitation associated with dementia.
- Reduces agggression and irritability in patients with dementia, brain injury, mental retardation.
- Used for anxiety in alcoholics or substance abusers (buspirone has low abuse potential).
- Reduces frequency of vascular headaches (does not relieve headache pain).
- Not useful in withdrawal from sedatives.

 DOSAGE & USAGE INFORMATION

How to take:
Tablets—Take with food.

When to take:
As directed. Usually 3 times daily. Food increases absorption.

If you forget a dose:
Take as soon as you remember, but skip this dose and don't double the next dose if it is almost time for the next dose.

What drug does:
Chemical family azaspirodecanedione; *not* a benzodiazepine. Probably has an effect on neurotransmitter systems.

Continued next column

 OVERDOSE

SYMPTOMS:
Severe drowsiness or nausea, vomiting, small pupils, unconsciousness.
WHAT TO DO:
- Dial 911 (emergency) or 0 (operator) for an ambulance or medical help. Then give first aid immediately.
- See emergency information at end of book.

Time lapse before drug works:
2 or 4 weeks before beneficial effects may be observed.

Don't take with:
Alcohol, other tranquilizers, antihistamines, muscle relaxants, sedatives or narcotics.

 POSSIBLE ADVERSE REACTIONS OR SIDE EFFECTS

SYMPTOMS	WHAT TO DO
Life-threatening: Chest pain; pounding, fast heartbeat (rare).	Discontinue. Seek emergency treatment.
Common: Lightheadedness, headache, nausea, restlessness, dizziness (if these side effects continue).	Discontinue.Call doctor right away.
Infrequent: Drowsiness, dry mouth, ringing in ears, nightmares or vivid dreams, unusual fatigue.	Continue. Call doctor when convenient.
Rare: Numbness or tingling in feet or hands; sore throat; fever; depression or confusion; uncontrollable movements of tongue, lips, arms and legs; slurred speech; psychosis; blurred vision.	Discontinue. Call doctor right away.

BUSPIRONE

 ## WARNINGS & PRECAUTIONS

Don't take if:
You are allergic to buspirone.

Before you start, tell your doctor:
- If you have ever been addicted to any substance.
- If you have chronic kidney or liver disease.
- If you are already taking *any* medicine.

Over age 60:
Adverse reactions and side effects may be more frequent and severe than in younger persons.

Pregnancy:
No problems expected, but better to avoid if possible. Consult doctor. Risk category B (see page 47).

Breast-feeding:
Buspirone passes into milk of lactating experimental animals. Avoid if possible.

Children & adolescents:
Safety and efficacy not established for under 18 years old.

Prolonged use:
- Not recommended for prolonged use. Adverse side effects more likely.
- Request follow-up studies to check kidney function, blood counts, and platelet counts.

Skin, sunlight & heat:
No problems expected.

Driving, piloting or hazardous work:
Don't drive or pilot aircraft until you learn how medicine affects you. Don't work around dangerous machinery. Don't climb ladders or work in high places. Danger increases if you drink alcohol or take medicine affecting alertness and reflexes, such as antihistamines, tranquilizers, sedatives, pain medicine, narcotics and mind-altering drugs.

Discontinuing:
No problems expected.

Others:
- Before elective surgery requiring local or general anesthesia, tell your dentist, surgeon or anesthesiologist that you take buspirone.
- Advise any doctor or dentist whom you consult that you take this medicine.
- This medication is expensive and is not available in a generic form.

 ## POSSIBLE INTERACTION WITH OTHER DRUGS

GENERIC NAME OR DRUG CLASS	COMBINED EFFECT
Antihistamines*	Increased sedative effect of both drugs.
Barbiturates*	Excessive sedation. Sedative effect of both drugs may be increased.
Benzodiazepines*	Recent use of benzodiazepines may lessen effect of buspirone.
Central nervous system (CNS) depressants*	Increased sedative effect.
Monoamine oxidase MAO inhibitors*	May increase blood pressure.
Narcotics*	Excessive sedation. Sedative effect of both drugs may be increased.

 ## POSSIBLE INTERACTION WITH OTHER SUBSTANCES

INTERACTS WITH	COMBINED EFFECT
Alcohol:	Excess sedation. Use caution.
Beverages: Caffeine-containing drinks.	Avoid. Decreased anti-anxiety effect of buspirone.
Cocaine:	Avoid. Decreased anti-anxiety effect of buspirone.
Foods:	None expected.
Marijuana:	Avoid. Decreased anti-anxiety effect of buspirone.
Tobacco:	Avoid. Decreased anti-anxiety effect of buspirone.

CAFFEINE

BRAND NAMES

See complete list of brand and generic names in the *Brand and Generic Name Directory*, page 169.

BASIC INFORMATION

Habit forming? Yes
Prescription needed? No
Available as generic? Yes
Drug class: Stimulant (xanthine), vasoconstrictor

 ## USES

- Treatment for drowsiness and fatigue (occasional use only).
- Treatment for migraine and other vascular headaches in combination with ergot.

 ## DOSAGE & USAGE INFORMATION

How to take:
- Tablet or liquid—Swallow with liquid or food to lessen stomach irritation. If you can't swallow whole, crumble tablet and take with liquid or food.
- Extended-release capsules—Swallow whole with liquid.

When to take:
At the same times each day.

If you forget a dose:
Take as soon as you remember up to 2 hours late. If more than 2 hours, wait for next scheduled dose (don't double this dose).

What drug does:
- Constricts blood vessel walls.
- Stimulates central nervous system.

Time lapse before drug works:
30 minutes.

Continued next column

 ## OVERDOSE

SYMPTOMS:
Excitement, insomnia, rapid heartbeat (infants can have slow heartbeat), confusion, fever, hallucinations, convulsions, coma.
WHAT TO DO:
- **Dial 911 (emergency) or 0 (operator) for an ambulance or medical help. Then give first aid immediately.**
- **See emergency information at end of book.**

Don't take with:
- Nonprescription drugs without consulting your doctor or pharmacist.
- See Interaction column and consult doctor.

 ## POSSIBLE ADVERSE REACTIONS OR SIDE EFFECTS

SYMPTOMS	WHAT TO DO
Life-threatening:	
In case of overdose, see previous column.	
Common:	
• Rapid heartbeat, low blood sugar (hunger, anxiety, cold sweats, rapid pulse) with tremor, irritability (mild).	Discontinue. Call doctor right away.
• Nervousness, insomnia.	Continue. Tell doctor at next visit.
• Increased urination.	No action necessary.
Infrequent:	
• Confusion, irritability (severe).	Discontinue. Call doctor right away.
• Nausea, indigestion, burning feeling in stomach.	Continue. Call doctor when convenient.
Rare:	
None expected.	

WARNINGS & PRECAUTIONS

Don't take if:
- You are allergic to any stimulant.
- You have heart disease.
- You have active peptic ulcer of stomach or duodenum.

Before you start, tell your doctor:
- If you have irregular heartbeat.
- If you have hypoglycemia (low blood sugar).
- If you have epilepsy.
- If you have a seizure disorder.
- If you have high blood pressure.
- If you have insomnia.

Over age 60:
Adverse reactions and side effects may be more frequent and severe than in younger persons.

Pregnancy:
Decide with your doctor if drug benefits justify risk to unborn child. Risk category C (see page 47).

Breast-feeding:
Drug passes into milk. Avoid drug or discontinue nursing until you finish medicine. Consult doctor for advice on maintaining milk supply.

Children & adolescents:
Not recommended.

Prolonged use:
Stomach ulcers.

Skin, sunlight & heat:
No problems expected.

Driving, piloting or hazardous work:
No problems expected.

Discontinuing:
Will cause withdrawal symptoms of headache, irritability, drowsiness. Discontinue gradually if you use caffeine for a month or more.

Others:
Consult your doctor if drowsiness or fatigue continues, recurs or is not relieved by caffeine.

POSSIBLE INTERACTION WITH OTHER DRUGS

GENERIC NAME OR DRUG CLASS	COMBINED EFFECT
Caffeine-containing drugs, other	Increased risk of overstimulation.
Central nervous system (CNS) stimulants*	Increased risk of overstimulation.
Cimetidine	Increased caffeine effect.
Contraceptives, oral*	Increased caffeine effect.
Isoniazid	Increased caffeine effect.
Monoamine oxidase (MAO) inhibitors*	Dangerous blood pressure rise.
Sympathomimetics*	Overstimulation.
Xanthines*	Increased risk of overstimulation.

POSSIBLE INTERACTION WITH OTHER SUBSTANCES

INTERACTS WITH	COMBINED EFFECT
Alcohol:	Decreased alcohol effect.
Beverages: Caffeine drinks (coffee, tea or soft drinks).	Increased caffeine effect. Use caution.
Cocaine	Convulsions or excessive nervousness.
Foods:	No proven problems.
Marijuana:	Increased effect of both drugs. May lead to dangerous, rapid heartbeat. Avoid.
Tobacco:	Increased heartbeat. Avoid. Decreased caffeine effect.

CALCIUM CHANNEL BLOCKERS

BRAND AND GENERIC NAMES

See complete list of brand and generic names in the *Brand and Generic Name Directory*, page 169.

BASIC INFORMATION

Habit forming? No
Prescription needed? Yes
Available as generic? Yes
Drug class: Calcium channel blocker, antiarrhythmic, antianginal

USES

- Possibly effective in treating bipolar (manic-depressive) disorder as directed by the doctor.
- Treats migraine.
- Nonpsychiatry use—Used for angina attacks, irregular heartbeat, high blood pressure.

DOSAGE & USAGE INFORMATION

How to take:
- Tablet or capsule—Swallow with liquid. You may chew or crush tablet.
- Extended-release tablets or capsules—Swallow each dose whole with liquid; do not crush.

When to take:
At the same times each day. Take verapamil with food.

If you forget a dose:
Take as soon as you remember up to 2 hours late. If more than 2 hours, wait for next scheduled dose (don't double this dose).

Continued next column

OVERDOSE

SYMPTOMS:
Unusually fast or unusually slow heartbeat, loss of consciousness, cardiac arrest.
WHAT TO DO:
- **Dial 911 (emergency) or 0 (operator) for an ambulance or medical help. Then give first aid immediately.**
- **If patient is unconscious and not breathing, give mouth-to-mouth breathing. If there is no heartbeat, use cardiac massage and mouth-to-mouth breathing (CPR). Don't try to make patient vomit. If you can't get help quickly, take patient to nearest emergency facility.**
- **See emergency information at end of book.**

What drug does:
- Reduces work that heart must perform.
- Reduces normal artery pressure.
- Increases oxygen to heart muscle.

Time lapse before drug works:
1 to 2 hours.

Don't take with:
Any other medicine without consulting your doctor or pharmacist.

POSSIBLE ADVERSE REACTIONS OR SIDE EFFECTS

SYMPTOMS	WHAT TO DO
Life-threatening:	
In case of overdose, see previous column.	
Common:	
Tiredness.	Continue. Tell doctor at next visit.
Infrequent:	
• Unusually fast or unusually slow heartbeat, wheezing, cough, shortness of breath.	Discontinue. Call doctor right away.
• Dizziness; numbness or tingling in hands and feet; swollen feet, ankles or legs; difficult urination.	Continue. Call doctor when convenient.
• Nausea, constipation.	Continue. Tell doctor at next visit.
Rare:	
• Fainting, depression, psychosis, rash, jaundice.	Discontinue. Call doctor right away.
• Headache, insomnia, vivid dreams, hair loss.	Continue. Tell doctor at next visit.

WARNINGS & PRECAUTIONS

Don't take if:
- You are allergic to calcium channel blockers.
- You have very low blood pressure.

Before you start, tell your doctor:
- If you have kidney or liver disease.
- If you have high blood pressure.
- If you have heart disease other than coronary artery disease.

Over age 60:
Adverse reactions and side effects may be more frequent and severe than in younger persons.

Pregnancy:
Decide with your doctor if drug benefits justify risk to unborn child. Risk category C (see page 47).

Breast-feeding:
Safety not established. Avoid if possible. Consult doctor.

Children & adolescents:
Not recommended.

Prolonged use:
Talk to your doctor about the need for follow-up medical examinations or laboratory studies to check blood pressure, liver function, kidney function, ECG*.

Skin, sunlight & heat:
One or more drugs in this group may cause rash or intensity sunburn in areas exposed to sun or ultraviolet light (photosensitivity reaction). Avoid overexposure. Notify doctor if reaction occurs.

Driving, piloting or hazardous work:
Avoid if you feel dizzy. Otherwise, no problems expected.

Discontinuing:
Don't discontinue without doctor's advice until you complete prescribed dose, even though symptoms diminish or disappear.

Others:
- Learn to check your own pulse rate. If it drops to 50 beats per minute or lower, don't take drug until your consult your doctor.
- Advise any doctor or dentist whom you consult that you take this medicine.

POSSIBLE INTERACTION WITH OTHER DRUGS

GENERIC NAME OR DRUG CLASS	COMBINED EFFECT
Angiotensin-converting enzyme (ACE) inhibitors*	Possible excessive potassium in blood. Dosages may require adjustment.
Antiarrhythmics*	Possible increased effect and toxicity of each drug.
Anticoagulants, oral*	Possible increased anticoagulant effect.
Anticonvulsants, hydantoin*	Increased anticonvulsant effect.
Antihypertensives*	Blood pressure drop. Dosages may require adjustment.
Beta-adrenergic blocking agents*	Possible irregular heartbeat and congestive heart failure.
Calcium (large doses)	Possible decreased effect of calcium channel blocker.

Carbamazepine	May increase carbamazepine effect and toxicity.
Cimetidine	Possible increased effect of calcium channel blocker.
Cyclosporine	Increased cyclosporine toxicity.
Digitalis preparations*	Increased digitalis effect. May need to reduce dose.
Disopyramide	May cause dangerously slow, fast or irregular heartbeat.
Diuretics*	Dangerous blood pressure drop. Dosages may require adjustment.
Encainide	Increased effect of toxicity on heart muscle.
Fluvoxamine	Slow heartbeat (with diltiazem).
Hypokalemia-causing medications*	Increased antihypertensive effect.
Lithium	Possible decreased lithium effect.
Metformin	Increased metformin effect.
Nicardipine	Possible increased effect and toxicity of each drug.

Continued on page 173

POSSIBLE INTERACTION WITH OTHER SUBSTANCES

INTERACTS WITH	COMBINED EFFECT
Alcohol:	Dangerously low blood pressure. Avoid.
Beverages: Grapefruit juice.	Possible increased drug effect.
Cocaine:	Possible irregular heartbeat. Avoid.
Foods:	None expected.
Marijuana:	Possible irregular heartbeat. Avoid.
Tobacco:	Possible rapid heartbeat. Avoid.

*See Glossary

CARBAMAZEPINE

BRAND NAMES

Apo-Carbamazepine   PMS Carbamazepine
Epitol   Tegretol
Mazepine   Tegretol Chewtabs
Novocarbamaz   Tegretol CR

BASIC INFORMATION

Habit forming? No
Prescription needed? Yes
Available as generic? Yes
Drug class: Analgesic, anticonvulsant, antimanic agent

 USES

- Decreases frequency, severity and duration of attacks of tic douloureux*.
- Treats bipolar (manic-depressive) disorder.
- Prevents seizures.
- Used for pain relief, alcohol withdrawal.

 DOSAGE & USAGE INFORMATION

How to take:
Regular or chewable tablet—Swallow with liquid or food to lessen stomach irritation.

When to take:
At the same times each day.

If you forget a dose:
Take as soon as you remember up to 2 hours late. If more than 2 hours, wait for next scheduled dose (don't double this dose).

Continued next column

 OVERDOSE

SYMPTOMS:
Involuntary movements, drowsiness, irregular heartbeat, irregular bleeding, decreased urination, decreased blood pressure, dilated pupils, flushed skin, stupor, coma.
WHAT TO DO:
- **Dial 911 (emergency) or 0 (operator) for an ambulance or medical help. Then give first aid immediately.**
- **If patient is unconscious and not breathing, give mouth-to-mouth breathing. If there is no heartbeat, use cardiac massage and mouth-to-mouth breathing (CPR). Don't try to make patient vomit. If you can't get help quickly, take patient to nearest emergency facility.**
- **See emergency information at end of book.**

What drug does:
Reduces excitability of nerve fibers in brain, thus inhibiting repetitive spread of nerve impulses. Reduces transmission of pain messages at certain nerve terminals.

Time lapse before drug works:
- Tic douloureux—24 to 72 hours.
- Bipolar disorder—Unknown.
- Seizures—1 to 2 weeks.

Don't take with:
Any other medicine without consulting your doctor or pharmacist. May inactivate other medications, such as birth control pills.

 POSSIBLE ADVERSE REACTIONS OR SIDE EFFECTS

SYMPTOMS	WHAT TO DO
Life-threatening:	
In case of overdose, see previous column.	
Common:	
• Blurred vision.	Continue. Call doctor when convenient.
• Back-and-forth eye movements.	Discontinue. Call doctor right away.
Infrequent:	
• Confusion, slurred speech, fainting, depression, headache, hallucinations, hives, rash, mouth sores, sore throat, fever, unusual bleeding or bruising, unusual fatigue, jaundice.	Discontinue. Call doctor right away.
• Diarrhea, nausea, vomiting, constipation, dry mouth, impotence.	Continue. Call doctor when convenient.
Rare:	
• Breathing difficulty; irregular, pounding or slow heartbeat; chest pain; uncontrollable body jerks; numbness, weakness or tingling in hands and feet; tender, bluish legs or feet; less urine; swollen lymph glands, blood disorder (symptoms of anemia, bleeding, frequent infections).	Discontinue. Call doctor right away.
• Frequent urination, muscle pains, joint aches.	Continue. Call doctor when convenient.

WARNINGS & PRECAUTIONS

Don't take if:
- You are allergic to carbamazepine or any tricyclic antidepressant*.
- You have had liver or bone marrow disease.
- You have taken a monoamine oxidase (MAO) inhibitor* in the past 2 weeks.

Before you start, tell your doctor:
- If you have high blood pressure, thrombophlebitis or heart disease.
- If you have glaucoma.
- If you have emotional or mental problems.
- If you have liver or kidney disease.
- If you have a history of blood disorders.
- If you are taking any other medications.
- If you drink more than 2 alcoholic drinks per day.

Over age 60:
Adverse reactions and side effects may be more frequent and severe than in younger persons.

Pregnancy:
Decide with your doctor whether drug benefits justify risk to unborn child. Risk category C (see page 47).

Breast-feeding:
Drug passes into milk. Avoid drug or discontinue nursing until you finish medicine. Consult doctor for advice on maintaining milk supply.

Children & adolescents:
Safety not established in children under 6.

Prolonged use:
- Lowers sex drive.
- Talk to your doctor about the need for follow-up medical examinations or laboratory studies to check complete blood counts (white blood cell count, platelet count, red blood cell count, hemoglobin, hematocrit), serum iron and serum levels.

Skin, sunlight & heat:
May cause rash or intensity sunburn in areas exposed to sun or ultraviolet light (photosensitivity reaction). Avoid overexposure and use sunscreen. Notify doctor if reaction occurs.

Driving, piloting or hazardous work:
Don't drive or pilot aircraft until you learn how medicine effects you. Don't work around dangerous machinery. Don't climb ladders or work in high places. Danger increases if you drink alcohol or take medicine affecting alertness and reflexes.

Discontinuing:
Don't discontinue without doctor's advice until you complete prescribed dose, even though symptoms diminish or disappear.

Others:
- Use only if less hazardous drugs are not effective. Stay under medical supervision.
- Periodic blood tests are needed.
- Advise any doctor or dentist whom you consult that you take this medicine.

POSSIBLE INTERACTION WITH OTHER DRUGS

GENERIC NAME OR DRUG CLASS	COMBINED EFFECT
Anticoagulants, oral*	Decreased anticoagulant effect.
Anticonvulsants, hydantoin* or succinimide*	Decreased effect of both drugs.
Antidepressants, tricyclic*	Confusion. Possible psychosis.
Barbiturates*	Possible increased barbiturate metabolism.
Cimetidine	Increased carbamazepine effect.
Cisapride	Decreased carbamazepine effect.
Clozapine	Toxic effect on bone marrow and central nervous system.
Contraceptives, oral*	Reduced contraceptive protection. Use barrier birth control method.

Continued on page 173

POSSIBLE INTERACTION WITH OTHER SUBSTANCES

INTERACTS WITH	COMBINED EFFECT
Alcohol:	Increased sedative effect of alcohol. Avoid.
Beverages:	None expected.
Cocaine:	Increased adverse effects of carbamazepine. Avoid.
Foods:	None expected.
Marijuana:	Increased adverse effects of carbamazepine. Avoid.
Tobacco:	None expected.

CHLORAL HYDRATE

BRAND NAMES

Aquachloral   **Novochlorhydrate**
Noctec

BASIC INFORMATION

Habit forming? Yes
Prescription needed? Yes
Available as generic? Yes
Drug class: Sedative-hypnotic agent

 ## USES

Relieves insomnia.

 ## DOSAGE & USAGE INFORMATION

How to take:
- Syrup or capsule—Swallow with liquid or food to lessen stomach irritation.
- Suppositories—Remove wrapper and moisten suppository with water. Gently insert smaller end into rectum. Push well into rectum with finger.

When to take:
At the same time each day.

If you forget a dose:
Take as soon as you remember up to 2 hours late. If more than 2 hours, wait for next scheduled dose (don't double this dose).

Continued next column

 ## OVERDOSE

SYMPTOMS:
Confusion, weakness, breathing difficulty, throat irritation, jaundice, stagger, slow or irregular heartbeat, unconsciousness, convulsions, coma.
WHAT TO DO:
- **Dial 911 (emergency) or 0 (operator) for an ambulance or medical help. Then give first aid immediately.**
- **If patient is unconscious and not breathing, give mouth-to-mouth breathing. If there is no heartbeat, use cardiac massage and mouth-to-mouth breathing (CPR). Don't try to make patient vomit. If you can't get help quickly, take patient to nearest emergency facility.**
- **See emergency information at end of book.**

What drug does:
Affects brain centers that control wakefulness and alertness.

Time lapse before drug works:
30 to 60 minutes.

Don't take with:
Any other medicine without consulting your doctor or pharmacist.

 ## POSSIBLE ADVERSE REACTIONS OR SIDE EFFECTS

SYMPTOMS	WHAT TO DO
Life-threatening: In case of overdose, see previous column.	
Common: Nausea, stomach pain, vomiting.	Discontinue. Call doctor right away.
Infrequent: "Hangover" effect, clumsiness or unsteadiness, drowsiness, dizziness, lightheadedness, diarrhea.	Continue. Call doctor when convenient.
Rare: • Hallucinations, agitation, confusion. leukopenia (white blood cells causing sore throat and fever).	Discontinue. Call doctor right away.
• Hives, rash.	Continue. Call doctor when convenient.

 ## WARNINGS & PRECAUTIONS

Don't take if:
You are allergic to chloral hydrate or you have porphyria.

Before you start, tell your doctor:
- If you have had liver, kidney or heart trouble.
- If you are prone to stomach upsets (if medicine is in oral form).
- If you are allergic to tartrazine dye.
- If you have colitis or a rectal inflammation (if medicine is in suppository form).

Over age 60:
Adverse reactions and side effects may be more frequent and severe than in younger persons. More likely to have "hangover" effect.

Pregnancy:
Decide with your doctor if drug benefits justify risk to unborn child. Risk category C (see page 47).

Breast-feeding:
Small amounts may filter into breast milk. Best to avoid.

Children & adolescents:
Use only under medical supervision.

Prolonged use:
- Drug loses its effectiveness as an antianxiety agent or sleep aid after about 2 weeks. Not recommended for longer use.
- Addiction and possible kidney damage may result if used long-term.

Skin, sunlight & heat:
No problems expected.

Driving, piloting or hazardous work:
Don't drive or pilot aircraft until you learn how medicine affects you. Don't work around dangerous machinery. Don't climb ladders or work in high places. Danger increases if you drink alcohol or take medicine affecting alertness and reflexes, such as antihistamines, tranquilizers, sedatives, pain medicine, narcotics and mind-altering drugs.

Discontinuing:
Don't discontinue without consulting doctor. Dose may require gradual reduction if you have taken drug for a long time. Doses of other drugs may also require adjustment.

Others:
- Frequent kidney function tests recommended when drug is used for long time.
- Advise any doctor or dentist whom you consult that you take this medicine.

POSSIBLE INTERACTION WITH OTHER DRUGS

GENERIC NAME OR DRUG CLASS	COMBINED EFFECT
Anticoagulants, oral*	Possible hemorrhaging.
Antidepressants*	Increased chloral hydrate effect.
Antihistamines*	Increased chloral hydrate effect.
Central nervous system (CNS) depressants*	Increased sedative effect.
Clozapine	Toxic effect on the central nervous system.
Fluoxetine	Increased depressant effects of both drugs.

Guanfacine	May increase depressant effects of either drug.
Leucovorin	High alcohol content of leucovorin may cause adverse effects.
Mind-altering drugs*	Increased chloral hydrate effect.
Molindone	Increased tranquilizer effect.
Monoamine oxidase (MAO) inhibitors*	Increased chloral hydrate effect.
Narcotics*	Increased chloral hydrate effect.
Phenothiazines*	Increased chloral hydrate effect.
Sertraline	Increased depressive effects of both drugs.

POSSIBLE INTERACTION WITH OTHER SUBSTANCES

INTERACTS WITH	COMBINED EFFECT
Alcohol:	Increased sedative effects of both. Avoid.
Beverages:	None expected.
Cocaine:	Decreased chloral hydrate effect. Avoid.
Foods:	None expected.
Marijuana:	May severely impair mental and physical functioning. Avoid.
Tobacco:	None expected.

*See Glossary

CLONIDINE

BRAND NAMES

Catapres   Dixarit
Catapres-TTS

BASIC INFORMATION

Habit forming? No
Prescription needed? Yes
Available as generic? Yes
Drug class: Antihypertensive

 ## USES

- Treatment of narcotic withdrawal syndrome.
- May be used for nicotine withdrawal.
- Prevention of migraine headaches.
- Control of overactivity and tics in children.

 ## DOSAGE & USAGE INFORMATION

How to take:
- Tablet—Swallow with liquid.
- Transdermal patch (attaches to skin)—Apply to clean, dry, hairless skin on arm or trunk. Follow all prescription instructions carefully.

When to take:
- Tablet—Once or twice a day as directed.
- Transdermal patch—Replace as directed, usually once a week.

Continued next column

 ## OVERDOSE

SYMPTOMS:
Vomiting, fainting, slow heartbeat, feeling cold, coma, diminished reflexes, shortness of breath, dizziness, extreme tiredness.

WHAT TO DO:
- Dial 911 (emergency) or 0 (operator) for an ambulance or medical help. Then give first aid immediately.
- If patient is unconscious and not breathing, give mouth-to-mouth breathing. If there is no heartbeat, use cardiac massage and mouth-to-mouth breathing (CPR). Don't try to make patient vomit. If you can't get help quickly, take patient to nearest emergency facility.
- See emergency information at end of book.

If you forget a dose:
- Take tablet as soon as you remember. If it is almost time for the next dose, wait for the next scheduled dose (don't double this dose). If you miss more than 2 doses in a row, call your doctor.
- If the once-a-week patch change is 3 days late, call your doctor.

What drug does:
- Reduces nervous system overactivity.
- Relaxes and allows expansion of blood vessel walls.

Time lapse before drug works:
2 to 3 weeks for full benefit.

Don't take with:
- Medicines containing alcohol; read labels carefully.
- Any other medicine without consulting your doctor or pharmacist.

 ## POSSIBLE ADVERSE REACTIONS OR SIDE EFFECTS

SYMPTOMS	WHAT TO DO
Life-threatening:	
In case of overdose, see previous column.	
Common:	
Dizziness, constipation drowsiness, irritated skin (with skin patch), dry mouth, tiredness, headache.	Continue. Call doctor when convenient.
Infrequent:	
• Depression, swollen hands or feet.	Discontinue. Call doctor right away.
• Darkened skin (with skin patch), light-headedness upon rising from sitting or lying, nausea, vomiting, dry or burning eyes, diminished sex drive or ability, appetite loss, nervousness.	Continue. Call doctor when convenient.
Rare:	
Cold fingers and toes, nightmares, slow heart rate.	Discontinue. Call doctor right away.

WARNINGS & PRECAUTIONS

Don't take if:
You are allergic to clonidine.

Before you start, consult your doctor:
- If you will have surgery within 2 months, including dental surgery, requiring general or spinal anesthesia.
- If you have heart disease or kidney disease.
- If you have a peripheral circulation disorder (intermittent claudication, Raynaud's syndrome, Buerger's disease).
- If you have history of depression.
- If you have a disorder affecting the skin or any skin irritation (with use of transdermal patch).

Over age 60:
Adverse reactions and side effects may be more frequent and severe than in younger persons.

Pregnancy:
Decide with your doctor whether drug benefits justify risk to unborn child. Risk category C (see page 47).

Breast-feeding:
Unknown whether safe or not. Consult doctor.

Children & adolescents:
Useful for controlling overactivity or tics.

Prolonged use:
- Don't discontinue without consulting doctor. Dose may require gradual reduction if you have taken drug for a long time. Doses of other drugs may also require adjustment.
- Request yearly eye examinations.
- Talk to your doctor about the need for follow-up medical examinations or laboratory studies.

Skin, sunlight & heat:
Use with caution in hot weather.

Driving, piloting or hazardous work:
Don't drive or pilot aircraft until you learn how medicine affects you. Don't work around dangerous machinery. Don't climb ladders or work in high places. Danger increases if you drink alcohol or take medicine affecting alertness and reflexes.

Discontinuing:
Don't discontinue abruptly. May cause a withdrawal syndrome including anxiety, chest pain, insomnia, headache, nausea, irregular heartbeat, flushed face, sweating. Consult doctor if any symptoms occur after discontinuing the medication.

Others:
- Advise any doctor or dentist whom you consult that you take this medicine.
- For dry mouth, suck sugarless hard candy or chew sugarless gum. If dry mouth continues, consult your dentist.

POSSIBLE INTERACTION WITH OTHER DRUGS

GENERIC NAME OR DRUG CLASS	COMBINED EFFECT
Antidepressants, tricyclic*	Decreased clonidine effect.
Antihypertensives*, other	Excessive blood pressure drop.
Appetite suppressants*	Decreased clonidine effect.
Beta-adrenergic blocking agents*	Possible precipitous change in blood pressure.
Central nervous system (CNS) depressants*	Increased depressive effects of both drugs.

POSSIBLE INTERACTION WITH OTHER SUBSTANCES

INTERACTS WITH	COMBINED EFFECT
Alcohol:	Increased sensitivity to sedative effect of alcohol and very low blood pressure. Avoid.
Beverages:	No problems expected.
Cocaine:	Increased risk of heart block and high blood pressure.
Foods:	No problems expected.
Marijuana:	Weakness on standing.
Tobacco:	No problems expected

*See Glossary

CLOZAPINE

BRAND NAMES

Clozaril   Leponex

BASIC INFORMATION

Habit forming? No
Prescription needed? Yes. Prescribed only
through a special program.
Available as generic? No
Drug class: Antipsychotic (new generation)

 ## USES

Treats severe schizophrenia in patients not
helped by other medicines.

 ## DOSAGE & USAGE INFORMATION

How to take:
Tablet—Swallow with liquid. If you can't swallow
whole, crumble tablet and take with liquid or
food.

When to take:
Once or twice daily as directed.

If you forget a dose:
Take as soon as you remember up to 2 hours
late. If more than 2 hours, wait for next
scheduled dose (don't double this dose).

What drug does:
Interferes with binding of dopamine. May
produce significant improvement, but may at
times also make schizophrenia worse.

Time lapse before drug works:
Weeks to months before improvement is evident.
Your doctor may increase the dosage to obtain
optimal effectiveness..

Don't take with:
Any other prescription drug, nonprescription drug
or alcohol without first checking with your doctor
or pharmacist.

 ## OVERDOSE

SYMPTOMS:
Heartbeat fast, slow, irregular; hallucinations;
restlessness; excitement; drowsiness;
breathing difficulty.
WHAT TO DO:
- **Dial 911 (emergency) or 0 (operator) for an
  ambulance or medical help. Then give first
  aid immediately.**
- **See emergency information at end of book.**

 ## POSSIBLE ADVERSE REACTIONS OR SIDE EFFECTS

SYMPTOMS	WHAT TO DO
Life-threatening: High fever, rapid pulse, profuse sweating, muscle rigidity, confusion and irritability, seizures; fever, chills, mouth sores.	Discontinue. Seek emergency treatment.
Common: Dry mouth, blurred vision, constipation, difficulty urinating; sedation, low blood pressure, dizziness.	Continue. Call doctor when convenient.
Infrequent: None expected.	
Rare: • Jerky or involuntary movements, especially of the face, lips, jaw, tongue; slow-frequency tremor of head or limbs, especially while moving; muscle rigidity, lack of facial expression and slow inflexible movements; seizures.	Discontinue. Call doctor right away.
• Pacing or restlessness; (akathisia); intermittent spasms of muscles of face, eyes, tongue, jaw, neck, body or limbs.	Continue. Call doctor when convenient.

WARNINGS & PRECAUTIONS

Don't take if:
- You are significantly mentally depressed.
- You have bone marrow depression from other drugs.
- You have an enlarged prostate.
- You have glaucoma.

Before you start, tell your doctor:
- If you have ever had seizures from any cause.
- If you have liver, heart or gastrointestinal disease or any type of blood disorder.

Over age 60:
Possible greater risk of weakness or dizziness upon standing after sitting or lying down. Greater risk of excitement, confusion. Great risk of difficulty in urination.

Pregnancy:
Risk category B (see page 47).

Breast-feeding:
May cause sedation, restlessness or irritability in the nursing infant. Avoid.

Children & adolescents:
Safety not established. Consult doctor.

Prolonged use:
Effects unknown.

Skin, sunlight & heat:
No problems expected.

Driving, piloting or hazardous work:
Don't drive or pilot aircraft until you learn how medicine affects you. Don't work around dangerous machinery. Don't climb ladders or work in high places. Danger increases if you drink alcohol or take medicine affecting alertness and reflexes.

Discontinuing:
Don't discontinue without consulting doctor. Dose may require gradual reduction if you have taken drug for a long time. Doses of other drugs may also require adjustment.

Others:
- This medicine is available only through a special management program for monitoring and distributing this drug.
- You will need laboratory studies each week for white blood cell and differential counts.

POSSIBLE INTERACTION WITH OTHER DRUGS

GENERIC NAME OR DRUG CLASS	COMBINED EFFECT
Antihypertensives*	Lower than expected blood pressure.
Bone marrow depressants*	Toxic bone marrow depression.
Carbamazepine	Decreased clozapine effect.
Central nervous system (CNS) depressants*	Toxic effects on the central nervous system.
Fluoxetine	Increased risk of adverse reactions.
Fluvoxamine	Increased risk of adverse reactions.
Haloperidol	Increased risk of seizures.
Lithium	Increased risk of seizures.
Phenytoin	Decreased clozapine effect.
Risperidone	Increased risperidone effect.
Valproic acid	Increased clozapine effect.

POSSIBLE INTERACTION WITH OTHER SUBSTANCES

INTERACTS WITH	COMBINED EFFECT
Alcohol:	Avoid. Increases toxic effect on the central nervous system.
Beverages: Caffeine drinks.	Excess (more than 3 cups of coffee or equivalent) increases risk of heartbeat irregularities.
Cocaine:	Increased risk of heartbeat irregularities.
Foods:	No special problems expected.
Marijuana:	Increased risk of heartbeat irregularities.
Tobacco:	Decreased serum concentration of clozapine. Avoid.

DIPHENHYDRAMINE

BRAND NAMES

See complete list of brand and generic names in the *Brand and Generic Name Directory*, page 170.

BASIC INFORMATION

Habit forming? No
Prescription needed? No, for most
Available as generic? Yes
Drug class: Antihistamine, antiemetic, antivertigo, antidyskinetic, sedative-hypnotic agent

USES

- Reduces allergic symptoms such as hay fever, hives, rash or itching.
- Prevents motion sickness, nausea, vomiting.
- Induces sleep.
- Reduces stiffness and tremors from Parkinson's disease or side effects of antipsychotics.

DOSAGE & USAGE INFORMATION

How to take:
Follow label directions.

When to take:
As a sleep aid, take 20-30 minutes before bedtime. For other uses, follow label directions.

If you forget a dose:
If using as a sleep aid, take as soon as you remember. Don't double a dose.

What drug does:
- Acts as a central nervous system depressant that helps induce sleep.
- Blocks brain's vomiting center.
- Blocks action of histamine after an allergic response triggers histamine release in sensitive cells.

Time lapse before drug works:
15 minutes to an hour.

Don't take with:
Any other medicine without consulting your doctor or pharmacist.

OVERDOSE

SYMPTOMS:
Convulsions, red face, hallucinations, coma.
WHAT TO DO:
- **Dial 911 (emergency) or 0 (operator)for an ambulance or medical help. Then give first aid immediately.**
- **See emergency information at end of book.**

POSSIBLE ADVERSE REACTIONS OR SIDE EFFECTS

SYMPTOMS	WHAT TO DO
Life-threatening: In case of overdose, see previous column.	
Common: Drowsiness; dizziness; dry mouth, nose or throat.	Continue. Tell doctor at next visit.
Infrequent: • Change in vision, clumsiness, rash.	Discontinue. Call doctor right away.
• Less tolerance for contact lenses, painful or difficult urination.	Continue. Call doctor when convenient.
• Appetite loss.	Continue. Tell doctor at next visit.
Rare: Nightmares, agitation, irritability, sore throat, fever, rapid heartbeat, unusual bleeding or bruising, fatigue, weakness, confusion, fainting, seizures.	Discontinue. Call doctor right away.

WARNINGS & PRECAUTIONS

Don't take if:
You are allergic to any antihistamine.

Before you start, tell your doctor:
- If you have glaucoma.
- If you have an enlarged prostate.
- If you have asthma.
- If you have kidney disease.
- If you have peptic ulcer.
- If you will have surgery within 2 months, including dental surgery, requiring general or spinal anesthesia.

Over age 60:
Don't exceed recommended dose. Adverse reactions and side effects may be more frequent and severe than in younger persons, especially urination difficulty, diminished alertness and other brain and nervous system symptoms.

Pregnancy:
Consult doctor. Risk category B. See page 47.

Breast-feeding:
Drug passes into milk. Avoid drug or discontinue nursing until you finish medicine. Consult doctor for advice on maintaining milk supply.

Children & adolescents:
Children may exhibit overexcited behavior when using this drug. Don't give to children under 12 without doctor's approval.

Prolonged use:
Not recommended for long-term use. Consult doctor.

Skin, sunlight & heat:
May cause rash or intensify sunburn in areas exposed to sun or sunlamp.

Driving, piloting or hazardous work:
Don't drive or pilot aircraft until you learn how medicine affects you. Don't work around dangerous machinery. Don't climb ladders or work in high places. Danger increases if you drink alcohol or take medicine affecting alertness and reflexes, such as antihistamines, tranquilizers, sedatives, pain medicine, narcotics and mind-altering drugs.

Discontinuing:
No problems expected.

Others:
Advise any doctor or dentist whom you consult that you take this medicine.

POSSIBLE INTERACTION WITH OTHER DRUGS

GENERIC NAME OR DRUG CLASS	COMBINED EFFECT
Anticholinergics*	Increased anticholinergic effect.
Antidepressants*	Excess sedation. Avoid.
Antihistamines*, other	Excess sedation. Avoid.
Carteolol	Decreased antihistamine effect.
Central nervous system (CNS) depressants*	May increase sedation.
Clozapine	Toxic effect on the central nervous system.
Mind-altering drugs*	Excess sedation. Avoid.
Molindone	Increased sedative and antihistamine effects.

Monoamine oxidase (MAO) inhibitors*	Increased antihistamine effect.
Narcotics*	Excess sedation. Avoid.
Procarbazine	May increase sedation.
Sedatives*	Excess sedation. Avoid.
Sertraline	Increased depressive effects of both drugs.
Sotalol	Increased antihistamine effect.

POSSIBLE INTERACTION WITH OTHER SUBSTANCES

INTERACTS WITH	COMBINED EFFECT
Alcohol:	Excess sedation. Avoid.
Beverages: Caffeine drinks.	Decreased sedation.
Cocaine:	Decreased antihistamine effect. Avoid.
Foods:	None expected.
Marijuana:	Excess sedation. Avoid.
Tobacco:	None expected.

DISULFIRAM

BRAND NAMES

Antabuse

BASIC INFORMATION

Habit forming? No
Prescription needed? Yes
Available as generic? Yes
Drug class: None

 USES

Treatment for alcoholism. Will not cure
alcoholism, but is a powerful deterrent to
drinking.

 DOSAGE & USAGE INFORMATION

How to take:
Tablet—Swallow with liquid.

When to take:
Morning or bedtime. Avoid if you have used *any*
alcohol, tonics, cough syrups, fermented vinegar,
after-shave lotion or backrub solutions within 12
hours.

If you forget a dose:
Take as soon as you remember up to 12 hours
late. If more than 12 hours, wait for next
scheduled dose (don't double this dose).

What drug does:
In combination with alcohol, produces a
metabolic change that causes severe,
temporary toxicity.

Time lapse before drug works:
3 to 12 hours.

Continued next column

 OVERDOSE

SYMPTOMS:
**Memory loss, behavior disturbances,
lethargy, confusion and headaches; nausea,
vomiting, stomach pain and diarrhea;
weakness and unsteady walk; temporary
paralysis.**
WHAT TO DO:
● **Dial 911 (emergency) or 0 (operator) for an
ambulance or medical help. Then give first
aid immediately.**
● **See emergency information at end of book.**

Don't take with:
● See Interaction column and consult doctor.
● Nonprescription drugs that contain *any*
alcohol.
● Any other central nervous system (CNS)
depressant drugs*.

 POSSIBLE ADVERSE REACTIONS OR SIDE EFFECTS

SYMPTOMS	WHAT TO DO
Life-threatening:	
In case of overdose, see previous column.	
Common:	
Drowsiness.	Continue. Tell doctor at next visit.
Infrequent:	
● Eye pain, vision changes, abdominal discomfort, throbbing headache, numbness in hands and feet.	Continue. Call doctor when convenient.
● Mood change, decreased sexual ability in men, tiredness.	Continue. Tell doctor at next visit.
● Bad taste in mouth (metal or garlic).	No action necessary.
Rare:	
Rash, jaundice.	Discontinue. Call doctor right away.

 WARNINGS & PRECAUTIONS

Don't take if:
● You are allergic to disulfiram (alcohol-
disulfiram combination is not an allergic
reaction).
● You have used alcohol in any form or amount
within 12 hours.
● You have taken paraldehyde within 1 week.
● You have heart disease.

Before you start, tell your doctor:
● If you have allergies.
● If you plan to become pregnant within
medication period.
● If no one has explained to you how disulfiram
reacts with alcohol.
● If you think you cannot avoid drinking.
● If you have diabetes, epilepsy, liver or kidney
disease.
● If you take other drugs.

Over age 60:
Adverse reactions and side effects may be more frequent and severe than in younger persons.

Pregnancy:
Decide with your doctor if drug benefits justify risk to unborn child. Risk category C (see page 47).

Breast-feeding:
Studies inconclusive. Consult your doctor.

Infants & children:
Not recommended.

Prolonged use:
Periodic blood cell counts and liver function tests recommended if you take this drug a long time.

Skin, sunlight & heat:
No problems expected.

Driving, piloting or hazardous work:
Avoid if you feel drowsy or have vision side effects. Otherwise, no restrictions.

Discontinuing:
Don't discontinue without consulting doctor. Dose may require gradual reduction if you have taken drug for a long time. Doses of other drugs may also require adjustment. Avoid alcohol at least 14 days following last dose.

Others:
- Check all liquids that you take or rub on for presence of alcohol.
- Advise any doctor or dentist whom you consult that you take this medicine.

POSSIBLE INTERACTION WITH OTHER DRUGS

GENERIC NAME OR DRUG CLASS	COMBINED EFFECT
Anticoagulants*	Possible unexplained bleeding.
Anticonvulsants*	Excessive sedation.
Barbiturates*	Excessive sedation.
Central nervous system (CNS) depressants*	Increased depressive effect.
Clozapine	Toxic effect on the central nervous system.
Guanfacine	May increase depressant effects of either drug.

Isoniazid	Unsteady walk and disturbed behavior.
Leucovorin	High alcohol content of leucovorin may cause disulfiram reaction*.
Methyprylon	Increased sedative effect, perhaps to dangerous level. Avoid.
Metronidazole	Disulfiram reaction*.
Nabilone	Greater depression of central nervous system.
Sedatives*	Excessive sedation.
Terfenadine	Increase terfenadine effect, possibly to dangerous level.
Theophylline	Increased theophylline effect; possibly toxic levels.

POSSIBLE INTERACTION WITH OTHER SUBSTANCES

INTERACTS WITH	COMBINED EFFECT
Alcohol: *Any* form or amount.	Possible life-threatening toxicity. See disulfiram reaction*.
Beverages: Punch or fruit drink that may contain alcohol.	Disulfiram reaction*.
Cocaine:	Increased disulfiram effect.
Foods: Sauces, fermented vinegar, marinades, desserts or other foods prepared with *any* alcohol.	Disulfiram reaction*.
Marijuana:	None expected.
Tobacco:	None expected.

FLUOXETINE

BRAND NAMES

Prozac

BASIC INFORMATION

Habit forming? No
Prescription needed? Yes
Available as generic? No
Drug class: Antidepressant (selective serotonin reuptake inhibitor)

 USES

- Treats mental depression, particularly in people who do not tolerate tricyclic antidepressants.
- Treats obsessive-compulsive disorder.
- Treats bulimia.
- May be used to treat obesity.

 DOSAGE & USAGE INFORMATION

How to take:
- Capsules—Swallow with liquid or food to lessen stomach irritation. If you can't swallow whole, open capsule and take with liquid or food.
- Oral solution—Follow instructions on prescription.

When to take:
In the morning at the same time each day.

If you forget a dose:
Take as soon as you remember up to 2 hours late. If more than 2 hours, wait for next scheduled dose (don't double this dose).

What drug does:
Affects serotonin, one of the chemicals in the brain called neurotransmitters, that plays a role in emotions and psychological disturbances.

Time lapse before drug works:
1 to 3 weeks.

Continued next column

 OVERDOSE

SYMPTOMS:
Seizures, agitation, violent vomiting.
WHAT TO DO:
- **Dial 911 (emergency) or 0 (operator) for an ambulance or medical help. Then give first aid immediately.**
- **See emergency information at end of book.**

Don't take with:
- Any monoamine oxidase (MAO) inhibitor* or within 14 days of stopping one. To do so may result in a serious or fatal reaction.
- Any other medicine without consulting your doctor or pharmacist.

 POSSIBLE ADVERSE REACTIONS OR SIDE EFFECTS

SYMPTOMS	WHAT TO DO
Life-threatening:	
Rash, itchy skin, breathing difficulty (allergic reaction), chest pain.	Seek emergency treatment immediately.
Common:	
Diarrhea, nervousness, drowsiness, headache, increased sweating, insomnia, anxiety.	Continue. Call doctor when convenient.
Infrequent:	
• Chills, fever, joint or muscle pain, enlarged lymph glands, unusual excitability, blurred vision, chest pain.	Discontinue. Call doctor right away.
• Nightmares, taste changes, vision changes, decreased sex drive, dry mouth, skin flushing, urinating frequently, painful menstruation, stuffy nose, tremors.	Continue. Call doctor when convenient.
Rare:	
• Seizures. (convulsions).	Discontinue. Seek emergency treatment.
• Fast heartbeat; abdominal pain; signs of low blood sugar (anxiety, nervousness, chills, increased sweating, difficulty concentrating).	Discontinue. Call doctor right away.
• Nausea, vomiting, constipation, cough, increased appetite.	Continue. Call doctor when convenient.

118

WARNINGS & PRECAUTIONS

Don't take if:
You are allergic to fluoxetine.

Before you start, tell your doctor:
- If you have a history of seizure disorders.
- If you have severe liver or kidney disease.

Over age 60:
Adverse reactions and side effects may be more frequent and severe than in younger persons. You may need smaller doses for shorter periods of time.

Pregnancy:
Don't take unless essential. Consult doctor. Risk category B (see page 47).

Breast-feeding:
Unknown effects. Consult doctor.

Children & adolescents:
Not recommended.

Prolonged use:
No problems expected, but stay under a doctor's care as long as you take this medicine.

Skin, sunlight & heat:
No problems expected.

Driving, piloting or hazardous work:
Don't drive or pilot aircraft until you learn how medicine affects you. Don't work around dangerous machinery. Don't climb ladders or work in high places. Danger increases if you drink alcohol or take medicine affecting alertness and reflexes.

Discontinuing:
Don't discontinue without consulting doctor. Dose may require gradual reduction if you have taken drug for a long time. Doses of other drugs may also require adjustment.

Others:
- Advise any doctor or dentist whom you consult about the use of this medicine.
- For dry mouth, suck on sugarless hard candy or chew sugarless gum. If dry mouth persists, see your dentist.

POSSIBLE INTERACTION WITH OTHER DRUGS

GENERIC NAME OR DRUG CLASS	COMBINED EFFECT
Anticoagulants, oral*	Increased risk of bleeding.
Anticonvulsants*	Increased risk of anticonvulsant toxicity.
Antidepressants, tricyclic*	Increased levels of tricyclic antidepressant; possible toxicity.
Central nervous system (CNS) depressants*	Increased depressant effects of both drugs.
Clozapine	Increased risk of adverse clozapine reactions.
Lithium	Risk of increased lithium effect.
Monoamine oxidase (MAO) inhibitors*	May cause confusion, agitation, convulsions, high blood pressure. Possibly life-threatening. Allow 4-5 weeks between use of these drugs.
Selegiline	Increased risk of adverse effects. May lead to convulsions and hypertensive crisis. Let 14 days elapse between taking the 2 drugs.

POSSIBLE INTERACTION WITH OTHER SUBSTANCES

INTERACTS WITH	COMBINED EFFECT
Alcohol:	Possible toxicity of both drugs. Avoid.
Beverages:	Decreases effect of fluoxetine.
Cocaine:	Decreases effect of fluoxetine.
Foods:	None expected.
Marijuana:	Decreases effect of fluoxetine.
Tobacco:	Decreases effect of fluoxetine.

*See Glossary

FLUVOXAMINE

BRAND NAMES

Luvox

BASIC INFORMATION

Habit forming? No
Prescription needed? Yes
Available as generic? No
Drug class: Antiobsessional agent

 USES

- Used to relieve the symptoms of obsessive-compulsive disorder (OCD), including recurrent disturbing thoughts (obsessions) and/or repetitive, ritualized behaviors (compulsions).
- Treatment for other disorders as determined by your doctor.

 DOSAGE & USAGE INFORMATION

How to take:
Tablet–Swallow with liquid. May be taken with or without food.

When to take:
1 dose a day–Take at bedtime. 2 doses a day–Take one at bedtime and one in the morning. Dosages may be increased gradually every 4-7 days to achieve maximum benefits.

If you forget a dose:
- 1 dose a day–Skip the missed dose and wait for the next scheduled dose (don't double this dose).
- 2 doses a day–Take as soon as you remember if it is almost time for the next dose, then skip the missed dose and wait for your next scheduled dose (don't double this dose).

What drug does:
Affects serotonin, one of the chemicals in the brain called neurotransmitters, that plays a role in emotions and psychological disturbances.

Continued next column

 OVERDOSE

SYMPTOMS:
Diarrhea, dizziness, drowsiness, vomiting, slow or irregular heartbeat, seizures, breathing difficulty, coma.
WHAT TO DO:
- **Dial 911 (emergency) or 0 (operator) for an ambulance or medical help. Then give first aid immediately.**
- **See emergency information at end of book.**

Time lapse before drug works:
May take several weeks for full effectiveness.

Don't take with:
- Any other medication without consulting your doctor or pharmacist.
- Any monoamine oxidase (MAO) inhibitor* or within 14 days of stopping one. May result in a serious or fatal reaction.
- See Interaction column and consult doctor.

 POSSIBLE ADVERSE REACTIONS OR SIDE EFFECTS

SYMPTOMS	WHAT TO DO
Life-threatening:	
In case of overdose, see previous column.	
Common:	
• Diarrhea, dizziness, nervousness, unusual tiredness or weakness, twitching or jerking movements, impotence, loss of sexual desire.	Discontinue. Call doctor right away.
• Constipation, dry mouth, drowsiness, headache, nausea, runny nose, trouble sleeping, loss of appetite, heartburn, flushing, increased sweating, weight loss, frequent urination, taste changes.	Continue. Call doctor when convenient.
• Yawning.	No action necessary.
Infrequent:	
• Mood or behavior changes, agitation, blurred vision, fast or pounding heartbeat, urination problems, skin rash or hives, uncontrolled excitable behavior, breathing problems, vomiting, shakiness, trouble swallowing, anxiety, forgetfulness.	Discontinue. Call doctor right away.
• Chills, swelling of hands or feet, gas, weight gain.	Continue. Call doctor when convenient.

Rare:

Unusual bleeding or bruising, chest pain, cold hands or feet, restlessness, clumsiness or unsteadiness, unusual feeling of well-being, hallucinations, eye problems, sensitivity to light, black or tarry stools, bloody vomit, swollen glands, menstrual changes.

Discontinue. Call doctor right away.

WARNINGS & PRECAUTIONS

Don't take if:
You are allergic to fluvoxamine.

Before you start, tell your doctor:
- If you have a seizure disorder, heart disease, kidney or liver disease.
- If you have or have had a history of drug dependence or drug abuse.
- If you have a history of mood disorders or thoughts of suicide.
- If you are allergic to any other medication, food or other substance.

Over age 60:
Adverse reactions and side effects may be more frequent and severe than in younger persons. Lower dosages may to be prescribed.

Pregnancy:
Decide with your doctor if drug benefits justify risks to unborn child. Risk category C (see page 47).

Breast-feeding:
Drug passes into milk. Avoid drug or discontinue nursing until you finish medicine. Consult doctor for advice on maintaining milk supply.

Children & adolescents:
Not recommended for children under age 18.

Prolonged use:
No special problems expected. Schedule regular doctor visits to determine if drug is continuing to be effective in controlling symptoms of OCD.

Skin, sunlight & heat:
May cause rash or intensify sunburn in areas exposed to sun or ultraviolet light (photosensitivity). Avoid overexposure and use sunscreen. Consult doctor if reaction occurs.

Driving, piloting or hazardous work:
Don't drive or pilot aircraft until you learn how medicine affects you. Don't work around dangerous machinery. Don't climb ladders or work in high places. Danger increases if you drink alcohol or take other medicines affecting alertness and reflexes such as antihistamines, tranquilizers, sedatives, pain medicine, narcotics and mind-altering drugs.

Discontinuing:
Since obsessive-compulsive disorder is a chronic condition, you may have a recurrence of symptoms if drug is discontinued.

Others:
Advise any doctor or dentist whom you consult that you take this medicine.

POSSIBLE INTERACTION WITH OTHER DRUGS

GENERIC NAME OR DRUG CLASS	COMBINED EFFECT
Anticoagulants, oral*	Increased risk of bleeding.
Antidepressants, tricyclic*	Increased antidepressant effect.
Astemizole	Serious heart problems. Avoid.
Benzodiazepines*	Increased benzodiazepine effect.
Beta-adrenergic blocking agents*	Increased beta blocker effect.
Carbamazepine	Possible toxicity of carbamazepine.
Clozapine	Increased risk of adverse reactions.
Lithium	Increased risk of seizures.
Methadone	Increased methadone effect.
Monoamine oxidase (MAO) inhibitors*	Potentially life-threatening. Allow 14 days between use of 2 drugs.

Continued on page 174

POSSIBLE INTERACTION WITH OTHER SUBSTANCES

INTERACTS WITH	COMBINED EFFECT
Alcohol:	Unknown. Avoid.
Beverages:	None expected.
Cocaine:	Unknown. Avoid.
Foods:	None expected.
Marijuana:	Increased sedation. Avoid.
Tobacco:	Decreased fluvoxamine effect.

*See Glossary

HALOPERIDOL

BRAND NAMES

Apo-Haloperidol	Halperon
Haldol	Novo-Peridol
Haldol Decanoate	Peridol
Haldol LA	PMS Haloperidol

BASIC INFORMATION

Habit forming? No
Prescription needed? Yes
Available as generic? Yes
Drug class: Antipsychotic

 ## USES

- Reduces severe anxiety, agitation and psychotic behavior.
- Treatment for Tourette's syndrome
- Treatment for infantile autism.
- Treatment for Huntington's chorea.

 ## DOSAGE & USAGE INFORMATION

How to take:
- Tablet—Swallow with liquid. If you can't swallow whole, crumble tablet and take with liquid or food.
- Drops—Dilute dose in beverage before swallowing.

When to take:
At the same times each day.

Continued next column

 ## OVERDOSE

SYMPTOMS:
Weak, rapid pulse; shallow, slow breathing; tremor or muscle weakness; very low blood pressure; convulsions; deep sleep ending in coma.
WHAT TO DO:
- Dial 911 (emergency) or 0 (operator) for an ambulance or medical help. Then give first aid immediately.
- If patient is unconscious and not breathing, give mouth-to-mouth breathing. If there is no heartbeat, use cardiac massage and mouth-to-mouth breathing (CPR). Don't try to make patient vomit. If you can't get help quickly, take patient to nearest emergency facility.
- See emergency information at end of book.

If you forget a dose:
Take as soon as you remember up to 2 hours late. If more than 2 hours, wait for next scheduled dose (don't double this dose).

What drug does:
Corrects an imbalance in nerve impulses from brain; blocks effect of dopamine*.

Time lapse before drug works:
Up to 4 weeks.

Don't take with:
- Nonprescription drugs without consulting doctor.
- Any other medicine without consulting your doctor or pharmacist.

 ## POSSIBLE ADVERSE REACTIONS OR SIDE EFFECTS

SYMPTOMS	WHAT TO DO
Life-threatening: High fever, rapid pulse, profuse sweating, muscle rigidity, confusion and irritability, seizures.	Discontinue. Seek emergency treatment.
Common: • Jerky or involuntary movements, especially of the face, lips, jaw, tongue; slow-frequency tremor of head or limbs, especially while moving; muscle rigidity, lack of facial expression and slow inflexible movements.	Discontinue. Call doctor right away.
• Pacing or restlessness; intermittent spasms of muscles of face, eyes, tongue, jaw, neck, body or limbs.	Continue. Call doctor when convenient.
Infrequent: Dry mouth, blurred vision, constipation, difficulty urinating; sedation, low blood pressure, dizziness.	Continue. Call doctor when convenient.
Rare: Other symptoms not listed above.	Continue. Call doctor when convenient.

WARNINGS & PRECAUTIONS

Don't take if:
- You have ever been allergic to haloperidol.
- You are depressed.
- You have Parkinson's disease.
- Patient is younger than 3 years old.

Before you start, tell your doctor:
- If you take sedatives, sleeping pills, tranquilizers, antidepressants, antihistamines, narcotics or mind-altering drugs.
- If you have a history of mental depression.
- If you have had kidney or liver problems.
- If you have diabetes, epilepsy, glaucoma, high blood pressure or heart disease, prostate trouble, overactive thyroid or asthma.
- If you drink alcoholic beverages frequently.

Over age 60:
Adverse reactions and side effects may be more frequent and severe than in younger persons.

Pregnancy:
Decide with your doctor if drug benefits justify risk to unborn child. Risk category C (see page 47).

Breast-feeding:
Drug passes into milk. Avoid drug or discontinue nursing until you finish medicine. Consult doctor about maintaining milk supply.

Children & adolescents:
Not recommended. Side effects may be more common.

Prolonged use:
- May develop tardive dyskinesia (involuntary movements of jaws, lips and tongue).
- Talk to your doctor about the need for follow-up medical examinations or laboratory studies to check blood pressure, liver function.

Skin, sunlight & heat:
- May cause rash or intensify sunburn in areas exposed to sun or ultraviolet light (photosensitivity). Avoid overexposure and use sunscreen. Consult doctor if reaction occurs.
- Avoid getting overheated. The drug affects body temperature and sweating.

Driving, piloting or hazardous work:
Don't drive or pilot aircraft until you learn how medicine affects you. Don't work around dangerous machinery. Don't climb ladders or work in high places. Danger increases if you drink alcohol or take medicine affecting alertness and reflexes.

Discontinuing:
Don't discontinue without consulting doctor. Dose may require gradual reduction if you have taken drug for a long time. Doses of other drugs may also require adjustment.

Others:
- For dry mouth, suck on sugarless hard candy or chew sugarless gum. If dry mouth persists, consult your dentist
- Advise any doctor or dentist whom you consult that you take this medicine.

POSSIBLE INTERACTION WITH OTHER DRUGS

GENERIC NAME OR DRUG CLASS	COMBINED EFFECT
Anticholinergics*	Increased anticholinergic effect. May cause elevated pressure within the eye.
Anticonvulsants*	Changed seizure pattern.
Antidepressants*	Excessive sedation.
Antihistamines*	Excessive sedation.
Antihypertensives*	May cause severe blood pressure drop.
Barbiturates*	Excessive sedation.
Bupropion	Increased risk of major seizures.
Central nervous system (CNS) depressants*	Increased CNS depression; increased blood pressure drop.
Clozapine	Toxic effect on the nervous system.

Continued on page 174

POSSIBLE INTERACTION WITH OTHER SUBSTANCES

INTERACTS WITH	COMBINED EFFECT
Alcohol:	Excessive sedation and depressed brain function. Avoid.
Beverages:	None expected.
Cocaine:	Decreased effect of haloperidol. Avoid.
Foods:	None expected.
Marijuana:	Occasional use—Increased sedation. Frequent use—Possible toxic psychosis.
Tobacco:	None expected.

*See Glossary

HYDROXYZINE

BRAND NAMES

See complete list of brand and generic names in the *Brand and Generic Name Directory*, page 170.

BASIC INFORMATION

Habit forming? No
Prescription needed? Yes
Available as generic? Yes
Drug class: Tranquilizer, antihistamine

 ## USES

- Treatment for anxiety, tension and agitation.
- Relieves itching from allergic reactions.

 ## DOSAGE & USAGE INFORMATION

How to take:
- Tablet, syrup or capsule—Swallow with liquid. If you can't swallow whole, crumble tablet or open capsule and take with liquid or food.
- Liquid—If desired, dilute dose in beverage before swallowing.

When to take:
At the same times each day.

If you forget a dose:
Take as soon as you remember up to 2 hours late. If more than 2 hours, wait for next scheduled dose (don't double this dose).

What drug does:
Blocks action of histamine after an allergic response triggers histamine release. Histamines cause itching, sneezing, runny nose and eyes and other symptoms.

Time lapse before drug works:
15 to 30 minutes.

Don't take with:
Any other medicine without consulting your doctor or pharmacist.

 ## OVERDOSE

SYMPTOMS:
Drowsiness, unsteadiness, agitation, purposeless movements, tremor, convulsions.
WHAT TO DO:
- Dial 911 (emergency) or 0 (operator) for an ambulance or medical help. Then give first aid immediately.
- See emergency information at end of book.

 ## POSSIBLE ADVERSE REACTIONS OR SIDE EFFECTS

SYMPTOMS	WHAT TO DO
Life-threatening: In case of overdose, see previous column.	
Common: Drowsiness; dizziness; dryness of mouth, nose or throat; nausea.	Continue. Call doctor when convenient.
Infrequent: • Change in vision, clumsiness, rash.	Discontinue. Call doctor right away.
• Less tolerance for contact lenses, painful or difficult urination.	Continue. Call doctor when convenient.
• Appetite loss.	Continue. Tell doctor at next visit.
Rare: Nightmares, agitation, irritability, sore throat, fever, rapid heartbeat, unusual bleeding or bruising, fatigue, weakness, confusion, fainting, seizures.	Discontinue. Call doctor right away.

 ## WARNINGS & PRECAUTIONS

Don't take if:
You are allergic to any antihistamine.

Before you start, tell your doctor:
- If you have asthma or kidney disease.
- If you will have surgery within 2 months, including dental surgery, requiring general or spinal anesthesia.

Over age 60:
- Adverse reactions and side effects may be more frequent and severe than in younger persons.
- Drug likely to increase urination difficulty caused by enlarged prostate gland.

Pregnancy:
Decide with your doctor if drug benefits justify risk to unborn child. Risk category C (see page 47).

Breast-feeding:
Drug passes into milk. Avoid drug or discontinue nursing until you finish medicine. Consult doctor for advice on maintaining milk supply.

Children & adolescents:
Use only under medical supervision.

Prolonged use:
Tolerance* develops and reduces effectiveness.

Skin, sunlight & heat:
No problems expected.

Driving, piloting or hazardous work:
Don't drive or pilot aircraft until you learn how medicine affects you. Don't work around dangerous machinery. Don't climb ladders or work in high places. Danger increases if you drink alcohol or take medicine affecting alertness and reflexes, such as antihistamines, tranquilizers, sedatives, pain medicine, narcotics and mind-altering drugs.

Discontinuing:
Don't discontinue without consulting doctor. Dose may require gradual reduction if you have taken drug for a long time. Doses of other drugs may also require adjustment.

Others:
Advise any doctor or dentist whom you consult that you take this medicine.

POSSIBLE INTERACTION WITH OTHER DRUGS

GENERIC NAME OR DRUG CLASS	COMBINED EFFECT
Antidepressants, tricyclic*	Increased effects of both drugs.
Antihistamines*	Increased hydroxyzine effect.
Attapulgite	Decreased hydroxyzine effect.
Carteolol	Decreased antihistamine effect.
Central nervous system (CNS) depressants*	Greater depression of central nervous system.
Clozapine	Toxic effect on the central nervous system.
Fluoxetine	Increased depressant effects of both drugs.
Guanfacine	May increase depressant effects of either drug.
Leucovorin	High alcohol content of leucovorin may cause adverse effects.
Narcotics*	Increased effects of both drugs.
Pain relievers*	Increased effects of both drugs.
Sertraline	Increased depressive effects of both drugs.
Sotalol	Increased antihistamine effect.

POSSIBLE INTERACTION WITH OTHER SUBSTANCES

INTERACTS WITH	COMBINED EFFECT
Alcohol:	Increased sedation and intoxication. Use with caution.
Beverages: Caffeine drinks.	Decreased tranquilizer effect of hydroxyzine.
Cocaine:	Decreased hydroxyzine effect. Avoid.
Foods:	None expected.
Marijuana:	None expected.
Tobacco:	None expected.

LITHIUM

BRAND NAMES

Carbolith	Lithane
Cibalith-S	Lithizine
Duralith	Lithobid
Eskalith	Lithonate
Eskalith CR	Lithotabs

BASIC INFORMATION

Habit forming? No
Prescription needed? Yes
Available as generic? Yes
Drug class: Mood stabilizer

 USES

- Normalizes mood and behavior in bipolar (manic-depressive) disorder.
- Treats alcohol toxicity and addiction.
- Treats schizoid personality disorders.

 DOSAGE & USAGE INFORMATION

How to take:
- Tablet or capsule—Swallow with liquid or food to lessen stomach irritation. If you can't swallow whole, crumble tablet or open capsule and take with liquid or food. Drink 2 or 3 quarts liquid per day, especially in hot weather.
- Extended-release tablets—Swallow each dose whole. Do not crush.
- Syrup—Take at mealtime. Follow with 8 oz. water.

When to take:
At the same times each day, preferably at mealtime.

If you forget a dose:
Take as soon as you remember up to 2 hours late. If more than 2 hours, wait for next scheduled dose (don't double this dose).

Continued next column

 OVERDOSE

SYMPTOMS:
Moderate overdose increases some side effects and may cause diarrhea, nausea. Large overdose may cause vomiting, muscle weakness, convulsions, stupor and coma.
WHAT TO DO:
- Dial 911 (emergency) or 0 (operator) for an ambulance or medical help. Then give first aid immediately.
- See emergency information at end of book.

What drug does:
May correct chemical imbalance in brain's transmission of nerve impulses that influence mood and behavior.

Time lapse before drug works:
1 to 3 weeks. May require 3 months before depressive phase of illness improves.

Don't take with:
Any other medication without consulting your doctor or pharmacist.

 POSSIBLE ADVERSE REACTIONS OR SIDE EFFECTS

SYMPTOMS	WHAT TO DO
Life-threatening:	
In case of overdose, see previous column.	
Common:	
• Dizziness, diarrhea, nausea, vomiting, shakiness, tremor.	Continue. Call doctor when convenient.
• Dry mouth, thirst, decreased sexual ability, increased urination, anorexia.	Continue. Tell doctor at next visit.
Infrequent:	
• Rash, stomach pain, fainting, heartbeat irregularities, shortness of breath, ear noises.	Discontinue. Call doctor right away.
• Swollen hands, feet; slurred speech; thyroid impairment (coldness; dry, puffy skin); muscle aches; headache; weight gain; fatigue; menstrual irregularities, acnelike eruptions.	Continue. Call doctor when convenient.
• Drowsiness, confusion, weakness.	Continue. Tell doctor at next visit.
Rare:	
• Blurred vision, eye pain.	Discontinue. Call doctor right away.
• Jerking of arms and legs, worsening of psoriasis, hair loss.	Continue. Call doctor when convenient.

 WARNINGS & PRECAUTIONS

Don't take if:
- You are allergic to lithium or tartrazine dye.
- You have kidney or heart disease.
- Patient is younger than 12.

Before you start, tell your doctor:
- About all medications you take.
- If you plan to become pregnant within medication period.

- If you have diabetes, low thyroid function, epilepsy or any significant medical problem.
- If you are on a low-salt diet or drink more than 4 cups of coffee per day.
- If you plan surgery within 2 months.

Over age 60:
Adverse reactions and side effects may be more frequent and severe than in younger persons.

Pregnancy:
Some fetal risk, but benefits may outweigh risks. Risk category D (see page 47).

Breast-feeding:
Drug passes into milk. Avoid drug or discontinue nursing until you finish medicine. Consult doctor for advice on maintaining milk supply.

Children & adolescents:
Don't give to children younger than 12.

Prolonged use:
- Enlarged thyroid with possible impaired function.
- Talk to your doctor about the need for follow-up medical examinations or laboratory studies to check lithium levels, ECG*, kidney function, thyroid, complete blood counts (white blood cell count, platelet count, red blood cell count, hemoglobin, hematocrit).

Skin, sunlight & heat:
No problems expected.

Driving, piloting or hazardous work:
Don't drive or pilot aircraft until you learn how medicine affects you. Don't work around dangerous machinery. Don't climb ladders or work in high places. Danger increases if you drink alcohol or take medicine affecting alertness and reflexes.

Discontinuing:
Don't discontinue without consulting doctor. Dose may require gradual reduction if you have taken drug for a long time. Doses of other drugs may also require adjustment. Quitting this medication when feeling well creates risk of relapse which may not respond to restarting the medication.

Others:
- Regular checkups, periodic blood tests, and tests of lithium levels and thyroid function recommended.
- Avoid exercise in hot weather and other activities that cause heavy sweating. This contributes to lithium poisoning. It is essential to take adequate fluids during hot weather to avoid toxicity.
- Call your doctor if you have an illness that causes heavy sweating, vomiting, or diarrhea. The loss of too much salt and water from your body could cause lithium toxicity.
- Advise any doctor or dentist whom you consult that you take this medicine.
- Some products contain tartrazine dye. Avoid, especially if allergic to aspirin.

POSSIBLE INTERACTION WITH OTHER DRUGS

GENERIC NAME OR DRUG CLASS	COMBINED EFFECT
Acetazolamide	Decreased lithium effect.
Antihistamines*	Possible excessive sedation.
Anti-inflammatory drugs, nonsteroidal (NSAIDs)*	Increased toxic effect of lithium.
Bupropion	Increased risk of major seizures.
Carbamazepine	Increased lithium effect.
Desmopressin	Possible decreased desmopressin effect.
Diazepam	Possible hypothermia.
Diclofenac	Possible increase in effect and toxicity.
Didanosine	Increased risk of peripheral neuropathy.
Diuretics*	Increased lithium effect or toxicity.

Continued on page 174

POSSIBLE INTERACTION WITH OTHER SUBSTANCES

INTERACTS WITH	COMBINED EFFECT
Alcohol:	Possible lithium poisoning.
Beverages: Caffeine drinks.	Decreased lithium effect.
Cocaine:	Possible psychosis.
Foods: Salt.	High intake could decrease lithium effect. Low intake could increase lithium effect. *Don't* restrict intake.
Marijuana:	Increased tremor and possible psychosis.
Tobacco:	None expected.

---

*See Glossary

LOXAPINE

BRAND NAMES

Loxapac   Loxitane C
Loxitane

BASIC INFORMATION

Habit forming? No
Prescription needed? Yes
Available as generic? Yes
Drug class: Tranquilizer, antidepressant

USES

- Treats serious mental illness.
- Treats anxiety and depression.

DOSAGE & USAGE INFORMATION

How to take:
- Oral solution—Take after meals with liquid to decrease stomach irritation.
- Tablets—Swallow with liquid or food to lessen stomach irritation. If you can't swallow whole, crumble tablet and take with liquid or food.
- Capsules—Swallow with liquid or food to lessen stomach irritation. If you can't swallow whole, open capsule and take with liquid or food.

When to take:
At the same times each day, according to instructions on prescription label.

If you forget a dose:
Take as soon as you remember up to 2 hours late. If more than 2 hours, wait for next scheduled dose (don't double this dose).

What drug does:
Probably blocks the effects of dopamine* in the brain.

Time lapse before drug works:
1/2 to 3 hours.

Don't take with:
Any other medicine without consulting your doctor or pharmacist.

OVERDOSE

SYMPTOMS:
Dizziness, drowsiness, severe shortness of breath, muscle spasms, coma.
WHAT TO DO:
- **Dial 911 (emergency) or 0 (operator) for an ambulance or medical help. Then give first aid immediately.**
- **See emergency information at end of book.**

POSSIBLE ADVERSE REACTIONS OR SIDE EFFECTS

SYMPTOMS	WHAT TO DO
Life-threatening: Severe shortness of breath, skin rash, heartbeat irregularities, profuse sweating, fever, convulsions (rare).	Seek emergency treatment immediately.
Common: • Increased dental problems because of dry mouth and less salivation.	Consult your dentist about a prevention program.
• Swallowing difficulty, expressionless face, stiff arms and legs, dizziness.	Discontinue. Call doctor right away.
Infrequent: • Chewing movements with lip smacking, loss of balance, shuffling walk, tremor of fingers and hands, uncontrolled tongue movements.	Discontinue. Call doctor right away.
• Constipation, difficult urination, blurred vision, confusion, loss of sex drive, headache, insomnia, menstrual irregularities, weight gain, light sensitivity, nausea.	Continue. Call doctor when convenient.
Rare: Rapid heartbeat, fever, sore throat, jaundice, unusual bleeding.	Discontinue. Call doctor right away.

WARNINGS & PRECAUTIONS

Don't take if:
- You are an alcoholic.
- You have liver disease.

Before you start, tell your doctor:
- If you have a seizure disorder.
- If you have an enlarged prostate, glaucoma, Parkinson's disease, heart disease.

Over age 60:
Adverse reactions and side effects may be more frequent and severe than in younger persons. You may need smaller doses for shorter periods of time.

Pregnancy:
Decide with your doctor if drug benefits justify risk to unborn child. Risk category C (see page 47).

Breast-feeding:
Drug may pass into milk. Avoid drug or discontinue nursing until you finish medicine. Consult doctor for advice on maintaining milk supply.

Children & adolescents:
Not recommended.

Prolonged use:
Talk to your doctor about the need for follow-up medical examinations or laboratory studies to check complete blood counts (white blood cell count, platelet count, red blood cell count, hemoglobin, hematocrit), liver function, eyes.

Skin, sunlight & heat:
May cause rash or intensify sunburn in areas exposed to sun or ultraviolet light (photosensitivity reaction). Avoid overexposure and use sunscreen. Notify doctor if reaction occurs.

Driving, piloting or hazardous work:
Don't drive or pilot aircraft until you learn how medicine affects you. Don't work around dangerous machinery. Don't climb ladders or work in high places. Danger increases if you drink alcohol or take medicine affecting alertness and reflexes.

Discontinuing:
- Don't discontinue without consulting doctor. Dose may require gradual reduction if you have taken drug for a long time. Doses of other drugs may also require adjustment.
- These symptoms may occur after medicine has been discontinued: dizziness; nausea; abdominal pain; uncontrolled movements of mouth, tongue and jaw.

Others:
Use careful oral hygiene.

POSSIBLE INTERACTION WITH OTHER DRUGS

GENERIC NAME OR DRUG CLASS	COMBINED EFFECT
Anticonvulsants*	Decreased effect of anticonvulsant.
Antidepressants, tricyclic*	May increase toxic effects of both drugs.
Bupropion	Increased risk of major seizures.
Central nervous system (CNS) depressants*	Increased sedative effects of both drugs.
Clozapine	Toxic effect on the central nervous system.
Epinephrine	Rapid heart rate and severe drop in blood pressure.

Extrapyramidal reaction*-causing drugs	Increased risk of side effects.
Fluoxetine	Increased depressant effects of both drugs.
Guanadrel	Decreased effect of guanadrel.
Guanethidine	Decreased effect of guanethidine.
Guanfacine	Increased effects of both drugs.
Haloperidol	May increase toxic effects of both drugs.
Leucovorin	High alcohol content of leucovorin may cause adverse effects.
Methyldopa	May increase toxic effects of both drugs.
Metoclopramide	May increase toxic effects of both drugs.
Molindone	May increase toxic effects of both drugs.
Pemoline	Increased central nervous stimulation.
Pergolide	Decreased pergolide effect.
Phenothiazines*	May increase toxic effects of both drugs.
Pimozide	May increase toxic effects of both drugs.

Continued on page 175

POSSIBLE INTERACTION WITH OTHER SUBSTANCES

INTERACTS WITH	COMBINED EFFECT
Alcohol:	May decrease effect of loxapine. Avoid.
Beverages:	None expected.
Cocaine:	May increase toxicity of both drugs. Avoid.
Foods:	None expected.
Marijuana:	May increase toxicity of both drugs. Avoid.
Tobacco:	May increase toxicity.

*See Glossary

MAPROTILINE

BRAND NAMES

Ludiomil

BASIC INFORMATION

Habit forming? No
Prescription needed? Yes
Available as generic? Yes
Drug class: Antidepressant

 USES

Treatment for depression or anxiety associated with depression.

 DOSAGE & USAGE INFORMATION

How to take:
Tablet—Swallow with liquid.

When to take:
At the same time each day, usually bedtime.

If you forget a dose:
Bedtime dose—If you forget your once-a-day bedtime dose, don't take it more than 3 hours late. If more than 3 hours, wait for next scheduled dose. Don't double this dose.

What drug does:
Probably affects part of brain that controls messages between nerve cells.

Time lapse before drug works:
Begins in 1 to 2 weeks. May require 4 to 6 weeks for maximum benefit.

Continued next column

 OVERDOSE

SYMPTOMS:
Respiratory failure, fever, cardiac arrhythmia, muscle stiffness, drowsiness, hallucinations, convulsions, coma.
WHAT TO DO:
- **Dial 911 (emergency) or 0 (operator) for an ambulance or medical help. Then give first aid immediately.**
- **If patient is unconscious and not breathing, give mouth-to-mouth breathing. If there is no heartbeat, use cardiac massage and mouth-to-mouth breathing (CPR). Don't try to make patient vomit. If you can't get help quickly, take patient to nearest emergency facility.**
- **See emergency information at end of book.**

Don't take with:
- Nonprescription drugs without consulting your doctor or pharmacist.
- See Interaction column and consult doctor.

 POSSIBLE ADVERSE REACTIONS OR SIDE EFFECTS

SYMPTOMS	WHAT TO DO
Life-threatening:	
Seizures.	Seek emergency treatment immediately.
Common:	
• Tremor.	Discontinue. Call doctor right away.
• Headache, dry mouth or unpleasant taste, constipation or diarrhea, nausea, indigestion, fatigue, weakness, drowsiness, nervousness, anxiety, excessive sweating.	Continue. Call doctor when convenient.
• Insomnia, craving sweets.	Continue. Tell doctor at next visit.
Infrequent:	
• Hallucinations, shakiness, dizziness, fainting, blurred vision, eye pain, vomiting, irregular heartbeat or slow pulse, inflamed tongue, abdominal pain, jaundice, hair loss, rash, chills, joint pain, palpitations, hiccups, vision changes.	Discontinue. Call doctor right away.
• Painful or difficult urination; fatigue; decreased sex drive; abnormal dreams; nasal congestion; back pain; muscle aches; frequent urination; painful, absent or irregular menstruation.	Continue. Call doctor when convenient.
Rare:	
Itchy skin; sore throat; jaundice; fever; involuntary movements of jaw, lips and tongue; nightmares; confusion; swollen breasts in men.	Discontinue. Call doctor right away.

WARNINGS & PRECAUTIONS

Don't take if:
- You are allergic to tricyclic antidepressants.
- You drink alcohol.
- You have had a heart attack within 6 weeks.
- You have glaucoma.
- You have taken a monoamine oxidase (MAO) inhibitor* within 2 weeks.

Before you start, tell your doctor:
- If you will have surgery within 2 months, including dental surgery, requiring general or spinal anesthesia.
- If you have an enlarged prostate, heart disease or high blood pressure, stomach or intestinal problems, overactive thyroid, asthma, liver disease, schizophrenia, urinary retention, respiratory disorders, seizure disorders, diabetes, kidney disease.

Over age 60:
More likely to develop urination difficulty and side effects such as hallucinations, shakiness, dizziness, fainting, headache or insomnia.

Pregnancy:
Consult doctor. Risk category B (see page 47).

Breast-feeding:
Drug passes into milk. Avoid drug or discontinue nursing until you finish medicine. Consult doctor for advice on maintaining milk supply.

Children & adolescents:
Don't give to children younger than 12.

Prolonged use:
Request blood cell counts, liver function studies; monitor blood pressure closely.

Skin, sunlight & heat:
May cause rash or intensify sunburn in areas exposed to sun or ultraviolet light (photosensitivity reaction). Avoid overexposure and use sunscreen. Notify doctor if reaction occurs.

Driving, piloting or hazardous work:
Don't drive or pilot aircraft until you learn how medicine affects you. Don't work around dangerous machinery. Don't climb ladders or work in high places. Danger increases if you drink alcohol or take medicine affecting alertness and reflexes.

Discontinuing:
Don't discontinue without consulting doctor. Dose may require gradual reduction if you have taken drug for a long time. Doses of other drugs may also require adjustment.

Others:
- Advise any doctor or dentist whom you consult that you take this drug.
- For dry mouth, suck sugarless hard candy or chew sugarless gum. If dry mouth persists, consult your dentist.

POSSIBLE INTERACTION WITH OTHER DRUGS

GENERIC NAME OR DRUG CLASS	COMBINED EFFECT
Anticholinergics*	Increased sedation.
Antihistamines*	Increased antihistamine effect.
Barbiturates*	Decreased antidepressant effect.
Benzodiazepines*	Increased sedation.
Central nervous system (CNS) depressants*	Increased sedation.
Cimetidine	Possible increased antidepressant effect and toxicity.
Clonidine	Decreased clonidine effect.
Clozapine	Toxic effect on the central nervous system.
Disulfiram	Delirium.
Diuretics, thiazide*	Increased maprotiline effect.
Ethchlorvynol	Delirium.
Fluoxetine	Increased depressant effects of both drugs.
Guanethidine	Decreased guanethidine effect.

Continued on page 175

POSSIBLE INTERACTION WITH OTHER SUBSTANCES

INTERACTS WITH	COMBINED EFFECT
Alcohol: Beverages or medicines with alcohol.	Excessive intoxication. Avoid.
Beverages:	None expected.
Cocaine:	Excessive intoxication. Avoid.
Foods:	None expected.
Marijuana:	Excessive drowsiness. Avoid.
Tobacco:	May decrease absorption of maprotiline. Avoid.

*See Glossary

MEPROBAMATE

BRAND NAMES

See complete list of brand and generic names in the *Brand and Generic Name Directory*, page 170.

BASIC INFORMATION

Habit forming? Yes
Prescription needed? Yes
Available as generic? Yes
Drug class: Tranquilizer, antianxiety agent

USES

Reduces mild anxiety, tension and insomnia.

DOSAGE & USAGE INFORMATION

How to take:
• Tablet—Swallow with liquid.
• Extended-release capsules—Swallow each dose whole.

When to take:
At the same times each day.

If you forget a dose:
Take as soon as you remember up to 2 hours late. If more than 2 hours, wait for next scheduled dose (don't double this dose).

What drug does:
Sedates brain centers that control behavior and emotions.

Time lapse before drug works:
1 to 2 hours.

Don't take with:
• Nonprescription drugs containing alcohol or caffeine without consulting doctor.
• Any other medicine without consulting your doctor or pharmacist.

OVERDOSE

SYMPTOMS:
Dizziness, slurred speech, stagger, confusion, depressed breathing and heart function, stupor, coma.
WHAT TO DO:
• **Dial 911 (emergency) or 0 (operator) for an ambulance or medical help. Then give first aid immediately.**
• **See emergency information at end of book.**

POSSIBLE ADVERSE REACTIONS OR SIDE EFFECTS

SYMPTOMS	WHAT TO DO
Life-threatening: Hives, rash, intense itching, faintness soon after a dose, wheezing (anaphylaxis).	Seek emergency treatment immediately.
Common: Dizziness, confusion, agitation, drowsiness, unsteadiness, fatigue, weakness.	Continue. Tell doctor at next visit.
Infrequent: • Rash, hives, itchy skin; change in vision; diarrhea, nausea or vomiting.	Discontinue. Call doctor right away.
• False sense of well-being, headache, slurred speech, blurred vision.	Continue. Call doctor when convenient.
Rare: Sore throat; fever; rapid, pounding, unusually slow or irregular heartbeat; difficult breathing; unusual bleeding or bruising.	Discontinue. Call doctor right away.

WARNINGS & PRECAUTIONS

Don't take if:
- You are allergic to meprobamate, tybamate, carbromal or carisoprodol.
- You have had porphyria.
- Patient is younger than 6.

Before you start, tell your doctor:
- If you have epilepsy.
- If you have impaired liver or kidney function.
- If you have tartrazine dye allergy.
- If you suffer from drug abuse or alcoholism, active or in remission.
- If you have porphyria.

Over age 60:
Adverse reactions and side effects may be more frequent and severe than in younger persons.

Pregnancy:
Risk to unborn child outweighs drug benefits. Don't use. Risk category D (see page 47).

Breast-feeding:
Drug filters into milk. May cause sedation in child. Avoid.

Children & adolescents:
Not recommended.

Prolonged use:
- Habit forming.
- May impair blood cell production.

Skin, sunlight & heat:
No problems expected.

Driving, piloting or hazardous work:
Don't drive or pilot aircraft until you learn how medicine affects you. Don't work around dangerous machinery. Don't climb ladders or work in high places. Danger increases if you drink alcohol or take medicine affecting alertness and reflexes, such as antihistamines, tranquilizers, sedatives, pain medicine, narcotics and mind-altering drugs.

Discontinuing:
Don't discontinue without consulting doctor. Dose may require gradual reduction if you have taken drug for a long time. Doses of other drugs may also require adjustment. Report to your doctor any unusual symptom that begins in the first week you discontinue this medicine. These symptoms may include convulsions, confusion, nightmares, insomnia.

Others:
- Advise any doctor or dentist whom you consult that you take this drug.
- For dry mouth, suck sugarless hard candy or sugarless gum. If dry mouth persists, consult your dentist.

POSSIBLE INTERACTION WITH OTHER DRUGS

GENERIC NAME OR DRUG CLASS	COMBINED EFFECT
Addictive drugs*	Increased risk of addictive effect.
Antidepressants, tricyclic*	Increased antidepressant effect.
Antihistamines*	Possible excessive sedation.
Central nervous system (CNS) depressants*	Increased depressive effects of both drugs.
Monoamine oxidase (MAO) inhibitors*	Increased meprobamate effect.
Narcotics*	Increased narcotic effect.
Sertraline	Increased depressive effects of both drugs.

POSSIBLE INTERACTION WITH OTHER SUBSTANCES

INTERACTS WITH	COMBINED EFFECT
Alcohol:	Dangerous increased effect of meprobamate.
Beverages: Caffeine drinks.	Decreased calming effect of meprobamate.
Cocaine:	Decreased meprobamate effect.
Foods:	None expected.
Marijuana:	Increased sedative effect of meprobamate.
Tobacco:	None expected.

*See Glossary

METHYLPHENIDATE

BRAND NAMES

PMS Methylphenidate   Ritalin SR
Ritalin

BASIC INFORMATION

Habit forming? Yes
Prescription needed? Yes
Available as generic? Yes
Drug class: Central nervous system
  stimulant, sympathomimetic

 ## USES

- Decreases overactivity and lengthens attention span in children with attention-deficit
  hyperactivity disorder (ADHD). It is used as
  part of the total management plan that
  includes educational, social and psychological
  treatment.
- Treatment of depression in adults.
- Treatment for narcolepsy (uncontrollable
  attacks of sleepiness) and other disorders.

 ## DOSAGE & USAGE
INFORMATION

How to take:
- Tablet—Swallow with liquid or food to lessen
  stomach irritation. If you can't swallow whole,
  crumble tablet and take with liquid or small
  amount of food.
- Extended-release tablet—Swallow whole with
  liquid.

Continued next column

 ## OVERDOSE

SYMPTOMS:
Rapid heartbeat, fever, confusion, vomiting,
agitation, hallucinations, convulsions, coma.
WHAT TO DO:
- **Dial 911 (emergency) or 0 (operator) for an**
  ambulance or medical help. Then give first
  aid immediately.
- **If patient is unconscious and not**
  breathing, give mouth-to-mouth breathing.
  If there is no heartbeat, use cardiac
  massage and mouth-to-mouth breathing
  (CPR). Don't try to make patient vomit. If
  you can't get help quickly, take patient to
  nearest emergency facility.
- **See emergency information at end of book.**

When to take:
- At the same times each day, preferably on an
  empty stomach.
- Take extended-release tablet in the morning.
  Regular tablet often taken at breakfast and
  lunch. Don't take late in evening.

If you forget a dose:
Take as soon as you remember up to 2 hours
late. If more than 2 hours, wait for next
scheduled dose (don't double this dose).

What drug does:
Stimulates brain to improve alertness,
concentration and attention span. Calms the
hyperactive child.

Time lapse before drug works:
- 1 month or more for maximum effect on child.
- 30 minutes to stimulate adults.

Don't take with:
Any other medicine without consulting your
doctor or pharmacist.

 ## POSSIBLE
ADVERSE REACTIONS
OR SIDE EFFECTS

SYMPTOMS	WHAT TO DO
Life-threatening: In case of overdose, see previous column.	
Common: Nervousness, trouble sleeping, dizziness, nausea, appetite loss, headache, drowsiness, stomach pain, weight loss.	Continue. Call doctor when convenient.
Infrequent: Rash or hives; chest pain; fast, irregular heartbeat; unusual bruising; joint pain; psychosis; uncontrollable movements; unexplained fever.	Discontinue. Call doctor right away.
Rare: Blurred vision, other vision change, sore throat, unusual tiredness, convulsions.	Discontinue. Call doctor right away.

WARNINGS & PRECAUTIONS

Don't take if:
- You are allergic to methylphenidate.
- You have glaucoma.

Before you start, tell your doctor:
- If you have epilepsy.
- If you have high blood pressure.
- If you take MAO inhibitors*.
- If you have emotional or psychotic problems.
- If you have a history of drug abuse.

Over age 60:
Adverse reactions and side effects may be more frequent and severe than in younger persons.

Pregnancy:
Decide with your doctor if drug benefits justify risk to unborn child. Risk category C (see page 47).

Breast-feeding:
No proven problems. Consult doctor.

Children & adolescents:
Use only under medical supervision for children 6 or older. Don't give to child younger than 6.

Prolonged use:
- Rare possibility of physical growth retardation in children.
- Talk to your doctor about the need for follow-up medical examinations or laboratory studies to check blood pressure, complete blood counts (white blood cell count, platelet count, red blood cell count, hemoglobin, hematocrit), growth charts.

Skin, sunlight & heat:
No problems expected.

Driving, piloting or hazardous work:
No problems expected.

Discontinuing:
Don't discontinue abruptly. Don't discontinue without doctor's advice until you complete prescribed dose, even though symptoms diminish or disappear. Report to your doctor any new symptoms of depression, unusual behavior, unusual weakness or tiredness.

Others:
- Dose must be carefully adjusted by doctor.
- Advise any doctor or dentist whom you consult about the use of this medicine.

POSSIBLE INTERACTION WITH OTHER DRUGS

GENERIC NAME OR DRUG CLASS	COMBINED EFFECT
Anticholinergics*	Increased anticholinergic effect.
Anticoagulants*, oral	Increased anticoagulant effect.
Anticonvulsants*	Increased anticonvulsant effect.
Antidepressants, tricyclic*	Increased antidepressant effect. Decreased methylphenidate effect.
Antihypertensives*	Decreased antihypertensive effect.
Central nervous system (CNS) stimulants*	Overstimulation.
Cisapride	Decreased methylphenidate effect.
Dextrothyroxine	Increased methylphenidate effect.
Guanadrel	Decreased guanadrel effect.
Guanethidine	Decreased guanethidine effect.
Minoxidil	Decreased minoxidil effect.
Monoamine oxidase (MAO) inhibitors*	Dangerous rise in blood pressure.
Nitrates*	Possible decreased effects of both drugs.
Pimozide	May mask the cause of tics.

POSSIBLE INTERACTION WITH OTHER SUBSTANCES

INTERACTS WITH	COMBINED EFFECT
Alcohol:	None expected.
Beverages: Caffeine drinks.	May raise blood pressure.
Cocaine:	High risk of heartbeat irregularities and high blood pressure.
Foods: Foods containing tyramine*.	May raise blood pressure.
Marijuana:	None expected.
Tobacco:	None expected.

MOLINDONE

BRAND NAMES

Moban   Moban Concentrate

BASIC INFORMATION

Habit forming? No
Prescription needed? Yes
Available as generic? No
Drug class: Antipsychotic

 USES

Treats severe emotional, mental or nervous problems.

 DOSAGE & USAGE INFORMATION

How to take:
Tablet or solution—Swallow with liquid or food to lessen stomach irritation. If you can't swallow tablet whole, crumble and take with food or liquid.

When to take:
Follow instructions on prescription label. Doses should be evenly spaced. For example, 4 times a day means every 6 hours.

If you forget a dose:
Take as soon as you remember up to 2 hours late. If more than 2 hours, wait for next scheduled dose (don't double this dose).

What drug does:
Corrects an imbalance in nerve impulses from the brain.

Time lapse before drug works:
Some benefit seen within a week; 4 to 6 weeks for full benefit.

Don't take with:
• Antacid or medicine for diarrhea.
• Nonprescription drugs for cough, cold or allergy.
• See Interaction column and consult doctor.

 OVERDOSE

SYMPTOMS:
Stupor, convulsions, coma.
WHAT TO DO:
• Dial 911 (emergency) or 0 (operator) for an ambulance or medical help. Then give first aid immediately.
• See emergency information at end of book.

 POSSIBLE ADVERSE REACTIONS OR SIDE EFFECTS

SYMPTOMS	WHAT TO DO
Life-threatening: High fever, rapid pulse, profuse sweating, muscle rigidity, confusion and irritability, seizures.	Discontinue. Seek emergency treatment.
Common: Sedation, low blood pressure and dizziness.	Continue. Call doctor when convenient.
Infrequent: • Jerky or involuntary movements, especially of the face, lips, jaw, tongue; slow-frequency tremor of head or limbs, especially while moving; muscle rigidity, lack of facial expression and slow, inflexible movements	Discontinue. Call doctor right away.
• Pacing or restlessness; intermittent spasms of muscles of face, eyes, tongue, jaw, neck, body or limbs; dry mouth, blurred vision, constipation, difficulty urinating.	Continue. Call doctor when convenient.
Rare: Other symptoms not listed above.	Continue. Call doctor when convenient.

 WARNINGS & PRECAUTIONS

Don't take if:
• You are allergic to any phenothiazine.
• You have a blood or bone marrow disease.

Before you start, tell your doctor:
• If you will have surgery within 2 months, including dental surgery, requiring general or spinal anesthesia.
• If you have asthma, emphysema or other lung disorder, glaucoma, prostate trouble, seizure disorders.
• If you take nonprescription ulcer medicine, asthma medicine or amphetamines.

Over age 60:
Adverse reactions and side effects may be more frequent and severe than in younger persons. More likely to develop involuntary movement of jaws, lips, tongue; chewing. Report this to your doctor immediately. Early treatment can help.

Pregnancy:
Decide with your doctor if drug benefits justify risk to unborn child. Risk category C (see page 47).

Breast-feeding:
Safety not established. Consult doctor.

Children & adolescents:
Don't give to children younger than 2.

Prolonged use:
- May lead to tardive dyskinesia (involuntary movement of jaws, lips, tongue; chewing).
- Talk to your doctor about the need for follow-up medical examinations or laboratory studies to check kidney function, eyes.

Skin, sunlight & heat:
Avoid getting overheated. The drug affects body temperature and sweating.

Driving, piloting or hazardous work:
Don't drive or pilot aircraft until you learn how medicine affects you. Don't work around dangerous machinery. Don't climb ladders or work in high places. Danger increases if you drink alcohol or take medicine affecting alertness and reflexes.

Discontinuing:
- Nervous and mental disorders—Don't discontinue without doctor's advice until you complete prescribed dose, even though symptoms diminish or disappear.
- Notify your doctor if any of the following occurs—Uncontrollable movements of tongue, arms and legs; lip smacking.

Others:
Advise any doctor or dentist whom you consult that you take this medicine.

POSSIBLE INTERACTION WITH OTHER DRUGS

GENERIC NAME OR DRUG CLASS	COMBINED EFFECT
Anticholinergics*	Increased anticholinergic effect.
Antidepressants, tricyclic*	Increased molindone effect.
Antihistamines*	Increased antihistamine effect.
Appetite suppressants*	Decreased appetite suppressant effect.

Beta-adrenergic blocking agents*	Increased tranquilizer effect.
Bupropion	Increased risk of major seizures.
Central nervous system (CNS) depressants*	Increased depressive effects of both drugs.
Clozapine	Toxic effect on the central nervous system.
Extrapyramidal reaction-causing medications*	Increased frequency and severity of extrapyramidal effects.
Fluoxetine	Increased depressant effects of both drugs.
Guanethidine	Decreased guanethidine effect.
Guanfacine	May increase depressant effects of either drug.
Leucovorin	High alcohol content of leucovorin may cause adverse effects.
Levodopa	Decreased levodopa effect.
Loxapine	May increase toxic effects of both drugs.
Mind-altering drugs*	Increased effect of mind-altering drugs.

Continued on page 175

POSSIBLE INTERACTION WITH OTHER SUBSTANCES

INTERACTS WITH	COMBINED EFFECT
Alcohol:	Dangerous oversedation.
Beverages:	None expected.
Cocaine:	Decreased molindone effect. Avoid.
Foods:	None expected.
Marijuana:	Drowsiness. May increase antinausea effect.
Tobacco:	None expected.

MONOAMINE OXIDASE (MAO) INHIBITORS

GENERIC AND BRAND NAMES

PHENELZINE (Nardil)
TRANYLCYPROMINE (Parnate)

BASIC INFORMATION

Habit forming? No
Prescription needed? Yes
Available as generic? No
Drug class: MAO (monoamine oxidase)
 inhibitor, antidepressant

USES

* Treatment for depression and panic disorder.
* Prevention of vascular or tension headaches.

DOSAGE & USAGE INFORMATION

How to take:
Tablet—Swallow with liquid. If you can't swallow
whole, crumble tablet and take with liquid or
food.

When to take:
At the same times each day.

If you forget a dose:
Take as soon as you remember up to 2 hours
late. If more than 2 hours, wait for next
scheduled dose (don't double this dose).

What drug does:
Inhibits nerve transmissions in brain that may
cause depression.

Time lapse before drug works:
4 to 6 weeks for maximum effect.

Continued next column

OVERDOSE

SYMPTOMS:
Restlessness, agitation, excitement, fever,
confusion, dizziness, heartbeat irregularities,
hallucinations, sweating, breathing
difficulties, insomnia, irritability,
convulsions, coma.
WHAT TO DO:
* Dial 911 (emergency) or 0 (operator) for an
 ambulance or medical help. Then give first
 aid immediately.
* See emergency information at end of book.

Don't take with:
* Nonprescription diet pills; nose drops;
 medicine for asthma, cough, cold or allergy;
 medicine containing caffeine or alcohol.
* Foods containing tyramine*. Life-threatening
 elevation of blood pressure may result.
* Any other medicine without consulting your
 doctor or pharmacist.

POSSIBLE ADVERSE REACTIONS OR SIDE EFFECTS

SYMPTOMS	WHAT TO DO
Life-threatening: In case of overdose, see previous column. Also see above regarding dangers associated with tyramine.	
Common:	
• Fatigue, weakness.	Continue. Call doctor when convenient.
• Dizziness when changing position, restlessness, tremors, dry mouth, constipation, difficult urination, blurred vision, "sweet tooth."	Continue. Tell doctor at next visit.
Infrequent:	
• Fainting, enlarged pupils, severe headache, chest pain, rapid or pounding heartbeat.	Discontinue. Seek emergency treatment.
• Hallucinations, insomnia, nightmares, diarrhea, swollen feet or legs, joint pain.	Continue. Call doctor when convenient.
• Diminished sex drive.	Continue. Tell doctor at next visit.
Rare: Rash, nausea, vomiting, stiff neck, jaundice, fever, increased sweating, dark urine, slurred speech, staggering gait.	Discontinue. Call doctor right away.

WARNINGS & PRECAUTIONS

Don't take if:
* You are allergic to any MAO inhibitor.
* You have heart disease, congestive heart
 failure, heart rhythm irregularities or high
 blood pressure.
* You have liver or kidney disease.

Before you start, tell your doctor:
* If you are alcoholic.
* If you have had a stroke.

MONOAMINE OXIDASE (MAO) INHIBITORS

- If you have diabetes, epilepsy, asthma, overactive thyroid, schizophrenia, Parkinson's disease, adrenal gland tumor.
- If you will have surgery within 2 months, including dental surgery, requiring general or spinal anesthesia.

Over age 60:
Not recommended. Adverse effects more likely.

Pregnancy:
Decide with your doctor if drug benefits justify risk to unborn child. Risk category C (see page 47).

Breast-feeding:
Safety not established. Consult doctor.

Children & adolescents:
Not recommended. Consult doctor.

Prolonged use:
- May be toxic to liver.
- Talk to your doctor about the need for follow-up medical examinations or laboratory studies to check blood pressure, liver function.

Skin, sunlight & heat:
No special problems expected.

Driving, piloting or hazardous work:
Don't drive or pilot aircraft until you learn how medicine affects you. Don't work around dangerous machinery. Don't climb ladders or work in high places. Danger increases if you drink alcohol or take medicine affecting alertness and reflexes.

Discontinuing:
- Don't discontinue without doctor's advice until you complete prescribed dose, even though symptoms diminish or disappear.
- Follow precautions regarding foods, drinks and other medicines for 2 weeks after discontinuing.
- Adverse symptoms caused by this medicine may occur even after discontinuation. If you develop any of the symptoms listed under Overdose, notify your doctor immediately.

Others:
- May affect blood sugar levels in patients with diabetes.
- Advise any doctor or dentist whom you consult about the use of this medicine.
- Fever may indicate that MAO inhibitor dose requires adjustment.

 POSSIBLE INTERACTION WITH OTHER DRUGS

GENERIC NAME OR DRUG CLASS	COMBINED EFFECT
Amphetamines*	Blood pressure rise to life-threatening level.
Anticholinergics*	Increased anticholinergic effect.
Anticonvulsants*	Changed seizure pattern.
Antidepressants, tricyclic*	Blood pressure rise to life-threatening level. Possible fever, convulsions, delirium.
Antidiabetic agents, oral* and insulin	Excessively low blood sugar.
Antihypertensives*	Excessively low blood pressure.
Beta-adrenergic blocking agents*	Possible blood pressure rise if MAO inhibitor is discontinued after simultaneous use with acebutolol.
Bupropion	Increased risk of bupropion toxicity.
Buspirone	Very high blood pressure.
Caffeine	Irregular heartbeat or high blood pressure.
Carbamazepine	Fever, seizures. Avoid.

Continued on page 176

 POSSIBLE INTERACTION WITH OTHER SUBSTANCES

INTERACTS WITH	COMBINED EFFECT
Alcohol:	Increased sedation to dangerous level.
Beverages: Caffeine drinks.	Irregular heartbeat or high blood pressure.
Drinks containing tyramine*.	Blood pressure rise to life-threatening level.
Cocaine:	Overstimulation. Possibly fatal.
Foods: Foods containing tyramine*.	Blood pressure rise to life-threatening level.
Marijuana:	Overstimulation. Avoid.
Tobacco:	No proven problems.

*See Glossary

NALTREXONE

BRAND NAMES

ReVia

BASIC INFORMATION

Habit forming? No
Prescription needed? Yes
Available as generic? No
Drug class: Narcotic antagonist

 USES

- Treats detoxified former narcotics addicts. It helps maintain a drug-free state.
- May be used to treat alcoholism (in conjunction with counseling).

 DOSAGE & USAGE INFORMATION

How to take:
- *Don't take at all until detoxification has been accomplished.*
- Tablets—Swallow with liquid or food to lessen stomach irritation. If you can't swallow whole, crumble tablet and take with liquid or food.

When to take:
At the same time every day or every other day as directed.

If you forget a dose:
Follow detailed instructions from the one who prescribed for you.

What drug does:
Binds to opioid receptors in the central nervous system and blocks the effects of narcotic drugs.

Time lapse before drug works:
1 hour.

Don't take with:
- Narcotics.
- Any other medicine without consulting your doctor or pharmacist.

 OVERDOSE

SYMPTOMS:
Seizures, coma.
WHAT TO DO:
- **Dial 911 (emergency) or 0 (operator) for an ambulance or medical help. Then give first aid immediately.**
- **See emergency information at end of book.**

 POSSIBLE ADVERSE REACTIONS OR SIDE EFFECTS

SYMPTOMS	WHAT TO DO
Life-threatening:	
Hallucinations, very fast heartbeat, fainting, breathing difficulties.	Seek emergency treatment immediately.
Common:	
Skin rash, chills, constipation, appetite loss, irritability, insomnia, anxiety, headache, nausea, vomiting.	Continue. Call doctor when convenient.
Infrequent:	
• Nosebleeds, joint pain.	Discontinue. Call doctor right away.
• Abdominal pain, blurred vision, confusion, earache, fever, depression, diarrhea, common cold symptoms.	Continue. Call doctor when convenient.
Rare:	
• Pain, tenderness or color change in feet.	Discontinue. Call doctor right away.
• Ringing in ears, swollen glands, decreased sex drive.	Continue. Call doctor when convenient.

WARNINGS & PRECAUTIONS

Don't take if:
- You don't have close medical supervision.
- You are currently dependent on drugs.
- You have severe liver disease.

Before you start, tell your doctor:
If you have mild liver disease.

Over age 60:
Adverse reactions and side effects may be more frequent and severe than in younger persons. You may need smaller doses for shorter periods of time.

Pregnancy:
Decide with your doctor whether drug benefits justify risk to unborn child. Risk category C (see page 47).

Breast-feeding:
Safety not established. Consult doctor.

Children & adolescents:
Not recommended.

Prolonged use:
- Not recommended.
- Talk to your doctor about the need for follow-up medical examinations or laboratory studies to check kidney function.

Skin, sunlight & heat:
No problems expected.

Driving, piloting or hazardous work:
Don't drive or pilot aircraft until you learn how medicine affects you. Don't work around dangerous machinery. Don't climb ladders or work in high places. Danger increases if you drink alcohol or take medicine affecting alertness and reflexes.

Discontinuing:
Don't discontinue without consulting doctor. Dose may require gradual reduction if you have taken drug for a long time. Doses of other drugs may also require adjustment.

Others:
- Probably not effective in treating people addicted to substances other than opium or morphine derivatives.
- Must be given under close supervision by people experienced in using naltrexone to treat addicts.
- Attempting to use narcotics to overcome effects of naltrexone may lead to coma and death.
- Advise any doctor or dentist whom you consult that you take this medicine.
- Withdraw from medication several days prior to expected surgery.

POSSIBLE INTERACTION WITH OTHER DRUGS

GENERIC NAME OR DRUG CLASS	COMBINED EFFECT
Narcotic medicines* (butorphanol, codeine, heroin, hydrocodone, hydromorphone, levorphanol, morphine, nalbuphine, opium, oxycodone, oxymorphone, paregoric, pentazocine, propoxyphene)	1. Precipitates withdrawal symptoms. May lead to cardiac arrest, coma and death (if naltrexone taken while person is dependent on these drugs). 2. If these drugs are taken while person is taking naltrexone, opioid effect (pain relief) will be blocked.
Isoniazid	Increased risk of liver damage.

POSSIBLE INTERACTION WITH OTHER SUBSTANCES

INTERACTS WITH	COMBINED EFFECT
Alcohol:	Unpredictable effects. Avoid.
Beverages:	None expected.
Cocaine:	Unpredictable effects. Avoid.
Foods:	None expected.
Marijuana:	Unpredictable effects. Avoid.
Tobacco:	None expected.

*See Glossary

NEFAZODONE

BRAND NAMES

Serzone

BASIC INFORMATION

Habit forming? No
Prescription needed? Yes
Available as generic? No
Drug class: Antidepressant
(phenylpiperazine)

USES

Treats symptoms of mental depression.

DOSAGE & USAGE INFORMATION

How to take:
Tablet—Swallow with liquid. May be taken with or without food.

When to take:
At the same times each day. The prescribed dosage may be increased weekly until maximum benefits are achieved.

If you forget a dose:
Take as soon as you remember up to 2 hours late. If more than 2 hours, wait for the next scheduled dose (don't double this dose).

What drug does:
The exact mechanism is unknown. It appears to block reuptake of serotonin and norepinephrine (stimulating chemicals in the brain that play a role in emotions and psychological distur-bances).

Time lapse before drug works:
Will take up to several weeks to relieve the depression.

Don't take with:
Any other medication without consulting your doctor or pharmacist.

OVERDOSE

SYMPTOMS:
Drowsiness, nausea, vomiting, low blood pressure (faintness, weakness, dizziness, lightheadedness) or increased severity of adverse reactions.
WHAT TO DO:
- Dial 911 (emergency) or 0 (operator) for an ambulance or medical help. Then give first aid immediately.
- See emergency information at end of book.

POSSIBLE ADVERSE REACTIONS OR SIDE EFFECTS

SYMPTOMS	WHAT TO DO
Life-threatening:	
In case of overdose, see previous column.	
Common:	
• Clumsiness or unsteadiness, blurred vision or other vision changes, fainting, lightheadedness, ringing in the ears, skin rash or itching.	Discontinue. Call doctor right away.
• Strange dreams, constipation or diarrhea, dry mouth, heartburn, fever, chills, flushing or feeling warm, headache, increased appetite, insomnia, coughing, tingling or prickly sensations, sore throat, trembling, drowsiness, confusion or agitation, memory lapses.	Continue. Call doctor when convenient.
Infrequent:	
• Tightness in chest; trouble breathing; wheezing; eye pain; combination of nausea, vomiting, diarrhea and stomach pain.	Discontinue. Call doctor right away.
• Joint pain, breast pain, increased thirst.	Continue. Call doctor when convenient.
Rare:	
Face swelling, hives, unusual tiredness or weakness, muscle pain or stiffness, chest pain, fast heartbeat, mood or mental changes, difficulty speaking, false sense of well-being, hallucinations, uncontrolled excited behavior, twitching, ear pain, increased hearing sensitivity, bleeding or bruising, irritated red eyes, eyes sensitive to light, pain in back or side, swollen glands, menstrual changes, change in sexual desire or function, problems with urination.	Discontinue. Call doctor right away.

WARNINGS & PRECAUTIONS

Don't use if:
You are allergic to nefazodone or trazodone (phenylpiperazine antidepressants).

Before you start, tell your doctor:
- If you have a seizure disorder, heart disease or blood circulation problem or have had a stroke.
- If you are dehydrated.
- If you have a history of drug dependence or drug abuse.
- If you have a history of mood disorders, such as mania, or thoughts of suicide.
- If you are allergic to any medication, food or other substances.

Over age 60:
A lower starting dosage is usually recommended until a response is determined.

Pregnancy:
Decide with your doctor if drug benefits justify risk to unborn child. Risk category C (see page 47).

Breast-feeding:
It is unknown if drug passes into milk. Avoid drug or discontinue nursing until you finish medicine. Consult doctor for advice on maintaining milk supply.

Children & adolescents:
Safety in children under age 18 has not been established.

Prolonged use:
Consult with your doctor on a regular basis while taking this drug to check your progress and to discuss any increase or changes in side effects and the need for continued treatment.

Skin, sunlight & heat:
May cause a rash or intensify sunburn in areas exposed to sun or ultraviolet light (photosensitivity reaction). Avoid excess sun exposure and use sunscreen. Consult doctor if reaction occurs.

Driving, piloting or hazardous work:
Don't drive or pilot aircraft until you learn how medicine affects you. Don't work around dangerous machinery. Don't climb ladders or work in high places. Danger increases if you drink alcohol or take medicine affecting alertness and reflexes.

Discontinuing:
Don't discontinue this drug without consulting doctor. Dosage may require a gradual reduction before stopping.

Others:
- Get up slowly from a sitting or lying position to avoid dizziness, faintness or lightheadedness.
- May affect the results of some medical tests.

- Advise any doctor or dentist whom you consult that you take this medicine.
- Take medicine only as directed. Do not increase or reduce dosage without doctor's approval.

POSSIBLE INTERACTION WITH OTHER DRUGS

GENERIC NAME OR DRUG CLASS	COMBINED EFFECT
Alprazolam	Increased effect of alprazolam.
Antihypertensives*	Possible too-low blood pressure.
Astemizole	Serious heart problems. Avoid.
Central nervous system (CNS) depressants*	Increased sedation. Avoid.
Digoxin	Increased digoxin effect.
Haloperidol	Unknown effect. May need dosage adjustment.
Monoamine oxidase (MAO) inhibitors*	Potentially life-threatening. Allow 14 days between use of 2 drugs.
Propranolol	Unknown effect. May need dosage adjustment of both drugs.
Selective serotonin reuptake inhibitors*	Potentially life-threatening serotonin syndrome (see Glossary). Avoid.
Terfenadine	Serious heart problems. Avoid.
Triazolam	Increased effects of both drugs.

POSSIBLE INTERACTION WITH OTHER SUBSTANCES

INTERACTS WITH	COMBINED EFFECT
Alcohol:	Increased sedative affect. Avoid.
Beverages:	None expected.
Cocaine:	Unknown. Avoid.
Foods:	None expected.
Marijuana:	Unknown. Best to avoid.

*See Glossary

PAROXETINE

BRAND NAMES

Paxil

BASIC INFORMATION

Habit forming? No
Prescription needed? Yes
Available as generic? No
Drug class: Antidepressant (selective serotonin reuptake inhibitor)

 USES

Treats mental depression.

 DOSAGE & USAGE INFORMATION

How to take:
Tablet—Swallow with liquid. May be taken with food to lessen gastric irritation.

When to take:
At the same times each day, usually in the morning.

If you forget a dose:
Take as soon as you remember up to 2 hours late. If more than 2 hours, wait for next scheduled dose (don't double this dose).

What drug does:
Affects serotonin, one of the chemicals in the brain called neurotransmitters, that plays a role in emotions and psychological disturbances.

Time lapse before drug works:
1 to 4 weeks.

Don't take with:
• Any other medication without consulting your doctor or pharmacist.
• Any monoamine oxidase (MAO) inhibitor* or within 14 days of stopping one. To do so may result in a serious or fatal reaction.
• See Interaction column and consult doctor.

 OVERDOSE

SYMPTOMS:
Vomiting, severe drowsiness, heart rhythm disturbances, dilated pupils, severe mouth dryness.
WHAT TO DO:
• Dial 911 (emergency) or 0 (operator) for an ambulance or medical help. Then give first aid immediately.
• See emergency information at end of book.

 POSSIBLE ADVERSE REACTIONS OR SIDE EFFECTS

SYMPTOMS	WHAT TO DO
Life-threatening: Rash, itchy skin, breathing difficulty (allergic reaction); chest pain.	Seek emergency treatment immediately.
Common: Weakness, sweating, nausea, sleepiness, dry mouth, dizziness, insomnia, tremor, male ejaculatory problems, male genital disorders, constipation, diarrhea, problems urinating, vomiting.	Continue. Call doctor when convenient.
Infrequent: Anxiety, nervousness, decreased or increased appetite, decreased libido, heart palpitations, taste changes, weight loss or gain.	Continue. Call doctor when convenient.
Rare: • Blurred vision.	Continue. Call doctor when convenient.
• Mania* symptoms.	Discontinue. Call doctor right away.

WARNINGS & PRECAUTIONS

Don't take if:
- You are allergic to paroxetine.
- You are taking astemizole, cisapride or terfenadine.
- You currently take (or have taken in the last 2 weeks) a monoamine oxidase (MAO) inhibitor*.

Before you start, tell your doctor:
- If you have a history of seizure disorders.
- If you have thoughts of suicide.
- If you have kidney or liver disease.
- If you have a history of drug abuse or mania.

Over age 60:
Adverse reactions and side effects may be more frequent and severe than in younger persons. You may need smaller dosages for shorter periods of time.

Pregnancy:
Consult doctor. Risk category B (see page 47).

Breast-feeding:
Drug passes into milk. Avoid drug or discontinue nursing until you finish medicine. Consult doctor for advice on maintaining milk supply.

Children & adolescents:
Safety and effectiveness not yet determined.

Prolonged use:
No problems expected. Your doctor should periodically evaluate your response to the drug and adjust the dosage if necessary.

Skin, sunlight & heat:
No problems expected.

Driving, piloting or hazardous work:
Don't drive or pilot aircraft until you learn how medicine affects you. Don't work around dangerous machinery. Don't climb ladders or work in high places. Danger increases if you drink alcohol or take other medicines affecting alertness and reflexes such as antihistamines, tranquilizers, sedatives, pain medicine, narcotics and mind-altering drugs.

Discontinuing:
- Don't discontinue without consulting doctor. Dose may require gradual reduction if you have taken drug for a long time. Doses of other drugs may also require adjustment.
- Consult doctor if the following symptoms appear after you discontinue the drug: dizziness, lightheadedness, agitation, confusion, restlessness, vision changes, insomnia, headache, muscle aches, runny nose, unusual tiredness or weakness, nausea or vomiting.

Others:
Advise any doctor or dentist whom you consult that you take this medicine.

POSSIBLE INTERACTION WITH OTHER DRUGS

GENERIC NAME OR DRUG CLASS	COMBINED EFFECT
Anticoagulants, oral*	Increased risk of bleeding.
Antidepressants*, other	Increased effects of both drugs.
Cimetidine	Increased levels of paroxetine in blood.
Digoxin	Decreased digoxin effect.
Lithium	Unknown effect. Consult doctor.
Monoamine oxidase (MAO) inhibitors*	Can cause a life-threatening reaction. Avoid.
Phenytoin	Decreased effect of phenytoin.
Selegiline	Increased risk of adverse effects. May lead to convulsions and hypertensive crisis. Let 14 days elapse between taking the 2 drugs.

POSSIBLE INTERACTION WITH OTHER SUBSTANCES

INTERACTS WITH	COMBINED EFFECT
Alcohol:	Contributes to depression. Avoid.
Beverages:	None expected.
Cocaine:	Effects unknown. Avoid.
Foods:	None expected.
Marijuana:	Effects unknown. Avoid.
Tobacco:	None expected.

*See Glossary

PEMOLINE

BRAND NAMES

Cylert   Cylert Chewable

BASIC INFORMATION

Habit forming? Yes
Prescription needed? Yes
Available as generic? No
Drug class: Central nervous system
  stimulant

 ## USES

- Decreases overactivity and lengthens attention span in children with attention-deficit hyperactivity disorder (ADHD). It is used as part of the total management plan that includes educational, social and psychological treatment.
- Treats minimal brain dysfunction.

 ## DOSAGE & USAGE INFORMATION

How to take:
- Tablet—Swallow with liquid or food to lessen stomach irritation. If you can't swallow whole, crumble tablet and take with liquid or food.
- Chewable tablets—Chew well before swallowing.

When to take:
Daily in the morning.

Continued next column

 ## OVERDOSE

SYMPTOMS:
Agitation, confusion, fast heartbeat, hallucinations, severe headache, high fever with sweating, large pupils, muscle twitching or trembling, uncontrolled eye or body movements, vomiting.
WHAT TO DO:
- Dial 911 (emergency) or 0 (operator) for an ambulance or medical help. Then give first aid immediately.
- If patient is unconscious and not breathing, give mouth-to-mouth breathing. If there is no heartbeat, use cardiac massage and mouth-to-mouth breathing (CPR). Don't try to make patient vomit. If you can't get help quickly, take patient to nearest emergency facility.
- See emergency information at end of book.

If you forget a dose:
Take as soon as you remember up to 2 hours late. If more than 2 hours, wait for next scheduled dose (don't double this dose).

What drug does:
Stimulates brain to improve alertness, concentration and attention span. Calms the hyperactive child.

Time lapse before drug works:
- 1 month or more for maximum effect on child.
- 30 minutes to stimulate adults.

Don't take with:
Any other medicine without consulting your doctor or pharmacist.

 ## POSSIBLE ADVERSE REACTIONS OR SIDE EFFECTS

SYMPTOMS	WHAT TO DO
Life-threatening: In case of overdose, see previous column.	
Common: Trouble sleeping, loss of appetite, weight loss.	Continue. Call doctor when convenient.
Infrequent: Irritability, depression dizziness, headache, drowsiness, skin rash, stomach ache.	Continue. Call doctor when convenient.
Rare: Yellow skin or eyes; symptoms of overdose (agitation, confusion, fast heartbeat, hallucinations, severe headache, high fever with sweating, large pupils, muscle twitching or trembling, uncontrolled eye or body movements, vomiting).	Discontinue. Call doctor right away.

WARNINGS & PRECAUTIONS

Don't take if:
You are allergic to pemoline.

Before you start, tell your doctor:
- If you have liver disease.
- If you have kidney disease.
- If patient is younger than 6 years.
- If there is marked emotional instability.

Over age 60:
Adverse reactions and side effects may be more frequent and severe than in younger persons.

Pregnancy:
No proven harm to unborn child. Avoid if possible. Consult doctor. Risk category B (see page 47).

Breast-feeding:
Effect unknown. Consult doctor.

Children & adolescents:
Use only under close medical supervision.

Prolonged use:
- Rare possibility of physical growth retardation.
- Talk to your doctor about the need for follow-up medical examinations or laboratory studies to check liver function, growth charts.

Skin, sunlight & heat:
No problems expected.

Driving, piloting or hazardous work:
Don't drive or pilot aircraft until you learn how medicine affects you. Don't work around dangerous machinery. Don't climb ladders or work in high places. Danger increases if you drink alcohol or take medicine affecting alertness and reflexes, such as antihistamines, tranquilizers, sedatives, pain medicine, narcotics and mind-altering drugs.

Discontinuing:
- Don't discontinue without consulting doctor. Dose may require gradual reduction if you have taken drug for a long time. Doses of other drugs may also require adjustment.
- If you notice any of the following symptoms after discontinuing, notify your doctor: mental depression (severe), tiredness or weakness.

Others:
- Dose must be carefully adjusted by doctor. Don't give more or less than prescribed dose.
- Be sure you and the doctor discuss benefits and risks of this drug before starting.
- Consult doctor if no improvement is noticed after 1 month of drug use.
- Advise any doctor or dentist whom you consult about the use of this medicine.

POSSIBLE INTERACTION WITH OTHER DRUGS

GENERIC NAME OR DRUG CLASS	COMBINED EFFECT
Anticonvulsants*	Dosage adjustment for anticonvulsant may be necessary.
Central nervous system (CNS) stimulants*, other	May increase toxic effects of both drugs.

POSSIBLE INTERACTION WITH OTHER SUBSTANCES

INTERACTS WITH	COMBINED EFFECT
Alcohol:	More chance of depression. Avoid.
Beverages: Caffeine drinks.	Overstimulation. Avoid.
Cocaine:	Convulsions or excessive nervousness.
Foods:	No problems expected.
Marijuana:	Unknown.
Tobacco:	Unknown.

PHENOTHIAZINES

BRAND AND GENERIC NAMES

See complete list of brand and generic names in the *Brand and Generic Name Directory*, page 170.

BASIC INFORMATION

Habit forming? No
Prescription needed? Yes
Available as generic? Yes, for some.
Drug class: Tranquilizer, antiemetic (phenothiazine)

USES

- Reduces anxiety, agitation.
- Stops nausea, vomiting, hiccups.

DOSAGE & USAGE INFORMATION

How to take:
- Tablet or extended-release capsule—Swallow with liquid or food to lessen stomach irritation.
- Suppositories—Remove wrapper and moisten suppository with water. Gently insert into rectum, pointed end first.
- Drops or liquid—Dilute dose in beverage.

When to take:
- Nervous and mental disorders—Take at the same times each day.
- For other uses, take as directed by your doctor.

If you forget a dose:
Nervous and mental disorders—Take up to 2 hours late. If more than 2 hours, wait for next scheduled dose (don't double this dose).

What drug does:
- Suppresses brain centers that control abnormal emotions and behavior.
- Suppresses brain's vomiting center.

Continued next column

OVERDOSE

SYMPTOMS:
Stupor, convulsions, coma.
WHAT TO DO:
- Dial 911 (emergency) or 0 (operator) for an ambulance or medical help. Then give first aid immediately.
- See emergency information at end of book.

Time lapse before drug works:
Some benefit seen within a week; takes 4 to 6 weeks for full effect.

Don't take with:
- Antacid or medicine for diarrhea.
- Nonprescription drug for cough, cold or allergy.
- Any other medicine without consulting your doctor or pharmacist.

POSSIBLE ADVERSE REACTIONS OR SIDE EFFECTS

SYMPTOMS	WHAT TO DO
Life-threatening: High fever, rapid pulse, profuse sweating, muscle rigidity, confusion and irritability, seizures.	Discontinue. Seek emergency treatment.
Common: Dry mouth, blurred vision, constipation, difficulty urinating; sedation, dizziness, low blood pressure.	Continue. Call doctor when convenient.
Infrequent: • Continuous jerky or involuntary movements, especially of the face, lips, jaw, tongue; slow-frequency tremor of head or limbs, especially while moving; muscle rigidity, lack of facial expression and slow, inflexible movements.	Discontinue. Call doctor right away.
• Pacing or restlessness; intermittent spasms of muscles of face, eyes, tongue, jaw, neck, body or limbs; jaundice (yellow skin or eyes).	Continue. Call doctor when convenient.
Rare: Other symptoms not listed above.	Continue. Call doctor when convenient.

WARNINGS & PRECAUTIONS

Don't take if:
- You are allergic to any phenothiazine.
- You have a blood or bone marrow disease.

Before you start, tell your doctor:
- If you will have surgery within 2 months, including dental surgery, requiring general or spinal anesthesia.
- If you have asthma, emphysema or other lung disorder; glaucoma; or prostate trouble.
- If you take nonprescription ulcer medicine, asthma medicine or amphetamines.

Over age 60:
Adverse reactions and side effects may be more frequent and severe than in younger persons. More likely to develop involuntary movement of jaws, lips, tongue; chewing. Report this to your doctor immediately. Early treatment can help.

Pregnancy:
Risk factors vary for drugs in this group. See category list on page 47 and consult doctor.

Breast-feeding:
Drug passes into milk. Avoid drug or discontinue nursing until you finish medicine. Consult doctor for advice on maintaining milk supply.

Children & adolescents:
- Don't give to children younger than 2.
- Children more likely than adults to develop adverse reactions from these drugs.

Prolonged use:
May lead to tardive dyskinesia (involuntary movement of jaws, lips, tongue; chewing).

Skin, sunlight & heat:
- One or more drugs in this group may cause rash or intensify sunburn in areas exposed to sun or ultraviolet light (photosensitivity reaction). Use sunscreen and avoid overexposure. Notify doctor if reaction occurs. Sensitivity may remain for 3 months after discontinuing drug.
- Avoid getting overheated or chilled. These drugs affect body temperature and sweating.

Driving, piloting or hazardous work:
Don't drive or pilot aircraft until you learn how medicine affects you. Don't work around dangerous machinery. Don't climb ladders or work in high places. Danger increases if you drink alcohol or take medicine affecting alertness and reflexes.

Discontinuing:
- Nervous and mental disorders—Don't discontinue without doctor's advice until you complete prescribed dose, even though symptoms diminish or disappear.
- Other disorders—Follow doctor's instructions about discontinuing.

- Adverse reactions may occur after drug is discontinued. Consult doctor if new symptoms develop, such as dizziness, nausea, stomach pain, trembling or tardive dyskinesia*.

Others:
- To relieve mouth dryness, chew or suck sugarless gum, candy, or ice.
- Avoid getting the liquid form of the drug on the skin. It may cause a skin rash or irritation.
- Advise any doctor or dentist whom you consult that you take this medicine.

POSSIBLE INTERACTION WITH OTHER DRUGS

GENERIC NAME OR DRUG CLASS	COMBINED EFFECT
Anticholinergics*	Increased phenothiazine effect
Anticonvulsants*	Increased risk of seizures. May need to increase dosage of anticonvulsant.
Antidepressants, tricyclic*	Increased antidepressant effect.
Antihistamines*	Increased antihistamine effect.
Antihypertensives*	Severe low blood pressure.
Appetite suppressants*	Decreased appetite suppressant effect.
Bupropion	Increased risk of major seizures.

Continued on page 177

POSSIBLE INTERACTION WITH OTHER SUBSTANCES

INTERACTS WITH	COMBINED EFFECT
Alcohol:	Dangerous oversedation. Avoid
Beverages:	None expected.
Cocaine:	Decreased phenothiazine effect. Avoid.
Foods:	None expected.
Marijuana:	Drowsiness. May increase antinausea effect.
Tobacco:	None expected.

RISPERIDONE

BRAND NAMES

Risperdal

BASIC INFORMATION

Habit forming? No
Prescription needed? Yes
Available as generic? No
Drug class: Antipsychotic

USES

Treats nervous, mental and emotional conditions. Helps in managing the signs and symptoms of schizophrenia.

DOSAGE & USAGE INFORMATION

How to take:
Tablet—Swallow with liquid. May be taken with or without food.

When to take:
At the same times each day. The prescribed dosage will gradually be increased over the first few days of use.

If you forget a dose:
Take as soon as you remember. If it is almost time for the next dose, wait for the next scheduled dose (don't double this dose).

What drug does:
The exact mechanism is unknown. It appears to block certain nerve impulses between nerve cells.

Time lapse before drug works:
One to 7 days. A further increase in the dosage amount may be necessary to relieve symptoms for some patients.

Don't take with:
Any other medication without consulting your doctor or pharmacist.

OVERDOSE

SYMPTOMS:
Extreme drowsiness, rapid heartbeat, faintness, convulsions, excessive sweating, difficulty breathing, loss of muscular control.
WHAT TO DO:
• Dial 911 (emergency) or 0 (operator) for an ambulance or medical help. Then give first aid immediately.
• See emergency information at end of book.

POSSIBLE ADVERSE REACTIONS OR SIDE EFFECTS

SYMPTOMS	WHAT TO DO
Life-threatening: High fever, rapid pulse, profuse sweating, muscle rigidity, confusion and irritability, seizures (malignant neuroleptic syndrome - rare).	Discontinue. Seek emergency treatment.
Common: Anxiety, drowsiness, dizziness, digestive problems, rash, sexual dysfunction.	Continue. Call doctor when convenient.
Infrequent: • Jerky or involuntary movements, especially of the face, lips, jaw, tongue (with higher doses only); slow-frequency tremor of head, face, or limbs, especially while moving; muscle rigidity, lack of facial expression and slow, inflexible movements.	Discontinue. Call doctor right away.
• Dry mouth, blurred vision, constipation, difficulty urinating; sedation, dizziness and low blood pressure; pacing or restlessness, intermittent spasms of muscles of face, eyes, tongue, jaw, neck, body or limbs.	Continue. Call doctor when convenient.
Rare: Other symptoms not listed above.	Continue. Call doctor when convenient.

WARNINGS & PRECAUTIONS

Don't take if:
You are allergic to risperidone.

Before you start, tell your doctor:
* If you have liver or kidney disease or heart disease.
* If you are allergic to any other medications.
* If you have a history of seizures.

Over age 60:
Adverse reactions and side effects may be more severe than in younger persons. A lower starting dosage is usually recommended until a response is determined.

Pregnancy:
Decide with your doctor if drug benefits justify any possible risk to unborn child. Risk category C (see page 47).

Breast-feeding:
It is unknown if drug passes into milk. Avoid nursing until you finish medicine. Consult doctor for advice on maintaining milk supply.

Children & adolescents:
Safety in children under age 12 has not been established. Use only under close medical supervision.

Prolonged use:
Consult with your doctor on a regular basis while taking this drug to check your progress or to discuss any increase or changes in side effects and the need for continued treatment.

Skin, sunlight & heat:
* May cause rash or intensify sunburn in areas exposed to sun or ultraviolet light (photosensitivity reaction). Use sunscreen and avoid overexposure. Notify doctor if reaction occurs.
* Hot temperatures and exercise, hot baths can increase risk of heatstroke. Drug may affect body's ability to maintain normal temperature.

Driving, piloting or hazardous work:
Don't drive or pilot aircraft until you learn how medicine affects you. Don't work around dangerous machinery. Don't climb ladders or work in high places. Danger increases if you drink alcohol or take medicine affecting alertness and reflexes.

Discontinuing:
Don't discontinue this drug without consulting doctor. Dosage may require a gradual reduction before stopping.

Others:
* Get up slowly from a sitting or lying position to avoid any dizziness, faintness or lightheadedness.

* Advise any doctor or dentist whom you consult that you take this medicine.
* Take medicine only as directed. Do not increase or reduce dosage without doctor's approval.

POSSIBLE INTERACTION WITH OTHER DRUGS

GENERIC NAME OR DRUG CLASS	COMBINED EFFECT
Antihypertensives*	Increased antihypertensive effect.
Carbamazepine	Decreased effect of risperidone.
Clozapine	Increased effect of risperidone.
Central nervous system (CNS) depressants*, other	Increased sedative effect.
Levodopa	May decrease levodopa effect.

POSSIBLE INTERACTION WITH OTHER SUBSTANCES

INTERACTS WITH	COMBINED EFFECT
Alcohol:	Increased sedative affect. Avoid.
Beverages:	None expected.
Cocaine:	Effect not known. Best to avoid.
Foods:	None expected.
Marijuana:	Effect not known. Best to avoid.
Tobacco:	None expected.

SERTRALINE

BRAND NAMES

Zoloft

BASIC INFORMATION

Habit forming? No
Prescription needed? Yes
Available as generic? No
Drug class: Antidepressant (selective
serotonin reuptake inhibitor)

 USES

Treats mental depression.

 **DOSAGE & USAGE
INFORMATION**

How to take:
Tablets—Swallow with liquid. If you can't
swallow whole, crumble tablet and take with
liquid or food.

When to take:
Once daily, either in the morning or in the
evening as directed by your doctor.

If you forget a dose:
Take as soon as you remember up to 2 hours
late. If more than 2 hours, wait for next
scheduled dose (don't double this dose).

What drug does:
It affects serotonin, one of the chemicals in the
brain called neurotransmitters, that plays a role
in emotions and psychological disturbances.

Time lapse before drug works:
1 to 4 weeks.

Don't take with:
- Any monoamine oxidase (MAO) inhibitor* (or
  within 14 days of discontinuing an MAO
  inhibitor). To do so may cause serious or even
  fatal reactions.
- Any other medication without consulting your
  doctor or pharmacist.

 OVERDOSE

SYMPTOMS:
Seizures, agitation, violent vomiting.
WHAT TO DO:
- **Dial 911 (emergency) or 0 (operator) for an
  ambulance or medical help. Then give first
  aid immediately.**
- **See emergency information at end of book.**

 **POSSIBLE
ADVERSE REACTIONS
OR SIDE EFFECTS**

SYMPTOMS	WHAT TO DO
Life-threatening: Rash, itchy skin, breathing difficulty (allergic reaction); chest pain.	Seek emergency treatment immediately.
Common: Diarrhea, nervousness, drowsiness, headache, increased sweating, insomnia, anxiety.	Continue. Call doctor when convenient.
Infrequent: • Chills, fever, joint or muscle pain, enlarged lymph glands, unusual excitability, blurred vision, chest pain.	Discontinue. Call doctor right away.
• Nightmares, taste changes, vision changes, decreased sex drive, dry mouth, skin flushing, urinating frequently, painful menstruation, stuffy nose, tremors.	Continue. Call doctor when convenient.
Rare: • Convulsions.	Discontinue. Seek emergency treatment.
• Fast heartbeat; abdominal pain; signs of low blood sugar (anxiety, nervousness, chills, increased sweating, difficulty concentrating).	Discontinue. Call doctor right away.
• Nausea, vomiting, constipation, cough, increased appetite.	Continue. Call doctor when convenient.

WARNINGS & PRECAUTIONS

Don't take if:
- You have epilepsy.
- You have an allergy to sertraline.

Before you start, tell your doctor:
If you have severe liver or kidney disease.

Over age 60:
Adverse reactions may be more frequent and severe than in younger persons. You may need smaller doses for shorter periods of time.

Pregnancy:
Don't take unless essential. Consult doctor. Risk category B (see page 47).

Breast-feeding:
Unknown effects. Consult doctor.

Children & adolescents:
Not recommended.

Prolonged use:
No special problems expected.

Skin, sunlight & heat:
No special problems expected.

Driving, piloting or hazardous work:
Don't drive or pilot aircraft until you learn how medicine affects you. Don't work around dangerous machinery. Don't climb ladders or work in high places. Danger increases if you drink alcohol or take medicine affecting alertness and reflexes.

Discontinuing:
Don't discontinue without consulting doctor. Dose may require gradual reduction if you have taken drug for a long time. Doses of other drugs may also require adjustment.

Others:
- Advise any doctor or dentist whom you consult that you take this medicine.
- May affect results of some medical tests.

POSSIBLE INTERACTION WITH OTHER DRUGS

GENERIC NAME OR DRUG CLASS	COMBINED EFFECT
Antidepressants, tricyclic*	Increased levels of tricyclic antidepressant; possible toxicity.
Central nervous system (CNS) depressants*	Increased depressive effects of both drugs.
Lithium	May increase risk of side effects.
Monoamine oxidase (MAO) inhibitors*	Increased risk of adverse effects. May lead to convulsions and hypertensive crisis. Let 14 days elapse between taking the 2 drugs.
Selegiline	Increased risk of adverse effects. May lead to convulsions and hypertensive crisis. Let 14 days elapse between taking the 2 drugs.
Warfarin	Increased anticoagulant effect.

POSSIBLE INTERACTION WITH OTHER SUBSTANCES

INTERACTS WITH	COMBINED EFFECT
Alcohol:	May increase depression.
Beverages:	No proven problems.
Cocaine:	Decreased effect of sertraline.
Foods:	No proven problems.
Marijuana:	Decreased effect of sertraline.
Tobacco:	No proven problems.

TACRINE

BRAND NAMES

Cognex

BASIC INFORMATION

Habit forming? No
Prescription needed? Yes
Available as generic? No
Drug class: Cholinesterase inhibitor

 USES

Treatment for symptoms of mild to moderate Alzheimer's disease. May improve memory, reasoning and other cognitive functions slightly in some patients or slow the progress of Alzheimer's disease. It will not reverse the disease.

 DOSAGE & USAGE INFORMATION

How to take:
Capsule—Swallow with liquid.

When to take:
At the same times each day. Take 1 hour before or 2 hours after eating. Follow doctor's instructions.

If you forget a dose:
Take as soon as you remember up to 2 hours late. If more than 2 hours, wait for next scheduled dose (don't double this dose).

Continued next column

 OVERDOSE

SYMPTOMS:
Severe nausea and vomiting, excessive saliva, sweating, blood pressure decrease, slow heartbeat, collapse, convulsions, muscle weakness (including respiratory muscles, which could lead to death).
WHAT TO DO:
- **Dial 911 (emergency) or 0 (operator) for an ambulance or medical help. Then give first aid immediately.**
- **If patient is unconscious and not breathing, use cardiac massage and mouth-to-mouth breathing (CPR). Don't try to make patient vomit. If you can't get help quickly, take patient to nearest emergency facility.**
- **See emergency information at end of book.**

What drug does:
Slows breakdown of a brain chemical (acetylcholine) that gradually disappears from the brains of people with Alzheimer's disease.

Time lapse before drug works:
May take several months before beneficial results are observed. Dosage is normally increased over a period of time to help prevent adverse reactions.

Don't take with:
- Any other medication without consulting your doctor or pharmacist.
- See Interaction column and consult doctor.

 POSSIBLE ADVERSE REACTIONS OR SIDE EFFECTS

SYMPTOMS	WHAT TO DO
Life-threatening: In case of overdose, see previous column.	
Common: Nausea, vomiting, diarrhea, lack of coordination.	Continue. Call doctor when convenient.
Infrequent: Rash, indigestion, headache, muscle aches, loss of appetite, stomach pain, nervousness, chills, dizziness, drowsiness, dry or itching eyes, increased sweating, joint pain, runny nose, sore throat, swelling of feet or legs, insomnia, weight loss, unusual tiredness or weakness, flushing of face.	Continue. Call doctor when convenient.
Rare: Changes in liver function (yellow skin or eyes; black, very dark or light stool color); lack of coordination, convulsions.	Continue. Call doctor right away.

WARNINGS & PRECAUTIONS

Don't take if:
You are allergic to tacrine or acridine derivatives*.

Before you start, tell your doctor:
- If you have heart rhythm problems.
- If you have a history of ulcer disease or are at risk of developing ulcers.
- If you have a history of liver disease.
- If you have epilepsy or seizure disorder.
- If you have a history of asthma.
- If you have had previous treatment with tacrine that caused jaundice (yellow skin and eyes) or elevated bilirubin.

Over age 60:
No problems expected.

Pregnancy:
Unknown effect. Drug is usually not prescribed for women of childbearing age. Risk category C (see page 47).

Breast-feeding:
Unknown effect. Not recommended for women of childbearing age.

Children & adolescents:
Not used in this age group.

Prolonged use:
- Drug may lose its effectiveness.
- Talk to your doctor about the need for follow-up medical examinations or laboratory studies to check blood chemistries and liver function.

Skin, sunlight & heat:
No problems expected.

Driving, piloting or hazardous work:
Don't drive or pilot aircraft until you learn how medicine affects you. Don't work around dangerous machinery. Don't climb ladders or work in high places. Danger increases if you drink alcohol or take other medicines affecting alertness and reflexes such as antihistamines, tranquilizers, sedatives, pain medicine, narcotics and mind-altering drugs.

Discontinuing:
Do not discontinue drug unless advised by doctor. Abrupt decreases in dosage may cause a cognitive decline.

Others:
- Advise any doctor or dentist whom you consult that you take this medicine.
- May affect the results in some medical tests.
- Do not increase dosage without doctor's approval.
- Treatment with tacrine may need to be discontinued or the dosage lowered if weekly blood tests indicate a sensitivity to the drug or liver toxicity develops.

POSSIBLE INTERACTION WITH OTHER DRUGS

GENERIC NAME OR DRUG CLASS	COMBINED EFFECT
Anticholinergics*	Decreased anticholinergic effect.
Cimetidine	Increased tacrine effect, especially adverse effects.
Theophylline	Increased theophylline effect or toxicity.

POSSIBLE INTERACTION WITH OTHER SUBSTANCES

INTERACTS WITH	COMBINED EFFECT
Alcohol:	None expected.
Beverages:	None expected.
Cocaine:	None expected.
Foods:	None expected.
Marijuana:	None expected.
Tobacco:	May decrease tacrine effect.

*See Glossary

THIOTHIXENE

BRAND NAMES

Navane

Thiothixene HCl
Intensol

BASIC INFORMATION

Habit forming? No
Prescription needed? Yes
Available as generic? Yes
Drug class: Antipsychotic (thioxanthine)

 USES

Reduces anxiety, agitation, psychosis.

 DOSAGE & USAGE INFORMATION

How to take:
- Capsule—Swallow with liquid. If you can't swallow whole, open capsule and take with liquid or food.
- Syrup—Dilute dose in beverage before swallowing.

When to take:
At the same times each day.

If you forget a dose:
Take as soon as you remember up to 2 hours late. If more than 2 hours, wait for next scheduled dose (don't double this dose).

What drug does:
Corrects imbalance of nerve impulses.

Continued next column

 OVERDOSE

SYMPTOMS:
Drowsiness, dizziness, weakness, muscle rigidity, twitching, tremors, confusion, dry mouth, blurred vision, rapid pulse, shallow breathing, low blood pressure, convulsions, coma.
WHAT TO DO:
- **Dial 911 (emergency) or 0 (operator) for an ambulance or medical help. Then give first aid immediately.**
- **If patient is unconscious and not breathing, give mouth-to-mouth breathing. If there is no heartbeat, use cardiac massage and mouth-to-mouth breathing (CPR). Don't try to make patient vomit. If you can't get help quickly, take patient to nearest emergency facility.**
- **See emergency information at end of book.**

Time lapse before drug works:
3 weeks.

Don't take with:
Any other medicine without consulting your doctor or pharmacist.

 POSSIBLE ADVERSE REACTIONS OR SIDE EFFECTS

SYMPTOMS	WHAT TO DO
Life-threatening: High fever, rapid pulse, profuse sweating, muscle rigidity, confusion and irritability, seizures.	Discontinue. Seek emergency treatment.
Common: • Jerky or involuntary movements, especially of the face, lips, jaw, tongue; slow-frequency tremor of head or limbs, especially while moving; muscle rigidity, lack of facial expression and slow, inflexible movements.	Discontinue. Call doctor right away.
• Pacing or restlessness; intermittent spasms of muscles of face, eyes, tongue, jaw, neck, body or limbs; dry mouth, blurred vision, constipation, difficulty urinating.	Continue. Call doctor when convenient.
Infrequent: Sedation, low blood pressure and dizziness.	Continue. Call doctor when convenient.
Infrequent: Other symptoms not listed above.	Continue. Call doctor when convenient.

 WARNINGS & PRECAUTIONS

Don't take if:
- You are allergic to any thioxanthine or phenothiazine tranquilizer.
- You have serious blood disorder.
- You have Parkinson's disease.
- Patient is younger than 12.

Before you start, tell your doctor:
- If you have had liver or kidney disease.
- If you have epilepsy, glaucoma, prostate trouble.
- If you have high blood pressure or heart disease (especially angina).
- If you use alcohol daily.
- If you will have surgery within 2 months, including dental surgery, requiring general or spinal anesthesia.

Over age 60:
Adverse reactions and side effects may be more frequent and severe than in younger persons.

Pregnancy:
Decide with your doctor if drug benefits justify risk to unborn child. Risk category C (see page 47).

Breast-feeding:
Studies inconclusive. Consult your doctor.

Children & adolescents:
Not recommended.

Prolonged use:
- Pigment deposits in lens and retina of eye.
- Involuntary movements of jaws, lips, tongue (tardive dyskinesia).
- Talk to your doctor about the need for follow-up medical examinations or laboratory studies to check complete blood counts (white blood cell count, platelet count, red blood cell count, hemoglobin, hematocrit), liver function, eyes.

Skin, sunlight & heat:
- May cause rash or intensify sunburn in areas exposed to sun or ultraviolet light (photosensitivity reaction). Use sunscreen and avoid overexposure. Notify doctor if reaction occurs.
- Hot temperatures and exercise, hot baths can increase risk of heatstroke. Drug may affect body's ability to maintain normal temperature.

Driving, piloting or hazardous work:
Don't drive or pilot aircraft until you learn how medicine affects you. Don't work around dangerous machinery. Don't climb ladders or work in high places. Danger increases if you drink alcohol or take medicine affecting alertness and reflexes.

Discontinuing:
Don't discontinue without consulting doctor. Dose may require gradual reduction if you have taken drug for a long time. Doses of other drugs may also require adjustment.

Others:
- Advise any doctor or dentist whom you consult that you take this medicine.
- For dry mouth, suck sugarless hard candy or chew sugarless gum. If dry mouth persists, consult your dentist.

POSSIBLE INTERACTION WITH OTHER DRUGS

GENERIC NAME OR DRUG CLASS	COMBINED EFFECT
Anticonvulsants*	Change in seizure pattern.
Antidepressants, tricyclic*	Increased thiothixene effect. Excessive sedation.
Antihistamines*	Increased thiothixene effect. Excessive sedation.
Antihypertensives*	Excessively low blood pressure.
Barbiturates*	Increased thiothixene effect. Excessive sedation.
Bupropion	Increased risk of major seizures.
Epinephrine	Excessively low blood pressure.
Guanethidine	Decreased guanethidine effect.
Levodopa	Decreased levodopa effect.
Mind-altering drugs*	Increased thiothixene effect. Excessive sedation.
Monoamine oxidase (MAO) inhibitors*	Excessive sedation.
Narcotics*	Increased thiothixene effect. Excessive sedation.

Continued on page 177

POSSIBLE INTERACTION WITH OTHER SUBSTANCES

INTERACTS WITH	COMBINED EFFECT
Alcohol:	Excessive brain depression. Avoid.
Beverages:	None expected.
Cocaine:	Decreased thiothixene effect. Avoid.
Foods:	None expected.
Marijuana:	Daily use—Fainting likely, possible psychosis.
Tobacco:	None expected.

TRAZODONE

BRAND NAMES

Desyrel   Trialodine
Trazon

BASIC INFORMATION

Habit forming? No
Prescription needed? Yes
Available as generic? Yes
Drug class: Antidepressant (nontricyclic)

 ## USES

- Treats mental depression.
- Treats anxiety.
- Helps promote sleep.
- Treats some types of chronic pain.

 ## DOSAGE & USAGE INFORMATION

How to take:
Tablet—Swallow with liquid or food to lessen stomach irritation. If you can't swallow whole, crumble tablet and take with liquid or food.

When to take:
According to prescription directions. Bedtime dose usually higher than other doses.

If you forget a dose:
Take as soon as you remember up to 2 hours late. If more than 2 hours, wait for next scheduled dose (don't double this dose).

What drug does:
Inhibits serotonin* uptake in brain cells.

Continued next column

 ## OVERDOSE

SYMPTOMS:
Fainting, irregular heartbeat, respiratory arrest, chest pain, seizures, coma.
WHAT TO DO:
- Dial 911 (emergency) or 0 (operator) for an ambulance or medical help. Then give first aid immediately.
- If patient is unconscious and not breathing, give mouth-to-mouth breathing. If there is no heartbeat, use cardiac massage and mouth-to-mouth breathing (CPR). Don't try to make patient vomit. If you can't get help quickly, take patient to nearest emergency facility.
- See emergency information at end of book.

Time lapse before drug works:
2 to 4 weeks for full effect.

Don't take with:
Any other medicine without consulting your doctor or pharmacist.

 ## POSSIBLE ADVERSE REACTIONS OR SIDE EFFECTS

SYMPTOMS	WHAT TO DO
Life-threatening: In case of overdose, see previous column.	
Common: Drowsiness.	Continue. Call doctor when convenient.
Infrequent:	
• Prolonged penile erections that may be very painful (priapism).	Seek emergency treatment immediately.
• Tremor, fainting, incoordination, blood pressure rise or drop, rapid heartbeat, shortness of breath.	Discontinue. Call doctor right away.
• Disorientation, confusion, fatigue, dizziness on standing, headache, nervousness, rash, itchy skin, blurred vision, ringing in ears, dry mouth, bad taste, diarrhea, nausea, vomiting, constipation, aching, menstrual changes, diminished sex drive, nightmares, vivid dreams.	Continue. Call doctor when convenient.
Rare: Unusual excitement	Discontinue. Call doctor right away.

 ## WARNINGS & PRECAUTIONS

Don't take if:
- You are allergic to trazodone.
- You are thinking about suicide.

Before you start, tell your doctor:
- If you have heart rhythm problem.
- If you have any heart disease.
- If you will have surgery within 2 months, including dental surgery, requiring general or spinal anesthesia.
- If you have bipolar (manic-depressive) disorder.
- If you have liver or kidney disease.

Over age 60:
Adverse reactions and side effects may be more frequent and severe than in younger persons.

Pregnancy:
Decide with your doctor if drug benefits justify risk to unborn child. Risk category C (see page 47).

Breast-feeding:
Drug passes into milk. Avoid drug or discontinue nursing until you finish medicine. Consult doctor for advice on maintaining milk supply.

Children & adolescents:
Not recommended.

Prolonged use:
See your doctor for occasional blood counts, especially if you have fever and sore throat.

Skin, sunlight & heat:
May cause rash or intensity sunburn in areas exposed to sun or ultraviolet light (photosensitivity reaction). Use sunscreen and avoid overexposure. Notify doctor if reaction occurs.

Driving, piloting or hazardous work:
Don't drive or pilot aircraft until you learn how medicine affects you. Don't work around dangerous machinery. Don't climb ladders or work in high places. Danger increases if you drink alcohol or take medicine affecting alertness and reflexes, such as antihistamines, tranquilizers, sedatives, pain medicine, narcotics and mind-altering drugs.

Discontinuing:
Don't discontinue without consulting doctor. Dose may require gradual reduction if you have taken drug for a long time. Doses of other drugs may also require adjustment.

Others:
- Electroconvulsive therapy* should be avoided. Combined effect is unknown.
- Advise any doctor or dentist whom you consult that you take this medicine.
- For dry mouth, suck on sugarless hard candy or chew sugarless gum.

POSSIBLE INTERACTION WITH OTHER DRUGS

GENERIC NAME OR DRUG CLASS	COMBINED EFFECT
Antidepressants*, other	Excess drowsiness.
Antihistamines*	Excess drowsiness.
Antihypertensives*	Possible too-low blood pressure. Avoid.
Barbiturates*	Too-low blood pressure and drowsiness. Avoid.
Central nervous system (CNS) depressants*	Increased sedation.
Digoxin	Possible increased digitalis level in blood.
Guanabenz	Increased effects of both medicines.
Monoamine oxidase (MAO) inhibitors*	May add to toxic effect of each.
Narcotics*	Excess drowsiness.
Phenytoin	Possible increased phenytoin level in blood.

POSSIBLE INTERACTION WITH OTHER SUBSTANCES

INTERACTS WITH	COMBINED EFFECT
Alcohol:	Excess sedation. Avoid.
Beverages: Caffeine.	May add to heartbeat irregularity. Avoid.
Cocaine:	May add to heartbeat irregularity. Avoid.
Foods:	No problems expected.
Marijuana:	May add to heartbeat irregularity. Avoid.
Tobacco:	May add to heartbeat irregularity. Avoid.

*See Glossary

TRIAZOLAM

BRAND NAMES

Apo-Triazo   Novo-Triolam
Halcion   Nu-Triazo

BASIC INFORMATION

Habit forming? Yes
Prescription needed? Yes
Available as generic? Yes
Drug class: Sedative-hypnotic agent

 USES

- Treatment for insomnia (short term).
- Prevention or treatment of transient insomnia associated with sudden sleep schedule changes, such as travel across several time zones.

 DOSAGE & USAGE INFORMATION

How to take:
Tablet—Swallow with liquid. If you can't swallow whole, crumble tablet and take with liquid or food.

When to take:
At the same time each day, according to instructions on prescription label. You should be in bed when you take your dose.

If you forget a dose:
Take as soon as you remember up to 2 hours late. If more than 2 hours, wait for next scheduled dose (don't double this dose).

Continued next column

 OVERDOSE

SYMPTOMS:
Drowsiness, weakness, tremor, stupor, coma.
WHAT TO DO:
- **Dial 911 (emergency) or 0 (operator) for an ambulance or medical help. Then give first aid immediately.**
- **If patient is unconscious and not breathing, give mouth-to-mouth breathing. If there is no heartbeat, use cardiac massage and mouth-to-mouth breathing (CPR). Don't try to make patient vomit. If you can't get help quickly, take patient to nearest emergency facility.**
- **See emergency information at end of book.**

What drug does:
Affects limbic system of brain, the part that controls emotions.

Time lapse before drug works:
Within 30 minutes.

Don't take with:
Any prescription or nonprescription drugs without consulting your doctor or pharmacist.

 POSSIBLE ADVERSE REACTIONS OR SIDE EFFECTS

SYMPTOMS	WHAT TO DO
Life-threatening:	
In case of overdose, see previous column.	
Common:	
Clumsiness, drowsiness, dizziness.	Continue. Call doctor when convenient.
Infrequent:	
• Amnesia, hallucinations, confusion, depression, irritability, rash, itch, vision changes, sore throat, fever, chills, dry mouth.	Discontinue. Call doctor right away.
• Constipation or diarrhea, nausea, vomiting, difficult urination, vivid dreams, behavior changes, abdominal pain, headache.	Continue. Call doctor when convenient.
Rare:	
• Slow heartbeat, breathing difficulty.	Discontinue. Seek emergency treatment.
• Mouth, throat ulcers; jaundice.	Discontinue. Call doctor right away.
• Decreased sex drive.	Continue. Call doctor when convenient.

 WARNINGS & PRECAUTIONS

Don't take if:
- You are allergic to any benzodiazepine.
- You have myasthenia gravis.
- You are an active or recovering alcoholic.
- Patient is younger than 6 months.

Before you start, tell your doctor:
- If you have liver, kidney or lung disease.
- If you have diabetes, epilepsy or porphyria.
- If you have glaucoma.

Over age 60:
Adverse reactions and side effects may be more frequent and severe than in younger persons. You may need smaller doses for shorter periods of time. You may develop agitation, rage or a "hangover" effect.

Pregnancy:
Risk to unborn child outweighs drug benefits. Don't use. Risk category X (see page 47).

Breast-feeding:
Drug may pass into milk. Avoid drug or discontinue nursing until you finish medicine. Consult doctor for advice on maintaining milk supply.

Children & adolescents:
Not recommended.

Prolonged use:
May impair liver function.

Skin, sunlight & heat:
No problems expected.

Driving, piloting or hazardous work:
Don't drive or pilot aircraft until you learn how medicine affects you. Don't work around dangerous machinery. Don't climb ladders or work in high places. Danger increases if you drink alcohol or take medicine affecting alertness and reflexes.

Discontinuing:
Don't discontinue without consulting doctor. Dose may require gradual reduction if you have taken drug for a long time. Doses of other drugs may also require adjustment.

Others:
- Hot weather, heavy exercise and profuse sweating may reduce excretion and cause overdose.
- Blood sugar may rise in diabetics, requiring insulin adjustment.
- Don't use for insomnia more than 4-7 days.
- Advise any doctor or dentist whom you consult that you take this medicine.
- Triazolam has a very short duration of action in the body.

POSSIBLE INTERACTION WITH OTHER DRUGS

GENERIC NAME OR DRUG CLASS	COMBINED EFFECT
Anticonvulsants*	Change in seizure frequency or severity.
Antidepressants*	Increased sedative effects of both drugs.
Antihistamines*	Increased sedative effects of both drugs.
Antihypertensives*	Excessively low blood pressure.
Central nervous system (CNS) depressants*, other	Increased central nervous system depression.
Cimetidine	Increased triazolam effect. May be dangerous.
Clozapine	Toxic effect on the central nervous system.
Contraceptives, oral*	Increased triazolam effect and toxicity.
Disulfiram	Increased triazolam effect and toxicity.
Erythromycins*	Increased triazolam effect and toxicity.
Isoniazid	Increased triazolam effect and toxicity.
Ketoconazole	Increased triazolam effect and toxicity.
Levodopa	Possible decreased levodopa effect and toxicity.
Molindone	Increased tranquilizer effect.
Monoamine oxidase (MAO) inhibitors*	Convulsions, deep sedation, rage.
Narcotics*	Increased sedative effects of both drugs.
Nefazodone	Increased effects of both drugs.

Continued on page 177

POSSIBLE INTERACTION WITH OTHER SUBSTANCES

INTERACTS WITH	COMBINED EFFECT
Alcohol:	Heavy sedation or amnesia. Avoid.
Beverages:	None expected.
Cocaine:	Decreased triazolam effect.
Foods:	None expected.
Marijuana:	Heavy sedation. Avoid.
Tobacco:	Decreased triazolam effect.

VALPROIC ACID

BRAND AND GENERIC NAMES

Depakene
Depakote
Depakote Sprinkle

DIVALPROEX
Epival
Myproic Acid

BASIC INFORMATION

Habit forming? No
Prescription needed? Yes
Available as generic? Yes
Drug class: Anticonvulsant

USES

- Treatment of various types of epilepsy.
- Treatment for bipolar (manic-depressive) disorder.

DOSAGE & USAGE INFORMATION

How to take:
Capsule or syrup—Swallow with liquid or food to lessen stomach irritation.

When to take:
Once a day.

If you forget a dose:
Take as soon as you remember. Don't ever double dose.

What drug does:
Increases concentration of gamma aminobutyric acid, which inhibits nerve transmission in parts of brain.

Time lapse before drug works:
1 to 4 hours, but full effect may take weeks.

Continued next column

OVERDOSE

SYMPTOMS:
Coma
WHAT TO DO:
- Dial 911 (emergency) or 0 (operator) for an ambulance or medical help. Then give first aid immediately.
- If patient is unconscious and not breathing, give mouth-to-mouth breathing. If there is no heartbeat, use cardiac massage and mouth-to-mouth breathing (CPR). Don't try to make patient vomit. If you can't get help quickly, take patient to nearest emergency facility.
- See emergency information at end of book.

Don't take with:
Any other medicine without consulting your doctor or pharmacist.

POSSIBLE ADVERSE REACTIONS OR SIDE EFFECTS

SYMPTOMS	WHAT TO DO
Life-threatening: In case of overdose, see previous column.	
Common: Loss of appetite, indigestion, nausea, vomiting, abdominal cramps, diarrhea, tremor, unusual weight gain or loss, menstrual changes in girls.	Continue. Call doctor when convenient.
Infrequent: Clumsiness, or unsteadiness, constipation, skin rash, dizziness, drowsiness, unusual excitement or irritability.	Continue. Call doctor when convenient.
Rare: Mood or behavior changes; continued nausea, vomiting and appetite loss; increase in number of seizures; swelling of face, feet or legs; yellow skin or eyes; tiredness or weakness; back-and-forth eye movements (nystagmus); seeing double or seeing spots; severe stomach cramps; unusual bleeding or bruising.	Continue, but call doctor right away.

WARNINGS & PRECAUTIONS

Don't take if:
You are allergic to valproic acid.

Before you start, tell your doctor:
- If you have blood, kidney or liver disease.
- If you will have surgery within 2 months, including dental surgery, requiring general or spinal anesthesia.

Over age 60:
Adverse reactions and side effects may be more frequent and severe than in younger persons.

Pregnancy:
Risk to unborn child exists. Use only if benefits of drug greatly exceed fetal risk. Risk category D (see page 47).

Breast-feeding:
Drug passes into milk. Avoid drug or discontinue nursing until you finish medicine. Consult doctor for advice on maintaining milk supply.

Children & adolescents:
Use under close medical supervision only.

Prolonged use:
Request periodic blood tests, liver and kidney function tests. These tests are necessary for safe and effective use.

Skin, sunlight & heat:
No problems expected.

Driving, piloting or hazardous work:
Don't drive or pilot aircraft until you learn how medicine affects you. Don't work around dangerous machinery. Don't climb ladders or work in high places. Danger increases if you drink alcohol or take medicine affecting alertness and reflexes, such as antihistamines, tranquilizers, sedatives, pain medicine, narcotics and mind-altering drugs.

Discontinuing:
Don't discontinue without consulting doctor. Dose may require gradual reduction if you have taken drug for a long time. Doses of other drugs may also require adjustment.

Others:
Advise any doctor or dentist whom you consult that you take this drug.

POSSIBLE INTERACTION WITH OTHER DRUGS

GENERIC NAME OR DRUG CLASS	COMBINED EFFECT
Anticoagulants*, oral	Increased chance of bleeding.
Anticonvulsants*	Unpredictable. May require increase or decrease in dosage of valproic acid or other anticonvulsant.
Anti-inflammatory drugs, nonsteroidal* (NSAIDs)	Increased risk of bleeding problems.
Antivirals, HIV/AIDS*	Increased risk of pancreatitis.
Carbamazepine	Decreased valproic acid effect.
Central nervous system (CNS) depressants*	Increased sedative effect.
Clonazepam	May prolong seizure.

Felbamate	Increased side effects and adverse reactions of valproic acid.
Hepatotoxics*	Increased risk of liver toxicity.
Lamotrigine	Increased lamotrigine effect. Possibly decrease effect valproic acid.
Levocarnitine	Decreased levocarnitine. Patients taking valproic acid may need to take the supplement levocarnitine.
Phenobarbital	Increased phenobarbital levels; possibly toxic or beneficial effect.
Phenytoin	Unpredictable. Dose may require adjustment.
Primidone	Increased primidone effect. Possible toxicity.
Salicylates*	Increased effect of valproic acid.
Sertraline	Increased depressive effects of both drugs.
Sodium benzoate & sodium phenylacetate	May reduce effect of sodium benzoate & sodium phenylacetate.

Continued on page 177

POSSIBLE INTERACTION WITH OTHER SUBSTANCES

INTERACTS WITH	COMBINED EFFECT
Alcohol:	Deep sedation. Avoid.
Beverages:	No problems expected.
Cocaine:	Increased brain sensitivity. Avoid.
Foods:	No problems expected.
Marijuana:	Increased brain sensitivity. Avoid.
Tobacco:	Decreased valproic acid effect.

*See Glossary

VENLAFAXINE

BRAND NAMES

Effexor

BASIC INFORMATION

Habit forming? Not known
Prescription needed? Yes
Available as generic? No
Drug class: Antidepressant (bicyclic)

 USES

Treats mental depression.

 DOSAGE & USAGE INFORMATION

How to use:
Tablet—Swallow with liquid and take with food to lessen stomach irritation.

When to use:
At the same times each day (usually with meals or with a snack).

If you forget a dose:
Take as soon as you remember up to 2 hours late. If more than 2 hours, wait for the next scheduled dose (don't double this dose).

What drug does:
Increases the amount of certain chemicals in the brain that are required for the transmission of messages between nerve cells.

Time lapse before drug works:
Begins in 1 to 3 weeks, but may take 4 to 6 weeks for maximum benefit.

Don't take with:
Any other medication without consulting your doctor or pharmacist.

 OVERDOSE

SYMPTOMS:
May cause no symptoms, or there may be extreme drowsiness, convulsions or rapid heartbeat.
WHAT TO DO:
* **Dial 911 (emergency) or 0 (operator) for an ambulance or medical help. Then give first aid immediately.**
* **See emergency information at end of book.**

 POSSIBLE ADVERSE REACTIONS OR SIDE EFFECTS

SYMPTOMS	WHAT TO DO
Life-threatening:	
In case of overdose, see previous column.	
Common:	
• Fast heartbeat, blurred vision, increased blood pressure.	Discontinue. Call doctor right away.
• Stomach pain, gas, insomnia or drowsiness, dizziness, decreased sexual drive, impotence, nausea or vomiting, headache, diarrhea or constipation, dryness of mouth, skin flushing, rash, loss of appetite, unusual tiredness, weakness, strange dreams, sweating, tremors, nervousness, headache.	Continue. Call doctor when convenient.
Infrequent:	
• Lightheadedness or faintness when arising from a sitting or lying position, mood or behavior changes, mental changes, difficulty urinating.	Continue. Call doctor when convenient.
• Weight loss or gain, changes in taste, ringing in ears.	Continue. Tell doctor at next visit.
Rare:	
Seizures.	Discontinue. Seek emergency help.

WARNINGS & PRECAUTIONS

Don't take if:
You are allergic to venlafaxine.

Before you start, tell your doctor:
- If you have liver or kidney disease.
- If you have high blood pressure.
- If you have thoughts about suicide.
- If you are allergic to any other medications.
- If you have a history of seizures.

Over age 60:
Adverse reactions and side effects may be more severe than in younger persons.

Pregnancy:
Decide with your doctor if drug benefits justify any possible risk to unborn child. Risk category C (see page 47).

Breast-feeding:
It is unknown if drug passes into milk. Avoid nursing until you finish medicine. Consult doctor for advice on maintaining milk supply.

Children & adolescents:
Safety in children under age 18 has not been established. Use only under close medical supervision.

Prolonged use:
Consult with your doctor on a regular basis while taking this drug to check your progress, to monitor your blood pressure and to determine the need for continued treatment.

Skin, sunlight & heat:
No special problems expected.

Driving, piloting or hazardous work:
Don't drive or pilot aircraft until you learn how medicine affects you. Don't work around dangerous machinery. Don't climb ladders or work in high places. Danger increases if you drink alcohol or take medicine affecting alertness and reflexes.

Discontinuing:
Don't discontinue this drug without consulting doctor. Dosage may require a gradual reduction before stopping.

Others:
- Get up slowly from a sitting or lying position to avoid any dizziness, faintness or lightheadedness.
- Advise any doctor or dentist whom you consult that you take this medicine.
- Take medicine only as directed. Do not increase or reduce dosage without doctor's approval.

POSSIBLE INTERACTION WITH OTHER DRUGS

GENERIC NAME OR DRUG CLASS	COMBINED EFFECT
Antidepressants*, other	Increased sedative effect. Not recommended.
Central nervous system (CNS) depressants*, other	Increased sedative effect.
Cimetidine	Increased risk of adverse reactions.
Monoamine oxidase (MAO) inhibitors*	Increased risk and severity of adverse reactions. Allow 14 days between use of the two drugs.

POSSIBLE INTERACTION WITH OTHER SUBSTANCES

INTERACTS WITH	COMBINED EFFECT
Alcohol:	Increased sedative affect. Avoid.
Beverages:	None expected.
Cocaine:	Effect not known. Best to avoid.
Foods:	None expected.
Marijuana:	Effect not known. Best to avoid.
Tobacco:	None expected.

ZOLPIDEM

BRAND NAMES

Ambien

BASIC INFORMATION

Habit forming? Yes
Prescription needed? Yes
Available as generic? No
Drug class: Sedative-hypnotic agent

 ## USES

Short-term (less than 2 weeks) treatment for insomnia.

 ## DOSAGE & USAGE INFORMATION

How to take:
Tablets—Swallow with liquid.

When to take:
Take immediately before bedtime. For best results, do not take with a meal or immediately after eating a meal.

If you forget a dose:
Take as soon as you remember. Take drug only when you are able to get 7 to 8 hours of sleep before your daily activity begins. Do not exceed prescribed dosage.

What drug does:
Acts as a central nervous system depressant, decreasing sleep problems such as trouble falling asleep, waking up too often during the night and waking up too early in the morning.

Time lapse before drug works:
Within 1 to 2 hours.

Don't take with:
Any other prescription or nonprescription drug without consulting your doctor or pharmacist.

 ## OVERDOSE

SYMPTOMS:
Drowsiness, weakness, stupor, coma.
WHAT TO DO:
- Dial 911 (emergency) or 0 (operator) for an ambulance or medical help. Then give first aid immediately.
- If patient is unconscious and not breathing, use cardiac massage and mouth-to-mouth breathing (CPR). Don't try to make patient vomit. If you can't get help quickly, take patient to nearest emergency facility.
- See emergency information at end of book.

 ## POSSIBLE ADVERSE REACTIONS OR SIDE EFFECTS

SYMPTOMS	WHAT TO DO
Life-threatening: In case of overdose, see previous column.	
Common: Daytime drowsiness, lightheadedness, dizziness, clumsiness, headache, diarrhea, nausea.	Continue. Call doctor when convenient.
Infrequent: Dry mouth, muscle aches or pain, tiredness, indigestion, joint pain, memory problems.	Continue. Call doctor when convenient.
Rare: Behavioral changes, agitation, confusion, hallucinations, worsening of depression, bloody or cloudy urine, painful or difficult urination, increased urge to urinate, skin rash or hives, itching.	Discontinue. Call doctor right away.

WARNINGS & PRECAUTIONS

Don't take if:
You are allergic to zolpidem.

Before you start, tell your doctor:
- If you have respiratory problems.
- If you have kidney or liver disease.
- If you suffer from depression.
- If you are an active or recovering alcoholic or substance abuser.

Over age 60:
Adverse reactions and side effects may be more frequent and severe than in younger persons. You may need smaller doses for shorter periods of time.

Pregnancy:
Consult doctor. Risk category B (see page 47).

Breast-feeding:
Drug passes into milk. Avoid drug or discontinue nursing until you finish medicine. Consult doctor for advice on maintaining milk supply.

Children & adolescents:
Not recommended for patients under age 18.

Prolonged use:
Not recommended for long-term usage. Don't take for longer than 1 to 2 weeks unless under doctor's supervision.

Skin, sunlight & heat:
No special problems expected.

Driving, piloting or hazardous work:
Don't drive or pilot aircraft until you learn how medicine affects you. Don't work around dangerous machinery. Don't climb ladders or work in high places. Danger increases if you drink alcohol or take other medicines affecting alertness and reflexes.

Discontinuing:
- Don't discontinue without consulting doctor. Dose may require gradual reduction if you have taken drug for a long time.
- You may have sleeping problems for 1 or 2 nights after stopping drug.

Others:
- Advise any doctor or dentist whom you consult that you take this medicine.
- Don't take drug if you are traveling on an overnight airplane trip of less than 7 or 8 hours. A temporary memory loss may occur (traveler's amnesia).

POSSIBLE INTERACTION WITH OTHER DRUGS

GENERIC NAME OR DRUG CLASS	COMBINED EFFECT
Central nervous system (CNS) depressants*	Increased sedative effect. Avoid.
Chlorpromazine	Increased sedative effect. Avoid.
Imipramine	Increased sedative effect. Avoid.

POSSIBLE INTERACTION WITH OTHER SUBSTANCES

INTERACTS WITH	COMBINED EFFECT
Alcohol:	Increased sedation. Avoid.
Beverages:	None expected.
Cocaine:	None expected.
Foods:	Decreased sedative effect if taken with a meal or right after a meal.
Marijuana:	None expected.
Tobacco:	None expected.

Brand and Generic Name Directory

How to Read the Lists Below

The following drugs are alphabetized by generic name or drug class name, shown in large capital letters. The generic names and brand names that follow each title in this list are the complete list referred to on the drug chart. Generic names are in all capital letters on these lists; brand names are lower case.

Some main headings below, such as *AMPHETAMINES* (a drug class name), are followed by generic names, which are numbered, and then by brand names, each of which is followed by a superscript number. By matching numbers, you can determine the generic drug(s) in each brand-name drug. For example, under *AMPHETAMINES*, the brand-name drug Dexedrine[2] contains the generic drug *DEXTROAMPHETAMINE*, which is numbered 2.

Other main heads below, such as MEPROBAMATE, are simple generic names, followed by brand-name drugs containing that generic drug.

AMPHETAMINES

GENERIC NAMES
1. AMPHETAMINE
2. DEXTROAMPHETAMINE
3. METHAMPHETAMINE

BRAND NAMES
Biphetamine[1, 2]
Desoxyn[3]
Desoxyn Gradumet[3]
Dexedrine[2]
Dexedrine Spansule[2]
DextroStat[2]
Oxydess[2]

ANTIDEPRESSANTS, TRICYCLIC

GENERIC NAMES
1. AMITRIPTYLINE
2. AMOXAPINE
3. CLOMIPRAMINE
4. DESIPRAMINE
5. DOXEPIN
6. IMIPRAMINE
7. NORTRIPTYLINE
8. PROTRIPTYLINE
9. TRIMIPRAMINE

BRAND NAMES
Adapin[5]
Anafranil[3]
Apo-Amitriptyline[1]
Apo-Imipramine[6]
Apo-Trimip[9]
Asendin[2]
Aventyl[7]
Elavil[1]
Elavil Plus[1]
Emitrip[1]
Endep[1]

Enovil[1]
Etrafon[1]
Etrafon Forte[1]
Etrafon-A[1]
Etrafon-D[1]
Etrafon-F[1]
Impril[6]
Janimine[6]
Levate[1]
Limbitrol[1]
Limbitrol DS[1]
Norfranil[6]
Norpramin[4]
Novo-Doxepin[5]
Novopramine[6]
Novo-Tripramine[9]
Novotriptyn[1]
Pamelor[7]
Pertofrane[4]
PMS Amitriptyline[1]
PMS Imipramine[6]
PMS Levazine[1]
Rhotrimine[9]
Sinequan[5]
Surmontil[9]
Tipramine[6]
Tofranil[6]
Tofranil-PM[6]
Triadapin[5]
Triavil[1]
Triptil[8]
Vivactil[8]

BARBITURATES

GENERIC NAMES
1. AMOBARBITAL
2. APROBARBITAL
3. BUTABARBITAL
4. BUTALBITAL
5. MEPHOBARBITAL
6. METHARBITAL
7. PENTOBARBITAL
8. PHENOBARBITAL
9. SECOBARBITAL
10. SECOBARBITAL & AMOBARBITAL
11. TALBUTAL

BRAND NAMES
Alurate[2]
Amaphen[4]
Amytal[1]
Ancalixir[8]
Anolor-300[4]
Anoquan[4]
Arcet[4]
Bancap[4]
Barbita[8]
Bucet[4]
Busodium[3]
Butace[4]
Butalan[3]
Butisol[3]
Dolmar[4]
Endolor[4]
Esgic[4]
Esgic-Plus[1, 4]
Ezol[4]
Femcet[4]
Fioricet[4]
G-1[4]
Gemonil[6]
Isocet[4]
Isopap[4]
Luminal[8]
Mebaral[5]
Medigesic[4]
Nembutal[7]
Nova Rectal[7]
Novopentobarb[7]
Novosecobarb[9]

Pacaps[4]
Phrenilin[4]
Phrenilin Forte[4]
Repan[4]
Sarisol No. 2[3]
Seconal[9]
Sedapap[4]
Solfoton[8]
Tencet[4]
Triad[4]
Triaprin[4]
Tuinal[10]
Two-Dyne[4]

BENZODIAZEPINES

GENERIC NAMES
1. ALPRAZOLAM
2. BROMAZEPAM
3. CHLORDIAZEPOXIDE
4. CLONAZEPAM
5. CLORAZEPATE
6. DIAZEPAM
7. ESTAZOLAM
8. FLURAZEPAM
9. HALAZEPAM
10. KETAZOLAM
11. LORAZEPAM
12. MIDAZOLAM
13. NITRAZEPAM
14. OXAZEPAM
15. PRAZEPAM
16. QUAZEPAM
17. TEMAZEPAM

BRAND NAMES
Alprazolam Intensol[1]
Apo-Alpraz[1]
Apo-Chlordiazepoxide[3]
Apo-Clorazepate[5]
Apo-Diazepam[6]
Apo-Flurazepam[8]
Apo-Lorazepam[11]
Apo-Oxazepam[14]
Ativan[17]
Centrax[15]
Clindex[3]
Clinoxide[3]
Dalmane[8]
Diazemuls[6]
Diazepam Intensol[6]
Doral[16]
Klonopin[4]
Lectopam[2]
Librax[3]
Libritabs[3]
Librium[3]
Lidoxide[3]
Limbitrol[3]
Limbitrol DS[3]
Lipoxide[3]
Loftran[16]
Lorazepam Intensol[11]
Medilium[3]
Meval[6]
Mogadon[15]

Novo-Alprazol[1]
Novoclopate[5]
Novodipam[6]
Novoflupam[8]
Novolorazem[11]
Novopoxide[3]
Novoxapam[14]
Nu-Alpraz[1]
Nu-Loraz[11]
Paxipam[9]
PMS Diazepam[6]
ProSom[7]
Restoril[17]
Rivotril[4]
Serax[14]
Solium[3]
Somnol[8]
T-Quil[6]
Tranxene[5]
Tranxene T-Tab[5]
Tranxene-SD[5]
Valium[6]
Valrelease[6]
Vivol[6]
Xanax[1]
Zapex[14]
Zebrax[3]
Zetran[6]

BETA-ADRENERGIC BLOCKING AGENTS

GENERIC NAMES
1. ACEBUTOLOL
2. ATENOLOL
3. BETAXOLOL
4. BISOPROLOL
5. CARTEOLOL
6. LABETALOL
7. METOPROLOL
8. NADOLOL
9. OXPRENOLOL
10. PENBUTOLOL
11. PINDOLOL
12. PROPRANOLOL
13. SOTALOL
14. TIMOLOL

BRAND NAMES
Apo-Atenolol[2]
Apo-Metoprolol[7]
Apo-Metoprolol (Type L)[7]
Apo-Propranolol[12]
Apo-Timol[14]
Betaloc[7]
Betaloc Durules[7]
Betapace[13]
Blocadren[14]
Cartrol[5]
Corgard[8]
Detensol[12]
Inderal[12]
Inderal LA[12]
Kerlone[3]
Levatol[10]
Lopresor[7]

Lopresor SR[7]
Lopressor[7]
Monitan[1]
Normodyne[6]
Novo-Atenol[2]
Novometoprol[7]
Novo-Pindol[11]
Novopranol[12]
Novo-Timol[14]
NuMetop[7]
pms Propranolol[12]
Sectral[1]
Slow-Trasicor[9]
Sotacor[13]
Syn-Nadolol[8]
Syn-Pindolol[11]
Tenormin[2]
Toprol XL[7]
Trandate[6]
Trasicor[9]
Visken[11]
Zebeta[4]

CAFFEINE

BRAND NAMES
Caffedrine
Caffefrine Caplets
Chewable NoDoz
Dexitac
Enerjets
Keep Alert
Kolephrin
Korigesic
NoDoz
NoDoz Maximum Strength
  Caplets
Pep-Back
Quick Pep
Ultra Pep-Back
Vivarin
Wake-Up

CALCIUM CHANNEL BLOCKERS

GENERIC NAMES
1. AMLODIPINE
2. BEPRIDIL
3. DILTIAZEM
4. FELODIPINE
5. FLUNARIZINE
6. ISRADIPINE
7. NICARDIPINE
8. NIFEDIPINE
9. NISOLDIPINE
10. VERAPAMIL

BRAND NAMES
Adalat[8]
Adalat CC[8]
Adalat FT[8]
Adalat P.A.[8]
Apo-Diltiaz[3]
Apo-Nifed[8]
Apo-Verap[10]

Bepadin[2]
Calan[10]
Calan SR[10]
Cardene[7]
Cardizem[3]
Cardizem CD[3]
Cardizem SR[3]
Dilacor-XR[3]
Dyna Circ[6]
Isoptin[10]
Isoptin SR[10]
Lotrel[1]
Norvasc[1]
Novo-Diltazem[3]
Novo-Nifedin[8]
Novo-Veramil[10]
Nu-Diltiaz[3]
Nu-Nifed[8]
Nu-Verap[10]
Plendil[4]
Procardia[8]
Procardia XL[8]
Renedil[4]
Sibelium[5]
Syn-Diltiazem[3]
Vascor[2]
Verelan[10]

DIPHENHYDRAMINE

BRAND NAMES

Allerdryl
AllerMax Caplets
Aller-med
Banophen
Banophen Caplets
Beldin
Belix
Benadryl
Benadryl 25
Benadryl Kapseals
Bendylate
Benylin Cough
Bydramine Cough
Compoz
DiaHist
Diphen Cough
Diphendryl
Diphenhist
Diphenhist Captabs
Dormarex 2
Dormin
Fenylhist
Fynex
Genahist
Gen-D-phen
Hydramin
Hydramine
Hydramine Cough
Hydril
Insomnal
Nervine Nighttime Sleep-Aid
Nidryl
Noradryl
Nordryl

Nordryl Cough
Nytol with DPH
Nytol Maximum Strength
Phendry
Robalyn
Siladryl
Silphen Cough
Sleep-Eze 3
SleepGels Maximum Strength
Sominex Formula
Sominex Formula 2
Tusstat
Twilite Caplets
UniBent Cough
Unisom

HYDROXYZINE

BRAND NAMES

Anxanil
Apo-Hydroxyzine
Atarax
Novo-Hydroxyzin
Vistaril

MEPROBAMATE

BRAND NAMES

Acabamate
Apo-Meprobamate
Equanil
Equanil Wyseals
Medi-Tran
Meprospan 200
Meprospan 400
Miltown
Neuramate
Novomepro
Novo-Mepro
Pax 400
Probate
Sedabamate
Trancot
Tranmep

PHENOTHIAZINES

GENERIC NAMES

1. ACETOPHENAZINE
2. CHLORPROMAZINE
3. FLUPHENAZINE
4. MESORIDAZINE
5. METHOTRIMEPRAZINE
6. PERICYAZINE
7. PERPHENAZINE
8. PIPOTIAZINE
9. PROCHLORPERAZINE
10. PROMAZINE
11. THIOPROPAZATE
12. THIOPROPERAZINE
13. THIORIDAZINE
14. TRIFLUOPERAZINE
15. TRIFLUPROMAZINE

BRAND NAMES

Apo-Fluphenazine[3]
Apo-Perphenazine[7]

Apo-Thioridazine[13]
Apo-Trifluoperazine[14]
Chlorpromanyl-5[2]
Chlorpromanyl-20[2]
Chlorpromanyl-40[2]
Compazine[9]
Compazine Spansule[9]
Dartal[11]
Elavil Plus[7]
Etrafon[7]
Etrafon Forte[7]
Etrafon-A[7]
Etrafon-D[7]
Etrafon-F[7]
Largactil[2]
Largactil Liquid[2]
Largactil Oral Drops[2]
Levoprome[5]
Majeptil[12]
Mellaril[13]
Mellaril Concentrate[13]
Mellaril-S[13]
Modecate[3]
Modecate Concentrate[3]
Moditen Enanthate[3]
Moditen HCl[3]
Moditen HCl-H.P[3]
Neuleptil[6]
Novo-Chlorpromazine[2]
Novo-Flurazine[14]
Novo-Ridazine[13]
Nozinan[5]
Nozinan Liquid[5]
Nozinan Oral Drops[5]
Permitil[3]
Permitil Concentrate[3]
Piportil L₄[8]
PMS Levazine[7]
PMS Thioridazine[13]
Prolixin[3]
Prolixin Concentrate[3]
Prolixin Decanoate[3]
Prolixin Enanthate[3]
Prorazin[9]
Prozine [10]
Serentil[4]
Serentil Concentrate[4]
Solazine[14]
Stelazine[14]
Stelazine Concentrate[14]
Stemetil[9]
Stemetil Liquid[9]
Suprazine[14]
Terfluzine[14]
Terfluzine Concentrate[14]
Thorazine[2]
Thorazine Concentrate[2]
Thorazine Spansule[2]
Thor-Prom[2]
Tindal[2]
Triavil[7]
Trilafon[7]
Trilafon Concentrate[7]
Ultrazine-10[9]
Vesprin[5]

Additional Drug Interactions

The following lists of drugs and their interactions with other drugs are continuations of lists found in the alphabetized drug charts. These lists are alphabetized by generic name or drug class name, shown in large capital letters. Only those lists too long for the drug charts are included in this section. For complete information about any generic drug or drug class, see the alphabetized charts.

GENERIC NAME OR DRUG CLASS	COMBINED EFFECT	GENERIC NAME OR DRUG CLASS	COMBINED EFFECT
ANTIDEPRESSANTS, TRICYCLIC			
Benzodiazepines*	Increased sedation.	Leucovorin	High alcohol content of leucovorin may cause adverse effects.
Bupropion	Increased risk of major seizures.		
Central nervous system (CNS) depressants*	Excessive sedation.	Levodopa	May increase blood pressure. May decrease levodopa effect.
Cimetidine	Possible increased tricyclic antidepressant effect and toxicity.	Lithium	Possible decreased seizure threshold.
		Methyldopa	Possible decreased methyldopa effect.
Clonidine	Blood pressure increase. Avoid combination.	Methylphenidate	Possible increased tricyclic antidepressant effect and toxicity.
Clozapine	Toxic effect on the central nervous system.		
		Molindone	Increased molindone effect.
Contraceptives, oral*	Increased depression.	Monoamine oxidase (MAO) inhibitors*	Fever, delirium, convulsions.
Dextrothyroxine	Increased antidepressant effect. Irregular heartbeat.	Narcotics*	Oversedation.
		Nicotine	Increased effect of antidepressant (with imipramine).
Disulfiram	Delirium.		
Ethchlorvynol	Delirium.		
Fluoxetine	Increased effect of tricyclic antidepressant. Possible toxicity.	Phenothiazines*	Possible increased tricyclic antidepressant effect and toxicity.
Fluvoxamine	Increased antidepressant effect.	Phenytoin	Decreased phenytoin effect.
Furazolidine	Sudden, severe increase in blood pressure.	Procainamide	Possible irregular heartbeat.
		Quinidine	Possible irregular heartbeat.
Guanabenz	Decreased guanabenz effect.	Sertraline	Increased depressive effects of both drugs.
Guanadrel	Decreased guanadrel effect.	Sympathomimetics*	Increased sympathomimetic effect.
Guanethidine	Decreased guanethidine effect.	Thyroid hormones*	Irregular heartbeat.
Haloperidol	Decreased lamotrigine effect.	Zolpidem	Increased sedative effect. Avoid.

GENERIC NAME OR DRUG CLASS	COMBINED EFFECT	GENERIC NAME OR DRUG CLASS	COMBINED EFFECT

BARBITURATES

Dextrothyroxine	Decreased barbiturate effect.	Monoamine oxidase (MAO) inhibitors*	Increased barbiurate effect.
Divalproex	Dangerous sedation. Avoid.	Narcotics*	Dangerous sedation. Avoid.
Doxycycline	Decreased doxycycline effect.	Sertraline	Increased depressive effects of both drugs.
Griseofulvin	Decreased griseofulvin effect.		
Lamotrigine	Decreased lamotrigine effect.	Sotalol	Increased barbiturate effect. Dangerous sedation.
Mind-altering drugs*	Dangerous sedation. Avoid.	Valproic acid	Increased barbiturate effect.

BENZODIAZEPINES

Nicotine	Increased benzo-diazepine effect.	Probenecid	Increased benzo-diazepine effect.
Omeprazole	Delayed excretion of benzodiazepine causing increased amount of benzo-diazepine in blood.	Sertraline	Increased depressive effects of both drugs.
		Zidovudine	Increased toxicity of zidovudine.

BETA-ADRENERGIC BLOCKING AGENTS

Diazoxide	Additional blood pressure drop.	Nefazodone	Dosages of both drugs may require adjustment.
Digitalis preparations*	Can either increase or decrease heart rate. Improves irregular heartbeat.	Nitrates*	Possible excessive blood pressure drop.
Flecainide	Increased effect of toxicity on heart muscle.	Phenytoin	Decreased beta blocker effect.
		Propafenone	Increased beta blocker effect.
Fluvoxamine	Increased benzo-diazepine effect.	Quinidine	Slows heart excessively in some patients.
Indomethacin	Decreased effect of beta blocker.		
Insulin	Hypoglycemic effects may be prolonged.	Reserpine	Increased reserpine effect. Excessive sedation and depression. Additional blood pressure drop.
Levobunolol eyedrops	Possible increased beta blocker effect.		
Molindone	Increased tranquilizer effect.	Sympathomimetics*	Decreased effects of both drugs.
Monoamine oxidase (MAO) inhibitors*	High blood pressure following MAO discontinuation.	Timolol eyedrops	Possible increased beta blocker effect.
Narcotics*	Increased narcotic effect. Dangerous sedation.	Tocainide	May worsen congestive heart failure.

172

GENERIC NAME OR DRUG CLASS	COMBINED EFFECT	GENERIC NAME OR DRUG CLASS	COMBINED EFFECT

BETA-ADRENERGIC BLOCKING AGENTS continued

Warfarin	Increased warfarin effect.	Xanthines (aminophylline, theophylline)	Decreased effects of both drugs.

CALCIUM CHANNEL BLOCKERS

Nimodipine	Dangerous blood pressure drop.	Quinidine	Increased quinidine effect.
Nitrates*	Reduced angina attacks.	Rifampin	Decreased effect of calcium channel blocker.
Phenytoin	Possible decreased calcium channel blocker effect.	Theophylline	May increase effect and toxicity of theophylline.
Propafenone	Increased effects of both drugs and increased risk of toxicity.	Vitamin D	Decreased effect of calcium channel blocker.

CARBAMAZEPINE

Cortisone*	Decreased cortisone effect.	Isoniazid	Increased risk of liver damage.
Desmopressin	May increase desmopressin effect.	Itraconazole	Decreased itraconazole effect.
Digitalis preparations*	Excessive slowing of heart.	Lamotrigine	Decreased lamotrigine effect. Increased risk of side effects.
Diltiazem	Increased effect of carbamzepine.		
Doxepin (topical)	Increased risk of toxicity of both drugs.	Leucovorin	High alcohol content of leucovorin may cause adverse effects.
Doxycycline	Decreased doxycycline effect.		
Estrogens*	Decreased estrogen effect.	Mebendazole	Decreased effect of mebendazole.
Erythromycins*	Increased carbamazepine effect.	Monoamine oxidase (MAO) Inhibitors*	Dangerous over-stimulation. Avoid.
Ethinamate	Dangerous increased effects of ethinamate. Avoid combining.	Nicardipine	May increase carbamazepine effect and toxicity.
Felbamate	Increased side effects and adverse reactions.	Nimodipine	May increase carbamazepine effect and toxicity.
Fluoxetine	Increased carbamazepine effect.	Nizatidine	Increased carbamazepine effect and toxicity.
Fluvoxamine	Possible toxicity of carbamazepine.	Phenytoin	Decreased carbamazepine effect.
Guanfacine	May increase depressant effects of either drug.	Phenobarbital	Decreased carbamazepine effect.

173

GENERIC NAME OR DRUG CLASS	COMBINED EFFECT	GENERIC NAME OR DRUG CLASS	COMBINED EFFECT

CARBAMAZEPINE continued

GENERIC NAME OR DRUG CLASS	COMBINED EFFECT	GENERIC NAME OR DRUG CLASS	COMBINED EFFECT
Primidone	Decreased carbamazepine effect.	Tiopronin	Increased risk of toxicity to bone marrow.
Propoxyphene (Darvon)	Increased toxicity of both. Avoid.	Tramadol	Decreased tramadol effect.
Risperidone	Decreased risperidone effect.	Verapamil	Possible increased carbamazepine effect.
Sertraline	Increased depressive effects of both drugs.		

FLUVOXAMINE

GENERIC NAME OR DRUG CLASS	COMBINED EFFECT	GENERIC NAME OR DRUG CLASS	COMBINED EFFECT
Selegiline	Increased risk of adverse effects. May lead to convulsions and hypertensive crisis. Let 14 days elapse between taking the 2 drugs.	Terfenadine	Serious heart problems. Avoid.
		Theophylline	Increased theophylline effect.

HALOPERIDOL

GENERIC NAME OR DRUG CLASS	COMBINED EFFECT	GENERIC NAME OR DRUG CLASS	COMBINED EFFECT
Fluoxetine	Increased depressant effects of both drugs.	Levodopa	Decreased levodopa effect.
Guanethidine	Decreased guanethidine effect.	Lithium	Increased toxicity.
Guanfacine	May increase depressant effects of either drug.	Loxapine	May increase toxic effects of both drugs.
		Methyldopa	Possible psychosis.
		Narcotics*	Excessive sedation.
Leucovorin	High alcohol content of leucovorin may cause adverse effects.	Nefazodone	Unknown effect. May require dosage adjustment.
Nefazodone	Unknown effect. May need dosage adjustment.	Pergolide	Decreased pergolide effect.
Leucovorin	High alcohol content of leucovorin may cause adverse effects.	Procarbazine	Increased sedation.
		Sertraline	Increased depressive effects of both drugs.

LITHIUM

GENERIC NAME OR DRUG CLASS	COMBINED EFFECT	GENERIC NAME OR DRUG CLASS	COMBINED EFFECT
Fluvoxamine	Increased risk of seizure.	Iodide salts	Increased lithium effects on thyroid function.
Haloperidol	Increased toxicity of both drugs.	Ketoprofen	May increase lithium in blood.
Indomethacin	Increased lithium effect.		

GENERIC NAME OR DRUG CLASS	COMBINED EFFECT	GENERIC NAME OR DRUG CLASS	COMBINED EFFECT

LITHIUM continued

GENERIC NAME OR DRUG CLASS	COMBINED EFFECT	GENERIC NAME OR DRUG CLASS	COMBINED EFFECT
Methyldopa	Increased lithium effect.	Potassium iodide	Increased potassium iodide effect.
Molindone	Brain changes.	Sodium bicarbonate	Decreased lithium effect.
Oxyphenbutazone	Increased lithium effect.	Sumatriptan	Adverse effects unknown. Avoid.
Phenothiazines*	Decreased lithium effect.	Theophylline	Decreased lithium effect.
Phenylbutazone	Increased lithium effect.	Tiopronin	Increased risk of toxicity to kidneys.
Phenytoin	Increased lithium effect.		

LOXAPINE

GENERIC NAME OR DRUG CLASS	COMBINED EFFECT	GENERIC NAME OR DRUG CLASS	COMBINED EFFECT
Rauwolfia	May increase toxic effects of both drugs.	Thioxanthenes*	May increase toxic effects of both drugs
Sertraline	Increased depressive effects of both drugs.		

MAPROTILINE

GENERIC NAME OR DRUG CLASS	COMBINED EFFECT	GENERIC NAME OR DRUG CLASS	COMBINED EFFECT
Guanfacine	May increase depressant effects of either drug.	Narcotics*	Dangerous oversedation.
Leucovorin	High alcohol content of leucovorin may cause adverse effects.	Phenothiazines*	Possible increased antidepressant effect and toxicity.
Levodopa	Decreased levodopa effect.	Phenytoin	Decreased phenytoin effect.
Lithium	Possible decreased seizure threshold.	Quinidine	Irregular heartbeat.
Methyldopa	Decreased methyldopa effect.	Selegiline	Fever, delirium, convulsions.
Methylphenidate	Possible increased antidepressant effect and toxicity.	Sertraline	Increased depressive effects of both drugs.
Molindone	Increased tranquilizer effect.	Sympathomimetics*	Increased sympathomimetic effect.
Monoamine oxidase (MAO) inhibitors*	Fever, delirium, convulsions.	Thyroid hormones*	Irregular heartbeat.

MOLINDONE

GENERIC NAME OR DRUG CLASS	COMBINED EFFECT	GENERIC NAME OR DRUG CLASS	COMBINED EFFECT
Narcotics*	Increased narcotic effect.	Sertraline	Increased depressive effects of both drugs.
Phenytoin	Increased or decreased phenytoin effect.	Sotalol	Increased tranquilizer effect. Increased sotalol effect.

GENERIC NAME OR DRUG CLASS	COMBINED EFFECT	GENERIC NAME OR DRUG CLASS	COMBINED EFFECT

MONOAMINE OXIDASE (MAO) INHIBITORS

GENERIC NAME OR DRUG CLASS	COMBINED EFFECT	GENERIC NAME OR DRUG CLASS	COMBINED EFFECT
Central nervous system (CNS) depressants*	Excessive depressant action.	Methyldopa	Sudden, severe blood pressure rise.
Clozapine	Toxic effect on the central nervous system.	Methylphenidate	Increased blood pressure.
Doxepin (topical)	Potentially life-threatening. Allow 14 days between use of the 2 drugs.	Monoamine oxidase (MAO) inhibitors (others, when taken together)	High fever, convulsions, death
Dextromethorphan	Very high blood pressure.	Narcotics*	Severe high blood pressure.
Diuretics*	Excessively low blood pressure.	Nefazodone	Potentially life-threatening. Allow 14 days between use of the 2 drugs.
Ephedrine	Increased blood pressure.	Paroxetine	Can cause a life-threatening reaction. Avoid. Increased risk and severity of side effects. Allow 4 weeks between use of the 2 drugs.
Fluoxetine	Serotonin syndrome (muscle rigidity, confusion, high fever). Avoid. Increased risk and severity of side effects. Allow 4 weeks between use of the 2 drugs.		
		Phenothiazines*	Possible increased phenothiazine toxicity.
Fluvoxamine	Potentially life-threatening. Allow 14 days between use of the 2 drugs.	Phenylpropanolamine	Increased blood pressure.
		Pseudoephedrine	Increased blood pressure.
Furazolidine	Sudden, severe increase in blood pressure.	Sertraline	Serotonin syndrome (muscle rigidity, confusion, high fever). Avoid. Increased risk and severity of side effects. Allow 4 weeks between use of the 2 drugs.
Guanadrel	High blood pressure.		
Guanethidine	Blood pressure rise.		
Guanfacine	May increase depressant effects of either drug.		
Indapamide	Increased indapamide effect.	Sympathomimetics*	Blood pressure rise to life-threatening level.
Insulin	Increased hypoglycemic effect.	Tramadol	Increased risk of seizures.
Leucovorin	High alcohol content of leucovorin may cause adverse effects.	Trazodone	Increased risk of mental status changes.
Levodopa	Sudden, severe blood pressure rise.	Venlafaxine	Increased risk and severity of side effects. Allow 4 weeks between use of the 2 drugs.
Maprotiline	Dangerous blood pressure rise.		

GENERIC NAME OR DRUG CLASS	COMBINED EFFECT	GENERIC NAME OR DRUG CLASS	COMBINED EFFECT

PHENOTHIAZINES

GENERIC NAME OR DRUG CLASS	COMBINED EFFECT	GENERIC NAME OR DRUG CLASS	COMBINED EFFECT
Clozapine	Toxic effect on the central nervous system.	Mind-altering drugs*	Increased effect of mind-altering drug.
Doxepin (topical)	Increased risk of toxicity of both drugs.	Molindone	Increased tranquilizer effect.
Guanethidine	Increased guanethidine effect.	Narcotics*	Increased narcotic effect.
Isoniazid	Increased risk of liver damage.	Procarbazine	Increased sedation.
		Tramadol	Increased sedation.
Levodopa	Decreased levodopa effect.	Zolpidem	Increased sedation. Avoid.
Lithium	Decreased lithium effect.		

THIOTHIXENE

GENERIC NAME OR DRUG CLASS	COMBINED EFFECT	GENERIC NAME OR DRUG CLASS	COMBINED EFFECT
Pergolide	Decreased pergolide effect.	Sertraline	Increased depressive effects of both drugs.
Quinidine	Increased risk of heartbeat irregularities.	Tranquilizers*	Increased thiothixene effect. Excessive sedation.

TRIAZOLAM

GENERIC NAME OR DRUG CLASS	COMBINED EFFECT	GENERIC NAME OR DRUG CLASS	COMBINED EFFECT
Omeprazole	Delayed excretion of triazolam causing increased amount of triazolam in blood.	Probenecid	Increased triazolam effect.
		Zidovudine	Increased toxicity of zidovudine.

VALPROIC ACID

GENERIC NAME OR DRUG CLASS	COMBINED EFFECT	GENERIC NAME OR DRUG CLASS	COMBINED EFFECT
Sulfinpyrazone	Increased chance of bleeding.	Tocainide	Possible decreased blood cell production in bone marrow.

Glossary

A

ACE Inhibitors—See Angiotensin-Converting Enzyme Inhibitors.

Acquired Immunodeficiency Syndrome (AIDS)—A disease caused by the human immunodeficiency virus (HIV) that suppresses the body's immune system. People with AIDS are vulnerable to a variety of "opportunistic" infections and diseases. To date, there is no cure, but some medications can help relieve symptoms and prolong life.

Acridine Derivatives—Dyes or stains (usually yellow or orange) used for some medical tests and as antiseptic agents.

Acute—Having a short and relatively severe course, e.g., acute illness as opposed to chronic illness.

Addiction—A chronic disease caused by genetic, psychosocial and environmental factors involving preoccupation with mood-altering substances (drugs, alcohol, food) or behaviors (gambling, sex) in which there is a loss of self-control and a compulsion to continue despite adverse personal and social consequences. For other information on this disorder, see the disorder chart on Substance Abuse and Addiction.

Addictive Drugs—Any drugs that can lead to physiological dependence on the drugs. These include alcohol, cocaine, marijuana, nicotine, opium, morphine, codeine, heroin (and other narcotics) and others.

Addison's Disease—Changes in the body caused by a deficiency of hormones manufactured by the adrenal gland. Usually fatal if untreated.

ADHD—See Attention-Deficit Hyperactivity Disorder.

Adjustment Disorders—Emotional or behavioral responses (occurring within 3 months) to stressful events or traumas that are considered excessive or abnormally persistent in light of the provoking situations. These disorders are common and usually temporary. For other information on this disorder, see the disorder chart on Adjustment Disorders.

Adrenal Cortex—Center of the adrenal gland.

Adrenal Gland—Gland next to the kidney that produces cortisone and epinephrine (adrenaline).

Affect—The external expressions of emotion displayed by a person. Appropriate affect properly reflects emotion (smiling when one is happy); inappropriate affect is considered an abnormal response (laughing at a sad event).

Affective Disorders—A group of disorders characterized by mood disturbances such as depression and bipolar disorder (manic-depressive disorder).

Aggression—A term used to describe a wide variety of acts of hostility (physical or verbal) considered to be outside the range of normal behavior.

Agitation—An inability to be still; excessive physical activity. Usually associated with tension.

Agonist—(1) A drug that acts to enhance or facilitate the action of another drug; (2) a muscle whose contraction is counteracted by the opposite movement of another muscle.

Agranulocytosis—A symptom complex characterized by (1) a sharply decreased number of granulocytes (one of the types of white blood cells), (2) lesions of the throat and other mucous membranes, (3) lesions of the gastrointestinal tract and (4) lesions of the skin. Sometimes also called granulocytopenia.

AIDS—See Acquired Immunodeficiency Syndrome.

Akathisia—Compulsive, uncontrollable restlessness and agitation; a side effect of some medications.

Alcoholism—A psychological and physiological dependence on alcohol resulting in chronic disease and disruption of interpersonal, family and work relationships. For other information on this disorder, see the disorder chart on Alcoholism.

Alkalizers—A group of drugs that neutralize acidic properties of the blood and urine by making them more alkaline (or basic).

Alkylating Agent—Chemical used to treat malignant diseases.

Allergy—Excessive sensitivity to a substance.

Alpha-Adrenergic Blocking Agents—A group of drugs used to treat hypertension.

Alzheimer's Disease—A brain disorder characterized by gradual mental deterioration. For other information on this disorder, see the disorder chart on Alzheimer's Disease.

Amebiasis—Infection with amebas, one-celled organisms. Causes diarrhea, fever and abdominal cramps.

Aminoglycosides—A family of antibiotics used for serious infections. Their usefulness is limited because of relative toxicity compared to some other antibiotics.

Amnesia—A loss of memory that may be temporary or permanent.

Amphetamines—A family of drugs that stimulates the central nervous system, prescribed to treat attention-deficit disorders in children and also narcolepsy. They are habit-forming, are controlled under U.S. law and are no longer prescribed as appetite suppressants. For a list of the generic and brand names, see Brand Name Directory. For other information on these drugs, see the drug chart on Amphetamines. They may be ingredients of several combination drugs.

ANA Titers—A test to evaluate the immune system and to detect antinuclear antibodies (ANAs), substances that appear in the blood of some patients with autoimmune disease.

Analgesics—Agents that reduce pain without reducing consciousness.

Analysis—In psychiatry, a synonym for psychoanalysis.

Anaphylaxis—Severe allergic response to a substance. Symptoms are wheezing, itching, hives, nasal congestion, intense burning of hands and feet, collapse, loss of consciousness and cardiac arrest. Symptoms appear within a few seconds or minutes after exposure. Anaphylaxis is a severe medical emergency. Without appropriate treatment, it can cause death. Instructions for home treatment for anaphylaxis are at the back of this book.

Androgens—Male hormones, including fluoxymesterone, methyltestosterone, testosterone.

Anemia—Not enough healthy red blood cells in the bloodstream or too little hemoglobin in the red blood cells. Anemia is caused by an imbalance between blood loss and blood production.

Anemia, Aplastic—A form of anemia in which the bone marrow is unable to manufacture adequate numbers of blood cells of all types—red cells, white cells and platelets.

Anemia, Hemolytic—Anemia caused by a shortened lifespan of red blood cells. The body can't manufacture new cells fast enough to replace old cells.

Anemia, Iron-Deficiency—Anemia caused when iron necessary to manufacture red blood cells is not available.

Anemia, Pernicious—Anemia caused by a vitamin B-12 deficiency. Symptoms include weakness, fatigue, numbness and tingling of the hands or feet and degeneration of the central nervous system.

Anemia, Sickle-Cell—Anemia caused by defective hemoglobin that deprives red blood cells of oxygen, making them sickle-shaped.

Anesthesias, General—Gases that are used in surgery to render patients unconscious and able to withstand the pain of surgical cutting and manipulation.

Anesthetics—Drugs that eliminate the sensation of pain. These drugs are normally administered by a health care professional.

Angina (Angina Pectoris)—Chest pain with a sensation of suffocation and impending death. Caused by a temporary reduction in the amount of oxygen to the heart muscle through diseased coronary arteries.

Angiotensin-Converting Enzyme (ACE) Inhibitors—A family of drugs used to treat hypertension and congestive heart failure. Inhibitors decrease the rate of conversion of angiotensin I into angiotensin II, which is the normal process for the angiotensin-converting enzyme. These drugs include benazepril, captopril, enalapril, fosinopril, lisinopril, quinapril, ramipril.

Anhedonia—An inability to experience pleasure.

Anorexia Nervosa—A psychological eating disorder in which a person refuses to eat adequately—in spite of hunger—and loses enough weight to become emaciated. For other information on this disorder, see the disorder chart on Anorexia Nervosa.

Anorgasmic—In females, the inability to achieve orgasm.

Antacids—A large family of drugs prescribed to treat hyperacidity, peptic ulcer, esophageal reflux and other conditions. These drugs include alumina and magnesia; alumina, magnesia and calcium carbonate; alumina, magnesia and simethicone; alumina and magnesium carbonate; alumina and magnesium trisilicate; alumina, magnesium trisilicate and sodium bicarbonate; aluminum carbonate; aluminum hydroxide; bismuth subsalicylate; calcium carbonate; calcium carbonate and magnesia; calcium carbonate, magnesia and simethicone; calcium and magnesium carbonates; calcium and magnesium carbonates and magnesium oxide; calcium carbonate and simethicone; dihydroxyaluminum aminoacetate; dihydroxyaluminum sodium carbonate; magaldrate; magaldrate and simethicone; magnesium carbonate and sodium bicarbonate; magnesium hydroxide; magnesium oxide; magnesium trisilicate, alumina and magnesia; simethicone, alumina, calcium carbonate and magnesia; simethicone, alumina, magnesium carbonate and magnesia; sodium bicarbonate.

Antagonists—Muscles, drugs, etc., that act in opposition to or counteract another.

Antiadrenals—Medicines or drugs that prevent the effects of the hormones liberated by the adrenal glands.

Antianginals—A group of drugs used to treat angina pectoris (chest pain that comes and goes, caused by coronary artery disease).

Antianxiety Drugs—A group of drugs prescribed to treat anxiety. These drugs include alprazolam, buspirone, chlordiazepoxide, chlordiazepoxide and amitriptyline, chlorpromazine, clomipramine, clorazepate, diazepam, hydroxyzine, lorazepam, loxapine, maprotiline, oxazepam.

Antiarrhythmics—A group of drugs used to treat heartbeat irregularities (arrhythmias). These drugs include acebutolol, adenosine, amiodarone, atenolol, atropine, bretylium, digitalis, digitoxin, diltiazem, disopyramide, edrophonium, encainide, esmolol, flecainide, lidocaine, metoprolol, mexiletine, moricizine, nadolol, oxprenolol, phenytoin, procainamide, propafenone, propranolol, quinidine, scopolamine, sotalol, timolol, tocainide, verapamil.

Antiasthmatics—Medicines used to treat asthma, which may be tablets, liquids or aerosols (to be inhaled to get directly to the bronchial tubes rather than being absorbed through the bloodstream).

Antibacterials (Antibiotics)—A group of drugs (e.g., penicillins, tetracyclines) prescribed to treat bacterial infections. These drugs are not used to treat viral infections such as colds or flu.

Anticholinergics—Drugs that work against acetylcholine, a chemical found in many locations in the body, including connections between nerve cells and connections between muscle and nerve cells. Anticholinergic drugs used in conjunction with therapeutic drugs include anisotropine, atropine, belladonna, clidinium, dicyclomine, glycopyrrolate, homatropine, hyoscyamine, ipratropium, mepenzolate, methantheline, methscopolamine, pirenzepine, propantheline, scopolamine. Other medication with anticholinergic activity include antihistamines (some), benzotropine, biperiden, buclizine, bupropion, carbamzepine, clozapine, cyclobenzaprine, digoxin, disopyramide, dronbinol, ethopropazine, loxapine, MAO inhibitors, maprotiline, meclizine, molindone, orphenadrine, phenothiazines, pimozide, procainamide, procyclidine, quinidine, thioxanthenes, tricyclic antidepressants, trihexyphenidyl.

Anticoagulants—A family of drugs prescribed to slow the rate of blood clotting. These drugs include acenocoumarol, anisindione, dicumarol, dihydroergotamine and heparin, heparin, warfarin.

Anticonvulsants—A group of drugs prescribed to treat or prevent seizures (convulsions). These drugs include acetazolamide, amobarbital, carbamazepine, clonazepam, clorazepate, diazepam, dichlorphenamide, divalproex, ethosuximide, ethotoin, felbamate, gabapentin, lamotrigine, lorazepam, magnesium (chloride and sulfate), mephenytoin, mephobarbital, metharbital, methazolamide, methsuximide, metocurine, nitrazepam, paraldehyde, paramethadione, pentobarbital, phenobarbital, phensuximide, phenytoin, primidone, secobarbital, trimethadione, tubocurarine, valproic acid.

Anticonvulsants, Hydantoin—A group of drugs prescribed to treat or prevent seizures (convulsions). These drugs include ethotoin, mephenytoin, phenytoin.

Anticonvulsants, Succinimide—A group of drugs prescribed to treat or prevent seizures (convulsions). These drugs include ethosuximide, methsuximide, phensuximide.

Antidepressants—A group of medicines prescribed to treat mental depression. The three classess of antidepressants are monoamine oxidase inhibitors, selective serotonin reuptake inhibitors and tricyclic antidepressants.

Antidepressants, MAO (Monoamine Oxidase Inhibitors)—See Monoamine Oxidase Inhibitors.

Antidepressants, Tricyclic —A group of medicines with similar chemical structure and pharmacologic activity used to treat mental depression. For a list of the generic and brand names, see Brand Name Directory. For other information on these drugs, see the drug chart on Antidepressants, Tricyclic.

Antidiabetic Agents, Oral —A group of drugs used in the treatment of diabetes mellitus. These medicines all reduce blood sugar. These drugs include acetohexamide, chlorpropamide, glipizide, glyburide, metformin, tolazamide, tolbutamide.

Antidyskinetics—A group of drugs used for treatment of Parkinsonism (*paralysis agitans*) and drug-induced extrapyramidal reactions (see elsewhere in Glossary).

Antiemetics—A group of drugs used to treat nausea and vomiting.

Antifibrinolytic Drugs—Drugs that are used to treat serious bleeding.

Antifungals—A group of drugs used to treat fungus infections. They may be systemic (taken orally), topical or given by injection.

Antigout Drugs—Drugs to treat the metabolic disease called gout. Gout causes recurrent attacks of joint pain caused by deposits of uric acid in the joints.

Antihistamines—A family of drugs used to treat allergic conditions, such as hay fever, allergic conjunctivitis, itching, sneezing, runny nose, motion sickness, dizziness, sedation, insomnia and others. These drugs include astemizole, azatadine, brompheniramine, carbinoxamine, cetirizine, chlorpheniramine, clemastine, cyproheptadine, dexchlorpheniramine, dimenhydrinate, diphenhydramine, diphenylpyraline, doxylamine, hydroxyzine, loratadine, phenindamine, pyrilamine, terfenadine, tripelennamine, triprolidine.

Antihypertensives—Drugs used to treat high blood pressure. These medicines can be used singly or in combination with other drugs. They work best if accompanied by a low-salt, low-fat diet plus an active exercise program. These drugs include acebutolol, amiloride, amiloride and hydrochlorothiazide, amlodipine, atenolol, atenolol and chlorthalidone, benazepril, bendroflumethiazide, benzthiazide, betaxolol, bisoprolol, bumetanide, captopril, captopril and hydrochlorothiazide, carteolol, chlorothiazide, chlorthalidone, clonidine, clonidine and chlorthalidone, cyclothiazide, debrisoquine, deserpidine, deserpidine and hydrochlorothiazide, deserpidine and methyclothiazide, diazoxide, diltiazem, doxazosin, enalapril, enalapril and hydrochlorothiazide, ethacrynic acid, felodipine, fosinopril, furosemide, guanabenz, guanadrel, guanethidine, guanethidine and hydrochlorothiazide, guanfacine, hydralazine, hydralazine and hydrochlorothiazide, hydrochlorothiazide, hydroflumethiazide, indapamide, isradipine, labetalol, labetalol and hydrochlorothiazide, lisinopril, lisinopril and hydrochlorothiazide, losartan and hydrochlorothiazide, mecamylamine, methyclothiazide, methyldopa, methyldopa and chlorothiazide, methyldopa and hydrochlorothiazide, metolazone, metoprolol, metoprolol and hydrochlorothiazide, minoxidil, moexipril, nadolol, nadolol and bendroflumethiazide, nicardipine, nifedipine, nitroglycerin, nitroprusside, oxprenolol, penbutolol, pindolol, pindolol and hydrochlorothiazide, polythiazide, prazosin, prazosin and polythiazide, propranolol, propranolol and hydrochlorothiazide, quinapril, quinethazone, ramipril, rauwolfia serpentina, rauwolfia serpentina and bendroflumethiazide, reserpine, reserpine and chlorothiazide, reserpine and chlorthalidone, reserpine and hydralazine, reserpine, hydralazine and hydrochlorothiazide, reserpine and hydrochlorothiazide, reserpine and hydroflumethiazide, reserpine and methyclothiazide, reserpine and polythiazide, reserpine and trichlormethiazide, sotalol, spironolactone, spironolactone and hydrochlorothiazide, ţerazosin, timolol, timolol and hydrochlorothiazide, torsemide, triamterene, triamterene and hydrochlorothiazide, trichlormethiazide, trimethaphan, verapamil.

Anti-Inflammatory Drugs, Nonsteroidal (NSAIDs)—A family of drugs not related to cortisone or other steroids that decrease inflammation wherever it occurs in the body. Used for treatment of pain, fever, arthritis, gout, menstrual cramps and vascular headaches. These drugs include aspirin; aspirin, alumina and magnesia tablets; buffered aspirin; choline salicylate; choline and magnesium salicylates; diclofenac, diflunisal; etodolac; fenoprofen; flurbiprofen, ibuprofen; indomethacin; ketoprofen; magnesium salicylate; meclofenamate; mefenamic acid; mesalamine; nabumetone; naproxen; olsalazine; oxaprozin; oxyphenbutazone; piroxicam; salsalate; sodium salicylate; sulindac; tenoxicam; tolmetin.

Anti-Inflammatory Drugs, Steroidal—A family of drugs with pharmacologic characteristics similar to those of cortisone and cortisonelike drugs. They are used for many purposes to help the body deal with inflammation, no matter what the cause. Steroidal drugs may be taken orally or by injection (systemic) or applied locally for the skin, eyes, ears, bronchial tubes (topical) and others.

Antimania Drugs—Drugs used to treat hypomania and bipolar disorder (manic-depressive disorder).

Antimuscarines—Drugs that block the muscarinic action of acetylcholine and therefore decrease spasms of the smooth muscles. They are prescribed for peptic ulcers, painful menstruation, dizziness, seasickness, bedwetting, slow heart rate, treatment of toxicity from pesticides made from organophosphates and other medical problems.

Antimyasthenics—Medicines to treat myasthenia gravis, a muscle disorder (especially of the face and head) with increasing fatigue and weakness as muscles tire from use.

Antineoplastics—Potent drugs used for malignant diseases.

Antiobsessional Drugs—Drugs used to treat the symptoms of obsessive-compulsive disorder.

Antiparkisonism Drugs—Drugs used to treat Parkinson's disease. A disease of the central nervous system in older adults, it is characterized by gradual progressive muscle rigidity, tremors and clumsiness.

Antipsychotic Drugs—A group of drugs used to treat the mental disease of psychosis.

Antithyroid Drugs—A group of drugs that decrease the amount of thyroid hormone produced by the thyroid gland.

Antitussives—A group of drugs used to suppress cough.

Antiulcer Drugs—A group of medicines used to treat peptic ulcer in the stomach, duodenum or the lower end of the esophagus.

Antiurolithics—Medicines that prevent the formation of kidney stones.

Antiviral Drugs—A group of drugs used to treat viral infection.

Antiviral Drugs, HIV/AIDS—A group of drugs used to treat HIV and AIDS symptoms. These drugs include didanosine, stavudine, zalcitabine, zidovudine.

Anxiety—Feelings of apprehension, uneasiness or impending danger. The anxiety may be a normal response to danger or a threat, but in some cases, no danger or threat exists. For other information, see the disorder chart on Anxiety.

Anxiolytics—Medications that reduce anxiety. See Antianxiety Drugs.

Appendicitis—Inflammation or infection of the appendix. Symptoms include loss of appetite, nausea, low-grade fever and tenderness in the lower right part of the abdomen.

Appetite Suppressants—A group of drugs used to decrease the appetite as part of an overall treatment for obesity. These drugs include benzphetamine, diethylpropion, fenfluramine, mazindol, phendimetrazine, phenmetrazine, phentermine, phenylpropanolamine.

Artery—Blood vessel carrying blood away from the heart.

Assertiveness Training—A form of psychotherapy whereby individuals are trained to express their feelings, opinions and thoughts honestly and directly.

Asthenia—A term meaning loss of strength and energy, e.g., weakness.

Asthma—Recurrent attacks of breathing difficulty due to spasms and contractions of the bronchial tubes.

Asymptomatic—Showing or causing no symptoms; used to describe an individual who is diagnosed with a disease or disorder, but has no symptoms.

Ataxia—Inability to coordinate muscle movements. It can affect balance and gait, eye movements, limb movements and speech.

Attention-Deficit Hyperactivity Disorder (ADHD)—A pattern of behavior in children characterized by short attention spans and impulsivity, with or without hyperactivity. For other information on this disorder, see the disorder chart on Attention-Deficit Hyperactivity Disorder.

Atypical—A term used to describe a disorder that has symptoms not usually associated with that particular problem. For example, in atypical depression an individual may eat and sleep much more than usual rather than having no appetite and being unable to sleep.

Autism—A development disorder that appears in infancy or early childhood. It is characterized by self-absorption, inability to relate to others, avoidance of eye contact, playing alone, removal from reality and a wide range of other behaviors. However, many autisitc people lead nearly normal lives, and some are uniquely gifted.

Aversion Therapy—A form of psychotherapy used to help overcome unwanted behavior by making the person feel disgusted or repelled by the behavior.

B

Bacteria—Microscopic organisms. Some bacteria contribute to health; others (germs) cause disease.

Barbiturates—Powerful drugs used for sedation, to help induce sleep and sometimes to prevent seizures. Except for use in seizures (phenobarbital), barbiturates are being used less and less because there are better, less hazardous drugs that produce the same or better effects. For a list of the generic and brand names, see Brand Name Directory. For other information on these drugs, see the drug chart on Barbiturates.

Basal Area of Brain—Part of the brain that regulates muscle control and tone.

Behavior Therapy—Psychotherapy that focuses on ways to change the undesired behavior.

Benzethonium Chloride—A compound used as a preservative in some drug preparations. It is also used in various concentrations for cleaning cooking and eating utensils and as a disinfectant.

Benzodiazepines—A family of drugs prescribed to treat anxiety and alcohol withdrawal and sometimes prescribed for sedation. For a list of the generic and brand names, see Brand Name Directory. For other information on these drugs, see the drug chart on Benzodiazepines.

Bereavement—See Grief.

Beta Agonists—A group of drugs that act directly on cells in the body (beta-adrenergic receptors) to relieve spasms of the bronchial tubes and other organs consisting of smooth muscles. These drugs include albuterol, bitolterol, isoetharine, isoproterenol, metaproterenol, terbutaline.

Beta-Adrenergic Blocking Agents—A family of drugs with similar pharmacological actions with some variations. These drugs are prescribed for angina, heartbeat irregularities (arrhythmias), high blood pressure, hypertrophic subaortic stenosis, vascular headaches (as a preventative, not to treat once the pain begins) and others. For a list of the generic and brand names, see Brand Name Directory. For other information on these drugs, see the drug chart on Beta-Adrenergic Blocking Agents.

Bile Acids—Components of bile that are derived from cholesterol and formed in the liver. Bile acids aid the digestion of fat.

Biofeedback—A form of relaxation training that uses electronic monitoring to measure physiologic activities, such as pulse rate and muscle tension, to help a person learn how to control them.

Biological Clock—A term used to describe the internal regulating system that governs biological functions such as growth, the sleep-wake cycle and the menstrual cycle. This system operates according to a circadian rhythm. A circadian rhythm is one that is approximately 24 hours long.

Bipolar Disorder (Manic-Depressive Disorder)—A disorder that is characterized by extreme mood swings. Periods of unexplainable elation and overactivity (mania) alternate with deep depression. For other information on this disorder, see the disorder chart on Bipolar Disorder.

Bisexuality—Being attracted to members of both sexes.

Blood Alcohol Concentration (BAC)—The amount of alcohol in the blood. Used as an indicator of intoxication.

Blood Count—Laboratory studies to count white blood cells, red blood cells, platelets and other elements of the blood.

Blood Pressure, Diastolic—Pressure (usually recorded in millimeters of mercury) in the large arteries of the body when the heart muscle is relaxed and filling for the next contraction.

Blood Pressure, Systolic—Pressure (usually recorded in millimeters of mercury) in the large arteries of the body at the instant the heart muscle contracts.

Blood Sugar (Blood Glucose)—Element in the blood necessary to sustain life.

Bone Marrow Depressants—Medicines that affect the bone marrow to depress its normal function of forming blood cells. These medicines include aldesleukin, altretamine, amphotericin B (systemic), anticancer drugs, antithyroid drugs, azathioprine, busulfan, carboplatin, carmustine, chlorambucil, chloramphenicol, chromic phosphate, cisplatin, cladribine, clozapine, colchicine, cyclophosphamide, cytarabine, dacarbazine, dactinomycin, daunorubicin, didanosine, doxorubicin, eflornithine, etoposide, felbamate, floxuridine, flucytosine, fludarabine, fluorouracil, ganciclovir, hydroxyurea, idarubicin, ifosfamide, interferon, lomustine, mechlorethamine, melphalan, mercaptopurine, methotrexate, mitomycin, mitoxantrone, paclitaxel, pentostatin, plicamycin, procarbazine, streptozocin, sulfa drugs, thioguanine, uracil mustard, vidarabine (large doses), vinblastine, vincristine, zidovudine.

Brain Depressants—Drugs that depress brain function, such as tranquilizers, narcotics, alcohol, barbiturates.

Brain Imaging—Medical tests that visualize the structure or the function of the brain.

Brief Psychotherapy or Brief Dynamic Psychotherapy—Psychotherapy that lasts for a limited number of sessions, with emphasis on specific goals or objectives, such as eliminating a phobia.

Bronchodilators—A group of drugs used to dilate the bronchial tubes to treat such problems as asthma, emphysema, bronchitis, bronchiectasis, allergies and others.

Bruxism—Rhythmic grinding or clenching of the teeth, usually while sleeping, but may occur unconsciously when a person is awake.

Bulimia Nervosa—A psychological eating disorder characterized by abnormal perception of body image, constant craving for food and binge eating, followed by self-induced vomiting or laxative use. For other information on this disorder, see the disorder chart on Bulimia Nervosa.

BUN—Abbreviation for blood urea nitrogen. A test often used as a measurement of kidney function.

Burn-out—A term used to describe a state of physical, emotional and mental exhaustion, usually resulting from constant emotional pressure or stress.

C

Calcium Channel Blockers—A group of drugs used to treat angina and heartbeat irregularities and (rarely), some psychological symptoms. For a list of the generic and brand names, see Brand Name Directory. For other information on these drugs, see the drug chart on Calcium Channel Blockers.

Calcium Supplements—Supplements used to increase calcium concentration in the blood in an attempt to make bones denser (as in osteoporosis).

Capitation—A medical care plan whereby a certain amount of money is used to cover the cost of health care for a given individual.

Carbamates—A group of drugs derived from carbamic acid and used to reduce anxiety or as sedatives.

Carbonic Anhydrase Inhibitors—Drugs used to treat glaucoma and seizures and to prevent high-altitude sickness. They include acetazolamide, dichlorphenamide, methazolamide.

CAT Scan—See CT Scan.

Cataplexy—Sudden loss of muscular control and flexibility (lasting for a few seconds to minutes) without loss of consciousness. Usually triggered by strong emotional stimulation, such as anger, excitement or laughter.

Catatonia—A syndrome characterized by a motionless state with muscle rigidity and stupor; at other times, the person may be excessively active.

Cataract—Loss of transparency in the lens of the eye.

Catecholamines—A group of drugs used to treat excess catecholamine production (often a cause of hypertension).

Catharsis—Release of repressed emotions by talking or acting out feelings and memories. In more general terms, it is often used to describe any satisfying emotional experience.

Cell—Unit of protoplasm, the essential living matter of all plants and animals.

Central Nervous System (CNS)—The term used to describe the brain and spinal cord. The central nervous system works with the peripheral nervous system (PNS), which consists of all the nerves that carry signals between the CNS and the rest of the body.

Central Nervous System (CNS) Depressants—Drugs that cause sedation or otherwise diminish activity of the brain and other parts of the nervous system. These drugs include alcohol, aminoglutethimide, anesthetics (general and injection-local), anticonvulsants, antidepressants (MAO inhibitors and tricyclic types), antidyskinetics (except amantadine), antihistamines (some), apomorphine, baclofen, barbiturates, benzodiazepines, beta-adrenergic blocking agents, buclizine, carbamazepine, chlophedianol, chloral hydrate, chlorzoxazone, clonidine, clozapine, cyclizine, difenoxin and atropine, diphenoxylate and atropine, disulfiram, dronabinol, ethchlorvynol, ethinamate, etomidate, fenfluramine, fluoxetine, glutethimide, guanabenz, guanfacine, haloperidol, hydroxyzine, interferon, loxapine, maprotiline, meclizine, meprobamate, methyldopa, methyprylon, metoclopramide, metyrosine, mitotane, molindone, nabilone, opioid (narcotic) analgesics, oxybutynin, paraldehyde, paregoric, pargyline, paroxetine, phenothiazines, pimozide, procarbazine, promethazine, propiomazine, rauwolfia alkaloids, risperidone, scopolamine, sertraline, thioxanthenes, trazodone, trimeprazine, trimethobenzamide, zolpidem.

Central Nervous System (CNS) Stimulants—Drugs that cause excitation, anxiety and nervousness or otherwise stimulate the brain and other parts of the central nervous system. These drugs include amantadine, amphetamines, anesthetics (local), appetite suppressants (except fenfluramine), bronchodilators (xanthine-derivative), bupropion, caffeine, caffeine and sodium benzoate, chlophedianol, cocaine, dextroamphetamine, doxapram, dronabinol, ephedrine (oral), fluoxetine, methamphetamine, methylphenidate, nabilone, paroxetine, pemoline, selegiline, sertraline, sympathomimetics, tranylcypromine.

Cephalosporins—Antibiotics that kill many bacterial germs that penicillin and sulfa drugs can't destroy.

Character—The relatively fixed pattern of behavior or personality found in an individual.

Chemotherapy—A technique based on chemicals (drugs) used in the treatment of cancer.

Cholinergics (Parasympathomimetics)—Chemicals that facilitate passage of nerve impulses through the parasympathetic nervous system.

Cholinesterase Inhibitors—Drugs that prevent the action of cholinesterase, an enzyme that breaks down acetylcholine in the body.

Chromosomes—Microscopic structures within the cell that carry the genes that convey hereditary characteristics.

Chronic—Long-term, continuing. Chronic illnesses may not be curable, but they can often be prevented from becoming worse. Symptoms usually can be alleviated or controlled.

Chronic Fatigue Syndrome—A disorder characterized primarily by profound fatigue. For other information on this disorder, see the disorder chart on Chronic Fatigue Syndrome.

Chronic Pain Disorder (Somatoform Pain Disorder—Perceived pain that continues longer than 6 months without an accompanying injury or illness. There may be a medical problem, but it does not fully explain the pain. For other information on this disorder, see the disorder chart on Chronic Pain Disorder.

Circadian Rhythms—Behavioral or psychological rhythms associated with the 24-hour cycle of the earth's rotation. In humans, these involve metabolism, the sleep-wake cycle and glandular rhythms.

Cirrhosis—Disease that scars and destroys liver tissue.

Citrates—Medicines taken orally to make urine more acid.

Client-Orientated Therapy—A type of psychotherapy (founded by Carl Rogers) that helps an individual explore his or her emotional needs (rather than focusing diagnosis and treatment of specific disorders) and, with the support of the therapist, to work toward self-actualization (fulfilling one's potential).

Codependent—A person who "enables" another person to continue destructive habits, for example, a person who finds excuses for, denies or hides evidence of the spouse's alcoholism.

Cognitive Therapy—Psychotherapy that is based on the idea that the way we think about the world and ourselves affects our emotions and behavior. This therapy emphasizes changing behavior or distorted thinking that contributes to a problem.

Colitis, Ulcerative—Chronic, recurring ulcers of the colon that develop for unknown reasons.

Collagen—Support tissue of skin, tendon, bone, cartilage and connective tissue.

Colostomy—Surgical opening from the colon, the large intestine, to the outside of the body.

Comorbidity—The existence of two or more illness in an individual.

Complication—Undesirable event during disease or treatment that causes further symptoms and delay in recovery.

Compulsion—Repetitive behavior (e.g., washing hands over and over) or repetitive mental process (e.g., counting) that serves no useful purpose. The person with the compulsion feels anxiety if the act is not performed.

Conditioning—Changing behavior through learning. It involves the formation of a behavior in response to a specific stimulus.

Conduct Disorder—A personality disorder of children characterized by disruptive behaviors such as disobeying authority, stealing, lying and picking fights with other children.

Confusion—A disorganized mental state in which a person has reduced mental functioning, is not thinking clearly, has memory problems and is unable to reason clearly.

Congenital—Conditions that exist at and usually before birth, regardless of their cause.

Congestive—Characterized by excess accumulation of blood. In congestive heart failure, congestion occurs in the lungs, liver, kidneys and other parts of the body to cause shortness of breath, swelling of the ankles and feet, rapid heartbeat and other symptoms.

Consciousness—A state of awareness in which a person knows what he or she is doing and intends to do.

Constriction—Tightness or pressure.

Contraceptives, Oral (Birth Control Pills)—A group of hormones used to prevent ovulation, therefore preventing pregnancy. These hormones include ethynodiol diacetate and ethinyl estradiol, ethynodiol diacetate and mestranol, levonorgestrel and ethinyl estradiol, medroxyprogesterone, norethindrone tablets, norethindrone acetate and ethinyl estradiol, norethindrone and ethinyl estradiol, norethindrone and mestranol, norethyndrel and mestranol, norgestrel, norgestrel, ethinyl estradiol.

Convulsions—Violent, uncontrollable contractions of the voluntary muscles.

Coping Mechanisms—Methods of dealing with stress.

Coprophilia—A paraphilia characterized by an abnormal interest in feces.

Corticosteroids (Adrenocorticosteroids)—Steroid hormones produced by the body's adrenal cortex or their synthetic equivalents.

Cortisone (Adrenocorticoids, Glucocorticoids) and Other Adrenal Steroids—Medicines that mimic the action of the steroid hormone cortisone, which is manufactured in the cortex of the adrenal gland. These drugs decrease the effects of inflammation within the body. They are available for injection, oral use, topical use for the skin and nose and inhalation for the bronchial tubes. These drugs include alclometasone; amcinonide; beclomethasone; benzyl benzoate; betamethasone; bismuth; clobetasol; clobetasone 17-butyrate; clocortolone; corticotropin; cortisone; desonide; desoximetasone; desoxycorticosterone; dexamethasone; diflorasone; diflucortolone; fludrocortisone; flumethasone; flunisolide; fluocinonide; fluocinonide, procinonide and ciprocinonide; fluorometholone; fluprednisolone, flurandrenolide; halcinonide; hydrocortisone; medrysone; methylprednisolone; mometasone; paramethasone; peruvian balsam; prednisolone; prednisone; triamcinolone; zinc oxide.

Counseling—A term used to describe the process of interviewing, testing, giving advice and guidance and providing psychological support used by a health care professional to help an individual cope with life, solve problems and make future plans.

Countertransference—The projection of a therapist's emotions, wishes or thoughts onto a patient. See also transference.

Couple Therapy—Also called marriage therapy. It focuses on the relationship between two people. The therapy may be done with one couple or groups of couples.

Crisis Intervention—Emergency therapy that is brief and directed at a psychiatric crisis (a suicide attempt, violence or matter of similar urgency) to help restore coping mechanisms.

Cross Dressing—Dressing in clothing of the opposite sex. Usually describes men who like to dress in typical female clothing.

CT Scan, CAT Scan (Computerized Axial Tomography)—A computerized x-ray procedure that provides exceptionally clear images of parts of the body. It aids in diagnosis of diseases that cannot be diagnosed by ordinary x-ray methods.

Cushing Syndrome—A disease of the adrenal glands in which excessive hormones are excreted.

Cyclothymic Disorders—A type of mood disorder (affective disorder) characterized by mood swings similar to, but less severe than, those associated with bipolar (manic-depressive) disorder.

Cystitis—Inflammation of the urinary bladder.

D

Decongestants—Drugs used to open nasal passages by shrinking swollen membranes lining the nose.

Defense Mechanism—An automatic and unconscious response that enables a person to cope with conflicts arising from unacceptable impulses. Types of defense mechanisms include denial, displacement, humor, intellectualism, isolation of affect, projection, rationalization, reaction formation, repression, sublimation and suppression. See separate Glossary entries for explanation of each type.

Delirium—Temporary mental disturbance characterized by impaired and fluctuating ability to sustain attention, confusion, agitation and sometimes hallucinations.

Delusion—A false belief that a person clings to despite clear evidence that it is false. Occurs frequently in schizophrenia.

Delusional Disorders—Disorders characterized by consistent delusions, while other mental functioning is apparently unaffected. For other information on this disorder, see the disorder chart on Delusional Disorders.

Dementia (Senility)—Mental impairment caused by a variety of diseases that produce brain deterioration and loss of normal psychological functions. For other information on this disorder, see the disorder chart on Dementia.

Denial—A defense mechanism in which a person disclaims the existence of unpleasant realities.

Dependent Personality Disorder—A disorder characterized by a lack of self-confidence and decisiveness associated with a fear of separation. The person wants others to assume responsibility for his or her life.

Depersonalization—A state of feeling unreal, as if observing one's body or mental process from the outside.

Depression—A continuing feeling of sadness, despondency or hopelessness most days and most of every day for at least two weeks with accompanying symptoms. For other information on this disorder, see the disorder chart on Depression.

Depression, Low-Grade—See Dysthymia.

Desensitization—Treatment for phobias and other psychological disorders in which a patient gradually increases exposure to the source of fear while simultaneously learning to relax.

Detoxification—The controlled and gradual withdrawal of an abused substance (alcohol, drugs of abuse or other addictive substances) from the body. Detoxification may be done on an inpatient or outpatient basis. Medications and psychotherapy help ease the withdrawal symptoms.

Developmental Disability—Also known as mental retardation. A failure to develop age-appropriate intelligence, behavior and reasoning ability.

Diabetes—Metabolic disorder in which the body can't use carbohydrates efficiently. This leads to a dangerously high level of glucose (a carbohydrate) in the blood.

Diagnostic and Statistical Manual of Mental Disorders (DSM-IV)—A reference book that lists diagnostic criteria for all formally recognized mental disorders. The DSM is updated and revised regularly by the American Psychiatric Association.

Dialysis—Procedure to filter waste products from the bloodstream of a patient with kidney failure.

Differential Diagnosis—A list of disorders that could be the underlying cause of a particular symptom (or group of symptoms).

Digitalis Preparations (Digitalis Glycosides)—Important drugs to treat heart disease, such as congestive heart failure, heartbeat irregularities and cardiogenic shock. These drugs include digitoxin, digoxin.

Dilation—Enlargement.

Disorientation—In an individual, a loss of awareness or confusion about time, place, other persons or personal identity.

Displacement—A defense mechanism in which feelings are redirected from one person or object to another. For example, a person angry about being ill may direct that anger at a relative or medical professional.

Dissociative Disorders—A group of psychological illnesses that involve a sudden change in a person's state of consciousness, identity, behavior, thoughts, feelings and perception of external reality that cause that particular mental function to be separated or cut off from the mind as a whole. For other information on this disorder, see the disorder chart on Dissociative Disorders.

Disulfiram Reaction—Disulfiram (Antabuse) is a drug used to treat alcoholism. When alcohol in the bloodstream interacts with disulfiram, it causes a flushed face, severe headache, chest pains, shortness of breath, nausea, vomiting, sweating and weakness. Severe reactions may cause death. A disulfiram reaction is the interaction of any drug with alcohol or another drug to produce these symptoms.

Diuretics—Drugs that act on the kidneys to prevent reabsorption of electrolytes, especially chlorides. They are used to treat edema, high blood pressure, congestive heart failure, kidney and liver failure and others. These drugs include amiloride, amiloride and hydrochlorothiazide, bendroflumethiazide, benzthiazide, bumetanide, chlorothiazide, chlorthalidone, cyclothiazide, ethacrynic acid, furosemide, hydrochlorothiazide, hydroflumethiazide, indapamide, mannitol, methyclothiazide, metolazone, polythiazide, quinethazone, spironolactone, spironolactone and hydrochlorothiazide, triamterene, triamterene and hydrochlorothiazide, trichlormethiazide, urea.

Diuretics, Thiazide—Drugs that act on the kidneys to prevent reabsorption of electrolytes, especially chlorides. They are used to treat edema, high blood pressure, congestive heart failure, kidney and liver failure and others. These drugs include amiloride, bendroflumethiazide, benzthiazide, chlorthalidone, chlorothiazide, cyclothiazide, hydrochlorothiazide, hydroflumethiazide, methyclothiazide, metolazone, polythiazide, quinethazone, trichlormethiazide.

Dopamine—A neurotransmitter found in the brain. Abnormalities of dopamine may cause depression or psychosis.

Down Syndrome—A congenital form of mental retardation caused by a chromosome abnormality. It can have varying degrees of severity. Children with the disorder have an abnormal appearance.

Dreaming—Mental activity that takes place during sleep.

Dream Analysis—The interpretation of a person's dream as part of psychoanalysis or psychotherapy.

Drug Interaction—Change in the body's response to one drug when another is taken. An interaction may decrease the effect of one or both drugs, increase the effect of one or both drugs or cause toxicity.

Dysfunctional Family—A family with negative and destructive patterns of behavior between the parents or between parents and children.

Dyskinesia—Abnormal muscle movements caused by a brain disorder.

Dyslexia—A learning disability that is basically a failure to learn to read. Children with the problem often place letters in a word in reverse order, read letters backward or may be unable to associate sounds with symbols.

Dyspareunia—Pain felt by females during sexual intercourse.

Dysphoria—A generalized feeling of ill-being (moods or feelings of discontent, unrest, anxiety, depression, restlessness or other physical discomfort).

Dyssomnias—A group of sleep disorders that involve the amount, quality or timing of sleep.

Dysthymia (Low-Grade Depression)—A chronic depressive mood with symptoms that are milder, but longer lasting, than those of a major depressive episode. For other information on this disorder, see the disorder chart on Dysthymia.

Dystonia—An abnormal muscle rigidity that causes painful muscle spasms, fixed postures or strange movement patterns; associated with antipsychotic medications.

E

Eating Disorder—Any disorder associated with a disturbance in eating behavior. They include anorexia nervosa, bulimia and pica.

ECG (or EKG)—Abbreviation for electrocardiogram or electrocardiograph. An ECG is a graphic tracing representing the electrical current produced by impulses passing through the heart muscle.

ECT—See Electroconvulsive Therapy.

Eczema—Disorder of the skin with redness, itching, blisters, weeping and abnormal pigmentation.

EEG—Electroencephalogram or electroencephalograph. An EEG is a graphic recording of electrical activity generated spontaneously from nerve cells in the brain. This test is useful in the diagnosis of brain dysfunction, particularly in studying seizure disorders.

Ego—The conscious sense and awareness of oneself. In Freudian theory, one of the three divisions of the psyche. The other two are the id and the superego.

EKG—See ECG.

Elective Mutism—A rare disorder in children in which they withdraw by not speaking at all or speaking only to family members.

Electroconvulsive Therapy (ECT)—A type of therapy that uses an electric shock to induce a seizure that affects the central nervous system and helps bring relief of the symptoms. Used for severely depressed patients and other select disorders that have not responded to standard treatments. General anesthesia and special muscle-relaxing medicines are used to prevent physical harm and pain, and the effects are limited primarily to the brain. ECT has an 80-90% success rate and is quite safe when done by an experienced psychiatrist.

Electrolytes—Substances that can transmit electrical impulses when dissolved in body fluids.

Embolism—Sudden blockage of an artery by a clot or foreign material in the blood.

Emotional Problems—A term used to describe a wide range of psychological difficulties, especially the problems associated with living or psychological reaction patterns (e.g., grief) as opposed to those problems that are diagnosed as psychological or psychiatric disorders (e.g., depression).

Emphysema—Disease in which the lungs' air sacs lose elasticity and air accumulates in the lungs.

Endometriosis—Condition in which uterus tissue is found outside the uterus. Can cause pain, abnormal menstruation and infertility.

Endorphins—Chemical substances produced in the body that relieve pain and are thought to be involved with controlling the body's response to stress. They have a chemical structure similar to that of morphine.

Enzymes—Protein chemicals that can accelerate chemical reactions in the body.

Epilepsy—Episodes of brain disturbance that cause convulsions and loss of consciousness.

Epinephrine—A substance produced by the adrenal glands in response to fear, stress or anxiety (also called adrenaline).

Ergot Preparations—Medicines used to treat migraine and other types of throbbing headaches. Also used after delivery of babies to make the uterus clamp down and reduce excessive bleeding.

Erythromycins—A group of drugs with similar structure used to treat infections. These drugs include erythromycin, erythromycin estolate, erythromycin ethylsuccinate, erythromycin gluceptate, erythromycin lactobionate, erythromycin stearate.

Esophagitis—Inflammation of the lower part of the esophagus, the tube connecting the throat and the stomach.

Estrogens—Female hormones used to replenish the body's stores after the ovaries have been removed or become nonfunctional after menopause. Also used with progesterone in some birth control pills and for other purposes.

Etiology—The cause of a disease or disorder.

Euphoria—An exaggerated feeling of well-being.

Eustachian Tube—Small passage from the middle ear to the sinuses and nasal passages.

Extrapyramidal Reactions—Abnormal reactions in the power and coordination of posture and muscular movements in which movements are not under voluntary control. Some drugs associated with producing extrapyramidal reactions include amoxapine, haloperidol, loxapine, molindone, paroxetine, phenothiazines, pimozide, risperidone, tacrine, thioxanthenes.

Extremity—Arm, leg, hand or foot.

F

Factitious Disorders—A group of disorders in which feigned or invented symptoms or symptoms that are under the control of the patient mimic true symptoms of illnesses. The patient does this willingly in order to assume the sick role and receive the attention given to a patient. The disorders include Munchausen syndrome, which involves physical symptoms, and Ganser syndrome, in which the symptoms are psychological.

Family History—Information about illnesses that tend to occur within a family. This information is used to determine the likelihood of diseases occurring in other members of the family.

Family Therapy—Psychotherapy that involves the entire family rather than just one individual.

Fetal Alcohol Syndrome—A group of congenital abnormalities (birth defects) caused by the mother's consumption of alcohol during pregnancy. The baby may die or be physically and mentally retarded to some degree. Even small amounts of alcohol may be harmful to an unborn child.

Fetishism—A paraphilia in which objects (e.g., underclothes, shoes) are used to obtain sexual gratification.

Fever—Above-normal body temperature; normal is approximately 98.6°F (37°C) by mouth, 99.6°F (37.6°C) rectally.

Fibrocystic Breast Problems—Overgrowth of fibrous tissue in the breast, producing nonmalignant cysts.

Fibroid Tumors—Nonmalignant tumors of the muscular layer of the uterus.

Flashback—An episode of reexperiencing a traumatic event.

Flooding—A drastic form of psychotherapy used for treatment of phobias. A patient is suddenly confronted with the feared object or placed in the feared situation with no chance of escape. Having experienced the phobia at its fullest intensity, a person comes to realize that the dreaded thing is not dangerous. Only a competent therapist should subject a phobic person to this therapy.

Flu (Influenza)—A viral infection of the respiratory tract that lasts three to ten days. Symptoms include headache, fever, runny nose, cough, tiredness and muscle aches.

Fluoroquinolones—A class of drugs used to treat bacterial infections, such as urinary tract infections and some types of bronchitis.

Folliculitis—Inflammation of a follicle.

Free Association—A technique used in psychoanalytic therapy in which thoughts are expressed without censorship.

Freud, Sigmund—The founder of psychoanalysis, who developed its fundamental techniques and concepts.

Freudian—Pertaining to Sigmund Freud or his psychological theories and his method of psychotherapy.

Freudian Slip—A mistake made in speaking in which the speaker unconsciously reveals his or her true motives and desires.

G

G6PD—Deficiency of glucose 6-phosphate, which is necessary for glucose metabolism.

Ganglionic Blockers—Medicines that block the passage of nerve impulses through a part of the nerve cell called a ganglion. Ganglionic blockers are used to treat urinary retention and other medical problems.

Gastritis—Inflammation of the stomach.

Gastrointestinal—Of the stomach and intestinal tract.

Gender Identity—A person's sense of himself or herself as male or female. It is distinct from sexual identity, which is determined by sexual organs.

Gender Identity Disorder—In children, a preference to be the opposite sex (usually affects boys more than girls). Boys with the disorder are preoccupied with activities and clothing that are typically those of girls. In adolescents and adults, this disorder is characterized by a person's persistent feelings of discomfort about his or her sexual identity. Transsexualism is the most common example of this problem.

Genes—The biologic units of heredity. Physical traits (such as hair and eye color, height, etc.) are passed on depending on the gene match-up between the two parents.

Genetic Counseling—The testing, advising and counseling of couples at risk of transmitting genetic diseases to their children.

Genetics—Science of determining inherited factors that result in the unique make-up of every human being; also, the science that traces the patterns of appearance of genetic (inherited) disease.

Geriatrics—The branch of medicine concerned with the aging process and with problems and disorders of the older adults.

Gestalt Therapy—A type of psychotherapy based on the idea that the whole is more than the sum of its parts; that is, a sense of wholeness is more important than individual pieces of perception and behavior. It aims to increase self-awareness by integrating all aspects of an individual.

Gland—Organ that manufactures and excretes materials not required for its own metabolic needs.

Glaucoma—Eye disease in which increased pressure inside the eye damages the optic nerve, causes pain and changes vision.

Glucagon—Injectable drug that immediately elevates blood sugar by mobilizing glycogen from the liver.

Gold Compounds—Medicines that use gold as their base and are typically used to treat joint or arthritic disorders.

Grief (Bereavement)—The emotional reaction following the death of a loved person, a divorce, loss of a body part or function, loss of self-esteem or other significant loss. Grief is a normal, appropriate reaction to loss. Occasionally grief is so intense or prolonged that professional help is needed. For other information, see the disorder chart on Grief.

Group Therapy—Therapy sessions that are conducted with two or more people at the same time. The dynamics of the group becomes part of the therapy process.

H

H_2 Antagonists—Antihistamines that work against H_2 histamine. H_2 histamine may be liberated at any point in the body, but most often in the skin, bronchial tubes and gastrointestinal tract.

Hallucination—A false perception that has no grounding in reality. The hallucination may be a false perception of sounds, sights, physical sensations, or smells.

Hangover Effect—The same feelings as a "hangover" after too much alcohol consumption. Symptoms include headache, irritability and nausea.

Health Maintenance Organization—See HMO.

Hemochromatosis—Disorder of iron metabolism in which excessive iron is deposited in and damages body tissues, particularly those of the liver and pancreas.

Hemoglobin—Pigment that carries oxygen in red blood cells.

Hemolytics—Drugs that separate hemoglobin from the blood cells.

Hemorrhage—Heavy bleeding.

Hemorrheologic Agents—Medicines to help control bleeding.

Hemosiderosis—Increase of iron deposits in body tissues without tissue damage.

Hepatitis—Inflammation of liver cells, usually accompanied by jaundice.

Hepatotoxics—Medications that can possibly cause toxicity or decreased normal function of the liver. These drugs include acetaminophen (with long-term use); alcohol; amiodarone; anabolic steroids; androgens; angiotensin-converting enzyme (ACE) inhibitors; anti-inflammatory drugs, nonsteroidal (NSAIDs); asparaginase; carbamazepine; carmustine; dantrolene; dapsone; daunorubicin; disulfiram; divalproex; erythromycins; estrogens; ethionamide; etretinate; felbamate; fluconazole; flutamide; gold compounds; halothane; HMG-CoA reductase inhibitors; isoniazid; itraconazole; ketoconazole (oral); labetalol; mercaptopurine; methimazole; methotrexate; methyldopa; naltrexone; niacin (high doses); nitrofurans; phenothiazines; phenytoin; plicamycin; rifampin; sulfamethoxazole-trimethoprim, sulfonamides; tacrine; valproic acid; zidovudine.

Hiatal Hernia—Section of stomach that protrudes into the chest cavity.

Histamine—Chemical in body tissues that dilates the smallest blood vessels, constricts the smooth muscle surrounding the bronchial tubes and stimulates stomach secretions.

History—Past medical events in a patient's life.

HIV—See Human Immunodeficiency Virus.

Hives—Elevated patches on the skin that are redder or paler than surrounding skin and often itch severely.

HMO (Health Maintenance Organization)—A group of health care professionals joined together in a group to provide a broad coverage of medical care services for individuals.

Homophobia—Fear or dislike of homosexuals.

Homosexuality—Sexual preference for members of one's own sex.

Hormone Replacement Therapy (HRT)—A combination of medications (estrogen and progestin or estrogen and androgen) used for the treatment of premenopausal and menopausal symptoms and for prevention of diseases that affect women in their later years.

Hormones—Chemical substances produced in the body to regulate other body functions.

Hospice—A program of care for terminally ill individuals.

Hotlines—Telephone numbers that individuals can call to obtain help and information about a variety of medical topics. These information sources are maintained by various organizations, hospitals, universities and governmental agencies.

HRT—See Hormone Replacement Therapy.

Human Immunodeficiency Virus (HIV)—A retrovirus transmitted via body fluids (blood, semen, vaginal fluids, breast milk). HIV is the cause of acquired immunodeficiency syndrome (AIDS).

Human-Potential Therapy—See Client-Orientated Therapy.

Humor—A type of defense mechanism in which a person uses humor to help counter painful feelings.

Huntington's Chorea—A progressive hereditary disease characterized by chorea (rapid, jerky, involuntary movements) and dementia (progressive mental impairment).

Hyperactivity—A behavior pattern that involves overactivity and difficulty concentrating.

Hypercalcemia—Too much calcium in the blood. This happens with some malignancies and in calcium overdose.

Hyperkalemia-Causing Medications—Medicines that cause too much potassium in the bloodstream.

Hypersensitivity—Serious reactions to many medications. The effects of hypersensitivity may be characterized by wheezing, shortness of breath, rapid heart rate, severe itching, faintness, unconsciousness and severe drop in blood pressure.

Hypersomnia—Prolonged sleep or excessive daytime sleepiness.

Hypertension—High blood pressure.

Hypervitaminosis—A condition due to an excess of one or more vitamins. Symptoms may include weakness, fatigue, loss of hair and changes in the skin.

Hypnagogia—The semiconscious state that immediately precedes sleep. A hypnagogia hallucination is a hallucination that occurs just before falling asleep.

Hypnosis—A trancelike state of altered awareness. It causes an individual to be extremely suggestible. Hypnosis is sometimes used as a therapy in helping to break undesirable habits such as smoking.

Hypnotics—Drugs used to induce a sleeping state.

Hypocalcemia—Abnormally low level of calcium in the blood.

Hypochondriasis—A disorder characterized by a person's conviction that he or she has a serious or fatal disease, despite evidence to the contrary from thorough medical examinations and tests. For other information on this disorder, see the disorder chart on Hypochondriasis.

Hypoglycemia—Low blood sugar (blood glucose). A critically low blood sugar level will interfere with normal brain function and can damage the brain permanently.

Hypoglycemics—Drugs that reduce blood sugar.

Hypokalemia-Causing Medications—Medicines that cause a depletion of potassium in the bloodstream. These include adrenocorticoids (systemic), alcohol, amphotericin B (systemic), bronchodilators (adrenergic), carbonic anhydrase inhibitors, diuretics (loop and thiazide), foscarnet, indapamide, insulin, laxatives (if dependent on), penicillins (some), salicylates, sodium bicarbonate, urea.

Hypomania—An abnormal mood that is similar to mania, but not as severe. Symptoms include excited behavior, unrealistic optimism, rapid speech and activity and a decreased need for sleep.

Hypotension—Blood pressure below normal. Symptoms may include weakness, lightheadedness and dizziness. Orthostatic hypotension occurs when a person stands suddenly from a sitting or reclining position.

Hypotension-Causing Drugs—Medications that might cause hypotension (low blood pressure).

Hypothermia-Causing Drugs—Medications (including most antipsychotic drugs) that can cause a significant lowering of body temperature.

I

Iatrogenic—An illness, injury, disease or disorder induced inadvertently by medical treatment.

Ichthyosis—Skin disorder with dryness, scaling and roughness.

Id—One of the three parts of personality as described by Sigmund Freud. The other two are the ego and the superego. The id is the primitive, unconscious store of energy involving basic instincts and needs.

Identity—An individual's sense of who he or she is.

Identity Disorder—Any disorder in which there is a loss of self.

Idiopathic—Of unknown cause; used to describe a disease or disorder whose cause is unknown or uncertain.

Ileitis—Inflammation of the ileum, the last section of the small intestine.

Ileostomy—Surgical opening from the ileum, the end of the small intestine, to the outside of the body.

Illusions—A misperception of a real occurrence or a distorted perception of a material object.

Immunosuppressants—Powerful drugs that suppress the immune system. Immunosuppressants are used in patients who have had organ transplants or severe disease associated with the immune system.

Impotence—Males' inability to achieve or sustain erection of the penis for sexual intercourse.

Impulse Control Disorders—A group of disorders characterized by a person's inability to resist an impulse or temptation to do something that ultimately proves harmful to the person or to others. For other information on this disorder, see the disorder chart on Impulse Control Disorders.

Incoherence—Speech that is incomprehensible, e.g., words may be made up, there are distortions of syntax and grammar and the person jumps from one thought to another without making anything clear.

Incontinence—Inability to control urination and/or bowel movements.

Influenza—See Flu.

Informed Consent—A voluntarily signed agreement by a mentally competent person to accept treatment or undergo a procedure after being informed by a medical professional about the nature of the procedure, the risks and benefits involved and any alternatives available.

Inhalants—Substances that produce vapors that are inhaled orally or nasally. The inhalants may be appropriately prescribed medications or substances of abuse that produce psychoactive effects when inhaled.

Inhibition—A mental or psychological process that restrains or suppresses an action, emotion or thought.

Insanity—A term once used to describe serious mental disorders. It is used today only in a legal context, such as "insanity defense" (whereby a person cannot be convicted of a crime if it can be shown that he or she lacked criminal responsibility).

Insomnia—Sleeplessness.

Institutionalize—Place a person in a nursing home or other care facility or prison, usually for a long period of time.

Intellectualism—A type of defense mechanism in which a person attempts to avoid painful feelings by taking refuge in "thinking" (takes an objective or abstract view of the feelings).

Interaction—See Drug Interaction.

Interpersonal Psychotherapy (IPT)—A form of therapy that concentrates on a person's interactions and relationships with other people. Used most often in treating depression.

Interview—In psychology, a process between interviewer and patient for purposes of gathering information to help in diagnosing and assessment and in determining optimum treatment.

Intoxication—The condition resulting from an overdosage of a chemical substance. Most often refers to the effects caused by excessive use of alcohol.

Intrapsychic—Taking place in the mind.

IPT—See Interpersonal Psychotherapy.

Iron Supplements—Products that contain iron in a form that can be absorbed from the intestinal tract.

Isolation of Affect—A type of defense mechanism in which a person removes the disturbing affect from an idea or an event and leaves the nondisturbing aspects.

J

Jaundice—Symptoms of liver damage, bile obstruction or destruction of red blood cells. Symptoms include yellowed whites of the eyes, yellow skin, dark urine and light stool.

Jealousy, Morbid—A preoccupation with the sexual infidelity of one's partner. It usually occurs in a male and is often associated with another psychological disorder, such as personality disorder or depression.

Jungian Theory—A form of psychoanalysis named after Carl Jung, at one time an associate of Sigmund Freud. This therapy pays greater attention than other therapies to the mythical dimensions of dreams and fantasies.

K

Keratosis—Growth that is an accumulation of cells from the outer skin layers.

Kidney Stones—Small, solid stones made from calcium, cholesterol, cysteine and other body chemicals.

L

Labile—Unstable; likely to undergo change. A term sometimes used to describe emotional instability.

Latent—Existing in hidden form; unconscious, but not actively so (e.g., latent homosexual).

Laxatives—Medicines used to treat constipation.

LD—See Learning Disability.

LDH—Abbreviation for lactate dehydrogenase. It is a measurement of cardiac enzymes used to confirm some heart conditions.

Learning Disability (LD)—An inability to read (dyslexia), write (dysgraphia) or do grade-appropriate mathematics (dyscalculia) in children of normal or above-average intelligence. Most experts feel that these disabilities stem from some form of minimal brain dysfunction.

Lesbian—A female homosexual.

Libido—Sexual desire.

Lincomycins—A family of antibiotics used to treat certain infections.

Living Will—A mentally competent person's written statement instructing family and medical personnel about the use of life-sustaining procedures in the event of terminal illness or trauma.

Lupus—Serious disorder of connective tissue that primarily affects women. Varies in severity, with skin eruptions, joint inflammation, low white blood cell count and damage to internal organs, especially the kidneys.

Lymph Glands—Glands in the lymph vessels throughout the body that trap foreign and infectious matter and protect the bloodstream from infection.

M

Macrolides—A class of antibiotic (antibacterial) drugs.

Male Hormones—Chemical substances secreted by the testicles, ovaries and adrenal glands in humans. Some male hormones used by humans are derived synthetically.

Magnetic Resonance Imaging—See MRI.

Maladaptive Behavior—Behavior that is not suited or properly adapted to a situation or a function. The behavior interferes with a person's ability to adjust or cope with changes in life's circumstances.

Malingering—Deliberate simulation or exaggeration of physical or psychological symptoms for a particular purpose (time off from work, receiving insurance compensation and others).

Mania—A mood disturbance characterized by euphoria, agitation, elation, irritability, rapid and confused speech and excessive activity. Mania usually occurs as part of bipolar (manic-depressive) disorder.

Manic-Depressive Disorder—See Bipolar Disorder.

MAO Inhibitors—See Monoamine Oxidase (MAO) Inhibitors.

Marital Therapy—Psychotherapy for a married couple or established partners to help resolve problems in their relationship.

Masochism, Sexual—A form of paraphilia in which a person needs to suffer physical or psychological pain in order to gain sexual gratification.

Mast Cell—Connective tissue cell.

Masturbation—Sexual arousal by self-stimulation of one's own genitals, usually to orgasm.

Meditation—A state of extended reflection or contemplation. There are a variety of forms of meditation. Most involve sitting quietly for 15 to 20 minutes once or twice a day, concentrating on a word or an image and breathing slowly and rhythmically. The experience is relaxing and produces a state of calm. Meditation is often recommended as a stress-management technique.

Melancholia—A pronounced depression with feelings of foreboding and a lack of response to any stimulus, e.g., lack of pleasure in any of the joys in life.

Menopause—The end of menstruation in the female, often accompanied by irritability, hot flashes, changes in the skin and bones and vaginal dryness.

Mental Health—The state of psychological well-being that enables a person to function effectively.

Mental Retardation—Impaired intellectual development resulting in an inability to cope with the responsibilities of life. For other information on this disorder, see the disorder chart on Mental Retardation.

Mental Status Examination—The evaluation of a person's mental functioning.

Metabolism—Process of using nutrients and energy to build and break down wastes.

Migraines—Periodic headaches caused by constriction of arteries to the skull. Symptoms include severe pain, vision disturbances, nausea, vomiting and sensitivity to light.

Mind-Altering Drugs—Any drugs that changes alertness, perception, concentration, contact with reality or muscular coordination.

Mineral Supplements—Mineral substances added to the diet to treat or prevent mineral deficiencies.

Modeling—Acquiring a behavior by following the pattern or behavior of others. A therapist may perform the desired behavior, which is then imitated by the patient.

Monoamine Oxidase (MAO) Inhibitors—Drugs that prevent the activity of the enzyme monoamine oxidase (MAO) in brain tissue, thus affecting mood. MAO inhibitors include antidepressants, the use of which is frequently restricted because of severe side effects. MAO inhibitors include phenelzine and tranylcypromine, which are discussed on the drug chart for Monoamine Oxidase (MAO) Inhibitors. Other drugs that are MAO Inhibitors include furazolidone, procarbazine, and selegiline.

Mood Disorders—A group of disorders characterized by disturbances in mood, such as in depression or bipolar (manic-depressive) disorder.

MRI (Magnetic Resonance Imaging)—A method of studying the body's internal structures that employs a strong magnetic field (rather than x-rays) and a computer to produce detailed pictures.

Munchausen Syndrome—A form of factitious disorder in which a person has symptoms that are totally fabricated, pretended, or self-inflicted. The person wants the attention given to a patient. *Munchausen by proxy* is the term used to describe a parent who artificially creates physical symptoms in a child.

Muscle Blockers—Same as muscle relaxants or skeletal muscle relaxants.

Muscle Relaxants—Medicines used to lessen painful contractions and spasms of muscles.

Mutism—The absence of speech.

Myasthenia Gravis—Disease of the muscles characterized by fatigue and progressive paralysis. It is usually confined to muscles of the face, lips, tongue and neck.

N

Narcissism—An exaggerated sense of self-importance, self-admiration or self-love, and an oversensitivity to the opinion of others.

Narcolepsy—A sleep disorder characterized by excessive daytime sleepiness with recurrent episodes of sleep throughout the day. Cataplexy (sudden loss of muscle tone) may occur. Nighttime sleep is disrupted.

Narcotics—A group of habit-forming, addicting drugs used for treatment of pain, diarrhea, cough, acute pulmonary edema and others. They are all derived from opium, a milky exudate in capsules of the poppy *Papaver somniferum*. Law requires licensed physicians to dispense by prescription. These drugs include alfentanil, butorphanol, codeine, fentanyl, hydrocodone, hydromorphone, levorphanol, meperidine, methadone, morphine, nalbuphine, opium, oxycodone, oxymorphone, paregoric, pentazocine, propoxyphene, sufentanil.

Necrophilia—A type of paraphilia in which intense sexual urges and/or sexual fantasies involve corpses.

Nephrotoxic (Kidney-Poisoning) Medications—Medicines that, under some circumstances, can be toxic to the kidneys.

Nervous Breakdown—A nontechnical term for mental illness serious enough to interfere with daily activities.

Neuritis—Inflammation of a nerve.

Neurodegenerative Disease — A disease that involves deterioration in the function and forms of nerves and related structures. Alzheimer's disease and multiple sclerosis are examples.

Neuroleptic Malignant Syndrome—A life-threatening complication associated with antipsychotic medications. It is characterized by high fever, rapid pulse, profuse sweating, muscle rigidity, irritability and confusion and seizures.

Neurological—Relating to the body's nervous system.

Neurologist—Doctor specially trained to diagnose and treat diseases of the nervous system.

Neuron—Nerve cell.

Neurosis—A term used to describe a range of relatively mild psychiatric disorders in which the person remains in touch with reality. It has generally been replaced by terms that describe specific mental disorders.

Neurotoxic Medications—Medicines that cause toxicity to the nerve tissues in the body.

Neurotransmitters—Chemicals produced by the nerve cells that have a role in communication between nerve cells (neurons) or from a nerve cell to a muscle cell.

Night Terror—Abrupt arousal from sleep in a terrified state. It occurs mainly in children. Though it has no serious significance, it can be upsetting to parents.

Nitrates—Medicines made from a chemical with a nitrogen base. Nitrates include erythrityl tetranitrate, isosorbide dinitrate, nitroglycerin, pentaerythritol tetranitrate.

Noncompliance—Failure of a patient to follow a health care professional's recommended treatment plan, e.g., not taking prescribed medications, not losing weight, or not taking steps to stop smoking.

Nonsteroidal Anti-Inflammatory Drugs (NSAIDs)—See Anti-Inflammatory Drugs, Nonsteroidal.

Nutritional Supplements—Substances used to treat and prevent deficiencies (in vitamins, minerals and others) when the body is unable to absorb them by eating a well-balanced, nutritional diet.

Nystagmus—Abnormal, involuntary movements of the eyes; usually horizontal movements, but can be vertical or rotary.

O

Obsession—A recurrent, seemingly involuntary thought, idea or feeling. It often leads to compulsion (repetitive behavior).

Obsessive-Compulsive Disorder (OCD)—A disorder characterized by recurrent, intrusive thoughts (obsessions) and repetitive, ritualistic behaviors (compulsions). For other information on this disorder, see the disorder chart on Obsessive-Compulsive Disorder.

Occupational Therapy—Treatment aimed at helping patients learn or relearn behaviors that help them cope with everyday tasks or to resume some type of work.

OCD—See Obsessive-Compulsive Disorder.

Operant Conditioning—See Conditioning.

Opiates—Pain-killing medicines derived from opium that are highly addictive.

Oppositional Defiant Disorder—A childhood disorder characterized by a pattern of negative, hostile and defiant behavior. The child is usually argumentative, angry and resentful.

Organic Brain Syndrome—A mental disorder caused by physical or chemical brain damage (as opposed to psychiatric origin).

Organic Disease—Physical illness.

Orgasm—Sexual climax.

Orientation—Awareness of self with respect to time, place or person (as opposed to disorientation).

Osteoporosis—Softening of bones caused by a loss of chemicals usually found in bones.

Ototoxic Medications—Medicines that may possibly cause hearing damage.

Ovary—Female sexual gland where eggs mature and ripen for fertilization.

Overanxious Disorder—A childhood anxiety disorder that varies in severity and is characterized by excessive worry about almost everything, extreme self-consciousness, inability to relax, a need for excessive reassurance and self-doubts.

Over-the-Counter (OTC) Drugs—Nonprescription medications.

P

Pain Relievers—Non-narcotic medicines used to treat pain.

Palpitations—Rapid heartbeat noticeable to the patient.

Pancreatitis—Serious inflammation or infection of the pancreas that causes upper abdominal pain.

Panic—Severe anxiety.

Panic Disorder—A severe, spontaneous form of anxiety that is recurrent and unpredictable. For other information on this disorder, see the disorder chart on Panic Disorder.

Paranoia—A delusion of persecution, characterized by exaggerated suspiciousness.

Paraphilias—A group of disorders in which unusual or bizarre objects or acts are required for sexual enjoyment. For other information on this disorder, see the disorder chart on Paraphilias.

Paraphrenia—A mental disorder with a primary symptom of paranoia; occurs in older adults.

Parkinson's Disease or Parkinson's Syndrome—Disease of the central nervous system. Characteristics are a fixed, emotionless expression of the face, tremor, slower muscle movements, weakness, changed gait and a peculiar posture.

Pathological—Pertaining to disease.

Pavlov, Ivan—Russian physiologist known for his work on conditioning (see separate entry in Glossary).

Pellagra—Disease caused by a deficiency of the water-soluble vitamin thiamine (vitamin B-1). Symptoms include brain disturbance, diarrhea and skin inflammation.

Penicillin—Chemical substance (antibiotic) originally discovered as a product of mold, which can kill some bacterial germs.

Performance Anxiety—Anxiety about making a speech, competitive situations, performing music, taking examinations and others. Physical symptoms include rapid breathing, rapid heartbeat, dry mouth, tingling in hands, "butterflies in the stomach."

Personality—Fixed ways of behaving, thinking and feeling.

Personality Disorders—A group of conditions that are not illnesses, but ways of behaving. They are classified according to the predominant symptoms. For these symptoms and other information on this disorder, see the disorder chart on Personality Disorders.

Pharmacotherapy—Treatment of diseases with medications.

Phenothiazines—Drugs used to treat mental psychosis. For a list of the generic and brand names, see Brand Name Directory. For other information on these drugs, see the drug chart on Phenothiazines

Pheochromocytoma—A tumor of the adrenal gland that produces chemicals that cause high blood pressure, headache, nervousness and other symptoms.

Phlegm—Thick mucus secreted by glands in the respiratory tract.

Phobia—Fear that is persistent and irrational of a particular object, activity or situation. The method for naming phobias comes from the combination of the name of the feared subject (in Greek or English), followed by *phobia*, e.g., claustrophobia is fear of closed places, computerphobia is fear of computers or using them. For other information on this disorder, see the disorder chart on Phobias. Also, a word may end in *phobia*, but have a different meaning, such as photophobia (see next Glossary entry).

Photophobia—Increased or abnormal sensitivity to light as perceived by the human eye. Drugs that can cause photophobia include antidiabetic drugs, atropine, belladonna, bromides, chloroquine, ciprofloxacin, chlordiazepoxide, clidinium, clomiphene, dicyclomine, digitalis drugs, doxepin, ethambutol, ethionamide, ethosuximide, etretinate, glycopyrrolate, hydroxychloroquine, hydroxyzine, hyoscyamine, mephenytoin, methenamine, methsuximide, monoamine oxidase (MAO) inhibitors, nalidixic acid, norfloxacin, oral contraceptives, orphenadrine, paramethadione, phenothiazines, propantheline, quinidine, quinine, scopolamine, tetracyclines, tridihexethyl, trimethadione.

Photosensitizing Medications—Medicines that can cause abnormally heightened skin reactions to the effects of sunlight and ultraviolet light. These medicines include acetazolamide, acetohexamide, alprazolam, amantadine, amiloride, amiodarone, amitriptyline, amoxapine, antidiabetic agents (oral), barbiturates, bendroflumethiazide, benzocaine, benzoyl peroxide, benzthiazide, captopril, carbamazepine, chlordiazepoxide, chloroquine, chlorothiazide, chlorpromazine, chlorpropamide, chlortetracycline, chlorthalidone, ciprofloxacin, clindamycin, clofazimine, clofibrate, clomipramine, coal tar, contraceptives (estrogen-containing), cyproheptadine, dacarbazine, dapsone, demeclocycline, desipramine, desoximetasone, diethylstilbestrol, diflunisal, diltiazem, diphenhydramine, disopyramide, doxepin, doxycycline, enoxacin, estrogens, etretinate, flucytosine, fluorescein, fluorouracil, fluphenazine, flutamide, furosemide, glipizide, glyburide, gold preparations, griseofulvin, haloperidol, hexachlorophene, hydrochlorothiazide, hydroflumethiazide, ibuprofen, imipramine, indomethacin, isotretinoin, ketoprofen, lincomycin, lomefloxacin, maprotiline, mesoridazine, methacycline, methotrexate, methoxsalen, methyclothiazide, methyldopa, metolazone, minocycline, minoxidil, nabumetone, nalidixic acid, naproxen, nifedipine, norfloxacin, nortriptyline, ofloxacin, oral contraceptives, oxyphenbutazone, oxytetracycline, perphenazine, phenelzine, phenobarbital, phenylbutazone, phenytoin, piroxicam, polythiazide, prochlorperazine, promazine, promethazine, protriptyline, pyrazinamide, quinidine, quinine, sulfonamides, sulindac, tetracycline, thiabendazole, thioridazine, thiothixene, tolazamide, tolbutamide, tranylcypromine, trazodone, tretinoin, triamterene, trichlormethiazide, trifluoperazine, triflupromazine, trimeprazine, trimethoprim, trimipramine, triprolidine, vinblastine.

Pica—An eating disorder in which a person repeatedly eats non-nutritive substances (e.g., clay, paint, dirt). Occurs most often in children and sometimes in pregnant women.

Pick's Disease—A hereditary disease characterized by dementia.

Pinworms—Common intestinal parasites that cause rectal itching and irritation.

Pituitary Gland—Gland at the base of the brain that secretes hormones to stimulate growth and other glands to produce hormones.

Placebo—A substance that contains no medicine (inert ingredients) and is given in place of a medication. Placebos are often used in drug studies. In some cases, benefit is gained from taking a placebo because the person taking it believes it will have a positive effect.

Platelet—Disc-shaped element of the blood, smaller than a red or white blood cell, that is necessary for blood clotting.

Play Therapy—A type of psychotherapy used for children in which children are encouraged to engage in play activities to communicate their problems and as a means for the therapist to provide counseling.

Polymixins—A family of antibiotics that kill bacteria.

Polyp—Growth on a mucous membrane.

Polysomnography—A medical technique used to diagnose sleep-related disorders. It is conducted overnight while the patient is asleep and records various functions of the body, such as heart and respiratory rates, eye movements, brain waves and others.

Porphyria—Inherited metabolic disorder characterized by changes in the nervous system and kidneys. May cause pain patterns that physicians may not recognize and incorrectly attribute to the patient's mental status.

Positron Emission Tomography (PET)—A diagnostic imaging technique that is often used to study brain function in various mental illnesses.

Postnatal Depression—See Postpartum Depression.

Postpartum—Following delivery of a baby.

Postpartum Depression (Postnatal Depression)—Emotional changes following the birth of a baby. Such changes affect almost half of all new mothers. For other information on this disorder, see the disorder chart on Postpartum Depression.

Post-Traumatic Stress Disorder (PTSD)—A type of anxiety seen in people who have experienced an event that would be extremely distressing to most human beings that is characterized by a persistent reexperiencing of the trauma and associated symptoms. For other information on this disorder, see the disorder chart on Post-Traumatic Stress Disorder.

Potassium—Important chemical found in body cells.

Potassium Foods—Foods high in potassium content, including dried apricots and peaches, lentils, raisins, citrus and whole-grain cereals.

Potassium Supplements—Medicines needed by people who don't have enough potassium in their diets or by those who develop a deficiency due to illness or taking diuretics and other medicines.

Prodrome—An early warning symptom of an illness.

Projection—A defense mechanism in which a person attributes unacceptable feelings or impulses on another individual or situation. The feelings are then "out there" rather than in oneself.

Prostaglandins—A group of drugs used for a variety of therapeutic purposes.

Prostate—Gland in the male that surrounds the neck of the bladder and the urethra.

Prothrombin—Blood substance essential in clotting.

Prothrombin Time (Pro Time)—Laboratory study used to follow prothrombin activity and keep coagulation safe.

Pseudodementia—A group of symptoms that mimic dementia; often caused by depression in the elderly. These symptoms do not arise from brain damage and are reversible.

Psoriasis—Chronic, inherited skin disease. Symptoms are lesions with silvery scales on the edges.

Psyche—A term meaning the mind (as opposed to the body).

Psychiatry—The medical science that deals with the study, cause, treatment, and prevention of mental illness and emotional and behavior problems.

Psychoanalysis—A type of psychotherapy developed by Sigmund Freud. It is based on Freudian theories about the unconscious mind and defense mechanisms. Its purpose is to recover experiences repressed in the unconscious mind and integrate them into the individual's personality.

Psychogenic—Anything that is produced or caused by psychic or mental factors rather than by organic factors, e.g., a symptom with an emotional origin instead of an organic origin.

Psychology—The study of mental processes and behaviors.

Psychomotor—The combination of physical and mental activity.

Psychomotor Agitation—An increase in physical activity due to mental unrest.

Psychomotor Retardation—A decrease in physical and mental activity.

Psychopathology—The medical study of the causes and nature of mental disease.

Psychopharmacology—The science of treating mental disorders with medications.

Psychosis—A mental disorder that may be manifested by loss of contact with reality, delusions, hallucinations or illusions, disorganized speech and bizarre behavior.

Psychosocial—Pertaining to psychological and social (cultural) factors; influences of society on growth and development.

Psychosomatic Illness—An illness that seems to be caused or worsened by mental or emotional factors.

Psychotherapist—Professional specially trained to diagnose and treat some mental illnesses.

Psychotropic Drugs—Drugs that work on the brain and affect the functioning of the mind.

PTSD—See Post-Traumatic Stress Disorder.

Purine Foods—Foods that are metabolized into uric acid. Foods high in purines include anchovies, liver, brains, sweetbreads, sardines, kidneys, oysters, gravy and meat extracts.

R

Rape—Forced sexual relations without the other person's consent.

Rapid Eye Movement (REM)—A stage of sleep during which the most active dreaming takes place.

Rationalization—A defense mechanism in which a person has an acceptable explanation for a feeling or behavior that replaces or hides the real underlying motive or impulse.

Rauwolfia Alkaloids—Drugs that belong to the family of antihypertensives (drugs that lower blood pressure). Rauwolfia alkaloids are not used as extensively as in years past.

RDA—Recommended daily allowance of a vitamin or mineral.

Reaction Formation—A defense mechanism in which a person adopts attitudes or behaviors that are the opposite of what is really felt.

Rebound Phenomenon—A reversed response to the withdrawal of a stimulus. A common rebound phenomenon occurs when discontinuing excessive use of alcohol; instead of being sedated, the individual becomes overactive.

Recall—To bring back to mind; to remember.

Receptors—Sensory nerve cells that convert stimuli into nerve impulses.

Recreational Drugs—Drugs that are taken for pleasurable effect rather than for medicinal purposes.

Rehabilitation—In psychiatry, the term used to describe therapy that focuses on a patient's functional status, access to resources and quality of life (social and vocational functioning). Clinical therapy is concerned with the person's symptoms, relapse, psychological well-being and problem behaviors.

REM Sleep—See Rapid Eye Movement.

Renal—Pertaining to the kidneys.

Repression—A defense mechanism in which a person's disturbing or painful memories, feelings, or wishes are kept from conscious awareness.

Resistance—A person's conscious or unconscious defense against bringing repressed thoughts to light.

Retardation, Mental—See Mental Retardation.

Retina—Innermost covering of the eyeball on which the image is formed.

Retinoids—A group of drugs that are synthetic vitamin A-like compounds used to treat skin conditions.

Reye Syndrome—Rare, sometimes fatal, disease of children that causes brain and liver damage.

Rickets—Bone disease caused by vitamin D deficiency in which the bones become bent and distorted during infancy or childhood.

S

SAD—See Seasonal Affective Disorder.
Sadism—A form of paraphilia in which pleasure or sexual gratification is obtained by inflicting physical or psychological suffering on another person.
Salicylates—Medicines used to relieve pain and reduce fever.
Schizophrenic Disorders—A group of emotional disorders including catatonic, paranoid, disorganized, undifferentiated and residual schizophrenia. *Schizo* means split, and *phrenia* refers to the mind. Schizophrenia is often referred to as split personality disorder because the person's thoughts and feelings do not relate to each other in a logical fashion. For other information on this disorder, see the disorder chart on Schizophrenic Disorders.
Secondary Gain—The practical benefit gained from being ill, such as extra attention, sympathy or financial reward.
Sedatives-Hypnotics—Drugs that reduce excitement or anxiety.
Seizure—Brain disorder causing changes in consciousness or convulsions.
Selective serotonin reuptake inhibitors (SSRIs)—Medications used for treatment of depression that work by increasing the serotonin levels in the brain. Serotonin is a neurotransmitter (brain chemical) having to do with mood and behavior. These drugs include fuoxetine, fluvoxamine, paroxetine, sertraline. More information can be found on the individual drug chart for each drug.
Self-Actualization—Living to one's full potential.
Self-Esteem—Belief in oneself; self-respect.
Self-Help Group—Group of people with the same physical or psychological problem who band together to provide each other help, understanding and support.
Self-Talk—A form of therapy in which various techniques are used to teach a patient to repeat a therapist's instructions or directions aloud (or whispered) as he or she does a task or repeats positive self-

statements. It is often used for children with problems such as hyperactivity and for adults to help them relax, improve performance, increase motivation or become more aware and alert.
Seasonal Affective Disorder (SAD)—A seasonal disruption of mood that occurs during the winter months and ceases with the advent of spring. For other information on this disorder, see the disorder chart on Seasonal Affective Disorder.
Senility—See Dementia.
Separation Anxiety—Feeling of distress that occurs in a child when parted from his or her parents or home. It is part of a normal development phase for babies. Separation anxiety disorder is a condition in which the reaction to separation is greater than that expected or inappropriate for the child's level of development.
Serotonin—A neurotransmitter (chemical) found in the brain that helps regulate mood and behavior. It appears to play a role in some mental disorders, such as depression.
Serotonin Reuptake Inhibitor, Selective—See Selective Serotonin Reuptake Inhibitor.
Serotonin Syndrome—A potentially very serious interaction between certain drugs. Symptoms include confusion, irritability, muscle rigidity, chills, high fever.
Sex Therapy—Treatment for sexual dysfunction that is usually not due to a physical cause.
Sexual Addiction—A chronic and intense preoccupation with sex.
Sexual Deviations—See Paraphilias.
Sexual Dysfunction—A group of disorders involving problems with sexual function (e.g., desire, enjoyment and response) that are usually not due to a physical cause. These disorders are common in both men and women. For other information on these disorders, see the disorder charts on Sexual Dysfunction, Female; Sexual Dysfunction, Male Impotence; and Sexual Dysfunction, Male Ejaculatory Disorders.
Sexual Orientation—An individual's gender preference for a sexual partner. Orientations include heterosexual (different sex), homosexual (same sex), both sexes (bisexual) or absent (asexual).
SGOT—Abbreviation for serum glutamic-oxaloacetic transaminase. Measuring the level in the blood helps demonstrate liver

disorders and diagnose recent heart damage.

SGPT—Abbreviation for a laboratory study measuring the blood level of serum glutamic-pyruvic transaminase. Deviations from a normal level may indicate liver disease.

Sick Sinus Syndrome—A complicated, serious heartbeat rhythm disturbance characterized by a slow heart rate alternating with a fast or slow heart rate with heart block.

Sinusitis—Inflammation or infection of the sinus cavities in the skull.

Skeletal Muscle Relaxants (Same as Skeletal Muscle Blockers)—A group of drugs prescribed to treat spasms of the skeletal muscles.

Sleep Apnea—A disorder in which a sleeping person stops breathing for short periods of time.

Sleep Disorders—Difficulty falling asleep or remaining asleep, intermittent wakefulness, early-morning awakening or a combination of these. For other information on this disorder, see the disorder chart on Sleep Disorders.

Sleep Inducers—Night-time sedatives to aid one in falling asleep.

Sleepwalking (Somnambulism)—Repeated episodes of arising from bed and walking around during periods of sleep.

Somatic—Pertaining to the body.

Somatic Therapy—In psychiatry, the treatment of mental disorders with medications or electroconvulsive therapy (physical treatments).

Somatoform Disorders—A group of disorders in which there are physical symptoms for which no medical cause can be found. Included in this group are somatization disorder, conversion disorder and body dysmorphic disorder. For other information on this disorder, see the disorder chart on Somatoform Disorders.

Somatoform Pain Disorder—See Chronic Pain Disorder.

Somnambulism—See Sleepwalking.

SSRI—See Selective Serotonin Reuptake Inhibitor.

Stereotypic Movement Disorder—A disorder characterized by repetitive behaviors such as rocking, headbanging and hitting, biting or scratching parts of the body. It is often associated with severe mental retardation and autism.

Stereotyping—An isolated, purposeless, repetitive movement often seen in catatonia and schizophrenia. Amphetamine drug intoxication also causes sterotypic movement.

Stigma—In a psychological context, negative attitudes of the public, as well as some medical professionals, toward individuals with severe mental illness. Families of individuals who are mentally ill often feel the stigma extends to them by virtue of association.

Stimulant Drugs—Medications that increase the activity of the brain and nervous system.

Stimulus—Any action or agent that causes or changes an activity in an organism, an organ or a part.

Streptococci—Bacteria that cause infections in the throat, respiratory system and skin. Improperly treated, can lead to disease in the heart, joints and kidneys.

Stress—The physical, mental and emotional reactions experienced as the result of changes and demands in one's life. For other information on this disorder, see the disorder chart on Stress.

Stressor—Something that causes stress.

Stroke—Sudden, severe attack. Usually sudden paralysis from injury to the brain or spinal cord caused by a blood clot or hemorrhage in the brain.

Stupor—Near-unconsciousness.

Sublimation—A defense mechanism in which a person's unacceptable impulse, drive or urge (e.g., sexual urge) is redirected into socially acceptable forms of behavior. For example, aggression may be channeled into sport.

Sublingual—Under the tongue. Some drugs are absorbed almost as quickly when given this way as when given by injection.

Substance—In psychopharmacological terms, a chemical agent that is used to change mood or behavior.

Substance Abuse and Addiction—Dependence, abuse, intoxication or withdrawal syndromes associated with occasional or regular use of certain chemical substances. For other information on this disorder, see the disorder chart on Substance Abuse and Addiction.

Suicide—Taking of one's own life. For other information, see the disorder chart on Suicide.

Sulfa Drugs—Shorthand for sulfonamide drugs, which are used to treat infections.

Sulfonamides—Sulfa drugs prescribed to treat infections. They include sulfacytine, sulfamethoxazole, sulfamethoxazole and trimethoprim, sulfasalazine, sulfisoxazole.

Sulfonureas—A family of drugs that lower blood sugar (hypoglycemic agents). Used in the treatment of some forms of diabetes.

Sundowning—Behavior in an individual that is normal during the day, but is inappropriate or uncontrolled at night.

Superego—In Freudian theory, one of the three divisions of the psyche. The other two are the id and the ego. The superego is associated with moral and ethical conduct and self-imposed standards of behavior.

Supportive Therapy—Psychotherapy in which the individual's relationship with the therapist and the emotional assistance the therapist provides are important to the outcome of the treatment. The therapy may include a variety of techniques used to help the individual cope with special situations or difficulties, reduce psychological symptoms and regain an emotional balance.

Suppression—A defense mechanism in which a person disturbing thoughts, impulses or feelings are deliberately put out of mind.

Sympathomimetics—A large group of drugs that mimic the effects of stimulation of the sympathetic part of the autonomic nervous system. These drugs include albuterol, amphetamine, benzphetamine, bitolterol, cocaine, dextroamphetamine, diethylpropion, dobutamine, ephedrine, epinephrine, ethylnorepinephrine, fenfluramine, ipratropium, isoproterenol, isoetharine, mazindol, mephentermine, metaproterenol, metaraminol, methoxamine, norepinephrine, phendimetrazine, phentermine, phenylephrine, phenylpropanolamine, pirbuterol, pseudoephedrine, ritodrine, terbutaline.

Syndrome—A group of signs and symptoms that, when combined, constitute a particular disorder.

Systemic—Affecting most or all of the body, in contrast to affecting only a limited area (local). For example, diabetes mellitus is a systemic condition; an abscess is a local condition.

T

Tardive Dyskinesia—Involuntary movements of the jaw, lips and tongue caused by an unpredictable drug reaction to antipsychotic medications.

Tartrazine Dye—A dye used in foods and medicine preparations that may cause an allergic reaction in some people.

Tetracyclines—A group of medicines with similar chemical structure used to treat infections.

Therapeutic Alliance—The relationship formed between a therapist and an individual undergoing treatment. The relationship allows them to work together effectively.

Therapist—One who provides therapy.

Thiazides—A group of chemicals that cause diuresis (loss of water through the kidneys). Frequently used to treat high blood pressure and congestive heart failure.

Thiothixenes—See Thioxanthenes.

Thioxanthenes—Drugs used to treat psychosis. These drugs include chlorprothixene, flupenthixol, thiothixene.

Thrombocytopenias—Diseases characterized by inadequate numbers of blood platelets circulating in the bloodstream.

Thrombolytic Agents—Drugs that help to dissolve blood clots.

Thrombophlebitis—Inflammation of a vein caused by a blood clot in the vein.

Thyroid—Gland in the neck that manufactures and secretes several hormones.

Thyroid Hormones—Medications that mimic the action of the thyroid hormone made in the thyroid gland. They include dextrothyroxine, levothyroxine, liothyronine, liotrix, thyroglobulin, thyroid.

Tic—Involuntary, recurring, abrupt, rapid movement of a muscle or group of muscles (usually in the face, shoulder or arms).

Tolerance—A decreasing response to repeated constant doses of a drug or a need to increase doses to produce the same physical or mental response.

Toxicity—Poisonous reaction to a drug or chemical substance that impairs body functions or damages cells.

Tranquilizers—Drugs that calm a person without clouding consciousness.

Transdermal Patches—Stick-on patches used to administer more and more medications. If you are using this form of medicine, follow these instructions: Choose an area of skin without cuts, scars or hair, such as the upper arm, chest or area behind the ear. Thoroughly clean the area where patch is to be applied. If the patch gets wet and loose, cover it with an additional piece of plastic. Apply a fresh patch if the first one falls off. Apply each dose to a different area of skin if possible.

Transference—In psychiatry, an unconscious assignment of emotions from important childhood figures, such as parents or siblings, to people in adult life. For example, an individual's feeling about a psychiatrist may reflect feelings about his or her parents.

Transsexual—A person who identifies himself or herself with the opposite sex and who may undergo surgery and hormone therapy to assume the physical characteristics of that sex.

Trauma—In psychiatry, a disturbing event or experience.

Tremor—Involuntary trembling.

Trichomoniasis—Infestation of the vagina by *trichomonas*, an infectious organism. The infection causes itching, vaginal discharge and irritation.

Trigeminal Neuralgia (Tic Douloureux)—Painful condition caused by inflammation of a nerve in the face.

Triglyceride—Fatty chemical manufactured from carbohydrates for storage in fat cells.

Twelve-Step Programs—Self-help group programs that are based on the 12 recovery guidelines developed by Alcoholics Anonymous.

Type-A Behavior—A pattern of aggressive and competitive behavior in an individual. This behavior pattern is frequently mentioned as a risk factor for some heart conditions.

Tyramine—Normal chemical component of the body that helps sustain blood pressure. Can rise to fatal levels in combination with some drugs. If you must be on a low-tyramine diet, get instructions from your doctor or from a dietician.

Tyramine is found in many foods:
Beverages—Alcohol beverages, especially Chianti or robust red wines, vermouth, ale, beer.

Breads—Homemade bread with a lot of yeast and breads or crackers containing cheese.

Fats—Sour cream.

Fruits—Bananas, red plums, avocados, figs, raisins, raspberries.

Meats and meat substitutes—Aged game, liver (if not fresh), canned meats, salami, sausage, aged cheese, salted dried fish, pickled herring, meat tenderizers.

Vegetables—Italian broad beans, green bean pods, eggplant.

Miscellaneous—Yeast concentrates or extracts, marmite, soup cubes, commercial gravy, soy sauce, any protein food that has been stored improperly or is spoiled.

U

Ulcer, Peptic—Open sore on the mucous membrane of the esophagus, stomach or duodenum caused by stomach acid.

Unconscious—The part of the mind that a person is not currently aware of, in which memories, perceptions or feelings are stored and actively processed.

Unipolar Disorder—A mood disorder involving symptoms of depression, as opposed to bipolar (manic-depressive) disorder, in which there are periods of mania (greatly elevated moods) as well as periods of depression.

Upper—A slang term used for any drug that has stimulating, arousing effects. Most of these drugs are amphetamines or amphetamine-derived.

Urethra—Hollow tube through which urine (and semen in men) is discharged.

Urethritis—Inflammation or infection of the urethra.

Uricosurics—A group of drugs that promote excretion of uric acid in the urine.

Urinary Acidifiers—Medications that cause urine to become acid.

Urinary Alkalizers—Medications that cause urine to become alkaline.

Uterus—Also called the womb. A hollow muscular organ in the female in which an embryo develops into a fetus.

V

Vascular—Pertaining to blood vessels.

Vascular Headache Preventatives—Medicines prescribed to prevent the occurrence of or reduce the frequency and severity of vascular headaches such as migraines.

Vascular Headache Treatment—Medicine prescribed to treat vascular headaches such as migraines.

Vasectomy—In males, a common method of sterilization. The surgical procedure involves cutting or tying off the *vas deferens* to prevent movement of the sperm from the testes.

Vasoconstriction—Narrowing of a blood vessel.

Vasodepression—Depression of the blood circulation.

Vasodilation—Expansion of a blood vessel.

Vasomotor—Pertaining to the nerves that control the muscular walls of the blood vessels. Vasoconstriction and vasodilation are the two forms of action of these nerves.

Venereal Disease—Any disease that is transmitted through sexual intercourse, e.g., gonorrhea, syphilis, HIV, trichomonas and others.

Virus—Infectious organism that reproduces in the cells of the infected host.

Visualization—A technique used for stress management whereby an individual uses his or her imagination to create mental pictures that can bring a feeling of calmness and promote relaxation. Visualization is also used by athletes and other performers to imagine themselves giving a peak performance and by individuals with illnesses or medical problems to imagine themselves returning to full health.

W

Withdrawal Symptoms—The psychological and physical effects that develop upon discontinuation of a substance a person has taken for an extended period of time or to which an individual is addicted.

X

Xanthines—Substances that stimulate muscle tissue, especially that of the heart. Types of xanthines include aminophylline, caffeine, dyphylline, oxtriphylline, theophylline.

Y

Yeast—A single-cell organism that can cause infections of the mouth, vagina, skin and parts of the gastrointestinal system.

Guide to Index

The alphabetical entries in the index include three categories of subject matter:

1. General information found in the introductory material at the front of the book.
2. Information in the disorder charts.
3. Information in the drug charts. These entries will be of three types—generic names, drug-class names and brand names.
   - Generic names appear in capital letters, followed by their drug-chart page numbers.
     BARBITURATES 92
   - Drug-class names appear in regular type, capital and lower-case letters. All generic drug names in this book that fall into a drug class are listed after the class name:
     Anticonvulsant - See
         BARBITURATES 92
         BENZODIAZEPINES 94
         CARBAMAZEPINE 106
         VALPROIC ACID 162

   Drug-class names that are used as the titles of drug charts appear in capital letters, followed by their page numbers:
       ANTIDEPRESSANTS, TRICYCLIC 90
   - Brand names appear in *italic*, followed by the names of the charts on which they appear and the chart page numbers:
       Elavil - See ANTIDEPRESSANTS, TRICYCLIC 90

   Some brand names contain two or more generic ingredients. These generic ingredients are listed in capital letters following the brand names:
       Elavil Plus - See
           ANTIDEPRESSANTS, TRICYCLIC 90
           PHENOTHIAZINES 148

Antidepressant (tricyclic) - See
     ANTIDEPRESSANTS, TRICYCLIC 90
ANTIDEPRESSANTS, TRICYCLIC 90
Antidyskinetic - See DIPHENHYDRAMINE 114
Antiemetic - See DIPHENHYDRAMINE 114
Antiemetic (phenothiazine) - See
     PHENOTHIAZINES 148
Antihistamine - See
     DIPHENHYDRAMINE 114
     HYDROXYZINE 124
Antihypertensive - See CLONIDINE 110
Antimanic agent - See CARBAMAZEPINE 106
Antiobsessional agent - See FLUVOXAMINE 120
Antipsychotic - See
     HALOPERIDOL 122
     MOLINDONE 136
     RISPERIDONE 150
Antipsychotic (new generation) - See CLOZAPINE
     112
Antipsychotic (thioxanthine) - See THIOTHIXENE
     156
Antisocial personality disorder - See Personality
     Disorders 73
Antivertigo - See DIPHENHYDRAMINE 114
Anxanil - See HYDROXYZINE 124
Anxiety 55; see also
     Panic Disorder 71
     Phobias 74
     Post-Traumatic Stress Disorder (PTSD) 76
     Stress 84
Anxiety, separation 10
Apo-Alpraz - See BENZODIAZEPINES 94
Apo-Amitriptyline - See ANTIDEPRESSANTS,
     TRICYCLIC 90
Apo-Atenolol - See BETA-ADRENERGIC
     BLOCKING AGENTS 96
Apo-Carbamazepine - See CARBAMAZEPINE 106
Apo-Chlordiazepoxide - See BENZODIAZEPINES 94
Apo-Clorazepate - See BENZODIAZEPINES 94
Apo-Diazepam - See BENZODIAZEPINES 94
Apo-Diltiaz - See CALCIUM CHANNEL
     BLOCKERS 104
Apo-Fluphenazine - See PHENOTHIAZINES 148
Apo-Flurazepam - See BENZODIAZEPINES 94
Apo-Haloperidol - See HALOPERIDOL 122
Apo-Hydroxyzine - See HYDROXYZINE 124
Apo-Imipramine - See ANTIDEPRESSANTS,
     TRICYCLIC 90
Apo-Lorazepam - See BENZODIAZEPINES 94
Apo-Meprobamate - See MEPROBAMATE 132
Apo-Metoprolol - See BETA-ADRENERGIC
     BLOCKING AGENTS 96
Apo-Metoprolol (Type L) - See BETA-
     ADRENERGIC BLOCKING AGENTS 96
Apo-Nifed - See CALCIUM CHANNEL BLOCKERS
     104
Apo-Oxazepam - See BENZODIAZEPINES 94
Apo-Perphenazine - See PHENOTHIAZINES 148
Apo-Propranolol - See BETA-ADRENERGIC
     BLOCKING AGENTS 96
Apo-Thioridazine - See PHENOTHIAZINES 148
Apo-Timol - See BETA-ADRENERGIC BLOCKING
     AGENTS 96
Apo-Triazo - See TRIAZOLAM 160
Apo-Trifluoperazine - See PHENOTHIAZINES 148
Apo-Trimip - See ANTIDEPRESSANTS,
     TRICYCLIC 90
Apo-Verap - See CALCIUM CHANNEL
     BLOCKERS 104
APROBARBITAL - See BARBITURATES 92
Aquachloral - See CHLORAL HYDRATE 108
Arcet - See BARBITURATES 92
Asendin - See ANTIDEPRESSANTS, TRICYCLIC 90

Atarax - See HYDROXYZINE 124
ATENOLOL - See BETA-ADRENERGIC
     BLOCKING AGENTS 96
Ativan - See BENZODIAZEPINES 94
Attention-Deficit Hyperactivity Disorder (ADHD) 56
Autism 10
Aventyl - See ANTIDEPRESSANTS, TRICYCLIC 90
Avoidant personality disorder - See Personality
     Disorders 73

B
Bancap - See BARBITURATES 92
Banophen - See DIPHENHYDRAMINE 114
Banophen Caplets - See DIPHENHYDRAMINE 114
Barbita - See BARBITURATES 92
BARBITURATES 92
Beldin - See DIPHENHYDRAMINE 114
Belix - See DIPHENHYDRAMINE 114
Benadryl - See DIPHENHYDRAMINE 114
Benadryl 25 - See DIPHENHYDRAMINE 114
Benadryl Kapseals - See DIPHENHYDRAMINE 114
Bendylate - See DIPHENHYDRAMINE 114
Benylin Cough - See DIPHENHYDRAMINE 114
BENZODIAZEPINES 94
Bepadin - See CALCIUM CHANNEL BLOCKERS
     104
BEPRIDIL - See CALCIUM CHANNEL BLOCKERS
     104
Bereavement - See Grief (Bereavement) 66
Beta-adrenergic blocker - See BETA-
     ADRENERGIC BLOCKING AGENTS 96
BETA-ADRENERGIC BLOCKING AGENTS 96
Betaloc - See BETA-ADRENERGIC BLOCKING
     AGENTS 96
Betaloc Durules - See BETA-ADRENERGIC
     BLOCKING AGENTS 96
Betapace - See BETA-ADRENERGIC BLOCKING
     AGENTS 96
BETAXOLOL - See BETA-ADRENERGIC
     BLOCKING AGENTS 96
Binge eating - See Bulimia Nervosa 58
Biphetamine - See AMPHETAMINES 88
Bipolar Disorder (Manic-Depressive Disorder) 57
BISOPROLOL - See BETA-ADRENERGIC
     BLOCKING AGENTS 96
Blocadren - See BETA-ADRENERGIC BLOCKING
     AGENTS 96
Body dysmorphic disorder - See Somatoform
     Disorders 83
Borderline personality disorder - See Personality
     Disorders 73
BROMAZEPAM - See BENZODIAZEPINES 94
Bucet - See BARBITURATES 92
Bulimia Nervosa 58
BUPROPION 98
Busodium - See BARBITURATES 92
BuSpar - See BUSPIRONE 100
BUSPIRONE 100
BUTABARBITAL - See BARBITURATES 92
Butace - See BARBITURATES 92
Butalan - See BARBITURATES 92
BUTALBITAL - See BARBITURATES 92
Butisol - See BARBITURATES 92
Bydramine Cough - See DIPHENHYDRAMINE 114

C
CAFFEINE 102
Caffedrine - See CAFFEINE 102
Caffedrine Caplets - See CAFFEINE 102
Calan - See CALCIUM CHANNEL BLOCKERS 104
Calan SR - See CALCIUM CHANNEL BLOCKERS
     104

Calcium channel blocker - See CALCIUM CHANNEL BLOCKERS 104
CALCIUM CHANNEL BLOCKERS 104
Cannabis, abuse of 25
CARBAMAZEPINE 106
Carbolith - See LITHIUM 126
Cardene - See CALCIUM CHANNEL BLOCKERS 104
Cardizem - See CALCIUM CHANNEL BLOCKERS 104
Cardizem CD - See CALCIUM CHANNEL BLOCKERS 104
Cardizem SR - See CALCIUM CHANNEL BLOCKERS 104
CARTEOLOL - See BETA-ADRENERGIC BLOCKING AGENTS 96
Cartrol - See BETA-ADRENERGIC BLOCKING AGENTS 96
Catapres - See CLONIDINE 110
Catapres-TTS - See CLONIDINE 110
Causes of psychological disorders 1
Central nervous system stimulant - See
 AMPHETAMINES 88
 METHYLPHENIDATE 134
 PEMOLINE 146
Centrax - See BENZODIAZEPINES 94
Chewable NoDoz - See CAFFEINE 102
CHLORAL HYDRATE 108
CHLORDIAZEPOXIDE - See BENZODIAZEPINES 94
Chlorpromanyl-5 - See PHENOTHIAZINES 148
Chlorpromanyl-20 - See PHENOTHIAZINES 148
Chlorpromanyl-40 - See PHENOTHIAZINES 148
CHLORPROMAZINE - See PHENOTHIAZINES 148
Cholinesterase inhibitor - See TACRINE 154
Chromium picolinate 21
Chronic Fatigue Syndrome 59
Chronic Pain Disorder (Somatoform Pain Disorder) 60
Cibalith-S - See LITHIUM 126
Clindex - See BENZODIAZEPINES 94
Clinoxide - See BENZODIAZEPINES 94
CLOMIPRAMINE - See ANTIDEPRESSANTS, TRICYCLIC 90
CLONAZEPAM - See BENZODIAZEPINES 94
CLONIDINE 110
CLORAZEPATE - See BENZODIAZEPINES 94
CLOZAPINE 112
Clozaril - See CLOZAPINE 112
Cocaine, abuse of 25
Codeine, abuse of 26
Coenzymye Q10 21
Cognex - See TACRINE 154
Compazine - See PHENOTHIAZINES 148
Compazine Spansule - See PHENOTHIAZINES 148
Compoz - See DIPHENHYDRAMINE 114
Compulsion - See Obsessive-Compulsive Disorder (OCD) 70
Compulsive gambing - See Impulse Control Disorders 68
Compulsive personality disorder - See Personality Disorders 73
Conduct disorder 10
Control disorders - See Impulse Control Disorders 68
Conversion disorder - See Somatoform Disorders 83
Corgard - See BETA-ADRENERGIC BLOCKING AGENTS 96
Cylert - See PEMOLINE 146
Cylert Chewable - See PEMOLINE 146

D
Dalmane - See BENZODIAZEPINES 94
Dartal - See PHENOTHIAZINES 148
Death, self-inflicted - See Suicide 86
Delusion - See
 Delusional Disorders 61
 Schizophrenic Disorders 77

Delusional Disorders 61
Dementia (Senility) 62
Depakene - See VALPROIC ACID 162
Depakote - See VALPROIC ACID 162
Depakote Sprinkle - See VALPROIC ACID 162
Dependent personality disorder - See Personality Disorders 73
Depersonalization disorder - See Dissociative Disorders 64
Depression 63; see also
 Bipolar Disorder (Manic-Depressive Disorder) 57
 Dysthymia (Low-Grade Depression) 65
 Postpartum Depression (Postnatal Depression) 75
 Seasonal Affective Disorder (SAD) 78
DESIPRAMINE - See ANTIDEPRESSANTS, TRICYCLIC 90
Desoxyn - See AMPHETAMINES 88
Desoxyn Gradumet - See AMPHETAMINES 88
Desyrel - See TRAZODONE 158
Detensol - See BETA-ADRENERGIC BLOCKING AGENTS 96
Dexedrine - See AMPHETAMINES 88
Dexedrine Spansule - See AMPHETAMINES 88
Dexitac - See CAFFEINE 102
DEXTROAMPHETAMINE - See AMPHETAMINES 88
DextroStat - See AMPHETAMINES 88
DiaHist - See DIPHENHYDRAMINE 114
Diazemuls - See BENZODIAZEPINES 94
DIAZEPAM - See BENZODIAZEPINES 94
Diazepam Intensol - See BENZODIAZEPINES 94
Dilacor-XR - See CALCIUM CHANNEL BLOCKERS 104
DILTIAZEM - See CALCIUM CHANNEL BLOCKERS 104
Diphen Cough - See DIPHENHYDRAMINE 114
Diphendryl - See DIPHENHYDRAMINE 114
Diphenhist - See DIPHENHYDRAMINE 114
Diphenhist Captabs - See DIPHENHYDRAMINE 114
DIPHENHYDRAMINE 114
Dissociative Disorders 64
DISULFIRAM 116
DIVALPROEX - See VALPROIC ACID 162
Dixarit - See CLONIDINE 110
Dolmar - See BARBITURATES 92
Doral - See BENZODIAZEPINES 94
Dormarex 2 - See DIPHENHYDRAMINE 114
Dormin - See DIPHENHYDRAMINE 114
DOXEPIN - See ANTIDEPRESSANTS, TRICYCLIC 90
Drug abuse & addiction - See Substance Abuse & Addiction 85
Duralith - See LITHIUM 126
Dyna Circ - See CALCIUM CHANNEL BLOCKERS 104
Dysthymia (Low-Grade Depression) 65

E
Eating disorders - See
 Anorexia Nervosa 54
 Bulimia Nervosa 58
ECT (electroconvulsive therapy) 5
Effexor - See VENLAFAXINE 164
Ejaculatory disorders - See Sexual Dysfunction, Male
 Ejaculatory Disorders 80
Elavil - See ANTIDEPRESSANTS, TRICYCLIC 90
Elavil Plus - See
 ANTIDEPRESSANTS, TRICYCLIC 90
 PHENOTHIAZINES 148
Elective mutism 10
Electroconvulsive therapy (ECT) 5
Emitrip - See ANTIDEPRESSANTS, TRICYCLIC 90
Endep - See ANTIDEPRESSANTS, TRICYCLIC 90
Endolor - See BARBITURATES 92

Leponex - See CLOZAPINE 112
Levate - See ANTIDEPRESSANTS, TRICYCLIC 90
Levatol - See BETA-ADRENERGIC BLOCKING
    AGENTS 96
Levoprome - See PHENOTHIAZINES 148
Librax - See BENZODIAZEPINES 94
Libritabs - See BENZODIAZEPINES 94
Librium - See BENZODIAZEPINES 94
Lidoxide - See BENZODIAZEPINES 94
Limbitrol - See
    ANTIDEPRESSANTS, TRICYCLIC 90
    BENZODIAZEPINES 94
Limbitrol DS - See
    ANTIDEPRESSANTS, TRICYCLIC 90
    BENZODIAZEPINES 94
Lipoxide - See BENZODIAZEPINES 94
Lithane - See LITHIUM 126
LITHIUM 126
Lithizine - See LITHIUM 126
Lithobid - See LITHIUM 126
Lithonate - See LITHIUM 126
Lithotabs - See LITHIUM 126
Loftran - See BENZODIAZEPINES 94
Lopresor - See BETA-ADRENERGIC BLOCKING
    AGENTS 96
Lopresor SR - See BETA-ADRENERGIC BLOCKING
    AGENTS 96
Lopressor - See BETA-ADRENERGIC BLOCKING
    AGENTS 96
LORAZEPAM - See BENZODIAZEPINES 94
Lorazepam Intensol - See BENZODIAZEPINES 94
Lotrel - See CALCIUM CHANNEL BLOCKERS 104
Low-grade depression - See Dysthymia (Low-Grade
    Depression) 65
Loxapac - See LOXAPINE 128
LOXAPINE 128
Loxitane - See LOXAPINE 128
Loxitane C - See LOXAPINE 128
LSD, abuse of 26
Ludiomil - See MAPROTILINE 130
Luminal - See BARBITURATES 92
Luvox - See FLUVOXAMINE 120

M

Majeptil - See PHENOTHIAZINES 148
Male sexual dysfunction - See
    Sexual Dysfunction, Male Ejaculatory Disorders 80
    Sexual Dysfunction, Male Impotence 81
Mania - See Bipolar Disorder (Manic-Depressive
    Disorder) 57
Manic-depressive disorder - See Bipolar Disorder
    (Manic-Depressive Disorder) 57
MAO (monoamine oxidase) inhibitor - See
    MONOAMINE OXIDASE (MAO) INHIBITORS 138
MAPROTILINE 130
Marijuana, abuse of 25
Masochism - See Paraphilias (Sexual Deviations) 72
Mazepine - See CARBAMAZEPINE 106
Mebaral - See BARBITURATES 92
Medical problems that mimic psychological disorders 3
Medigesic - See BARBITURATES 92
Medilium - See BENZODIAZEPINES 94
Medi-Tran - See MEPROBAMATE 132
Melatonin 22
Mellaril - See PHENOTHIAZINES 148
Mellaril Concentrate - See PHENOTHIAZINES 148
Mellaril-S - See PHENOTHIAZINES 148
Memory & aging 12-13
Mental Retardation 69
MEPHOBARBITAL - See BARBITURATES 92
MEPROBAMATE 132
Meprospan 200 - See MEPROBAMATE 132
Meprospan 400 - See MEPROBAMATE 132

Mescaline, abuse of 26
MESORIDAZINE - See PHENOTHIAZINES 148
Methadone, abuse of 26
METHAMPHETAMINE - See AMPHETAMINES 88
METHARBITAL - See BARBITURATES 92
METHOTRIMEPRAZINE - See PHENOTHIAZINES
    148
METHYLPHENIDATE 134
METOPROLOL - See BETA-ADRENERGIC
    BLOCKING AGENTS 96
Meval - See BENZODIAZEPINES 94
MIDAZOLAM - See BENZODIAZEPINES 94
Miltown - See MEPROBAMATE 132
Moban - See MOLINDONE 136
Moban Concentrate - See MOLINDONE 136
Modecate - See PHENOTHIAZINES 148
Modecate Concentrate - See PHENOTHIAZINES 148
Moditen Enanthate - See PHENOTHIAZINES 148
Moditen HCl - See PHENOTHIAZINES 148
Moditen HCl-H.P - See PHENOTHIAZINES 148
Mogadon - See BENZODIAZEPINES 94
MOLINDONE 136
Monitan - See BETA-ADRENERGIC BLOCKING
    AGENTS 96
Monoamine oxidase (MAO) inhibitor - See
    MONOAMINE OXIDASE (MAO) INHIBITORS 138
MONOAMINE OXIDASE (MAO) INHIBITORS 138
Mood stabilizer - See LITHIUM 126
Morphine, abuse of 26
Multiple personality disorder - See Dissociative
    Disorders 64
Mutism, elective 10
Myproic Acid - See VALPROIC ACID 162

N

NADOLOL - See BETA-ADRENERGIC BLOCKING
    AGENTS 96
NALTREXONE 140
Narcissistic personality disorder - See Personality
    Disorders 73
Narcotic antagonist - See NALTREXONE 140
Nardil - See MONOAMINE OXIDASE (MAO)
    INHIBITORS 138
Navane - See THIOTHIXENE 156
NEFAZODONE 142
Nembutal - See BARBITURATES 92
Nervine Nighttime Sleep-Aid - See
    DIPHENHYDRAMINE 114
Neuleptil - See PHENOTHIAZINES 148
Neuramate - See MEPROBAMATE 132
NICARDIPINE - See CALCIUM CHANNEL
    BLOCKERS 104
Nicotine, abuse of 23
Nidryl - See DIPHENHYDRAMINE 114
NIFEDIPINE - See CALCIUM CHANNEL
    BLOCKERS 104
NISOLDIPINE - See CALCIUM CHANNEL
    BLOCKERS 104
NITRAZEPAM - See BENZODIAZEPINES 94
Nitrous oxide, abuse of 26
Noctec - See CHLORAL HYDRATE 108
NoDoz - See CAFFEINE 102
NoDoz Maximum Strength Caplets - See CAFFEINE
    102
Noradryl - See DIPHENHYDRAMINE 114
Nordryl - See DIPHENHYDRAMINE 114
Nordryl Cough - See DIPHENHYDRAMINE 114
Norfranil - See ANTIDEPRESSANTS, TRICYCLIC 90
Normodyne - See BETA-ADRENERGIC BLOCKING
    AGENTS 96
Norpramin - See ANTIDEPRESSANTS, TRICYCLIC
    90

TEMAZEPAM - See BENZODIAZEPINES 94
Tencet - See BARBITURATES 92
Tenormin - See BETA-ADRENERGIC BLOCKING
   AGENTS 96
Terfluzine - See PHENOTHIAZINES 148
Terfluzine Concentrate - See PHENOTHIAZINES 148
THIOPROPAZATE - See PHENOTHIAZINES 148
THIOPROPERAZINE - See PHENOTHIAZINES 148
THIORIDAZINE - See PHENOTHIAZINES 148
THIOTHIXENE 156
Thiothixene HCl Intensol - See THIOTHIXENE 156
Thorazine - See PHENOTHIAZINES 148
Thorazine Concentrate - See PHENOTHIAZINES 148
Thorazine Spansule - See PHENOTHIAZINES 148
Thor-Prom - See PHENOTHIAZINES 148
TIMOLOL - See BETA-ADRENERGIC BLOCKING
   AGENTS 96
Tindal - See PHENOTHIAZINES 148
Tipramine - See ANTIDEPRESSANTS, TRICYCLIC
   90
Tobacco, abuse of 23
Tofranil - See ANTIDEPRESSANTS, TRICYCLIC 90
Tofranil-PM - See ANTIDEPRESSANTS, TRICYCLIC
   90
Toprol XL - See BETA-ADRENERGIC BLOCKING
   AGENTS 96
T-Quil - See BENZODIAZEPINES 94
Trancot - See MEPROBAMATE 132
Trandate - See BETA-ADRENERGIC BLOCKING
   AGENTS 96
Tranmep - See MEPROBAMATE 132
Tranquilizer - See
   HYDROXYZINE 124
   LOXAPINE 128
   MEPROBAMATE 132
   PHENOTHIAZINES 148
Tranquilizer (benzodiazepine) - See
   BENZODIAZEPINES 94
Tranxene - See BENZODIAZEPINES 94
Tranxene T-Tab - See BENZODIAZEPINES 94
Tranxene-SD - See BENZODIAZEPINES 94
TRANYLCYPROMINE - See MONOAMINE
   OXIDASE (MAO) INHIBITORS 138
Trasicor - See BETA-ADRENERGIC BLOCKING
   AGENTS 96
TRAZODONE 158
Trazon - See TRAZODONE 158
Triad - See BARBITURATES 92
Triadapin - See ANTIDEPRESSANTS, TRICYCLIC
   90
Trialodine - See TRAZODONE 158
Triaprin - See BARBITURATES 92
Triavil - See
   ANTIDEPRESSANTS, TRICYCLIC 90
   PHENOTHIAZINES 148
TRIAZOLAM 160
Trichotillomania - See Impulse Control Disorders 68
Tricyclic antidepressant - See ANTIDEPRESSANTS,
   TRICYCLIC 90
TRIFLUOPERAZINE - See PHENOTHIAZINES 148
TRIFLUPROMAZINE - See PHENOTHIAZINES 148
Trilafon - See PHENOTHIAZINES 148
Trilafon Concentrate - See PHENOTHIAZINES 148
Triavil - See PHENOTHIAZINES 148
TRIMIPRAMINE - See ANTIDEPRESSANTS,
   TRICYCLIC 90
Triptil - See ANTIDEPRESSANTS, TRICYCLIC 90
Tuinal - See BARBITURATES 92
Two-Dyne - See BARBITURATES 92

U
Ultra Pep-Back - See CAFFEINE 102
Ultrazine-10 - See PHENOTHIAZINES 148

V
Valium - See BENZODIAZEPINES 94
VALPROIC ACID 162
Valrelease - See BENZODIAZEPINES 94
Vascor - See CALCIUM CHANNEL BLOCKERS 104
Vasoconstrictor - See CAFFEINE 102
VENLAFAXINE 164
VERAPAMIL - See CALCIUM CHANNEL
   BLOCKERS 104
Verelan - See CALCIUM CHANNEL BLOCKERS 104
Vesprin - See PHENOTHIAZINES 148
Violence, uncontrolled - See Impulse Control
   Disorders 68
Visken - See BETA-ADRENERGIC BLOCKING
   AGENTS 96
Vistaril - See HYDROXYZINE 124
Vivactil - See ANTIDEPRESSANTS, TRICYCLIC 90
Vivarin - See CAFFEINE 102
Vivol - See BENZODIAZEPINES 94
Volatile inhalants, abuse of 26
Voyeurism - See Paraphilias (Sexual Deviations) 72

W
Wake-Up - See CAFFEINE 102
Wellbutrin - See BUPROPION 98

X Y Z
Xanax - See BENZODIAZEPINES 94
Zapex - See BENZODIAZEPINES 94
Zebeta - See BETA-ADRENERGIC BLOCKING
   AGENTS 96
Zebrax - See BENZODIAZEPINES 94
Zetran - See BENZODIAZEPINES 94
Zoloft - See SERTRALINE 152
ZOLPIDEM 166

Diagnosis at Your Fingertips — From H. Winter Griffith, M.D.
One of America's Most Trusted Family Physicians

Complete Guide to Prescription & Nonprescription Drugs, 1997 Edition
The fourteenth edition of this best-selling reference book. "Comprehensive, easy-to-use and informative."—*Los Angeles Times.*

Complete Guide to Pediatric Symptoms, Illness & Medications
The most complete guide to treating sick children from infancy through adolescence, arranged in quick-reference health sections. Includes thousands of symptoms and medications.

Complete Guide to Prescription & Nonprescription Pediatric Drugs by H. Winter Griffith, M.D., and Victor A. Elsberry, Pharm.D.
Specifically for children from infancy through teenage years, this reference guide gives important information for over three hundred pediatric drugs.

Complete Guide to Sports Injuries
Dr. Griffith shows how to recognize and treat hundreds of the most common sports injuries. Highly recommended for all coaches, parents and athletes.

Complete Guide to Symptoms, Illness & Surgery, 3rd Edition
Helps you diagnose, understand, and seek treatment for any illness, from the common cold to life-threatening cancer or heart disease.

Complete Guide to Symptoms, Illness & Surgery for People Over 50
The most comprehensive medical reference for older Americans, featuring hundreds of symptoms and what they mean with suggestions for treatment.

These books are available at your bookstore or wherever books are sold,
or, for your convenience, we'll send them directly to you.
Call 1-800-788-6262 Ext.1.

Or fill out the coupon below and send it to:

The Berkley Publishing Group
390 Murray Hill Parkway, Department B
East Rutherford, NJ 07073

Emergency Guide for Anaphylaxis Victims

The following are *basic* steps in recognizing and treating immediate effects of severe allergic reaction, which is called *anaphylaxis.*

Some people may be highly sensitive to certain drugs. An anaphylactic reaction to a drug can be life-threatening! Persons suffering these allergic symptoms should receive immediate emergency treatment!

Study the information before you need it. If possible, take a course in first aid and learn external cardiac massage and mouth-to-mouth breathing techniques, called *cardiopulmonary resuscitation* (CPR).

SYMPTOMS OF ANAPHYLAXIS:

- Itching
- Rash
- Hives
- Runny nose
- Wheezing
- Increased breathing difficulty

- Paleness
- Cold sweats
- Low blood pressure
- Coma
- Cardiac arrest
- Swelling of lips or tongue

IF VICTIM IS UNCONSCIOUS, NOT BREATHING:

1. Yell for help, but don't leave victim unless absolutely necessary to summon help.

2. Dial 911 (emergency) or 0 (operator) for an ambulance or medical help. If the victim is a child, give mouth-to-mouth breathing for one minute, then dial 911 or 0.

3. Begin mouth-to-mouth breathing immediately.

4. If there is no heartbeat, give external cardiac massage.

5. Don't stop CPR until help arrives.

6. Take medicine or empty bottles with you to the emergency room.

IF VICTIM IS UNCONSCIOUS AND BREATHING:

1. Dial 911 (emergency) or 0 (operator) for an ambulance or emergency medical help.

2. If you can't get help immediately, take patient to nearest emergency room.

3. Take medicine or empty bottles with you to emergency room for analysis.

Emergency Guide for Overdose Victims

This section lists *basic* steps in recognizing and treating immediate effects of drug overdose.

Study the information before you need it. If possible, take a course in first aid and learn external cardiac massage and mouth-to-mouth breathing techniques, called *cardiopulmonary resuscitation* (CPR).

For quick reference, list emergency telephone numbers in the spaces provided on the inside front cover for fire department paramedics, ambulance, poison control center and your doctor. These numbers, except for that of a doctor, are usually listed on the inside cover of your telephone directory.

IF VICTIM IS UNCONSCIOUS, NOT BREATHING:

1. Yell for help, but don't leave victim unless absolutely necessary to summon help.

2. Dial 911 (emergency) or 0 (operator) for an ambulance or medical help. If the victim is a child, give mouth-to-mouth breathing for one minute, then dial 911 or 0.

3. Begin mouth-to-mouth breathing immediately.

4. If there is no heartbeat, give external cardiac massage.

5. Don't stop CPR until help arrives.

6. Don't try to make victim vomit.

7. If vomiting occurs, save vomit to take to emergency room for analysis.

8. Take medicine or empty bottles with you to emergency room.

IF VICTIM IS UNCONSCIOUS AND BREATHING:

1. Dial 911 (emergency) or 0 (operator) for an ambulance or medical help.

2. If you can't get help immediately, take victim to the nearest emergency room.

3. Don't try to make victim vomit.

4. If vomiting occurs, save vomit to take to emergency room for analysis.

5. Watch victim carefully on the way to the emergency room. If heart or breathing stops, use cardiac massage and mouth-to-mouth breathing (CPR).

6. Take medicine or empty bottles with you to emergency room.

IF VICTIM IS DROWSY:

1. Dial 911 (emergency) or 0 (operator) for an ambulance or medical help.

2. If you can't get help immediately, take victim to the nearest emergency room.

3. Don't try to make victim vomit.

4. If vomiting occurs, save vomit to take to emergency room for analysis.

5. Watch victim carefully on the way to the emergency room. If heart or breathing stops, use cardiac massage and mouth-to-mouth breathing (CPR).

6. Take medicine or empty bottles with you to emergency room.

IF VICTIM IS ALERT:

1. Dial 911 (emergency) or 0 (operator) for an ambulance or emergency medical help.

2. Call poison control center or doctor for specific instructions.

3. If you can't get instructions, make victim drink one glass of water to dilute drug in the stomach. Don't use milk or other beverages.

4. If you are instructed to make victim vomit, use syrup of ipecac according to instructions from your doctor, poison control center or ipecac label.

5. Save vomit for analysis.

6. If you can't get paramedic help quickly, take victim to nearest emergency room.

7. Take medicine or empty bottles with you to emergency room.

IF VICTIM HAS NO SYMPTOMS BUT YOU SUSPECT OVERDOSE:

1. Call poison control center.

2. Describe the suspect drug with as much information as you can quickly gather. The center will give emergency instructions.

3. Or call victim's doctor or your doctor for instructions.

4. If you have no telephone, take victim to the nearest emergency room.

5. Take medicine or empty bottles with you to emergency room.

EMERGENCY TELEPHONE NUMBERS

Fire Department (Paramedic)   Ambulance

Doctor   Poison Control Center

Guide for Psychiatric Emergencies

Psychiatric emergencies can include suicide attempts or threats, threats of violence or harm to others, violent assault or abuse and acute psychoses. Family members should be aware when these possibilities exist in someone with a psychological disorder.

The steps to take to prevent emergency situations should be discussed with the patient's doctor as part of the treatment, and all those who have contact with the patient should be instructed to recognize any warning signs that might precede an episode and what to do should one occur.

There are no easy guidelines for handling these psychiatric emergencies as there are for handling medical emergencies in which someone is injured or suffering a heart attack. Each patient's behavior and circumstances are different. A calm and reassuring response to a patient's agitated state is sometimes enough. Other times, help will be needed from police or other emergency services.

SUICIDE ATTEMPTS:

1. Don't waste time trying to determine if a suicide attempt is real or just a bid for attention. Seek help immediately.

2. Take person to nearest emergency room or call local suicide hotline or call 911.

SUICIDAL TALK OR SIGNALS:

1. Talk of suicide can be serious. Some people who talk about suicide follow through. People who are severely depressed or those with schizophrenia are at greater risk of suicide. Seek help immediately if you are concerned or unsure if suicidal talk may be acted upon.

2. Sometimes people give indirect signals of suicide, such as making out a will or getting one's affairs in order. Statements such as "You'd be better off without me" are danger signals. It may also be significant if a severely depressed person suddenly seems relaxed. The person may have decided to commit suicide.

AVAILABILITY OF WEAPONS:

Guns—Many depressed persons end their lives by shooting. If you own a gun or other potentially lethal instrument, be certain the depressed person cannot get to it, and don't leave a severely depressed individual alone.

VIOLENCE OR ABUSIVE BEHAVIOR:

1. If the person is violent or threatening or has a weapon, take action immediately. Lock the person in a room if possible. Get yourself and others away from the home.

2. Call 911 if necessary. Describe the situation to the person who answers, and say that the violent person has a mental disorder. Local law enforcement personnel (e.g., police) will provide an immediate response. They may take the patient to a hospital or psychiatric facility.